# LANGUAGE AND WOMAN'S PLACE

# Studies in Language and Gender

Mary Bucholtz, General Editor

*Reinventing Identities: The Gendered Self in Discourse*
Edited by Mary Bucholtz, A. C. Liang, and Laurel A. Sutton

*Pronoun Envy: Literary Uses of Linguistic Gender*
by Anna Livia

*Language and Woman's Place: Text and Commentaries*
Revised and Expanded Edition
by Robin Tolmach Lakoff
Edited by Mary Bucholtz

ROBIN TOLMACH LAKOFF

# LANGUAGE AND WOMAN'S PLACE

## TEXT AND COMMENTARIES

### REVISED AND EXPANDED EDITION

EDITED BY MARY BUCHOLTZ

**OXFORD**
UNIVERSITY PRESS

2004

# OXFORD
UNIVERSITY PRESS

Oxford  New York
Auckland  Bangkok  Buenos Aires  Cape Town  Chennai
Dar es Salaam  Delhi  Hong Kong  Istanbul  Karachi  Kolkata
Kuala Lumpur  Madrid  Melbourne  Mexico City  Mumbai  Nairobi
São Paulo  Shanghai  Taipei  Tokyo  Toronto

Published by Oxford University Press, Inc.
198 Madison Avenue, New York, New York 10016

www.oup.com

Oxford is a registered trademark of Oxford University Press

Library of Congress Cataloging-in-Publication Data
Lakoff, Robin Tolmach.
    Language and woman's place / Robin Tolmach Lakoff ; edited by Mary Bucholtz. — Rev.
and expanded ed.
      p. cm. — (Studies in language and gender ; 3)
    Originally published: New York: Harper & Row, 1975.
    Includes bibliographical references and index.
    ISBN -13 978-0-19-516758-0;  978-0-19-516757-3  (pbk.)
    ISBN 0-19-516758-9;  0-19-516757-0  (pbk.)
    1. Women — Language.   2. Sex role.   3. Sexism in language.   4. English language — Sex
differences.   I. Bucholtz, Mary, 1966–  II. Title.   III. Series.

HQ1206.L36  2004
305.4 — dc22      2003056479

9 8 7 6 5

Printed in the United States of America
on acid-free paper

To my students, past and present,

who have been an inspiration for all my work. — RTL

And for Barbara Bucholtz,

who refused to know her place. — MB

The way we understood things twenty years ago

is not how we see them now; yet that understanding

was fruitful and led to today's deeper understanding.

—Robin Tolmach Lakoff, *Talking Power*

# Contents

## ∷
## THE ORIGINAL TEXT *with Annotations by the Author*

*Language and Woman's Place*

## ∷
## COMMENTARIES

Part I: Contexts

# Contributors

**Rusty Barrett** teaches in the Department of Linguistics at the University of Michigan, Ann Arbor. His research has examined the relationship between queer theory and sociolinguistic theory, popular conceptions of "gay language," and expressions of identity in performances by African American drag queens.

**Judith Mattson Bean** is an associate professor of English at Texas Woman's University. Her essays on twentieth-century sociolinguistics and discourse appear in *Discourse Processes, Language and Society, SECOL Review,* and *Southwestern American Literature.* She also has written articles and chapters on the discourse of nineteenth-century writer Margaret Fuller.

**Mary Bucholtz** is an assistant professor of linguistics at the University of California, Santa Barbara. She is coeditor of *Gender Articulated: Language and the Socially Constructed Self* (1995) and *Reinventing Identities: The Gendered Self in Discourse* (1999). Her research focuses on language, gender, race, and youth.

**Jenny Cook-Gumperz** is a professor of education at the University of California, Santa Barbara. A sociologist and sociolinguist, she is well known for her work on literacy theory and the social context of children's language learning. She is the author of *The Social Construction of Literacy, Social Control and Socialization,* and *Children's Worlds and Children's Language* (with William Corsaro and Jurgen Streeck), as well as numerous articles on literacy and language socialization.

**Catherine Evans Davies** studied with Robin Tolmach Lakoff at the University of California, Berkeley. She is an associate professor in the English department at the University of Alabama. Her research explores gender issues, cross-cultural interaction, language socialization, humor, media and popular culture, and the discourse of the American South.

**Penelope Eckert** is a professor of linguistics at Stanford University. She is the author of *Jocks and Burnouts: Social Categories and Identity in the High School* (1989), *Language Variation as Social Practice* (2000), and *Language and Gender* (2003; with Sally McConnell-Ginet), as well as numerous articles on language, gender, sexuality, and adolescence.

**Susan Ehrlich** is a professor in the Department of Languages, Literatures, and Linguistics, York University. Her areas of research include language and gender, language and the law, and second language acquisition. Her work has appeared in journals such as *Discourse & Society*, *Forensic Linguistics*, and *Language in Society*. Her most recent book is *Representing Rape: Language and Sexual Consent* (2001).

**Rudolf P. Gaudio** teaches anthropology at Purchase College of the State University of New York. His research focuses on the moral and political economies of language, gender, sexuality, and space in northern Nigeria and the United States. His work has appeared in *American Speech*, *Journal of Linguistic Anthropology*, *Socialist Review*, and several edited volumes.

**Kira Hall** is an assistant professor in the Departments of Linguistics and Anthropology at the University of Colorado, Boulder. Her publications include the edited collections *Gender Articulated* (with Mary Bucholtz) and *Queerly Phrased* (with Anna Livia). She is currently completing a book on the linguistic and cultural practices of Hindi-speaking *hijras* in northern India.

**Susan C. Herring**, a leading expert on gender and computer-mediated communication, is a professor of information science and linguistics at Indiana University. She has edited three collections on computer-mediated communication and has written numerous articles on gender and the Internet. Her current research focuses on the representation of women and men in multimedia computer interfaces.

**Janet Holmes** is a professor of linguistics at Victoria University of Wellington and director of the Language in the Workplace Project. She is a Fellow of the Royal Society of New Zealand and has published on a wide range of topics, including language and gender, New Zealand English, and workplace communication.

**Sachiko Ide** is a professor of linguistics at Japan Women's University. She is coeditor of *Aspects of Japanese Women's Language* (Kurosio, 1990) and *Women's Languages in Various Parts of the World*, a special issue of the *International Journal of the Sociology of Language* (1998). Her research areas include sociolinguistics, contrastive pragmatics, and language and culture.

**Barbara Johnstone** is a professor of rhetoric and linguistics at Carnegie Mellon University. She is the author of several books, including *Stories, Community, and Place* (1990) and *The Linguistic Individual* (1996). Her work focuses on the role of the individual speaker in discourse and on links between language, identity, and place.

**Shari Kendall** is an assistant professor of linguistics in the Department of English, Texas A&M University. Her research addresses the discursive construction of gendered, professional, and parental identities in work and family discourse; the constitution of ideologies of gender in legal contexts and the media; and the theoretical frameworks of framing, positioning, and interactional sociolinguistics.

**Scott Fabius Kiesling** is an assistant professor of linguistics at the University of Pittsburgh. He has focused his language and gender research on the language used in an all-male American fraternity. He has also investigated language and ethnic identity in Sydney, Australia, and social patterns of language change in southwestern Pennsylvania.

**Robin Tolmach Lakoff** has been a professor of linguistics at the University of California at Berkeley since 1972. Among her writings are *Language and Woman's Place* (1975), *Talking Power* (1990), and *The Language War* (2000).

**William L. Leap** is a professor of anthropology and chair of the Department of Anthropology, American University. His long-term studies of language, culture, sexuality, and power have generated a series of essays exploring "gay men's English" and attacking proposals to erase the significance of speaker identity in linguistic practice. His current research examines (homo)sexual geography in Washington, D.C., and the linguistics of homophobia.

**Anna Livia** obtained her PhD in French linguistics from the University of California, Berkeley, where she now teaches. She is the author of *Pronoun Envy* and coeditor of *Queerly Phrased*, both published by Oxford University Press. Her current research focuses on collocations of gender, class, and race and representations of reverse anthropology in francophone film.

**Yoshiko Matsumoto**, an associate professor in the Department of Asian Languages at Stanford University, received her PhD in linguistics from the University of California, Berkeley. Her research focuses on pragmatic aspects of Japanese, politeness, and issues of gender and age. A related paper, "Alternative Femininity: Personae of Middle-Aged Mothers," is forthcoming in *Japanese Language, Gender, and Ideology* (Oxford University Press).

**Sally McConnell-Ginet** is a professor of linguistics at Cornell University, where she is also active in feminist, gender, and sexuality studies. She has been teaching and doing research on language and gender/sexuality since the time *LWP* first appeared; she also works in formal semantics and pragmatics. With Penelope Eckert, she has published *Language and Gender* (2003).

**Bonnie McElhinny** is an associate professor in the Department of Anthropology and the Institute for Women and Gender Studies at the University of Toronto. Her interests include feminist theory; language, gender, and political economy; linguistic, historical, and anthropological studies of child rearing; and language, place, and political ecology.

**Norma Mendoza-Denton** is an assistant professor of linguistic anthropology at the University of Arizona and the founder and director of the Linguistic Anthropology Teaching Laboratory. She is a recent recipient of a Rockefeller Foundation Bellagio Residence Fellowship and author of the forthcoming book *Homegirls: Symbolic Practices in the Making of Latina Youth Styles.*

**Miriam Meyerhoff** is reader in linguistics at the University of Edinburgh. She has published work looking at how gender relates to social identities in Vanuatu (Pacific) and is now participating in fieldwork in Bequia (Caribbean) looking at gender and ethnicity. She recently coedited *The Handbook of Language and Gender* (2003).

**Marcyliena Morgan** is an associate professor of African and African American Studies at Harvard University. Her books include *Language, Discourse and Power in African American Culture* and *Language and The Social Construction of Identity in Creole Situations.* Her research interests include African American English and language ideology, identity, gender, and youth in the African diaspora.

**Robin Queen** is an assistant professor of linguistics and Germanic linguistics at the University of Michigan. Her research concerns the intersections of language and sociocultural identity, focusing primarily on these intersections as they occur in Turkish communities in Germany, in American films dubbed into German, and within queer linguistics.

**Deborah Tannen** is University Professor at Georgetown University. Her books include *Talking Voices, Conversational Style, Gender and Discourse, Talking from 9 to 5, That's Not What I Meant!, The Argument Culture,* and *I Only Say This Because I Love You.* Her most recent research, supported by the Alfred P. Sloan Foundation, examines framing in family interaction.

**Sara Trechter** is an associate professor of linguistics in the Department of English at California State University, Chico. She has written on the grammar and pragmatics of gender in Lakhota discourse and on the construction of whiteness in Lakhota. She is currently completing a book manuscript titled *Gendered Voices in Lakhota.*

# LANGUAGE AND WOMAN'S PLACE

## ⠿

# Editor's Introduction

MARY BUCHOLTZ

The publication of Robin Tolmach Lakoff's groundbreaking book *Language and Woman's Place* (*LWP*) by Harper & Row in 1975 has long been heralded as the beginning of the linguistic subfield of language and gender studies, as well as ushering in the study of language and gender in related disciplines such as anthropology, communication studies, education, psychology, and sociology. First published in shorter form in the journal *Language in Society* in 1973, the book has been widely read, reviewed, and discussed since its appearance, as well as inspiring a vast body of research on a variety of fundamental questions first laid out in its pages:

- What linguistic practices and ideologies are associated with women's speech?
- How are gender ideologies made manifest in the ways women are spoken of?
- What is the role of gender-based power inequity in these sociolinguistic processes?
- What is the role of cultural institutions, including socialization in the nuclear family and into heterosexuality, representations in the media, and other large-scale social structures?
- How do linguistically based cultural systems, such as politeness, reproduce unequal gendered arrangements?

Lakoff's incisive questions and her insightful answers to them did not merely inaugurate but in fact anticipated over two decades of research on language and gender. The volume's continuing relevance — indeed, centrality — to the field is due to its almost prescient perceptiveness, while the clarity and wit with which Lakoff presented her ideas has made *LWP* as enjoyable as it is indispensable. It is a testament to the book's canonical status in linguistics that it has remained in print continuously for over twenty-five years.

The idea for this new and expanded edition of *LWP* was born of necessity: I was preparing to teach an undergraduate class in language and gender and discovered to my dismay that the text had recently gone out of print despite ongoing reader demand. I approached Robin with the idea of a second edition. It was obvious that the book had to be reissued, but it was equally clear that the text should be placed in context for a new generation of readers. We decided that, in addition to the complete original text, the volume would include annotations of the text by Robin and an introductory essay in which she reflects on the book's origins and impact, and brief essays by a wide range of prominent scholars of language and gender commenting on the diverse ways in which *LWP* has advanced scholarship in the field.

Due to the efforts of many feminists, Robin Lakoff among them, American society — and especially woman's place within it — has changed dramatically and for the better since the book was first published in 1975. Yet *LWP* continues to resonate powerfully with today's readers. This is not only an indication of how much further we have to go to achieve the feminist goal of gender equality but also a testament to Lakoff's astute and far-seeing analysis. A number of commentators in this volume remark on the changes in gendered language since Lakoff's initial observations, yet they also point to the many ways in which the issues Lakoff identified are with us still. The text continues to be widely cited by scholars and remains required reading in undergraduate and graduate courses on language and gender and related topics.

Like any pioneering text, *LWP* has been critiqued, by both feminist and antifeminist scholars, yet the fact that it persists as the single most influential work in language and gender indicates that its foundational role in the field is substantive rather than symbolic. A reassessment of Lakoff's book in the past decade has led scholars to read the text with greater sensitivity to the intellectual and political climate in which it was written and to express renewed appreciation for the valuable contributions it makes not only to the history of language and gender research but also to its present and future development. The commentaries by language and gender scholars in this second edition therefore consider the book from the dual standpoint of its historical context and its current relevance. The purpose is not to rehash tired critiques but to consider afresh the ways in which *LWP* has shaped our knowledge of gender and the ways in which it resonates with contemporary issues in the field.

Part 1, "Contexts," locates *LWP* within historical context both within language and gender research and within feminist scholarship more generally. The section opens with my own examination of the feminist roots of *LWP* and the ongoing development of Lakoff's ideas about gender from 1973 to the present. Responding to the tendency for contemporary critics of Lakoff's work to read the text ahistorically, as though her thinking about gender and language ended in 1975, I argue for a consideration of the full range of her research. My own reading of *LWP* alongside Lakoff's later scholarship demonstrates both significant continuities and important changes in her approach to feminist linguistics over the years.

Bonnie McElhinny then turns to the complex question of Lakoff's relationship to radical feminism. McElhinny points out that although Lakoff has never claimed this label for herself, her work is compatible with many of the principles of radical feminism, the form of feminist theory that predominated politically and intellectually during the time Lakoff was writing *LWP*. Yet McElhinny also notes the dangers in assigning Lakoff's or any other scholar's work a particular label, a practice that often serves to promote a single form of feminist thought as normative and "up-to-date."

In the next essay, Sally McConnell-Ginet revisits her own early critique of *LWP* in light of recent research on how gender ideologies are constructed through language. McConnell-Ginet observes that her differences with Lakoff over the best way to understand language and gender were based in a more general theoretical disagreement about the best way to understand language itself, due to the two scholars' association with different theories of the relationship between semantics, grammar, and context. Surveying research that responded to Lakoff's characterization of "women's language," she concludes that one of the most significant contributions of *LWP* was long overlooked and has only been rearticulated within feminist linguistic theory in the last decade: the fundamental relationship between subjectivity, stance, and language.

In the last essay in this section, Anna Livia reflects on the ways the world and its language users have changed since *LWP* first appeared in print. She shows how the gender asymmetry in titles and pronouns discussed by Lakoff has become less acute. Yet she also demonstrates that the gendered linguistic ideologies that Lakoff described continue to circulate in popular culture. In her own research on French lesbian personal ads, Livia uncovers the complex interplay of gender and class addressed in Lakoff's work, an indication of the unexpected ways that *LWP* continues to be relevant in new sociohistorical contexts.

Part 2, "Concepts," explores some of the key analytic tools Lakoff drew on in *Language and Woman's Place* and how her work helped develop new frameworks for the analysis of language and gender. The issue of gender in powerful, polite, and patronizing language is the topic of the first commentary in this section. Janet Holmes notes Lakoff's central role in the development of politeness theory within linguistics, a role often overlooked by scholars who missed the connection between the gendered linguistic features she identified, politeness, and power. Holmes also observes that Lakoff's little-discussed predictions about language used about, rather than by, women were often quite accurate: drawing on several linguistic corpora, she shows that the word *lady* has acquired a connotation of patronizing or trivializing women, an association Lakoff described for this word in 1975.

In the next essay, Deborah Tannen discusses the importance of cultural difference in the theoretical underpinnings of *LWP*. Tracing the development of her own work on cross-gender communication as cross-cultural communication, Tannen shows how Lakoff's theory of politeness was built on ideas about cultural variation and in turn contributed to a cultural understanding of gender. Tannen argues that both for her and for Lakoff, gender is fundamentally a component of conversational style, along with ethnicity, region, age, class, and other factors.

In the next contribution, Penelope Eckert examines how the insights of *LWP* intersect with the issue of gendered symbolic capital, a central tool in the analysis of language and gender. Eckert demonstrates that the "good woman" stereotype that underlies Lakoff's concept of "women's language" is a key figure to which girls and women must orient in shaping their own gender identities, whether "good" or not. Eckert builds on Lakoff's ideas by showing how both "good women" and those who choose to be "bad" face the same gender-based constraints on access to real-world power and hence must use the symbolic realm of language and other tools of self-presentation to construct authoritative identities.

The final essay in this section, by Kira Hall, considers how *LWP* advances gender theory within linguistics by focusing on exceptional speakers in addition to those who conform to gender ideologies. Although many researchers have wrongly claimed that Lakoff characterized "women's language" as exclusively used by female speakers, Hall shows that Lakoff's entire theory of "women's language" hinges on the insight that men who elect for various reasons to remove themselves from structures of power may also use these linguistic practices (hippies, gays, and academics are Lakoff's examples). Thus "women's language" is not fundamentally about gender but more basically about the displayed lack of power.

Part 3, "Femininities," investigates in more detail the question of "women's language" as a gender norm, examining the ways that "ladylike" language is used by female speakers in a variety of contexts. One of the clearest examples of this phenomenon is described in Sachiko Ide's commentary on how *LWP* contributed to her understanding of "Japanese women's language," a widely discussed linguistic phenomenon in Japan. Ide shows how cultural differences between the United States and Japan required her to rework Lakoff's theory when she introduced it into linguistic scholarship in Japan. Whereas in the United States, "women's language" marks the speaker's subordination, Ide argues, in Japan it is an index of prestige and even power.

The second commentary in this section likewise explores how "women's language" may be put to use for strategic purposes in the construction of a powerful feminine identity. Catherine Evans Davies examines how media icon and "lifestyle entrepreneur" Martha Stewart draws on numerous elements of "women's language" to construct a powerful and authoritative persona based on the domestic sphere traditionally associated with women. Davies shows that "women's language" may, in this corporate context, be synonymous with powerful language.

A somewhat different relationship between gender and power is further explored in the final two commentaries on language socialization. The first, by Jenny Cook-Gumperz, demonstrates the ways in which preschool girls experiment with and against powerful language: in enacting the role of mother in imaginative play, in interaction with other girls, and in confronting the powerful language and action of intrusive boys. Drawing on Lakoff's ideas about politeness and gender, Cook-Gumperz shows how girls use politeness to control and persuade others; thus as a little girl learns to become a "lady" she also learns how to use language strategically, though not always successfully.

The place of mothers in gendered language socialization is addressed by Shari Kendall. Kendall observes that the role of mothers is an unspoken presence in *LWP*, and she shows how Lakoff's description of politeness and "women's language" aids in understanding the difference between the roles that a mother and father assume in interacting with their daughter at dinnertime. Kendall notes that while the father exclusively takes up a joking position, the mother fills a variety of socializing roles, all of which involve the modeling of or explicit instruction in "ladylike" language.

In Part 4, "Power," the consequences of such gender inequity in normative language use are made visible. Miriam Meyerhoff's contribution addresses *LWP*'s insights on silence, a pivotal concept in feminist theory since the 1970s, yet one that, as Meyerhoff notes, is often not discussed in treatments of Lakoff's work. Meyerhoff identifies two kinds of silencing effects described in *LWP*: one in which women may not speak at all and one in which women's speech is misunderstood because it is evaluated according to biased norms. Using tools from feminist philosophy of language and social psychology, Meyerhoff points to the mechanisms and motivations underlying the silencing of women as characterized by Lakoff.

In Susan C. Herring's essay, the silencing effects discussed by Meyerhoff are examined in a specific discursive context: online interaction. Contrary to the "technological determinism" of some feminists, which holds that cyberspace renders gender invisible and hence irrelevant, Herring, summarizing her extensive research on gender and computer-mediated communication, reports sharp gender inequities in cyberspace. Many of the gendered linguistic practices she found in her own research correspond to those identified by Lakoff; and those that are different, Herring observes, nevertheless reinforce Lakoff's larger point: the gender hierarchy consistently subordinates women to men.

A particularly vivid example of such a gender hierarchy is put forward in Susan Ehrlich's contribution, which focuses on sexual harassment and assault. Challenging the traditional feminist notion that words are wholly symbolic and have no material effects, Ehrlich posits a fundamental relationship between linguistic and material inequities. She shows that restrictive definitions of *rape* lead to the underreporting of rape when it involves acquaintances or family members, as well as the linguistic positioning of victims of such rapes as inadequate in their resistance. Ehrlich argues for

undermining the dichotomy between words and their material consequences for women's lives and bodies. *LWP* contributes to this project, she
suggests, by raising the question of whether correcting linguistic inequities
can correct the social inequities that underlie them.

In this section's final essay, Scott Kiesling considers how a focus on
men and masculinity illuminates *LWP* and shows how these issues are
central to the book. Kiesling observes that Lakoff's implicit separation of
gendered norms from real speakers means that multiple forms of femininity
and masculinity are available to both women and men. He goes on to
examine men's relationship to power and how this sheds light on Lakoff's
own treatment of power as differential across genders. Finally, he describes
how attention to mainstream masculinity makes visible Lakoff's early understanding of the now fashionable view of gender identities, both mainstream and marginalized, as performative.

The final sets of commentaries raise issues that were not yet, or not
fully, on the horizon of linguistic research when *LWP* was published. They
therefore trace the newest developments in scholarship on language, gender, and sexuality, noting the ways in which Lakoff's work helped make
such research possible.

Part 5, "Women's Places," considers the diversity of ways that women
use language, especially speakers who do not match the white, middle-class
American demographic of Lakoff's book. Judith Mattson Bean and Barbara
Johnstone consider how one Texas woman negotiates gendered expectations with her public role as the state leader of a powerful labor union, a
traditionally male and working-class group. They describe how, in keeping
with Lakoff's characterization of "women's language" and "men's language," this powerful woman reports her use of profanity to express authority and strong emotion but mitigates her self-descriptions using hedges
and laughter. While arguing for a theory of identity as flexible and creative,
Bean and Johnstone also draw on Lakoff's insights on how gender identities
are culturally constrained.

As the second commentary by Yoshiko Matsumoto indicates, just as
"women's language" is not the only linguistic style available to women in
the United States, women in Japan do not only use "Japanese women's
language." Matsumoto points out how, in a discussion of a Western male
scholar's analysis of "Japanese women's language," Lakoff challenges both
the sexism and the exoticism of much Western scholarship on this topic.
Matsumoto traces recent changes in gender norms in Japanese society and
language use, showing that even middle-aged, middle-class women use language stereotypically associated with men, yet she notes, following Lakoff,
that shifts away from "women's language" in Japan as in the United States
do not inevitably ensure gender equality.

In the next essay, Marcyliena Morgan demonstrates that the place for
women that *LWP* opened up can serve as a model for a language and
gender theory that makes African American women central rather than an

afterthought. Morgan notes that the significant gaps in our knowledge of African American language and gender practice, such as the absence of work on ordinary interactions between women and men, are largely due to racist stereotypes about African American gender roles. Morgan demonstrates how features of "women's language" as described by Lakoff also characterized the racial subordination demanded of African Americans under slavery and shows how African American women today variously exploit and reject elements of white "women's language" in indexing their identities.

Norma Mendoza-Denton's contribution to the volume likewise examines a group of speakers who must negotiate both racist ideologies and gender stereotypes: Latinas and Latinos in the United States. Surveying the research on gender and language among Latinas and Latinos, Mendoza-Denton notes that despite the cultural expectation that Latina girls and women should conform to the "ladylike" norms identified by Lakoff, many speakers transgress normative gender expectations. Mendoza-Denton points to her own research on class, gender, and ethnicity, focusing on how recent-immigrant, working-class Mexican girls confront the stereotype of linguistic and cultural conservatism that Lakoff describes.

In the last essay in this section, Sara Trechter considers Lakoff's political and cultural approach to language as a model for descriptive linguists working with endangered languages. She notes that even the small amount of linguistic work on gender in Native American communities may unwittingly promote or prescribe gender norms—especially because as fluent speakers are disappearing, linguistic descriptions take on authoritative roles for those seeking to revitalize their language. Trechter suggests that dialogic fieldwork methods, long a staple of feminist research, may help ensure that indigenous women have a central place in linguistic scholarship.

The final section of the book turns to issues that have, since *Language and Woman's Place* was published, transformed the study of language and gender into the study of language, gender, and sexuality. The first contribution, by William L. Leap, traces the conceptual and political parallels between the linguistic variety that Lakoff calls "women's language" and a similarly stable set of norms for some gay men. Leap observes that Lakoff's approach to language and gender is both theoretically and methodologically consonant with parallel trends in cultural studies in the 1970s, especially in her use of personal experience as a central method. In his own work on gay men's linguistic practices, Leap also draws on these theories and methods. He notes that although both his research and Lakoff's have been critiqued for their focus on white, middle-class speakers, both offered a description of one sociocultural context for language use that could be compared with others in later scholarship.

The question of the place of gay men in Lakoff's book is addressed in the next commentary by Rudolf P. Gaudio. Drawing on his own experiences as a gay academic man, Gaudio recalls the resistance of his younger

9

self to Lakoff's invocation of the stereotype that gay men talk like (straight) women and notes that neither gay men nor male academics are as oppositional to hegemonic masculinity as Lakoff, writing in Berkeley in its radical heyday, might have hoped. He concludes that critics of Lakoff's handling of gender and sexuality fail to read her work in the political context of leftist activism of the 1960s and 1970s as well as in the historical context of linguists' theoretical practice in the same period.

In the following essay, Robin Queen addresses the relationship between stereotypes and sexual identity in greater detail by focusing on lesbian identity. Queen points out that Lakoff's emphasis on stereotypes of the language use of white, heterosexual, middle-class women may actually help call attention to other stances toward the category of women. In her own research on lesbian language use, she similarly examines cultural representations to demonstrate how media images of lesbians aimed at mainstream and lesbian audiences offer widely divergent perspectives on the diversity of lesbian identities and their relationship to both femininity and masculinity.

The section—and the book—concludes with Rusty Barrett's examination of the central role of social norms in Lakoff's theory of language and gender, particularly in the context of reactions to the term *queer* in the field of language and sexuality. Barrett contrasts Lakoff's emphasis on the role of the listener in assigning social meaning to language with gender theorist Judith Butler's position that previously negative words such as *queer* can be assigned new, positive meanings. The widespread rejection of *queer* as an identity label, Barrett argues, would be predicted by Lakoff given her attention to social constraints on language change, even as the goals of queer theory and queer linguistics continue to be both viable and necessary. As Barrett and other authors in the volume point out, Lakoff's initial salvo in *LWP*—"Language uses us as much as we use language" (this volume, 39)—continues to offer a rich theoretical basis for new work on the relationship of language, gender, and sexuality in social life.

The range and diversity of the essays in this volume hint at how much work remains to understand fully Lakoff's contribution to feminist linguistics. In light of the breadth of topics they address, it is striking that so many common themes emerge. And in many cases the authors have zeroed in on issues in *LWP* that have long been overlooked in the extensive commentaries on the book within feminist linguistics and related fields, or that have been misinterpreted by Lakoff's critics. Among the themes that are repeatedly addressed in these pages are the following.

## 1. "Women's Language" as Ideology

As many of the authors in this volume observe (e.g., Eckert, Kiesling, McConnell-Ginet, Queen), Lakoff's formulation of "women's language" is at least as much a characterization of a widespread cultural ideology (or, in Lakoff's terms, a stereotype) of how women ought to speak as it is a description of the actual linguistic practices of real women. Yet this obvious fact was overlooked for many years, and only recently have scholars, made newly aware of the importance of ideology in language, recognized this crucial component of Lakoff's framework. The centrality of cultural members' beliefs about gender and language has become pivotal in research in the field, opening up new theoretical vistas that take ideology as an issue to be explored in its own right, as Lakoff did, rather than, as many of her critics would have it, as an obstacle to the correct empirical description of gendered language use.

## 2. Lakoff's Theorizing of "Women's Language" as an Index of Powerlessness

Whereas critics have often charged that Lakoff considers gender the most basic factor in her description of "women's language," several of the contributors point out that it is clear that Lakoff views power as the fundamental issue (e.g., Hall, Holmes, McElhinny, Meyerhoff). Moreover, as Lakoff (1990) makes explicit in her more recent writings addressing this critique, as long as gender inequality exists power and gender are inseparable concepts. This simple fact is demonstrated by a variety of contributions to this volume (e.g., Ehrlich, Herring, Kendall). However, authors also show that elements of "women's language" may be put to powerful ends (e.g., Cook-Gumperz, Davies, Ide), thereby demonstrating that, as Lakoff suggested early on, the displayed lack of power need not inevitably correlate with real-world powerlessness.

## 3. Lakoff's Attention to Masculinity and Men's Use of Language

LWP is most often characterized as an examination of "women's language," yet as a number of authors note, it also includes an analysis of "men's language" (e.g., Gaudio, Kiesling, Livia). Lakoff's description of "men's language" suggested that gendered linguistic norms for men functioned as ways of displaying an engagement with power. She addressed this issue with respect not only to men of diverse social classes but also to men whose political or occupational identities separated them from masculine norms. Lakoff's work thus presaged the increasing attention to men and masculinity in studies of language, gender, and sexuality and opened the door for a consideration of those men who may choose to resist mainstream masculinity.

11

## 4. Lakoff's Focus on Linguistic Practices That Violate Linguistic Norms

Despite the frequent charge that *LWP* takes a normative approach to language and gender, Lakoff was also attentive to the ways in which speakers might challenge gender norms of language use. This issue is explored most fully with respect to men, who for Lakoff, writing in the 1970s, were granted more cultural agency to opt out of traditional gendered practices. Thus Lakoff identified the speech of hippies, gay men, male academics, and upper-class men as nonnormative in the use of elements of "women's language" (Hall). But as several essays in this volume demonstrate, as cultural norms have shifted, women have likewise taken up some of the resources associated with "men's language" (Bean and Johnstone, Matsumoto, Mendoza-Denton), a linguistic change that Lakoff anticipated would come in the wake of social changes in gender arrangements.

## 5. Lakoff's Interest in the Interaction of Gender and Social Class

A number of commentators remark on Lakoff's attention to the relationship between social class and gendered linguistic behavior (e.g., Livia, Morgan), a relationship that for many years within language and gender studies was restricted almost entirely to quantitative studies of phonological variation. Lakoff's work on this issue is thus an important early contribution to the qualitative analysis of speech and social class. Her approach is particularly significant in that she takes the upper classes, rather than the lower, as those whose linguistic behavior is most in need of explanation, a perspective that runs counter to most sociolinguistic research. By analyzing upper-class men's use of "women's language" as a way of symbolizing their distance from the concerns of middle-class corporate masculinity, Lakoff implies that such speakers do not conform to dominant gender ideologies and should not be considered the prestige norm to which members of other social classes orient their own speech. She thus also indicates that gendered identities might differ for people of different social classes, an issue that continues to require exploration within language and gender research.

## 6. Lakoff's Use of an Introspective Methodology

Perhaps the most frequent target of critics of Lakoff's book is her decision to use introspection as a central source of data for her study. Several essays in this volume emphasize, however, that this approach was in keeping with mainstream linguistics of the day (e.g., Gaudio), and others offer an even more forceful objection to this complaint: introspection can be an important political and intellectual tool. Such a method can signal a rejection of rigidly positivistic approaches in favor of more interpretive perspectives (Leap). It may, in foregrounding dominant gender stereotypes, paradoxically highlight alternatives to normative gender (Queen), and it can demonstrate the 1970s-era feminist principle "the personal is political" (Bucholtz). Indeed, many contributors directly demonstrate the intimate connection between personal experience and scholarly activity by framing their discussion of Lakoff in relation to issues of gender and sexuality in their own lives (e.g., Barrett, Eckert, Gaudio, Kendall, Queen, Tannen).

## 7. Lakoff's Commitment to Social Justice

Early critiques of Lakoff acknowledged her position as a feminist but framed her as misguided in her approach. This dismissal of Lakoff's engagement with political issues, however, misses the crucial fact that *LWP* offers a radical challenge to mainstream scholarship as well as to mainstream society. Lakoff's text was one of the earliest and most forceful calls for linguists to use their professional knowledge and abilities to effect political change. What is more, it emerged in an academic climate in which political and intellectual endeavors remained largely separated and in which feminism in particular was regularly trivialized or ignored. It is an indication of how much has changed in the academy in the intervening years that so many authors in this volume bring this vital but underexplored dimension of Lakoff's work to the center of their discussion (e.g., Ehrlich, Morgan, Tannen, Trechter).

The foregoing brief description cannot do justice to the wealth of ideas in the following pages, both those proposed by Lakoff and those that respond to her work. This volume makes considerable progress toward addressing the omissions and errors in previous treatments of Lakoff's work and toward demonstrating the book's utility for contemporary scholarship. Yet it is far from exhausting either issue; much still remains to be mined in *LWP*. As Lakoff herself wrote regarding her pioneering work (this volume, 40), the present book is intended not as "the final word" but as "a goad to further research" that considers the role of the field's inaugural text in the study of language, gender, and sexuality.

### NOTE

I am indebted to Peter Ohlin, linguistics editor at Oxford University Press, for his strong support of this project, and to production editor Christi Stanforth and copyeditor Robert Dilworth for the care and attention they gave to the manuscript. I offer my thanks to all the contributors for their enthusiastic participation and rich and thoughtful contributions to this volume. I am especially grateful to Robin Lakoff, who trusted me with her words and work.

REFERENCES

Lakoff, Robin (1973). Language and woman's place. *Language in Society* 2:45–80.

———— (1975). *Language and woman's place.* New York: Harper & Row.

———— (1990). *Talking power.* New York: Basic Books.

::

# Author's Introduction

## Language and Woman's Place *Revisited*

ROBIN TOLMACH LAKOFF

1975

It is hard to remember just how different the world was when *Language and Woman's Place* (*LWP*) was first published in 1975 and harder still to return (even in imagination) to that world. Rereading the book, I am struck equally by how much has changed and how much remains essentially the same. While the knowledge available to me (as a linguist and a feminist) back then was much sparser than what we have at our disposal today, work done then still has bearing on the ways we think now.

The original essay was situated at a revolutionary moment, in both linguistics and women's history (not to mention American history). There was the youth revolution against the Vietnam War and the pieties of the "Establishment." There was women's liberation, born out of the civil rights and antiwar movements, but by about 1968 taking off on its own. The third (and most obscure) revolution occurred within transformational linguistics, the creation of generative semantics. Each of these contributed to *LWP*.

I entered linguistics as transformational generative grammar (TGG) was being developed at MIT by Noam Chomsky and his students and collaborators. It is difficult now to remember what linguistics was like prior to the advent of TGG: an obscure field, hyperspecialized, hardly capable of providing Big Answers or even asking Pretty Big Questions. American structural linguistics, the dominant paradigm in the United States until the mid-1960s, discouraged questions that could be explored through the medium of the investigator's intuitions. Language had to be analyzed as an astrophysicist might examine a distant galaxy. There were good historical reasons for this stance; but by the 1960s it had made linguistics a sterile discipline.

Besides being a powerfully charismatic figure in linguistics (and other fields), Chomsky played an active role in the antiwar movement. It was impossible to do linguistics at MIT and remain neutral about events in the larger world. Chomsky's growing status as public intellectual grew out of his contributions to linguistics, and brought that previously obscure field to public notice. It was thrilling: in our small way, *we*, the young and powerless, could play a role, however tiny, in making the revolution. *We* could change the language, the discourse, of a field—and of a nation.

But it is often true of revolutions—certainly of all of the ones I have personally known—that, once they succeed, they factionalize. By the late 1960s it had become clear to several of us that Chomsky's linguistic revolution wasn't the revolution in which we had enlisted. Chomsky had promised us a theory and method that would make language a "window into the mind." But within standard transformational theory that possibility could be realized only to a very limited degree, if at all. While investigators could use their minds as interpretive instruments—to judge the grammaticality or semantic similarity of sentences—they were not permitted to investigate meaning, much less a speaker's intention in uttering a sentence in a particular form, or the effect of that utterance on an addressee. TGG permitted us to posit a formal relationship between active and passive sentences but not to talk about why English has a passive construction, or why a speaker would be moved to use it. Particles like *well, I mean*, or *like* were beyond analysis and beneath contempt, examples of "performance" rather than "competence" and hence not rule-governed. (Yet speakers know how to use them and knowledge of this kind is what the linguistic grammar represents.) Such cases began to multiply. Chomskyan theory eliminated the possibility of examining those parts of language that revealed the most about its users' minds and social relationships. If transformational theory was a window into the mind, that window was in need of cleaning. Some of us began to think about ways to build depth into TGG, in which we still counted ourselves true believers. We devised rules and representations to relate externally accessible linguistic forms to mental states—for example, desires, assumptions, and personal identities—while retaining the Chomskyan belief in the primacy of the syntactic component of the grammar. Deep structure simply got deeper, wider, and more complex.

Far from accepting these innovations as moves in the right direction, Chomsky and his loyal adherents objected strenuously, creating an irrevocable breach. The new theory, generative semantics, was impossible, they argued. It was—the ultimate dismissal—"too powerful": rather than being the most economical way to relate surface form to deeper structures, it forced into the theory more complex, messy, barely formalizable constructs; it required that there be many more—and more kinds of—transformational rules relating deep and surface structures than were required in the simple and general formulations of the standard theory. Chomsky's concept of "explanatory adequacy" required the linguist to choose the theory that related deep to surface in the simplest, most economical, way.

We riposted: simple and economical TGG might well be if the criteria for adequacy were minimal. But to relate language and mind, the grammar had to be more complex than was possible in the standard theory. That complexity, while messy, would permit deeper, more gratifying explanations: real explanatory adequacy. It would allow linguistics to relate form to meaning and intention, demonstrating (something notoriously missing in the Chomskyan systematics) a precise, rigorous linkage between thought, culture, and language—an ambitious but essential project.

Much too ambitious, the other side (by then known as Extended Standard Theory) groused. If you followed generative semantics to its logical conclusion, *everything* speakers know about the world would have to be included within the transformational component, which therefore would become infinite. And while the output of the grammar, the sentences of a language, constitute an infinite repertoire, the grammar itself could not be infinite, or it could not be learned, and no one would be able to internalize the grammar and speak a language.

Not necessarily, said the generative semanticists. The linguistic grammar need only include those aspects of the extralinguistic world that have direct bearing on grammatical form: just a small subset of *everything*. So for instance, the grammar would have to include some representation of the social status of participants, at least in those languages that force speakers to make distinctions between intimate and formal second person address. But it would not have to incorporate specific mention of participants' occupations, or heights, or religions. The project was achievable. But we still had to answer, at least to our own satisfaction, the question that these claims raised: What parts of our psychological and social reality *did* require linguistic encoding, in at least some languages?

While this brouhaha was going on in the rarefied world of linguistic theory, other fights were proceeding in the larger universe. By around 1968 the feminist movement (then most commonly called "women's liberation," or, often disparagingly, "women's lib") was coming into its own. It is often hard to locate the moment at which a revolution begins: the storming of the Bastille, the Boston Tea Party, or the moment at which the women's movement caught fire. The 1963 publication of Betty Friedan's *Feminine Mystique* was critical. Also important was the training many women received in revolutionary theory and practice in the civil rights and antiwar movements: not only the practical experience of distributing leaflets, striking, sitting-in, and otherwise protesting; but the less gratifying realization that they were being left to make the coffee and run the mimeograph machines while the men got credit for the intellectual heavy lifting. Rising out of these experiences, feminism emerged in the late 1960s as an articulate locus of protest of its own. What women had learned from participating, if often behind the scenes, in the earlier movements they brought to the new one, their own.

The women's movement first exploded taboos, speaking the unspeakable, thinking the unthinkable, occasionally even doing the undoable.

17

While bras may never have been burned, old constraints were incinerated in those early years of "sisterhood." It was recognized early that language was important, that there were consequences when grown women were "girls" and when the masculine pronoun was "normal" to refer to everybody.

Generative semantics and the women's movement thus both arose as protests against the status quo, against the assumption of the unmarked and the "normal" as unquestionable. Both generative semantics and the linguistic arm of the women's movement started on a small scale, looking at the smaller and more concrete aspects of language. Transformational theory (including generative semantics) had permitted the incorporation of syntax into linguistics (the antimentalism of structuralism largely kept levels above morphology off-limits for them), but the possibility of incorporating larger and more abstract units — conversational turns, paragraphs, discourse — into linguistic analysis was still well in the future. Linguists spoke on occasion of "structure above (or beyond) the sentence level," but mostly about how it couldn't be done. When we attempted it, we thought of larger units as concatenations of sentences: $S + S + S \ldots$, rather than as structures with rules of their own, wholes different from the sum of their parts. Likewise, when linguists began to address the relationship between language and gender, we started with the smallest and most concrete units: sounds and words. Later, in the mid-1970s, when linguistics (and allied disciplines) provided the means for larger-scale analyses, those of us working in this area were quick to put them to use.

So generative semantics and the women's movement had similarly revolutionary origins and a similar need to question and subvert established beliefs. For me at any rate they came together in another way as well. My interest in the intersection of language and gender arose on two fronts: my political involvement in the women's movement and my academic engagement in the transformational dispute.

If generative semantics could demonstrate that it could distinguish those concepts that required underlying structure representation (because they had, in at least some languages, explicit linguistic encoding) from those that did not, we could demonstrate that our grammar was finite. But what kinds of concepts required inclusion? One potential answer: gender.

The inclusion of gender as an area of linguistic investigation was less obvious thirty years ago than it seems today. Scholars were willing to acknowledge that in a few "exotic" languages (Japanese, Dyirbal, Arawak, and Koasati) the genders of participants and subjects of conversations required linguistic encoding and hence (arguably) underlying structure representation. But this seemed not to be true of English and other languages with which investigators were likely to be familiar. And if a case could not be made for the inclusion of gender in English, then arguably, gender was not a part of universal grammar and hence not a part of underlying struc-

ture. It would remain beyond what was defined as "interesting" (like "structure beyond the sentence level").

So my aim, in embarking on *LWP*, was threefold:

1. To demonstrate that *at least one* extralinguistic artifact (i.e., gender) required linguistic representation;
2. To demonstrate that gender required linguistic representation
   even in languages like English, where its presence was (perhaps)
   less clearly felt than in "exotic" languages
   (these were my concerns as a linguist);
3. To use linguistic discrepancies between women and men as a
   diagnostic of social and psychological inequities between the
   sexes.
   (This was my concern as a feminist.)

## 2003

We have come a long way (baby), to paraphrase an irritating advertising
slogan from the 1970s. Like the sentiments expressed in the commercial,
the changes in gender stereotypes may look encouraging but, when in-
spected more closely, are often depressing. Many of the expressions that
were commonplace back then, serving to keep women in their place, have
become marginal or nonexistent. The difference between the bad old ways
of speech and the problematic language that swirls around us now illustrates how far we have come:

- Allusions to former first lady Hillary Rodham Clinton (even today, long after her time in the White House) in the media, as a
  strident feminist and obstreperous bitch (while the current first
  lady, Laura Bush, is often presented, crypto-contrastively, as
  sweetly submissive);
- The continued sniping at "feminism" and "feminists" as the
  cause of all things evil (the high crime rate, drug addiction, the
  decline of the educational system, and as in Sommers [2000],
  discussed below, the problems facing males); and the frequent
  denials of feminist sympathies by younger women, even as they
  espouse feminist values;
- The nostalgia for a past when men were men, women were
  women, there was no divorce, and children were seen and not
  heard as a halcyon golden age—although historical research
  shows that such a time either never existed or was much less
  pleasant for many of us than the myth suggests.

Linguistics has also come of age. While a generation ago "structure
above the sentence level" had the status of the basilisk (mythical and toxic),

19

now it is an accepted area of linguistics, and methods of discovery and analysis have been developed to understand it. By the mid-1970s conversation analysis had been brought into sociolinguistics; during the 1970s pragmatics focused attention on the function of sentence-level phenomena rather than their form, recasting them as "utterances" rather than "sentences."

By the 1980s discourse analysts were examining many types of communication, often via conversation analysis: language in the courtroom, at dinner parties, between the sexes, in the workplace (to give a few examples). These analyses made it clear that discourse should be understood not as concatenations of S's, but as language directed toward particular interactive and psychological purposes. These changes were not universally accepted. Some are unhappy about the extension of linguistics to this broad domain: they still think of language as a string of forms unrelated to function. Some feel that only thus can linguistics remain properly academic, unpoliticized, and "objective." Some feel that only thus can linguistics be "scientific" and deserving of respect. But others feel that there is no such thing as language in the abstract, or in a vacuum; language can only be understood as the product of human need and desire. We note the enthusiastic attendance at language and gender conferences; the proliferation of journals on sociolinguistics, discourse, and pragmatics; and the fact that, when linguistics penetrates into the consciousness of the lay public, it is inevitably in one of its hyphenated variants (genderlect, "Ebonics," language preservation). So it seems safe to say that "structure beyond the sentence level" is here to stay as an area of study within linguistics, just as it seems safe to say that women are here to stay as public speakers and makers of general meaning. The grumblings against both demonstrate their inevitability.

The changes in both fields since I wrote *LWP* mean that, if I were writing it today, I would go about it quite differently. We might still consider the occasional word or phrase in isolation and contemplate its significance: we might consider the continuing complaints about "male-bashing" (when historically very little was ever heard about "misogyny," and much of that neutral or even positive); but we might note contrastively the acceptance of the notion of "spousal abuse" and "acquaintance rape" as negative, indeed criminally actionable, behaviors. We could comment more ambivalently on the frequent discussions of women's desire for "having it all" (as a particularly female form of greed) or the rise of the "supermom" and the "soccer mom." We might point out that such phrases indicate that women's status is still not equal to men's: men normally expect to "have it all," and are not ridiculed for trying. There are no analogous "superdads" or "soccer dads," or for that matter, "ballet-school dads." A woman trying to juggle family and career is shunted to the "mommy track" or warned to stay home and tend to her family, lest the "Nannycam" prove that her child-care worker is up to no good. A man with both career and family is just a successful person. The "stay-at-home mom" (a term happily replacing "just a housewife") is still *normal* — psychologically if not statistically. At the very least, even this sort of simple analysis indicates that language remains a window into the mind: the words we have constructed over the last couple of decades reflect our new uncertainties and our new possibilities.

But since we linguists have at our disposal today more powerful ways of connecting language to reality, a good way to rethink and recontextualize the claims of *LWP* would be to look not at words, or sentences, but at discourse on a larger scale. As a society, how do we talk about women, about feminists, about the genders and their respective roles?

We could look at discourse at a couple of levels: first, public discourse proper: what has been said, in the most public arenas, on the topics above. And, second, metadiscourse: what has been said about what has been said (reviews and think pieces). Contemplating either one, we should be at least as concerned with what is *not* said as with what is said.

We see that gender is on the front burner today as much as it was a generation ago. "Woman's lib" is not a done deal, gender relations are still in ferment, evolution, and revolution, progress and regression. We are still determining what language is "normal," what worthy of discussion or criticism; what novel attitudes, behaviors, or utterances mean, and how to categorize them. Our project is simply the reorganization of a primal aspect of our identities, our sexuality and gender — a reorganization facilitated and complicated by language.

A couple of articles that appeared in the *New York Times Magazine* while I was writing this essay illustrate our current dilemmas. While the topics they discuss existed in the 1970s, they would not have attracted the attention of such a prestigious venue. The content of the articles, the style in which they are written, and the fact that they have appeared when and where they have tell us something about our current ways of dealing with gender as individuals and as a culture.

First (chronologically) is an article by Margaret Talbot (2002) entitled "Supermom Fictions." It discusses the conflicts today's women encounter between family and career, the myth of "having it all." Talbot is surprised at modern women's surprise that life for working women tends to be "messy," that there is always juggling to be done, and a ball or two is sometimes dropped. Talbot makes a reasonable point — life *is* that way and most of us learn to deal with it well enough — but asks why we believed it could be otherwise. The answer: we were misled by "feminism." Her examples: a 1970s perfume ad (did "feminists" write it?) and Helen Reddy's "I Am Woman," which she calls "the anthem of 'having it all' " (2002: 11).

Well, maybe so. But the problem with Talbot's analysis is that, as so often, women's difficulties in the new world are ascribed either to women's unreasonableness and greed, or to the impossible demands of "feminism." But could there be a third answer? Perhaps women's lives are messy because no one gives them much help. In the 1970s it seemed reasonable for women to compare their situation to men's and ask: Why can't—shouldn't—female and male life trajectories be parallel? If men can have both families and careers without going crazy or being accused of greed, why can't women? (And by the same token, if men want to spend many years of their lives staying at home with the children, why should that virtually always be seen as risible or unmanly?) Here as often the prevailing rhetoric prevents even reasonable and savvy people like Talbot from seeing that their arguments are deceptive in their failure to consider the need for deep social change.

Another article from the *New York Times Magazine*, "Fierce Encounters," by Deborah Sontag (2002), questions the current treatment of spousal abusers by the legal system: automatic arrest and, typically, incarceration. It argues that many abused women would prefer for their abusers not to be arrested but to receive other forms of treatment. Many such women, says Sontag, feel that they bear at least some of the responsibility for the attack: they instigated it, they landed the first blow. Sontag (reasonably, I think) suggests that we reevaluate our absolutist stand: arrest as the only option. At the same time, she doesn't discuss the opposite argument: that if you (essentially) leave it up to the woman to determine her partner's punishment (or lack of it), you put her in a very vulnerable position, making her (should she opt for jail) even more in future danger. The unasked question is: Who decides who is responsible for things? Who gets the power to determine whose meaning?

This was a question that I couldn't approach in *LWP*. Meaning, power, and responsibility can only be analyzed and discussed through the analysis of discourse. And, at the time, the women's movement could not see things as we do today.

The pressing problem then was the fact that women had very little opportunity to speak for themselves in public so as to be heard and have an effect. If we got any response it tended to be belittling (as in, "You're so cute when you're mad"). To some, even today, this state of affairs is laden with comforting nostalgia: if you couldn't take responsibility for anything, you couldn't be blamed when it went wrong. But those nostalgic for the past forget that you also couldn't get credit when something went right; and somehow, from the Book of Genesis to *The Manchurian Candidate*, women—powerless though in fact they might be—received disproportionate blame for all kinds of disasters throughout human history. At least if we had really had the power and the responsibility, that might have been more bearable.

Today we have achieved a significant amount of meaning-making power and responsibility. When women agitate to punish spousal abusers, they are listened to. When women try to ban prostitution and pornography, they are taken seriously. Both of these cases unfortunately pit women against other women: abuse experts against abuse victims; antiporn and antiprostitution advocates (often feminists) against pornographers, lovers of erotica, and prostitutes (many of them women). The questions raised by these paradoxes—who can speak for whom? Who should be listened to, and on what grounds?—turn out to resist simple answers.

In demanding that all abusers be punished, with no input from the abused spouse; and in arguing that all prostitution is the result of, and contributes to the creation of, women's sexual slavery, powerlessness, and objectification, one (typically middle-class) group of women is—generally without meaning to—intruding on another's (usually working-class) autonomy and self-esteem, saying in effect that no matter what these women say, they should not be listened to because they are the dupes of men, or they don't know any better. Women, however, may find themselves in horrible positions as a result of powerlessness, prior abuse, dependency on men, and belief in misogynist stereotypes. That men once had the unquestioned right to make meaning for women, we can now clearly see as unjust. But how are feminists to deal with the temptation to make meaning for other women? Is it ever right? If so, when? If not, on what basis should policy decisions be made? These questions are about discourse rights, meaning-making, and the political function of language. They are difficult, but we have to find the tools to get answers to them.

One of the most valuable discovery procedures introduced into linguistics by transformational generative grammar is the use of the asterisk (*)—the recognition that nonoccurring cases define the limitations of the grammar and are therefore essential to a complete grammar. In sentence-level grammar, the asterisk could be used to mark a sentence (or a word, a combination of sounds, or a morphological ending) that could not occur in the language—one that would be recognized as aberrant by a fluent speaker. The rules of the grammar had to account for that gap in the paradigm. This was the point of entry of mentalism into linguistics: only the analyst's knowledge of the language under investigation could predict whether or not a form could occur. Without this significant broadening and deepening of the tasks and goals of linguistics, the great achievements of TGG could not have been realized.

If we are to extend the domain of the grammar into extrasentential structure, how would the asterisk, or an equivalent, function? Just as feminist argument must be made more supple and subtle, more open to ambiguity and indeterminacy, so linguistic argumentation needs to develop in order to be useful in exploring this new terrain. The analysis of discourse has been devised within many fields. Some, such as conversation analysis, deriving from small-group sociology via ethnomethodology, are aggressively empirical and antimentalistic. Strictly empirical analysis has proved a valuable tool; but it has made it impossible to explore many of the most interesting questions about ourselves that linguistic investigation is ideally designed to answer. Yet—and this is the same paradox faced by the early-twentieth-century developers of the social sciences—if we permit the attitudes and mindsets of analysts to enter their analyses, we may be inviting irresponsible and unfalsifiable conclusions, like the first analysts of "exotic" languages, the missionaries and travelers whose dubious claims led to the requirement of antimentalism in the first place.

Some aspects of Chomskyan TGG may reasonably be brought into discourse analysis. When I wrote *LWP*, I made this assumption without understanding that it was controversial. I had been trained as a transformational grammarian. At the time, I was not aware that, to people not trained as theoretical syntacticians, the extension of TGG to interaction and discourse (even as it existed inchoately then) would be seen as controversial, even outrageous. (And syntactic theorists saw the extension of the assumptions of TGG to interaction and discourse as equally outrageous — for opposite reasons.) I wish I had appreciated the controversial nature of what I was trying to do, in bringing asterisks and paradigms into sociolinguistic examination. But I thought that language was language: if a method of analysis yielded interesting results, it was justified. If a method worked in one area, perhaps it would work in others.

Without the application of mentalistic methods and intuitionist discovery procedures, the work I wanted to do could not be done. For all its great usefulness, conversation analysis is of no help in dealing with paradigm gaps: it cannot talk about what does not occur in the transcript. Nor can it talk about why something is absent from the data: Is the omission due to an accidental gap or to rule-governed necessity? So intuition and introspection must play a role in at least some kinds of analyses. Criticism of my method that stops (as much of it does) at the outraged discovery that it is not entirely "empirical" is, therefore, not to the point. Linguistics must have both mentalistic and empirical methods at its disposal.

If we are to be able to make predictions about what arguments or contributions occur in contiguity, we must talk about items that are absent from the text although logically we might expect to find them. There might be any number of reasons for their absence. They might be like true asterisked sentences, logically or rationally uninterpretable: *Sincerity admires John.* Or their absence might be due to culturally "normal" ways of thought: the absent argument might fail to occur to speakers because the stereotypes of their culture impose blinders on them, making them unable to see alternatives to the world they are assuming in their arguments.

Consider, as examples of this method of looking at discourse, two texts, or, better, a text and its metatext: Christina Hoff Sommers's (2000) *The War against Boys: How Misguided Feminism Is Harming Our Young Men* and reviews of it in the *New York Times* (daily and Sunday *Book Review*), and another review in the neoconservative journal *Commentary*. What I find surprising about the entire set is less what it says than what it does not say. Sommers's text is peppered with illogical conclusions, omitted considerations, and the like. Even purportedly negative reviews of the book do not confront these problems. The logical gaps in the basic text are especially curious: Sommers was trained as a philosopher and taught in a philosophy department before joining the conservative American Enterprise Institute. While philosophers are not known for statistical acumen or for painstaking collection of empirical data, they are expected to have a grasp of logical argumentation.

Sommers's argument starts from observations (not her own) of reality. In recent years, in the U.S. educational system (especially in primary and secondary schools), boys appear by several measures to be falling behind girls. They drop out at a higher rate; their grades in most subjects are lower; they are more prone to get involved in drugs, crime, and violence; and they do more poorly on Scholastic Aptitude Tests and other objective tests of achievement and aptitude.

Let us grant that these claims are correct (although many are open to alternative analyses). Why, according to Sommers, have these things happened since the 1960s? She has a simple, snappy answer: the "feminization" of education at the hands of "feminists." "Misguided" feminists, that is. "Misguided feminism" in her subtitle is syntactically ambiguous: Is the noun phrase derived from a restrictive ("[that kind of] feminism that is misguided") or nonrestrictive ("feminism, which is [necessarily] misguided") relative clause? From the evidence I suspect the latter.

Sommers claims first that primary and secondary school teachers, who tend to be female, have imposed female standards of behavior on their charges. (It is harder for little boys to sit still than for little girls, for instance, and school demands that children sit still for long periods.) Here Sommers makes use of obvious evidence: of course it's true that women dominate elementary and secondary school teaching. (A feminist plot? Hardly!) And it is likewise true that the kind of conduct demanded in school comes easier to girls than boys. But this has always been true — schools demanded the same kind of behavior even when teachers were male and women were not educated. Some might call it "middle-class training," rather than "feminization." Second, Sommers asserts that feminists and sympathetic educational and psychological theorists have "pathologized" normal rambunctious males. The book begins with a dazzling riff on this theme: "It's a bad time to be a boy in America. As the new millennium begins, the triumphant victory of our women's soccer team has come to symbolize the spirit of American girls. The defining event for boys is the shooting at Columbine High" (2002: 13).

A very grabby beginning, to be sure, and a scary one if you are male or a parent of young males. But an opening also full of hyperbole likely to encourage illegitimate conclusions. First, the events at Columbine cannot be — and never were — equated with "normal" male behavior. Next, Sommers makes a kind of implicit equation, soon to become an explicit part of her argument: *The "pathologization" of boys (as demonstrated by Columbine's being their "defining" event) is a direct outcome of the "triumph" of girls.* Post hoc, ergo propter hoc. Even if we take her two statements to be true at face value, is the second the necessary result of the first? Is it even related to the first? Is gender equity (as Sommers's argument implies) a zero-sum game: females win only if males lose?

The questions go deeper. Is it really true that these are the defining events of femaleness and maleness at the turn of the millennium? Certainly both were important, and both received a great deal of media attention—perhaps too great in the case of Columbine. Certainly most Americans cheered Mia Hamm and her team—but their victory defined *one set of options* for women. It did not exclusively symbolize the spirit of American girls. It—along with other events—did symbolize the fact that women have made great strides and are now in a position to do things they had not formerly been able to do. But there are other positive defining events for women: the increasing participation of high school girls in science contests, the electoral victory of Hillary Rodham Clinton and other women, the appointment of Madeleine Albright as Bill Clinton's secretary of state. And there are negatives, like the great success of the reality show *The Bachelor.*

But if those are evidence of women's success, we can easily find their male equivalents: many Olympic victories by all-male teams; the election victory of George W. Bush and his appointment of Colin Powell as secretary of state; and others too numerous to mention. If females and males are roughly equal in the population, then the achievements of men are still, proportionally, greater than those of women. So it is hard to claim statistically that men have lost by women's gains. Perhaps they get a sliver less of the pie. But their share is certainly no less than 50 percent of the total. What has begun to shift is society's definition of the *normal* or *unmarked* for women. Options previously unmarked for males (e.g., success in sports and politics) are increasingly *less marked than they used to be* (but still marked) for women. It's hard to see how this shift leads inexorably to Columbine, but for Sommers it does just that.

Sommers makes the claim that boys are now defined by Columbine. Columbine, as a horrible event, received an inordinate amount of attention. Some of that attention focused on *certain kinds of* boys: on the one hand, bullies; on the other, the targets of the bullies, who are (very occasionally, though you'd never guess this from the coverage) driven to avenge themselves in hideous ways. But there was, to my recollection (and Sommers provides no counterexamples) no media discourse to the effect that Columbine and similar events represent a "pathology" common to all or even the majority of young males—any more than there was a claim that all or most women could have won Olympic medals. At most, we might say that as the Olympic victory stood for *the best* women could achieve (in one area at any rate), Columbine illustrated *the worst* males could descend to. But that is far from a "defining event."

The rest of Sommers's case depends on just such flimsy argumentation. Its bases often look sturdy: tables of figures and authoritative quotations. But the juxtapositions that make the arguments superficially persuasive and the claims that Sommers derives from her data are all questionable. Yet they receive no serious questioning, even by the most purportedly "negative" reviewers.

Let us, for the sake of argument, take her statement (A) at face value: boys are failing in school and in society. Let us also accept her other premise (B): that, in part driven by feminism, women are becoming more successful in both areas. From those truths, can we safely draw the conclusion that A is the result of B?

Of course not: the relationship between A and B could take any of several forms. Further research is needed to determine which, if any, is the case:

1. Sommers's claim: B caused A.
2. A caused B.
3. Neither caused the other. The occurrence of both, at around the same time, is coincidence.
4. Neither caused the other. Both were caused by a third factor, C, not yet identified.

And there are probably other possibilities. No reputable scientist would stake her career on (1) being correct without examining the other possibilities and eliminating them. No reputable philosopher would support an argument based on logical errors. I'm not a philosopher. (I don't even play one on TV.) But I can detect a logical flaw when it is big enough to drive an SUV through.

But the flaws in Sommers's arguments are not the strangest thing in this set of texts. What is particularly odd is that few if any of the commentators on the book have noted these flaws. The negative reviews take issue with the interpretation of particular cases, or with Sommers's taste for hyperbole, but they never look at Sommers's overall logic. This is odd since (as any author knows) a reviewer likes nothing better than picking holes in authorial arguments: the bigger the hole, the smarter the reviewer looks. A neoconservative (Finn 2000) writing a strongly positive review in the neocon journal *Commentary* describes Robert Coles's review (2000) in the *New York Times Book Review* as "thrashing" Sommers. On this evidence, we might assume that Coles's review was particularly savage. But it isn't, by a long shot. He criticizes Sommers's "high, hectoring pitch" in her attack on Carol Gilligan. But his criticism is chiefly that we should be concerned about the future of girls and boys alike (as indeed we should). There is no analysis of Sommers's arguments themselves and nothing that qualifies, in my lexicon, as "thrashing."

How can we explain the absence from the public discourse of careful analysis of Sommers's arguments? I can only suppose that those flaws have gone unnoticed by critics and remain inaccessible to most readers. Here is a gap in the paradigm, a missing piece, analogous to an asterisked sen-

tence in the syntactic inventory of English. The absence needs to be explained, in order for the discourse (basic and meta-) of *The War against
Boys* to become "grammatical" — to make sense.

Here's one explanation: the culture still perceives male achievement
towering over female achievement as "normal," that is, not requiring explanation, and therefore misses the first point, that males aren't really falling behind — females are simply beginning to catch up. They don't see that
the true norm is for both women and men to succeed in equal proportions,
at the Olympics or anywhere else. So when the percentage of success edges
a little closer to that mythic 50 percent apiece, *that* (rather than rampant
inequality) is construed as abnormal, eliciting fear and requiring "explanation."

If we turn to the problem of male pathologization, neither Sommers
nor her critics notice that, over history, females have been "pathologized"
to a far greater degree than males are now. Think of Freud; think of the
*Malleus Maleficarum*; think of millennia of misogyny. What is shocking in
current discourse, to Sommers and similar traditionalists, is that males are
now receiving *some* of the pathologization, if indeed they are. Women are
still the recipients of at least their share. We are blind to female pathologization, because it's "normal." But serious social critiques, and critiques
of those critiques, need to be able to perceive the abnormality in normality,
and comment on the roles and expectations of both females and males
from a fully objective position. We need to remove the blinders that millennia of misogyny have normalized. While none of us can achieve this
yet, we must at least be aware of our unawareness and its causes.

Just as talking about *widow* versus *widower*, *master* versus *mistress*, and
differences in tag-question usage were ways that the linguistic sophistication
of thirty years ago provided to enable me to demonstrate inequality between
female and male roles in society, today's linguists have additional options,
permitting us to examine, through language, the possibilities open to
women and men in different and deeper ways. Our work is still before us.

REFERENCES

Coles, Robert (2000). Boys to men. *New York Times Book Review*, June 25:20.
Finn, Chester E. Jr. (2000). The war against boys. *Commentary* 110(2) (Septem-
     ber):68.
Friedan, Betty. (1963). *The feminine mystique.* New York: Dell.
Sommers, Christina Hoff (2000). *The war against boys: How misguided feminism
     is harming our young men.* New York: Simon & Schuster.
Sontag, Deborah (2002). Fierce entanglements. *New York Times Magazine*, No-
     vember 17:52.
Talbot, Margaret (2002). Supermom fictions. *New York Times Magazine*, October
     27:11.

THE ORIGINAL TEXT *with Annotations by the Author*

# LANGUAGE AND WOMAN'S PLACE

Robin Lakoff

1975

For Andy[1]

whose generation will, I hope, have transcended

these issues by the time it can read this book.

# Contents

∷

# Preface

One can look at woman's position in our society from any number of points of view and gain enlightenment from each. In this book I have tried to see what we can learn about the way women view themselves and everyone's assumptions about the nature and role of women from the use of language in our culture, that is to say, the language used by and about women. While my reasons for taking this particular tack are based on my training in linguistics, I feel that such study is quite justifiable in its own terms. Language is more amenable to precise reproduction on paper and unambiguous analysis than are other forms of human behavior; if we tell someone he[2] has done something sexist, we often don't know how to describe exactly what he's done so that we can argue meaningfully about the truth of that assertion: the evidence vanishes before it can be studied. But if we say to someone, "You said . . . , which is insulting to women," provided he agrees that he has made the statement, it is available and open to close analysis. Often, as psychoanalysis has shown in such detail, we say things without knowing their significance, but the fact that we have said them shows that there is more going on in our minds than we consciously take credit for. By looking at the way we customarily talk if we are women, or talk about women whoever we are, we can gain insight into the way we feel — about ourselves, about women — through close analysis of what we say and how we say it until in the end we can ask and perhaps even answer the question: *Why* did I say it? It is my hope, then, to look at some of these linguistic issues and see what they tell us.

The ideas that are discussed in the book are the result of many hours of mind-stretching and insightful discussion and argument with many people, mention of whose names here is scarcely a just reward for what each has contributed to my thinking. First of all, in both time and importance, George Lakoff has been my teacher, adviser, and friend, linguistically and otherwise, for many years; most of what I know about language can be traced to him. I have also learned by having to argue him out of male-chauvinist ways and assumptions many times over the years; probably I would never have started thinking about the questions posed here had he not forced me to defend myself in arguments about linguistic sexism.

Many of my colleagues and friends have also been helpful; let me single out a few for mention, though many others have been helpful as well: Charlotte Baker, Wallace Chafe, Louise Cherry, Herb and Eve Clark, Alan Dershowitz, Richard Diebold, James Fox, David Green, Georgia Green, John and Jenny Gumperz, Dell Hymes, Mary Ritchie Key, John and Sally Lawler, Susan Matisoff, James D. McCawley, Michelle Rosaldo, John R. Ross, Louis Sass, Julia Stanley, Emily Stoper, Elizabeth Traugott, Monica Wilson, and Philip Zimbardo.

I should also like to thank the Center for Advanced Study for the Behavioral Sciences, where I was a Fellow in 1971–72 and where I did most of the research and writing underlying the first part of this book; and the National Science Foundation, which has supported the research for these studies under grant GS-38476.

# PART I: LANGUAGE AND WOMAN'S PLACE

# 1 ::

## Introduction

Language uses us as much as we use language.[3] As much as our choice of
forms of expression is guided by the thoughts we want to express, to the
same extent the way we feel about the things in the real world governs the
way we express ourselves about these things. Two words can be synonymous
in their denotative sense, but one will be used in case a speaker feels
favorably toward the object the word denotes, the other if he is unfavorably
disposed. Similar situations are legion, involving unexpectedness, interest,
and other emotional reactions on the part of the speaker to what he is
talking about. Thus, while two speakers may be talking about the same
thing or real-world situation, their descriptions may end up sounding utterly
unrelated. The following well-known paradigm will be illustrative.

(1)   (a)  I am strong-minded.
      (b)  You are obstinate.
      (c)  He is pigheaded.

If it is indeed true that our feelings about the world color our expression of our thoughts, then we can use our linguistic behavior as a
diagnostic of our hidden feelings about things.[4] For often — as anyone with
even a nodding acquaintance with modern psychoanalytic writing knows
too well — we can interpret our overt actions, or our perceptions, in accordance with our desires, distorting them as we see fit. But the linguistic data
are there, in black and white, or on tape, unambiguous and unavoidable.
Hence, while in the ideal world other kinds of evidence for sociological
phenomena would be desirable along with, or in addition to, linguistic
evidence, sometimes at least the latter is all we can get with certainty. This
is especially likely in emotionally charged areas like that of sexism and
other forms of discriminatory behavior. This book, then, is an attempt to
provide diagnostic evidence from language use for one type of inequity that
has been claimed to exist in our society: that between the roles of men
and women. I will attempt to discover what language use can tell us about
the nature and extent of any inequity; and finally to ask whether anything
can be done, from the linguistic end of the problem: does one correct a
social inequity by changing linguistic disparities? We will find, I think, that
women experience linguistic discrimination in two ways: in the way they
are taught to use language, and in the way general language use treats
them. Both tend, as we shall see, to relegate women to certain subservient
functions: that of sex object, or servant; and therefore certain lexical items

mean one thing applied to men, another to women, a difference that cannot be predicted except with reference to the different roles the sexes play in society.

The data on which I am basing my claims have been gathered mainly by introspection: I have examined my own speech and that of my acquaintances, and have used my own intuitions in analyzing it. I have also made use of the media: in some ways, the speech heard, for example, in commercials or situation comedies on television mirrors the speech of the television-watching community: if it did not (not necessarily as an exact replica, but perhaps as a reflection of how the audience sees itself or wishes it were), it would not succeed.[5] The sociologist, anthropologist or ethnomethodologist familar with what seem to him more error-proof data-gathering techniques, such as the recording of random conversation, may object that these introspective methods may produce dubious results. But first, it should be noted that *any* procedure is at some point introspective: the gatherer must analyze his data, after all. Then, one necessarily selects a subgroup of the population to work with: is the educated, white, middle-class group that the writer of the book identifies with less worthy of study than any other? And finally, there is the purely pragmatic issue: random conversation must go on for quite some time, and the recorder must be exceedingly lucky anyway, in order to produce evidence of any particular hypothesis, for example, that there is sexism in language, that there is not sexism in language. If we are to have a good sample of data to analyze, this will have to be elicited artificially from someone; I submit I am as good an artificial source of data as anyone.

These defenses are not meant to suggest that either the methodology or the results are final, or perfect. I mean to suggest one possible approach to the problem, one set of facts. I do feel that the majority of the claims I make will hold for the majority of speakers of English; that, in fact, much may, *mutatis mutandis*, be universal. But granting that this study does in itself represent the speech of only a small subpart of the community, it is still of use in indicating directions for further research in this area: in providing a basis for comparison, a taking-off point for further studies, a means of discovering what is universal in the data and what is not, and why. That is to say, I present what follows less as the final word on the subject of sexism in language — anything but that! — than as a goad to further research.

If a little girl "talks rough" like a boy, she will normally be ostracized, scolded, or made fun of. In this way society, in the form of a child's parents and friends, keeps her in line, in her place. This socializing process is, in most of its aspects, harmless and often necessary, but in this particular instance — the teaching of special linguistic uses to little girls — it raises serious problems, though the teachers may well be unaware of this. If the little girl learns her lesson well, she is not rewarded with unquestioned acceptance on the part of society; rather, the acquisition of this special style of speech will later be an excuse others use to keep her in a demeaning position, to refuse to take her seriously as a human being. Because of the way she speaks, the little girl—now grown to womanhood—will be accused of being unable to speak precisely or to express herself forcefully.

I am sure that the preceding paragraph contains an oversimplified description of the language-learning process in American society. Rather than saying that little boys and little girls, from the very start, learn two different ways of speaking, I think, from observation and reports by others, that the process is more complicated. Since the mother and other women are the dominant influences in the lives of most children under the age of five, probably both boys and girls first learn "women's language" as their first language. (I am told that in Japanese, children of both sexes use the particles proper for women until the age of five or so; then the little boy starts to be ridiculed if he uses them, and so soon learns to desist.) As they grow older, boys especially go through a stage of rough talk, as described by Spock and others; this is probably discouraged in little girls more strongly than in little boys, in whom parents may often find it more amusing than shocking. By the time children are ten or so, and split up into same-sex peer groups, the two languages are already present, according to my recollections and observations. But it seems that what has happened is that the boys have unlearned their original form of expression, and adopted new forms of expression, while the girls retain their old ways of speech. (One wonders whether this is related in any way to the often-noticed fact that little boys innovate, in their play, much more than little girls.) The ultimate result is the same, of course, whatever the interpretation.

So a girl is damned if she does, damned if she doesn't. If she refuses to talk like a lady, she is ridiculed and subjected to criticism as unfeminine; if she does learn, she is ridiculed as unable to think clearly, unable to take part in a serious discussion: in some sense, as less than fully human. These two choices which a woman has—to be less than a woman or less than a person—are highly painful.

An objection may be raised here that I am overstating the case against women's language, since most women who get as far as college learn to switch from women's to neutral language under appropriate situations (in class, talking to professors, at job interviews, and such).[6] But I think this objection overlooks a number of problems. First, if a girl must learn two dialects, she becomes in effect a bilingual. Like many bilinguals, she may never really be master of either language, though her command of both is adequate enough for most purposes, she may never feel really comfortable using either, and never be certain that she is using the right one in the right place to the right person. Shifting from one language to another requires special awareness to the nuances of social situations, special alertness to possible disapproval. It may be that the extra energy that must be (subconsciously or otherwise) expended in this game is energy sapped from more creative work, and hinders women from expressing themselves as well, as fully, or as freely as they might otherwise. Thus, if a girl knows that a professor will be receptive to comments that sound scholarly, objective, unemotional, she will of course be tempted to use neutral language in class or in conference. But if she knows that, as a man, he will respond more approvingly to her at other levels if she uses women's language, and sounds frilly and feminine, won't she be confused as well as sorely tempted in two directions at once? It is often noticed that women participate less in class discussion than men — perhaps this linguistic indecisiveness is one reason why. (Incidentally, I don't find this true in my classes.)

It will be found that the overall effect of "women's language" — meaning both language restricted in use to women and language descriptive of women alone — is this: it submerges a woman's personal identity, by denying her the means of expressing herself strongly, on the one hand, and encouraging expressions that suggest triviality in subject matter and uncertainty about it; and, when a woman is being discussed, by treating her as an object — sexual or otherwise — but never a serious person with individual views.[7] Of course, other forms of behavior in this society have the same purpose; but the phenomena seem especially clear linguistically.

The ultimate effect of these discrepancies is that women are systematically denied access to power, on the grounds that they are not capable of holding it as demonstrated by their linguistic behavior along with other aspects of their behavior; and the irony here is that women are made to feel that they deserve such treatment, because of inadequacies in their own intelligence and/or education.[8] But in fact it is precisely because women have learned their lessons so well that they later suffer such discrimination. (This situation is of course true to some extent for all disadvantaged groups: white males of Anglo-Saxon descent set the standards and seem to expect other groups to be respectful of them but not to adopt them — they are to "keep in their place.")

I should like now to talk at length about some specific examples of linguistic phenomena I have described in general terms above. I want to talk first about the ways in which women's speech differs from men's speech; and then, to discuss a number of cases in which it seems clear that women are discriminated against (usually unconsciously) by the language everyone uses. I think it will become evident from this discussion that both types of phenomena reflect a deep bias on the part of our culture (and, indeed, of every culture I have ever heard of) against women being accorded full status as rational creatures and individuals in their own right; and finally, I would like to talk briefly about what might be done, and perhaps what should not be done, to remedy things.

# 2 ∷

# Talking Like a Lady

"Women's language" shows up in all levels of the grammar of English. We find differences in the choice and frequency of lexical items; in the situations in which certain syntactic rules are performed; in intonational and other supersegmental patterns. As an example of lexical differences, imagine a man and a woman both looking at the same wall, painted a pinkish shade of purple. The woman may say (2):

(2)    The wall is mauve,

with no one consequently forming any special impression of her as a result of the words alone; but if the man should say (2), one might well conclude he was imitating a woman sarcastically or was a homosexual or an interior decorator. Women, then, make far more precise discriminations in naming colors than do men; words like *beige, ecru, aquamarine, lavender,* and so on are unremarkable in a woman's active vocabulary, but absent from that of most men. I have seen a man helpless with suppressed laughter at a discussion between two other people as to whether a book jacket was to be described as "lavender" or "mauve." Men find such discussion amusing because they consider such a question trivial, irrelevant to the real world.

   We might ask why fine discrimination of color is relevant for women, but not for men. A clue is contained in the way many men in our society view other "unworldly" topics, such as high culture and the Church, as outside the world of men's work, relegated to women and men whose masculinity is not unquestionable. Men tend to relegate to women things that are not of concern to them, or do not involve their egos. Among these are problems of fine color discrimination. We might rephrase this point by saying that since women are not expected to make decisions on important matters, such as what kind of job to hold, they are relegated the noncrucial decisions as a sop. Deciding whether to name a color "lavender" or "mauve" is one such sop.

   If it is agreed that this lexical disparity reflects a social inequity in the position of women, one may ask how to remedy it.[9] Obviously, no one could seriously recommend legislating against the use of the terms "mauve" and "lavender" by women, or forcing men to learn to use them. All we can do is give women the opportunity to participate in the real decisions of life.

   Aside from specific lexical items like color names, we find differences between the speech of women and that of men in the use of particles that grammarians often describe as "meaningless." There may be no referent for them, but they are far from meaningless: they define the social context of an utterance, indicate the relationship the speaker feels between himself and his addressee, between himself and what he is talking about.

As an experiment, one might present native speakers of standard American English with pairs of sentences, identical syntactically and in terms of referential lexical items, and differing merely in the choice of "meaningless" particle, and ask them which was spoken by a man, which a woman. Consider:

(3)    (a)   Oh dear, you've put the peanut butter in the refrigerator again.
       (b)   Shit, you've put the peanut butter in the refrigerator again.

It is safe to predict that people would classify the first sentence as part of "women's language," the second as "men's language." It is true that many self-respecting women are becoming able to use sentences like (3) (b) publicly without flinching, but this is a relatively recent development, and while perhaps the majority of Middle America might condone the use of (b) for men, they would still disapprove of its use by women. (It is of interest, by the way, to note that men's language is increasingly being used by women, but women's language is not being adopted by men, apart from those who reject the American masculine image [for example, homosexuals]. This is analogous to the fact that men's jobs are being sought by women, but few men are rushing to become housewives or secretaries. The language of the favored group, the group that holds the power, along with its nonlinguistic behavior, is generally adopted by the other group, not vice versa. In any event, it is a truism to state that the "stronger" expletives are reserved for men, and the "weaker" ones for women.)

Now we may ask what we mean by "stronger" and "weaker" expletives. (If these particles were indeed meaningless, none would be stronger than any other.) The difference between using "shit" (or "damn," or one of many others) as opposed to "oh dear," or "goodness," or "oh fudge" lies in how forcefully one says how one feels—perhaps, one might say, choice of particle is a function of how strongly one allows oneself to feel about something, so that the strength of an emotion conveyed in a sentence corresponds to the strength of the particle. Hence in a really serious situation, the use of "trivializing" (that is, "women's") particles constitutes a joke, or at any rate, is highly inappropriate. (In conformity with current linguistic practice, throughout this work an asterisk [*] will be used to mark a sentence that is inappropriate in some sense, either because it is syntactically deviant or used in the wrong social context.)

(4)    (a)   *Oh fudge, my hair is on fire.
       (b)   *Dear me, did he kidnap the baby?

As children, women are encouraged to be "little ladies." Little ladies don't scream as vociferously as little boys, and they are chastised more severely for throwing tantrums or showing temper: "high spirits" are expected and therefore tolerated in little boys; docility and resignation are

44

the corresponding traits expected of little girls. Now, we tend to excuse a show of temper by a man where we would not excuse an identical tirade from a woman: women are allowed to fuss and complain, but only a man can bellow in rage. It is sometimes claimed that there is a biological basis for this behavior difference, though I don't believe conclusive evidence exists that the early differences in behavior that have been observed are not the results of very different treatment of babies of the two sexes from the beginning; but surely the use of different particles by men and women is a learned trait, merely mirroring nonlinguistic differences again, and again pointing out an inequity that exists between the treatment of men, and society's expectations of them, and the treatment of women. Allowing men stronger means of expression than are open to women further reinforces men's position of strength in the real world: for surely we listen with more attention the more strongly and forcefully someone expresses opinions, and a speaker unable — for whatever reason — to be forceful in stating his views is much less likely to be taken seriously. Ability to use strong particles like "shit" and "hell" is, of course, only incidental to the inequity that exists rather than its cause. But once again, apparently accidental linguistic usage suggests that women are denied equality partially for linguistic reasons, and that an examination of language points up precisely an area in which inequity exists. Further, if someone is allowed to show emotions, and consequently does, others may well be able to view him as a real individual in his own right, as they could not if he never showed emotion. Here again, then, the behavior a woman learns as "correct" prevents her from being taken seriously as an individual, and further is considered "correct" and necessary for a woman precisely because society does *not* consider her seriously as an individual.

Similar sorts of disparities exist elsewhere in the vocabulary. There is, for instance, a group of adjectives which have, besides their specific and literal meanings, another use, that of indicating the speaker's approbation or admiration for something. Some of these adjectives are neutral as to sex of speaker: either men or women may use them. But another set seems, in its figurative use, to be largely confined to women's speech. Representative lists of both types are below:

| neutral | women only |
|---------|------------|
| great | adorable |
| terrific | charming |
| cool | sweet |
| neat | lovely |
| | divine |

As with the color words and swear words already discussed, for a man to stray into the "women's" column is apt to be damaging to his reputation, though here a woman may freely use the neutral words. But it should not be inferred from this that a woman's use of the "women's" words is without

45

its risks. Where a woman has a choice between the neutral words and the women's words, as a man has not, she may be suggesting very different things about her own personality and her view of the subject matter by her choice of words of the first set or words of the second.

(5) (a) What a terrific idea!
    (b) What a divine idea!

It seems to me that (a) might be used under any appropriate conditions by a female speaker. But (b) is more restricted. Probably it is used appropriately (even by the sort of speaker for whom it was normal) only in case the speaker feels the idea referred to to be essentially frivolous, trivial, or unimportant to the world at large—only an amusement for the speaker herself. Consider, then, a woman advertising executive at an advertising conference. However feminine an advertising executive she is, she is much more likely to express her approval with (5) (a) than with (b), which might cause raised eyebrows, and the reaction: "That's what we get for putting a woman in charge of this company."

On the other hand, suppose a friend suggests to the same woman that she should dye her French poodles to match her cigarette lighter. In this case, the suggestion really concerns only her, and the impression she will make on people. In this case, she may use (b), from the "woman's language." So the choice is not really free: words restricted to "women's language" suggest that concepts to which they are applied are not relevant to the real world of (male) influence and power.

One may ask whether there really are no analogous terms that are available to men—terms that denote approval of the trivial, the personal; that express approbation in terms of one's own personal emotional reaction, rather than by gauging the likely general reaction. There does in fact seem to be one such word: it is the hippie invention "groovy," which seems to have most of the connotations that separate "lovely" and "divine" from "great" and "terrific" excepting only that it does not mark the speaker as feminine or effeminate.

(6) (a) What a terrific steel mill!
    (b) *What a lovely steel mill! (male speaking)
    (c) What a groovy steel mill!

I think it is significant that this word was introduced by the hippies, and, when used seriously rather than sarcastically, used principally by people who have accepted the hippies' values. Principal among these is the denial of the Protestant work ethic: to a hippie, something can be worth thinking about even if it isn't influential in the power structure, or moneymaking. Hippies are separated from the activities of the real world just as women are—though in the former case it is due to a decision on their parts, while this is not uncontroversially true in the case of women. For both these groups, it is possible to express approval of things in a personal way—though one does so at the risk of losing one's credibility with members of the power structure. It is also true, according to some speakers, that upper-class British men may use the words listed in the "women's" column, as well as the specific color words and others we have categorized as specifically feminine, without raising doubts as to their masculinity among other speakers of the same dialect. (This is not true for lower-class Britons, however.) The reason may be that commitment to the work ethic need not necessarily be displayed: one may be or appear to be a gentleman of leisure, interested in various pursuits, but not involved in mundane (business or political) affairs, in such a culture, without incurring disgrace. This is rather analogous to the position of a woman in American middle-class society, so we should not be surprised if these special lexical items are usable by both groups. This fact points indeed to a more general conclusion. These words aren't, basically, "feminine"; rather, they signal "uninvolved," or "out of power." Any group in a society to which these labels are applicable may presumably use these words; they are often considered "feminine," "unmasculine," because women are the "uninvolved," "out of power" group *par excellence.*

Another group that has, ostensibly at least, taken itself out of the search for power and money is that of academic men. They are frequently viewed by other groups as analogous in some ways to women—they don't really work, they are supported in their frivolous pursuits by others, what they do doesn't really count in the real world, and so on. The suburban home finds its counterpart in the ivory tower: one is supposedly shielded from harsh realities in both. Therefore it is not too surprising that many academic men (especially those who emulate British norms) may violate many of these sacrosanct rules I have just laid down: they often use "women's language." Among themselves, this does not occasion ridicule. But to a truck driver, a professor saying, "What a lovely hat!" is undoubtedly laughable, all the more so as it reinforces his stereotype of professors as effete snobs.[10]

When we leave the lexicon and venture into syntax, we find that syntactically too women's speech is peculiar. To my knowledge, there is no syntactic rule in English that only women may use. But there is at least one rule that a woman will use in more conversational situations than a man. (This fact indicates, of course, that the applicability of syntactic rules is governed partly by social context—the positions in society of the speaker and addressee, with respect to each other, and the impression one seeks to make on the other.) This is the rule of tag-question formation.[*][11]

---

*Within the lexicon itself, there seems to be a parallel phenomenon to tag-question usage, which I refrain from discussing in the body of the text because the facts are contro-

A tag, in its usage as well as its syntactic shape (in English) is midway between an outright statement and a yes-no question: it is less assertive than the former, but more confident than the latter. Therefore it is usable under certain contextual situations: not those in which a statement would be appropriate, nor those in which a yes-no question is generally used, but in situations intermediate between these.

One makes a statement when one has confidence in his knowledge and is pretty certain that his statement will be believed; one asks a question when one lacks knowledge on some point and has reason to believe that this gap can and will be remedied by an answer by the addressee. A tag question, being intermediate between these, is used when the speaker is stating a claim, but lacks full confidence in the truth of that claim. So if I say

(7)  Is John here?

I will probably not be surprised if my respondent answers "no"; but if I say:

(8)  John is here, isn't he?

instead, chances are I am already biased in favor of a positive answer, wanting only confirmation by the addressee. I still want a response from him, as I do with a yes-no question; but I have enough knowledge (or think I have) to predict that response, much as with a declarative statement. A tag question, then, might be thought of as a declarative statement without the assumption that the statement is to be believed by the addressee: one has an out, as with a question. A tag gives the addressee leeway, not forcing him to go along with the views of the speaker.

---

versial and I do not understand them fully. The intensive *so*, used where purists would insist upon an absolute superlative, heavily stressed, seems more characteristic of women's language than of men's, though it is found in the latter, particularly in the speech of male academics. Consider, for instance, the following sentences:

> (*a*) I feel *so* unhappy!
> (*b*) That movie made me *so* sick!

Men seem to have the least difficulty using this construction when the sentence is unemotional, or nonsubjective—without reference to the speaker himself:

> (*c*) That sunset is *so* beautiful!
> (*d*) Fred is *so* dumb!

Substituting an equative like *so* for absolute superlatives (like *very, really, utterly*) seems to be a way of backing out of committing oneself strongly to an opinion, rather like tag questions (cf. discussion below, in the text). One might hedge in this way with perfect right in making aesthetic judgments, as in (*c*), or intellectual judgments, as in (*d*). But it is somewhat odd to hedge in describing one's own mental or emotional state: who, after all, is qualified to contradict one on this? To hedge in this situation is to seek to avoid making any strong statement: a characteristic, as we have noted already and shall note further, of women's speech.

There are situations in which a tag is legitimate, in fact the only legitimate sentence form. So, for example, if I have seen something only indistinctly, and have reason to believe my addressee had a better view, I can say:

(9)   I had my glasses off. He was out at third, wasn't he?

Sometimes we find a tag question used in cases in which the speaker knows as well as the addressee what the answer must be, and doesn't need confirmation. One such situation is when the speaker is making "small talk," trying to elicit conversation from the addressee:

(10)   Sure is hot here, isn't it?

In discussing personal feelings or opinions, only the speaker normally has any way of knowing the correct answer. Strictly speaking, questioning one's own opinions is futile. Sentences like (11) are usually ridiculous.

(11)   *I have a headache, don't I?

But similar cases do, apparently, exist, in which it is the speaker's opinions, rather than perceptions, for which corroboration is sought, as in (12):

(12)   The way prices are rising is horrendous, isn't it?

While there are of course other possible interpretations of a sentence like this, one possibility is that the speaker has a particular answer in mind — "yes" or "no" — but is reluctant to state it baldly. It is my impression, though I do not have precise statistical evidence, that this sort of tag question is much more apt to be used by women than by men. If this is indeed true, why is it true?

These sentence types provide a means whereby a speaker can avoid committing himself, and thereby avoid coming into conflict with the addressee. The problem is that, by so doing, a speaker may also give the impression of not being really sure of himself, of looking to the addressee for confirmation, even of having no views of his own. This last criticism is, of course, one often leveled at women. One wonders how much of it reflects a use of language that has been imposed on women from their earliest years.

Related to this special use of a syntactic rule is a widespread difference perceptible in women's intonational patterns.* There is a peculiar sentence intonation pattern, found in English as far as I know only among

*For analogues outside of English to these uses of tag questions and special intonation patterns, cf. my discussion of Japanese particles in "Language in Context," *Language*, 48 (1972), 907–27. It is to be expected that similar cases will be found in many other languages as well. See, for example, M. R. Haas's very interesting discussion of differences between men's and women's speech (mostly involving lexical dissimilarities) in many languages, in D. Hymes, ed., *Language in Culture and Society* (New York: Harper & Row, 1964).

women, which has the form of a declarative answer to a question, and is used as such, but has the rising inflection typical of a yes-no question, as well as being especially hesitant.[12] The effect is as though one were seeking confirmation, though at the same time the speaker may be the only one who has the requisite information.

(13)  (a)  When will dinner be ready?
      (b)  Oh . . . around six o'clock . . . ?

It is as though (b) were saying, "Six o'clock, if that's OK with you, if you agree." (a) is put in the position of having to provide confirmation, and (b) sounds unsure. Here we find unwillingness to assert an opinion carried to an extreme. One likely consequence is that these sorts of speech patterns are taken to reflect something real about character and play a part in not taking a woman seriously or trusting her with any real responsibilities, since "she can't make up her mind" and "isn't sure of herself." And here again we see that people form judgments about other people on the basis of superficial linguistic behavior that may have nothing to do with inner character, but has been imposed upon the speaker, on pain of worse punishment than not being taken seriously.

Such features are probably part of the general fact that women's speech sounds much more "polite" than men's. One aspect of politeness is as we have just described: leaving a decision open, not imposing your mind, or views, or claims on anyone else. Thus a tag question is a kind of polite statement, in that it does not force agreement or belief on the addressee. A request may be in the same sense a polite command, in that it does not overtly require obedience, but rather suggests something be done as a favor to the speaker. An overt order (as in an imperative) expresses the (often impolite) assumption of the speaker's superior position to the addressee, carrying with it the right to enforce compliance, whereas with a request the decision on the face of it is left up to the addressee. (The same is true of suggestions: here, the implication is not that the addressee is in danger if he does not comply—merely that he will be glad if he does. Once again, the decision is up to the addressee, and a suggestion therefore is politer than an order.) The more particles in a sentence that reinforce the notion that it is a request, rather than an order, the politer the result. The sentences of (14) illustrate these points: (14) (a) is a direct order, (b) and (c) simple requests, and (d) and (e) compound requests.*

(14)  (a)  Close the door.
      (b)  Please close the door.
      (c)  Will you close the door?
      (d)  Will you please close the door?
      (e)  Won't you close the door?

*For more detailed discussion of these problems, see Lakoff, "Language in Context."

Let me first explain why (e) has been classified as a compound request. (A sentence like *Won't you please close the door* would then count as a doubly compound request.) A sentence like (14) *(c)* is close in sense to "Are you willing to close the door?" According to the normal rules of polite conversation, to agree that you are willing is to agree to do the thing asked of you. Hence this apparent inquiry functions as a request, leaving the decision up to the willingness of the addressee. Phrasing it as a positive question makes the (implicit) assumption that a "yes" answer will be forthcoming. Sentence (14) *(d)* is more polite than *(b)* or *(c)* because it combines them: *please* indicating that to accede will be to do something for the speaker, and *will you*, as noted, suggesting that the addressee has the final decision. If, now, the question is phrased with a negative, as in (14) *(e)*, the speaker seems to suggest the stronger likelihood of a negative response from the addressee. Since the assumption is then that the addressee is that much freer to refuse, (14) *(e)* acts as a more polite request than (14) *(c)* or *(d)*: *(c) (d)* put the burden of refusal on the addressee, as *(e)* does not.

Given these facts, one can see the connection between tag questions and tag orders and other requests. In all these cases, the speaker is not committed as with a simple declarative or affirmative. And the more one compounds a request, the more characteristic it is of women's speech, the less of men's. A sentence that begins *Won't you please* (without special emphasis on *please*) seems to me at least to have a distinctly unmasculine sound. Little girls are indeed taught to talk like little ladies, in that their speech is in many ways more polite than that of boys or men, and the reason for this is that politeness involves an absence of a strong statement, and women's speech is devised to prevent the expression of strong statements.

# 3 ::

# Talking about Women

We have thus far confined ourselves to one facet of the problem of women and the English language: the way in which women prejudice the case against themselves by their use of language. But it is at least as true that others—as well as women themselves—make matters so by the way in which they refer to women. Often a word that may be used of both men and women (and perhaps of things as well), when applied to women, assumes a special meaning that, by implication rather than outright assertion, is derogatory to women as a group.

When a word acquires a bad connotation by association with something unpleasant or embarrassing, people may search for substitutes that do not have the uncomfortable effect—that is, euphemisms. Since attitudes toward the original referent are not altered by a change of name, the new name itself takes on the adverse connotations, and a new euphemism must be found. It is no doubt possible to pick out areas of particular psychological strain or discomfort — areas where problems exist in a culture — by pinpointing items around which a great many euphemisms are clustered. An obvious example concerns the various words for that household convenience into which human wastes are eliminated: toilet, bathroom, rest room, comfort station, lavatory, water closet, loo, and all the others.

In the case of women, it may be encouraging to find no richness of euphemism; but it is discouraging to note that at least one euphemism for "woman" does exist and is very much alive. The word, of course, is "lady," which seems to be replacing "woman" in a great many contexts. Where both exist, they have different connotations; where only one exists, there is usually a reason, to be found in the context in which the word is uttered.

Related to the existence of euphemistic terms for "woman" is the existence of euphemistic terms for woman's principal role, that of "housewife." Most occupational terms do not have coexisting euphemisms: these seem to come into being only when the occupation is considered embarrassing or demeaning.[13] Thus there is no euphemism for "professor," "doctor," "bank president"; but we do find "mortician" and "funeral director" for "undertaker"; "custodian" and "sanitary engineer" for "janitor"; "domestic" for "cleaning woman"; and so forth. Similarly one keeps running into hopeful suggestions, principally in the pages of women's magazines, that the lot of the housewife would be immeasurably improved if she thought of herself as "homemaker," "household executive," "household engineer," or any of several others. I am not sure what to make of the fact that none of these (unlike those of the bona fide occupational euphemisms) have taken hold: is it because the "housewife" doesn't consider her status demeaning? Then why the search for euphemisms? Or does she feel that there is no escape through a change in nomenclature, or lack pride in her job to such an extent that she doesn't feel up to making the effort? This is a question for the sociologist.

It may be objected that *lady* has a masculine counterpart, namely *gentleman*, occasionally shortened to *gent*. But I don't think this is a fair comparison. *Lady* is much more common than *gent(leman)*, and, since *gent* exists, the reason is not ease of pronunciation. *Lady* is really a euphemism for *woman*, but *gentleman* is not nearly frequent enough to classify as a euphemism for *man*. Just as we do not call whites "Caucasian-Americans," there is no felt need to refer to men commonly as "gentlemen." And just as there is a need for such terms as "Afro-Americans," there is similarly a felt need for "lady." One might even say that when a derogatory epithet exists, a parallel euphemism is deemed necessary. (The term WASP, white Anglo-Saxon Protestant, may occur to the reader as a possible derogatory term which has no parallel euphemism. But in fact, WASP is not parallel in usage to *nigger, polack,* or *yid.* One can refer to himself as a WASP, as one cannot refer to himself as a *nigger* without either a total lack of self-pride or bitter sarcasm. Thus one can say: "Sure I'm a WASP, and proud of it!" but probably not: "Sure I'm a nigger, and proud of it!" without special sarcastic inflection in the voice suggesting that it is an imitation of the addressee.) To avoid having to resort to terms like "Afro-American," we need only get rid of all expressions like "nigger"; to banish "lady" in its euphemistic sense from the vocabulary of English, we need only first get rid of "broad" and its relations. But of course, as already pointed out, we cannot achieve this commendable simplification of the lexicon unless we somehow remove from our minds the idea that blacks *are* niggers, and that women *are* broads. The presence of the words is a signal that something is wrong, rather than (as too often interpreted by well-meaning reformers) the problem itself. The point here is that, unless we start feeling more respect for women and, at the same time, less uncomfortable about them and their roles in society in relation to men, we cannot avoid *ladies* any more than we can avoid *broads.*

In the past, some ethnic groups that today are relatively respectable were apparently considered less so. And in looking at reports of the terms used to describe those groups at the earlier time, we find two interesting facts: first, there is a much greater incidence of derogatory epithets for that group (as might be expected); and second (which one might not be led to expect automatically) there exist euphemistic terms for that group that are no longer in general use. One can only conclude that euphemisms vanish as they are no longer needed. The example I have in mind is that of the words used to describe Jews. Aside from the uncomplimentary epithets which still exist today, though not encountered very often, one finds, in reading novels written and set more than half a century ago, a number of euphemisms that are not found any more, such as "Hebrew gentleman" and "Israelite." The disappearance of the euphemisms concurrently with the derogatory terms suggests that women will be *ladies* until some more dignified status can be found for them.

It might also be claimed that *lady* is no euphemism because it has exactly the same connotations as woman, is usable under the same semantic and contextual conditions. But a cursory inspection will show that this is not always the case. The decision to use one term rather than the other may considerably alter the sense of a sentence. The following are examples:

(15) (*a*) A (woman) that I know makes amazing things out of
      (lady)
    shoelaces and old boxes.

   (*b*) A (woman) I know works at Woolworth's.
       (lady)

   (*c*) A (woman) I know is a dean at Berkeley.
      (lady)

(These facts are true for some speakers of English. For other, *lady* has taken over the function of *woman* to such an extent that *lady* can be used in all these sentences.)

In my speech, the use of *lady* in (15) *(c)* imparts a frivolous or non-serious tone to the sentence: the matter under discussion is one of not too great moment. In this dialect, then, *lady* seems to be the more colloquial word: it is less apt to be used in writing, or in discussing serious matters. Similarly in (15) *(a)*, using *lady* would suggest that the speaker considered the "amazing things" not to be serious art, but merely a hobby or an aberration. If *woman* is used, she might be a serious (pop art) sculptor.

Related to this is the use of *lady* in job terminology. For at least some speakers, the more demeaning the job, the more the person holding it (if female, of course) is likely to be described as a *lady*. Thus, *cleaning lady* is at least as common as *cleaning woman*, *saleslady* as *saleswoman*. But one says, normally, *woman doctor*. To say *lady doctor* is to be very condescending: it constitutes an insult. For men, there is no such dichotomy. *Garbageman* or *salesman* is the only possibility, never *\*garbage gentleman*. And of course, since in the professions the male is unmarked, we never have *\*man (male) doctor*.

Numerous other examples can be given, all tending to prove the same point: that if, in a particular sentence, both *woman* and *lady* might be used, the use of the latter tends to trivialize the subject matter under discussion, often subtly ridiculing the woman involved. Thus, for example, a mention in the San Francisco *Chronicle* of January 31, 1972, of Madalyn Murray O'Hair as the "lady atheist" reduces her position to that of scatter-brained eccentric, or at any rate, one who need not be taken seriously. Even *woman atheist* is scarcely defensible: first, because her sex is irrelevant to her philosophical position, and second, because her name makes it clear in any event. But *lady* makes matters still worse. Similarly a reference to a *woman sculptor* is only mildly annoying (since there is no term *\*male sculptor*, the discrepancy suggests that such activity is normal for a man, but not for a woman), but still it could be used with reference to a serious artist. *Lady sculptor*, on the other hand, strikes me as a slur against the artist, deliberate or not, implying that the woman's art is frivolous, something she does to fend off the boredom of suburban housewifery, or at any rate, nothing of moment in the art world. Serious artists have shows, not *dilettantes*. So we hear of *one-woman shows*, but never *one-lady shows*.

Another realm of usage in which *lady* contrasts with *woman* is in titles of organizations. It seems that organizations of women who have a serious purpose (not merely that of spending time with one another) cannot use the word *lady* in their titles, but less serious ones may. Compare the *Ladies' Auxiliary* of a men's group, or the *Thursday Evening Ladies Browning and Garden Society* with *\*Ladies' Lib* or *\*Ladies Strike for Peace*.

What is curious about this split is that *lady* is, as noted, in origin a euphemism for *woman*. What kind of euphemism is it that subtly denigrates the people to whom it refers, suggests that they are not to be taken seriously, are laughing stocks? A euphemism, after all, is supposed to put a better face on something people find uncomfortable. But this is not really contradictory. What a euphemism is supposed to do, actually, is to remove from thought *that part* of the connotations of a word that creates the discomfort. So each of the euphemisms for toilet, starting with *toilet*, seems to be trying to get further from the notion of excrement, by employing successively more elegant terminology that seems designed to suggest that the piece of furniture in question has really other primary uses, for performing one's toilette, for washing, for comfort, for resting, but never for those other things. Perhaps the notion of the nonseriousness of women is not the thing that makes men—the devisers of euphemism—as well as women, uncomfortable. Perhaps it is some other aspect of the man-woman relationship. How can we determine whether this is in fact the case?

One way of identifying the precise source of discomfort is, perhaps, by looking at the derogatory terms for something. Many of the terms for blacks refer to their physical characteristics. And the latest euphemism for blacks, *Afro-Americans*, seems to be a specific attempt to get away from color names. (The term *black* is not a euphemism, but rather an attempt to confront the issue squarely and make color into a source of pride.) And as has often been noted, derogatory terms for women are very often overtly sexual: the reader will have no difficulty recalling what I allude to here.

The distinction between *lady* and *woman*, in those dialects of American English in which it is found, may be traceable to other causes than the sexual connotations present in *woman*. Most people who are asked why they have chosen to use *lady* where *woman* would be as appropriate will reply that *lady* seemed more polite. The concept of politeness thus invoked is the politeness used in dignifying or ennobling a concept that normally is not thought of as having dignity or nobility. It is this notion of politeness that explains why we have *cleaning lady*, but not, normally, *lady doctor*. A doctor does not need to be exalted by conventional expressions: she has dignity enough from her professional status. But a cleaning woman is in a very different situation, in which her occupational category requires ennobling. Then perhaps we can say that the very notion of womanhood, as opposed to manhood, requires ennobling since it lacks inherent dignity of its own: hence the word *woman* requires the existence of a euphemism like *lady*. Besides or possibly because of being explicitly devoid of sexual connotation, *lady* carries with it overtones recalling the age of chivalry: the exalted stature of the person so referred to, her existence above the common sphere. This makes the term seem polite at first, but we must also remember that these implications are perilous: they suggest that a "lady" is helpless, and cannot do things for herself. In this respect the use of a word like *lady* is parallel to the act of opening doors for women—or ladies. At first blush it is flattering: the object of the flattery feels honored, cherished, and so forth; but by the same token, she is also considered helpless and not in control of her own destiny. Women who protest that they *like* receiving these little courtesies, and object to being liberated from them, should reflect a bit on their deeper meaning and see how much they like *that*.

This brings us to the consideration of another common substitute for *woman*, namely *girl*. One seldom hears a man past the age of adolescence referred to as a boy, save in expressions like "going out with the boys," which are meant to suggest an air of adolescent frivolity and irresponsibility. But women of all ages are "girls": one can have a man, not a boy, Friday, but a girl, never a woman or even a lady, Friday; women have girlfriends, but men do not — in a nonsexual sense — have boyfriends. It may be that this use of *girl* is euphemistic in the sense in which *lady* is a euphemism: in stressing the idea of immaturity, it removes the sexual connotations lurking in *woman*. Instead of the ennobling present in *lady*, *girl* is (presumably) flattering to women because of its stress on youth. But here again there are pitfalls: in recalling youth, frivolity, and immaturity, *girl* brings to mind irresponsibility: you don't send a girl to do a woman's errand (or even, for that matter, a boy's errand). It seems that again, by an appeal to feminine vanity (about which we shall have more to say later) the users of English have assigned women to a very unflattering place in their minds: a woman is a person who is both too immature and too far from real life to be entrusted with responsibilities and with decisions of any serious nature. Would you elect president a person incapable of putting on her own coat? (Of course, if we were to have a married woman president, we would not have any name for her husband parallel to *First Lady*, and why do you suppose that is?)

Perhaps the way in which *lady* functions as a euphemism for *woman* is that it does not contain the sexual implications present in *woman*: it is not "embarrassing" in that way. If this is so, we may expect that, in the future, *lady* will replace *woman* as the primary word for the human female, since *woman* will have become too blatantly sexual. That this distinction is already made in some contexts at least is shown in the following examples:

(16) (*a*) She's only twelve, but she's already a woman.
$\qquad\qquad\qquad\qquad\qquad\qquad$ *lady

(*b*) After ten years in jail, Harry wanted to find a woman.
$\qquad\qquad\qquad\qquad\qquad\qquad\qquad$ *lady

(*c*) She's my woman, see, so don't mess around with her.
$\qquad\qquad\qquad$ *lady

It may be, finally, that the reason the use of *lady* rather than *woman* in a sentence creates the impression of frivolity discussed above is precisely because of the euphemistic nature of *lady*. In serious discussion, one does not typically employ euphemisms. So, for instance, a sentence like (17) (*a*) is more suited to cocktail party chitchat by returning tourists than to learned discussion by anthropologists, who would be more likely to use a technical term, as in (17) (b):

(17)  (a)  When the natives of Mbanga want to use the little boys' room, first they find a large pineapple leaf. . . .
      (b)  When the natives of Mbanga wish to defecate, first they find a large pineapple leaf. . . .

Perhaps the discomfort men suffer in contemplating, more or less unconsciously, the sexuality of women is traceable to guilt feelings on their part. The guilt arises, I should think, not only because they think sex is inherently dirty (that is another problem) but because if one deals with women as primarily sexual beings, one is in effect automatically relegating them to object status; if women are there for the use and enjoyment of men, they are not fully human beings in their own right. But women are in most other respects evidently human. So a man feels somewhat ambivalent—more or less consciously—and reacts all the more strongly for that reason. Hence, perhaps, the rather hysterical ridicule heaped on Women's Lib in the media. In any case, throughout English one finds evidence of many sorts that women are viewed (by women as well as men) as secondary beings: as having an existence only when defined by a man.

These facts about women's position should cause us to question one of the commonest criticisms made of women's behavior, as opposed to men's: one often hears that women are vain and self-centered, concerned only about their appearance and how others view them. A little thought should convince anyone that, in fact, it is men who are self-centered and egocentric and that women's seeming vanity is not that at all.

As noted above, a woman's reputation and position in society depend almost wholly on the impression she makes upon others, how others view her. She must dress decoratively, look attractive, be compliant, if she is to survive at all in the world. Then her overattention to appearance and appearances (including, perhaps, overcorrectness and overgentility of speech and etiquette) is merely the result of being forced to exist only as a reflection in the eyes of others.[14] She does not, cannot, do anything in her own behalf or purely for her own pleasure or aggrandizement. (Rather ironically, the only way she can increase her own comfort, pleasure, and security is through her husband's advancement, and thus she can achieve material comforts only through someone else's efforts. What seem to be self-centered efforts are really aimed at the opinions of others, and what appear to be efforts for someone else are really the only ones permissible for a woman's own behalf. It is no wonder women lack an identity and feel they have no place of their own.)

In fact, men are the vain sex. Men may derive pleasure directly from their own works. Men do things purely for their own satisfaction, not caring nearly so much how it will look to others. This, surely, is the true egocentricity. Further, it seems to me that the ultimate vanity or self-centeredness is to be found in eccentricity. The eccentric alone truly cares only for himself and his own pleasure: he does not concern himself with how his actions affect others or look to others. And eccentricity is far more common and far more tolerated in men than in women. A strong personality in general, a mark of egocentricity, is again valued in men much more than in women. For these reasons, women are not very successful in business or politics, where both vanity and eccentricity of certain sorts can be marks of distinction rather than objects of ridicule.

Sociologically it is probably fairly obvious that a woman in most subcultures in our society achieves status only through her father's, husband's, or lover's position. What is remarkable is that these facts show up linguistically in nonobvious ways.

Suppose we take a pair of words which, in terms of the possible relationships in an earlier society, were simple male-female equivalents, analogous to bull: cow. Suppose we find that, for independent reasons, society has changed in such a way that the primary meanings now are irrelevant. Yet the words have not been discarded, but have acquired new meanings, metaphorically related to their original senses. But suppose these new metaphorical uses are no longer parallel to each other. By seeing where the parallelism breaks down, we can intuit something about the different roles played by men and women in this culture. One good example of such a divergence through time is found in the pair *master* and *mistress*. Once used with reference to one person's power over another, these words became unusable in their original sense as the master-servant relationship became nonexistent. But the words are still common as used in sentences (18) and (19):

(18)  (a)  He is a master of the intricacies of academic politics.
      (b)  *She is a mistress . . .

(19)  (a)  *Harry declined to be my master, and so returned to his wife.
      (b)  Rhonda declined to be my mistress, and so returned to her husband.

Unless used with reference to animals or slaves, *master* now generally refers to a man who has acquired consummate ability in some field, normally nonsexual. But its feminine counterpart cannot be used in this way. It is practically restricted to its sexual sense of "paramour." We start out with two terms, both roughly paraphrasable as "one who has power over another." But the masculine form, once one person is no longer able to have absolute power over another, becomes usable metaphorically in the sense of "have power over *something*." The feminine counterpart also acquired a metaphorical interpretation, but the metaphor here is sexual: one's mistress "has power over" one in a sexual sense. And this expression is probably chivalrous, rather than descriptive of the real-world relationship between lovers. In terms of choice, of economic control, and so forth, it is

58

generally the man who holds the power in such a relationship; to call a woman one's "mistress" is the equivalent of saying "please" in prefacing a request to a subordinate. Both are done for politeness and are done purely because both participants in the relationship, in both cases, know that the supposed inferiority of the mistress's lover and of the user of "please" is only a sham. Interesting too in this regard is the fact that "master" requires as its object only the name of some activity, something inanimate and abstract. But "mistress" requires a masculine noun in the possessive to precede it. One cannot say:

(20)   *Rhonda is a mistress.

One must be *someone's* mistress.

And obviously too, it is one thing to be an *old master*, like Hans Holbein, and another to be an *old mistress:* the latter, again, requires a masculine possessive form preceding it, indicating who has done the discarding. *Old* in the first instance refers to absolute age: the artist's lifetime versus the time of writing. But *old* in the second really means "discarded," "old" with respect to someone else.

Others, too, have been struck by the hidden assumptions in the word *mistress*. In an article on the Op-Ed page of the *New York Times*, July 20, 1972, Rebecca Reyher suggests that a way around this difficulty is to adopt a parallel term for the man in such a relationship: stud. But further thought will make it clear that the use of this new term will not obviate the problem: the roots lie deeper, in the social nature of the relationship itself. As long as it is the woman who is dependent on the man, socially and economically, in such relationships, there will be no possibility of coining a parallel term for *mistress*. Just as we will have the sorts of disparities illustrated by sentences (18)–(19), we will find further disparities, for the same reasons. Note, for instance, the difference in the acceptability of: He's a real stud! as contrasted to: *She's a real mistress![15]

So here we see several important points concerning the relationship between men and women illustrated: first, that men are defined in terms of what they do in the world, women in terms of the men with whom they are associated; and second, that the notion of "power" for a man is different from that of "power" for a woman: it is acquired and manifested in different ways. One might say then that these words have retained their principal meanings through time; what has changed is the kinds of interpersonal relationships to which they refer.

As a second example, the examples in (21) should be completely parallel semantically:

(21)   (*a*)   He's a professional.
       (*b*)   She's a professional.

Hearing and knowing no more about the subjects of the discourse than this, what would one assume about them in each case? Certainly in (*a*)

59

the normal conclusion the casual eavesdropper would come to was that "he" was a doctor or a lawyer or a member of one of the other professions. But it is much less likely that one would draw a similar conclusion in (b). Rather, the first assumption most speakers of English seem to make is that "she" is a prostitute, literally or figuratively speaking. Again, a man is defined in the serious world by what he does, a woman by her sexuality, that is, in terms of one particular aspect of her relationship to men.[16]

This discrepancy is not confined to English. Victor Wen has informed me that a similar situation pertains in Chinese. One may say of a man, "He's in business," and of a woman, "She's in business," lexically and grammatically parallel. The former means about what its English equivalent means. But the latter is synonymous to sentence (21) (b).

James Fox tells me that in many cultures, as in English, people may be referred to metaphorically by animal names, suggesting that they have some of the attributes of that animal, real or part of the folklore. What is interesting here is that where animal names may be applied to both men and women—whether or not there are separate terms for male and female in the animal—the former may have connotations in all sorts of areas, while the latter, whatever other connotations the term may suggest, nearly always makes sexual reference as well. Compare in this regard *dog* and *bitch*, *fox* and *vixen*, and the difference between *he's a pig* and *she's a pig*.

The sexual definition of women, however, is but one facet of a much larger problem. In every aspect of life, a woman is identified in terms of the men she relates to. The opposite is not usually true of men: they act in the world as autonomous individuals, but women are only "John's wife," or "Harry's girlfriend." Thus, meeting a woman at a party, a quite normal opening conversational gambit might be: "What does your husband do?" One very seldom hears, in a similar situation, a question addressed to a man: "What does your wife do?" The question would, to a majority of men, seem tautological: "She's my wife—that's what she does." This is true even in cases in which a woman is being discussed in a context utterly unrelated to her relationships with men, when she has attained sufficient stature to be considered for high public office. In fact, in a recent discussion of possible Supreme Court nominees, one woman was mentioned prominently. In discussing her general qualifications for the office, and her background, the *New York Times* saw fit to remark on her "bathing-beauty figure." Note that this is not only a judgment on a physical attribute totally removed from her qualifications for the Supreme Court, but that it is couched in terms of how a man would react to her figure. Some days later, President Nixon announced the nominations to his Price Board, among them one woman. In the thumbnail sketches the *Times* gave of each nominee, it was mentioned that the woman's husband was a professor of English. In the case of none of the other nominees was the existence of a spouse even hinted at, and much less was there any clue about the spouse's occupation. So here, although the existence of a husband was as irrelevant for this woman appointee as the existence of a wife was for any of the male appointees, the husband was mentioned, since a woman cannot be placed in her position in society by the readers of the *Times* unless they know her marital status. The same is not at all true of men. Similarly in the 1971 mayoral campaign in San Francisco, the sole woman candidate was repeatedly referred to as *Mrs. Feinstein*, never *Feinstein*, when her opponents were regularly referred to by first and last names or last names alone: *Joseph Alioto*, or *Alioto*, not *Mr. Alioto*. Again, the woman had to be identified by her relationship to a man, although this should bear no relevance to her qualifications for public office.

While sharp intellect is generally considered an unqualified virtue in a man, any character trait that is not related to a woman's utility to men is considered suspect, if not downright bad. Thus the word *brainy* is seldom used of men; when used of women it suggests (1) that this intelligence is unexpected in a woman; (2) that it isn't really a good trait. If one calls a woman "smart," outside of the sense of "fashionable," either one means it as a compliment to her domestic thrift and other housekeeping abilities or, again, it suggests a bit of wariness on the part of the speaker.

Also relevant here are the connotations (as opposed to the denotative meanings) of the words *spinster* and *bachelor*. Denotatively, these are, again, parallel to "cow" versus "bull": one is masculine, the other feminine, and both mean "one who is not married." But there the resemblance ends. *Bachelor* is at least a neutral term, often used as a compliment. *Spinster* normally seems to be used pejoratively, with connotations of prissiness, fussiness, and so on. Some of the differences between the two words are brought into focus in the following examples:

(22)  (a)  Mary hopes to meet an eligible bachelor.
      (b)  *Fred hopes to meet an eligible spinster.

It is the concept of an *eligible spinster* that is anomalous. If someone is a spinster, by implication she is not eligible (to marry); she has had her chance, and been passed by. Hence, a girl of twenty cannot be properly called a spinster: she still has a chance to be married. (Of course, *spinster* may be used metaphorically in this situation, as described below.) But a man may be considered a bachelor as soon as he reaches marriageable age: to be a bachelor implies that one has the choice of marrying or not, and this is what makes the idea of a bachelor existence attractive, in the popular literature. He has been pursued and has successfully eluded his pursuers. But a spinster is one who has not been pursued, or at least not seriously. She is old unwanted goods. Hence it is not surprising to find that a euphemism has arisen for *spinster*, a word not much used today, *bachelor girl*, which attempts to capture for the woman the connotations *bachelor* has for a man. But this, too, is not much used except by writers trying to give their (slick magazine) prose a "with-it" sound. I have not heard the word used in unselfconscious speech. *Bachelor,* however, needs no euphemisms.

When *bachelor* and *spinster* are used metaphorically, the distinction in connotation between the two becomes even clearer:

(23)   *(a)*   John is a regular bachelor.
      *(b)*   Mary is a regular spinster.

The metaphorical connotations of "bachelor" generally suggest sexual freedom; of "spinster," puritanism or celibacy. So we might use a sentence like (23) *(a)* if John was in fact married but engaged in extramarital affairs freely. It is hard to think of other circumstances in which it might be used. Certainly it could not be used if John were married but determined to remain celibate. (23) *(b)*, on the other hand, might be used under two conditions: first, if Mary were in fact unmarried, but still of marriageable age (that is, not yet a literal spinster), and very cold and prissy; second, if Mary were married, with the same characteristics. The use of "regular," then, seems to be an indicator that the noun it modifies is to be taken purely in its connotative rather than denotative sense.

These examples could be multiplied. It is generally considered a *faux pas,* in proper society, to congratulate a girl on her engagement, while it is correct to congratulate her fiancé. Why is this? The reason here seems to be that it is impolite to remind someone of something that may be uncomfortable to him. To remind a girl that she must catch someone, that perhaps she might not have caught anyone, is rude, and this is what is involved, effectively, in congratulating someone. To congratulate someone is to rejoice with him in his good fortune; but it is not quite nice to remind a girl that getting married is good fortune for her, indeed a veritable necessity; it is too close to suggesting the bad fortune that it would be for her had she not found someone to marry. In the context of this society's assumptions about women's role, to congratulate a girl on her engagement is virtually to say, "Thank goodness! You had a close call!" For the man, on the other hand, there was no such danger. His choosing to marry is viewed as a good thing, but not something essential, and so he may be congratulated for doing a wise thing. If man and woman were equal in respect to marriage, it would be proper to congratulate either both or neither.

Another thing to think about is the traditional conclusion of the marriage service: "I now pronounce you man and wife." The man's position in the world, and in relation to other people including the bride, has not been changed by the act of marriage. He was a "man" before the ceremony, and a "man" he still is (one hopes) at its conclusion. But the bride went into the ceremony a "woman," not defined by any other person, at least linguistically; she leaves it a "wife," defined in terms of the "man," her husband. There are many other aspects of traditional marriage ceremonies in our culture that might be used to illustrate the same point.

And, having discussed bachelorhood and spinsterhood, and the marital state, we arrive at widowhood. Surely a bereaved husband and a bereaved wife are equivalent: they have both undergone the loss of a mate. But in fact, linguistically at any rate, this is not true. It is true that we have two words, *widow* and *widower*; but here again, *widow* is far commoner in use. Widows, not widowers, have their particular roles in folklore and tradition, and mourning behavior of particular sorts seems to be expected more strongly, and for a longer time, of a widow than of a widower. But there is more than this, as evidenced by the following:

(24) (a) Mary is John's widow.
     (b) *John is Mary's widower.

Like *mistress, widow* commonly occurs with a possessive preceding it, the name of the woman's late husband. Though he is dead, she is still defined by her relationship to him. But the bereaved husband is no longer defined in terms of his wife. While she is alive, he is sometimes defined as Mary's husband (though less often, probably, than she is as "John's wife"). But once she is gone, her function for him is over, linguistically speaking anyway.[17] So once again, we see that women are always defined in terms of the men to whom they are related, and hence the worst thing that can happen to a woman is not to have a man in this relationship—that is, to be a spinster, a woman with neither husband nor lover, dead or alive.

What all these facts suggest is merely this, again: that men are assumed to be able to choose whether or not they will marry, and that therefore their not being married in no way precludes their enjoying sexual activity; but if a woman is not married, it is assumed to be because no one found her desirable. Hence if a woman is not married by the usual age, she is assumed to be sexually undesirable, prissy, and frigid.

The reason for this distinction seems to be found in the point made earlier: that women are given their identities in our society by virtue of their relationship with men, not vice versa.

It has been argued that this claim about disparities in use between *man/husband* and *woman/wife*, as well as *bachelor/spinster* and *widow/widower* does not apply in other languages, where they are not found, although otherwise the speakers of these languages are as sexist as any. Then, the argument continues, aren't these so-called proofs of linguistic sexism invalidated, in the face of, for example, the French *mari et femme* = "husband and woman"? Or in the face of the fact that *widower* is not morphologically marked vis-à-vis *widow*, in many languages?[18]

My answer to all these arguments is *no*. We must look at the total picture, not its individual parts. Perhaps the French speaker says *"mari et femme"*; can a female speaker of French say *"mon mari travaille"*? Only if she can (and if a large body of the other claims made here are invalidated in French) can we claim that the linguistic disparity between "man" and "woman" does not hold in French.

Further, it should be clear that the *presence* of a marked trait (like the special ending on the masculine *widower*) is linguistic evidence of a social disparity; but the absence of such a trait is not evidence of its opposite. A language generally makes a distinction, or utilizes a marked form, for a reason; but the lack of such marking may be mere accident. Obviously, any fairly inventive mind, given fifteen minutes, could point to a dozen uses in English that are not sexist, but might conceivably have been so; but no one will use these nonoccurrences as proof of the nonsexism of English.

Now it becomes clearer why there is a lack of parallelism in men's and women's titles. To refer to a man as *Mr.* does not identify his marital status; but there is no such ambiguous term for women: one must decide on *Mrs.* or *Miss.* To remedy this imbalance, a bill was proposed in the United States Congress by Bella Abzug and others that would legislate a change in women's titles: *Miss* and *Mrs.* would both be abolished in favor of *Ms.* Rather less seriously, the converse has been proposed by Russell Baker, that two terms should be created for men, *Mrm.* and *Srs.*, depending upon marital status.[19] We may ask several questions: *(a)* Why does the imbalance exist in the first place? *(b)* Why do we feel that Baker's suggestion (even if it did not come from Baker) is somehow not to be taken as seriously as Abzug's? And *(c)* does Abzug's proposal have a chance of being accepted in colloquial speech? (One must distinguish between acceptance in official use and documents, where *Ms.* is already used to some extent, and acceptance in colloquial conversation, where I have never heard it. I think the latter will be a long time in coming, and I do not think we can consider *Ms.* a real choice until this occurs.)

*(a)* A title is devised and used for a purpose: to give a clue to participants in social interaction how the other person is to be regarded, how he is to be addressed. In an avowedly class-conscious society, social ranking is a significant determining factor: once you know that your addressee is to be addressed as "lord," or "mister," or "churl," you know where he stands with respect to you; the title establishes his identity in terms of his relationship with the larger social group. For this reason, the recent suggestion that both *Mr.* and *Mrs./Miss* be abolished in favor of *Person* is unlikely to be successful: *Person* tells you only what you already know, and does not aid in establishing ranking or relationship between two people. Even in a supposedly classless society, the use of *Mr.* (as opposed to simple last name or first name) connotes a great deal about the relationship of the two participants in the discourse with respect to each other. To introduce yourself, "I'm Mr. Jones" puts the relationship you are seeking to establish on quite a different basis than saying, "I'm Jones," or "I'm John," and each is usable under quite different contextual conditions, socially speaking. As long as

social distinctions, overt or covert, continue to exist, we will be unable to rid our language of titles that make reference to them. It is interesting that the French and Russian revolutions both tried to do away with honorific titles that distinguished class by substituting "citizen(ess)" and "comrade." These, however, are not purely empty like "person": they imply that speaker and addressee share a relationship in that both are part of the state and hence, by implication, both equal. In France, the attempt was not long-lived. (Although *tovarishch* is normal today in the Soviet Union, I don't know whether it is really usable under all conditions, whether a factory worker, for instance, could use it to his foreman, or his foreman's wife.)

Although, in our society, naming conventions for men and women are essentially equal (both have first and last names, and both may have additional names, of lesser importance), the social conventions governing the choice of form of address is not parallel in both sexes. Thus, as noted, a man, Mr. John Jones, may be addressed as John, as Jones, as Mr. Jones, and as Mr. John Jones. The first normally implies familiarity, the second intimacy coupled with Jones's inferiority (except in situations of nondirect address, as in professional citation; or among intimates, as a possibly more intimate form of address even than first name alone, without inferiority being implied); the third distance and more or less equality. The last is never used in direct address, and again indicates considerable distance. To address someone by first name alone is to assume at least equality with the other person, and perhaps superiority (in which case the other person will respond with *Mr.* and last name). *Mr. Jones* is probably the least-marked form of address, a means of keeping distance with no necessary suggestions of status. To address someone as *Jones* socially or in business may be an indication of his inferior status, but to refer to someone that way professionally (as at a linguistics conference, generally in indirect reference rather than direct address) seems to be a mark of his acceptance, as a colleague and a person to be taken seriously as a fellow member of the profession. In this way, perhaps, it is related to the last-name-only of familiarity: it is "we know each other well; we are equals and pals, or equals and colleagues."

Possibly related to this is a discrepancy in the rules of professional naming. Among linguists, at any rate, there are rules, unwritten but generally understood, about when someone is referred to (orally in discussion, rather than cited in papers) by full name, by last name, by title (Dr., Professor, Mr.) plus last name. If one is speaking of a student, or of a close friend to someone else who, the speaker knows, is also a friend of the person referred to, and the name is unambiguous in context, the reference is often, though not necessarily, by first name, though one also hears last names if the person referred to is male: either *Fred* or *Smith* may be used to refer to Fred Smith under these circumstances. If the person is less well known, and therefore not considered somehow a full colleague, the reference is most often by full first and last name; *a paper by Smith's student,*

*Bill Snurd,* not *\*Snurd.* (Any title alone with either last or first and last name indicates that the speaker himself is not a full member of the club or that he considers the person referred to beyond the professional pale: "Gosh, I talked to Professor Chomsky!" is the effusion of a neophyte.) All of this suggests a kind of understood camaraderie among people who are understood to "belong," and may act as a covert means of screening out nonmembers. Then what of the women in the profession (who, we will recall, are not professionals)? One finds oneself more and more often in awkward situations, as women become more prevalent in the field, and one does not know how to refer to them appropriately. If we are in a situation in which first name alone might be used of a male linguist, we are in no trouble: first name alone is used of a woman as well. If we are in a situation where first plus last name is used of a man, this will also be used for a woman, with no trouble. But there is a shadow area: if someone is assumed to be an equal and a colleague, but the speaker is not really a personal friend, or he knows the addressee is not, or he merely wishes to keep the conversation on a strictly impersonal note. Here, if the person referred to is a man, we normally find last name alone used. But for a woman, this is much less common. (I am, again, not referring to citation in writing, where last name alone is common for women as well as men.) There are two ways out: first name alone (Jane) or both names (Jane Jones), and I have encountered both, while I have virtually never encountered last name alone (Jones) for women.[20] But the use of the first name alone, in situations in which it is not warranted, such as if the speaker really is not a personal friend with the person referred to, sounds patronizing, and the second awkward in suggesting that the person referred to is not accepted as a colleague. Yet these are the only normal options.

I am speaking here only of prevailing tendencies. Exceptions obviously exist, and are the more apt to be made the better known a woman is in her field. But certainly, in common conversational use among linguists speaking colloquially, we might expect to find sentence *(a)* below rather more than we might expect *(b)*.

> Say, what did you think of Lakoff's latest paper, where *(a)* he
> *(b)* she
> makes the claim that logical structure is to be formally thought of as a 100-pound purple orangutan?

Ordinarily, the hearer of the sentence above would be somewhat jarred by encountering the feminine pronoun later in the sentence, since last name alone sets up a strong assumption that it is a male colleague being referred to. Probably the majority of linguists, in this situation, would also resort to circumlocution to avoid the following sentence:

> *(c)* I understand Green is claiming that Morgan thinks with a fork.

It would seem as though male members of the profession are, sub-consciously or otherwise, loath to admit women to full membership in their club, and this trouble in terms of address — limiting the choice to address-ing a woman either by first name, in this situation implying her inferiority to the speaker, or by both names, suggesting she is not quite a full col-league — is symptomatic of deeper problems of which we are all aware.

I think this tendency to use first names sooner and be more apt to use them, rather than last name alone or title plus last name, in referring to and addressing women, is evident in other areas than academia. On television discussion shows, or commentary, or topical comedy (of the Bob Hope kind), a woman will be called or referred to by her first name where a man might not. Again, this is not a hard-and-fast rule, but depends upon the respect accorded to the woman due to her age, position, and attrac-tiveness: it seems as though the more attractive a woman is, the less she can be taken seriously, and the more she is considered a decoration, able to be addressed by first name only. I feel that, other things being equal, there is a greater likelihood of hearing Gloria Steinem called "Gloria" by someone who does not know her very well than of hearing Norman Mailer called "Norman" under the same conditions. (Of course, nobody is likely to call the former Prime Minister of Israel "Golda.") This usage is perhaps to be compared with the tradition of calling children freely by their first names, and may be parallel to the use of "girl" for "woman" discussed earlier.

Aside from making apparent a dilemma arising from a social inequity, the facts noted above are of interest for other reasons: they show that titles are very much alive in our supposedly classless society, and apparently small differences in their use reflect great chasms in social position among users. The use (or misuse) of titles supplies much information to people, and hence titles are important in our language as in our society, and not about to be lightly discarded.

If then, we can reasonably assume that a title supplies information about the person to whose name it is attached, we may further assume that this information is necessary in telling people how to interact with this person. And if this sort of information is felt to be necessary for one class of people and not another, we may expect to find a distinction made in the titles for the first class, if at all, but not the second.

So it is with *Mrs.*, *Miss*, and *Mr*. Since a significant part of the opinion one normally forms about a woman's character and social station depends on her marital status — as is not the case with men — it is obvious that the title of address should supply this information in the case of women, but not of men.

(It may seem as though a man's marital status is, under certain con-ditions, of crucial interest to a woman, and therefore this point is suspect. But I think we have to distinguish between importance in the eyes of a single person in a particular situation, and importance in the eyes of society at large, in a great many possible situations. At almost every turn, because of the way social and business events are arranged, one needs to know a woman's marital status, and the position held by her husband. But one does not need the same information about a man, since his social status can be gauged, generally, purely by reference to his own accomplishments.) Once again, it would seem that trying to legislate a change in a lexical item is fruitless. The change to *Ms.* will not be generally adopted until a woman's status in society changes to assure her an identity based on her own accomplishments. (Perhaps even more debasing than the *Mrs./Miss* distinction is the fact that the woman in marrying relinquishes her own name, while the man does not. This suggests even more firmly that a woman is her husband's possession, having no other identity than that of his wife. Not only does she give up her last name [which, after all, she took from her father], but often her first name as well, to become *Mrs. John Smith.*)

Although blacks are not yet fully accorded equal status with whites in this society, nevertheless *black*, a term coined to elicit racial pride and sense of unity, seems to have been widely adopted both by blacks and whites, both in formal use and in the media, and increasingly in colloquial conversation. Does this constitute a counterexample to my claim here? I think not, but rather an element of hope. My point is that linguistic and social change go hand in hand: one cannot, purely by changing language use, change social status. The word *black*, in its current sense, was not heard until the late 1960s or even 1970, to any significant extent. I think if its use had been proposed much earlier, it would have failed in accep- tance. I think the reason people other than blacks can understand and sympathize with black racial pride is that they were made aware of the depths of their prejudice during the civil rights struggles of the early 1960s. It took nearly ten years from the beginning of this struggle for the use of *black* to achieve wide acceptance, and it is still often used a bit self- consciously, as though italicized. But since great headway was made first in the social sphere, linguistic progress could be made *on that basis*; and now this linguistic progress, it is hoped, will lead to new social progress in turn. The women's movement is but a few years old, and has, I should think, much deeper ingrained hostility to overcome than the civil rights movement ever did. (Among the intelligentsia, the black civil rights struggle was never a subject for ridicule, as women's liberation all too often is, among those very liberals who were the first on their blocks to join the NAACP.)[21] The parallel to the black struggle should indicate that social change must precede lexical change: women must achieve some measure of greater social independence of men before *Ms.* can gain wider accep- tance.

(b) There is thus a very good reason why a distinction is made in the case of women, but not men, in the matter of marital status. But this fact suggests an answer to the second question posed above, regarding why *Ms.* is felt to be a more serious proposal than Baker's suggestion. It is obviously easier to imagine obliterating an extant distinction than creating a new one: easier to learn to ignore the marital status of a woman than to begin to pay attention to that of a man. Moreover, we may also assume that for a woman, the use of *Ms.* is a liberating device, one to be desired. But (as Baker suggests) the use of two titles for men is an encumbrance, a remover of certain kinds of liberties, and something definitely undesirable. So the two suggestions are not equivalent, and if either were ever to be accepted, the choice of *Ms.* is the probable candidate.

(*c*) The third question regarding the chances *Ms.* has for real acceptance has, in effect, already been answered. Until society changes so that the distinction between married and unmarried women is as unimportant in terms of their social position as that between married and unmarried men, the attempt in all probability cannot succeed. Like the attempt to substitute any euphemism for an uncomfortable word, the attempt to do away with *Miss* and *Mrs.* is doomed to failure if it is not accompanied by a change in society's attitude to what the titles describe.

# 4 ::

## Conclusion

Linguistic imbalances are worthy of study because they bring into sharper focus real-world imbalances and inequities. They are clues that some external situation needs changing, rather than items that one *should* seek to change directly. A competent doctor tries to eliminate the germs that cause measles, rather than trying to bleach the red out with peroxide. I emphasize this point because it seems to be currently fashionable to try, first, to attack the disease by attempting to obliterate the external symptoms; and, second, to attack *every* instance of linguistic sexual inequity, rather than selecting those that reflect a real disparity in social treatment, not mere grammatical nonparallelism. We should be attempting to single out those linguistic uses that, by implication and innuendo, demean the members of one group or another, and should be seeking to make speakers of English aware of the psychological damage such forms do. The problem, of course, lies in deciding which forms are really damaging to the ego, and then in determining what to put in their stead.

A good example, which troubles me a lot at present, is that of pronominal neutralization. In English, as indeed in the great majority of the world's languages, when reference is made individually to members of a sexually mixed group, the normal solution is to resolve the indecision as to pronoun choice in favor of the masculine:* the masculine, then, is "unmarked" or "neutral," and therefore will be found referring to men and women both in sentences like the following:

(25)  (a)  Everyone take his seat.
     (b)  If a person wants to ingratiate himself with Harry, he
                                  *herself              *she
         should cook him moo-shu pork.

In (25) (a), her could of course be used in an all-female group; the point is that in a mixed group, even one predominantly female, his will normally be the "correct" form. Many speakers, feeling this is awkward and perhaps even discriminatory, attempt a neutralization with their, a usage frowned upon by most authorities as inconsistent or illogical. In (25) (b), herself and she might conceivably replace himself and he, but the effect of the sentence would be changed, not too surprisingly: the ingratiation would be understood as an attempt at (sexual) seduction, or an attempt to persuade Harry to marry the "person."

That is, although semantically both men and women are included in the groups referred to by the pronouns in these sentences, only he and related masculine forms are commonly possible. An analogous situation occurs in many languages with the words for human being: in English, we find man and mankind, which of course refer to women members of the species as well. This of course permits us innumerable jokes involving "man-eating sharks," and the widespread existence of these jokes perhaps points up the problem that these forms create for a woman who speaks a language like English.

I feel that the emphasis upon this point, to the exclusion of most other linguistic points, by writers within the women's movement is misguided. While this lexical and grammatical neutralization is related to the

---

*Wallace Chafe has given me an interesting example relative to this discussion of pronominal neutralization and sexism. In Iroquoian, neutralization is through the use of the feminine pronoun. The Iroquoian society is sometimes (inaccurately) referred to as matriarchal; in any case, women play a special role. These two facts together would seem to be a vindication for those who claim that neutralization in favor of the masculine pronoun, as in English, is a mark of the sexism rampant in our culture. But elsewhere in Iroquoian, this claim is belied. There are numerous prefixes attached to nouns, distinguishing number, gender, and case. When the noun refers to masculine human beings, these prefixes are kept separate of one another. But in referring to feminine human beings, animals, and inanimate objects, these numerous prefixes may be collapsed. This suggests that here women are considered in the category of animals and things, and lower or less important than men, contradicting the implications of the pronominal system. So this shows that even in a matriarchal society, sexism exists and has grammatical reflexes. It also suggests that pronoun neutralization is not really the crucial issue: there are other aspects of language—in English as well as Iroquoian—which are better indicators of the relationship between linguistic usage and cultural assumptions.

fact that men have been the writers and the doers, I don't think it by itself specifies a particular and demeaning role for women, as the special uses of *mistress* or *professional,* to give a few examples, do. It is not insidious in the same way: it does not indicate to little girls how they are expected to behave. Even if it did, surely other aspects of linguistic imbalance should receive equal attention. But more seriously, I think one should force oneself to be realistic: certain aspects of language are available to the native speaker's conscious analysis, and others are too common, too thoroughly mixed throughout the language, for the speaker to be aware each time he uses them. It is realistic to hope to change only those linguistic uses of which speakers themselves can be made aware, as they use them. One chooses, in speaking or writing, more or less consciously and purposefully among nouns, adjectives, and verbs; one does not choose among pronouns in the same way. My feeling is that this area of pronominal neutralization is both less in need of changing and less open to change than many of the other disparities that have been discussed earlier, and we should perhaps concentrate our efforts where they will be most fruitful.

But many nonlinguists disagree. I have read and heard dissenting views from too many anguished women to suppose that this use of *he* is really a triviality. The claim is that the use of the neutral *he* with such frequency makes women feel shut out, not a part of what is being described, an inferior species, or a nonexistent one. Perhaps linguistic training has dulled my perception, and this really is a troublesome question. If so, I don't know what to advise, since I feel in any case that an attempt to change pronominal usage will be futile. My recommendation then would be based purely on pragmatic considerations: attempt to change only what can be changed, since this is hard enough.

I think in any case that linguists should be consulted before any more fanciful plans are made public for reforming the inequities of English. Many of these are founded on misunderstanding and create well-deserved ridicule, but this ridicule is then carried over into other areas which are not ludicrous at all, but suffer guilt by association. For instance, there have been serious suggestions lately that women have not had much influence on the affairs of the world because the term for the thing is *his-tory.* They suggest that the problem could be solved by changing the word to *her-story.*

It should not be necessary to spend time demolishing this proposal, but it is so prevalent that it must be stopped soon. First of all, the argument at very best confuses cause and effect: it is very seldom the case that a certain form of behavior results from being given a certain name, but rather, names are given on the basis of previously observed behavior. So anteaters are so called because they were observed to eat ants; it is not the case that the name "anteater" was given them randomly, and they rewarded the giver of the name by eating ants, which they had not previously done. But in any event, the argument is fallacious. The word *history* is not derived from two English words, *his* + *story*; rather it comes from the Greek word

71

*historia,* from a root meaning "know." The Greeks, in coining the word, did not think it had anything to do with men versus women; so it could not have been so called because men were the only ones who played a part in it, nor could it have been so called in order to ensure that only men would have this role. In many languages, the equivalent of the English word *history* is related to it in appearance and origin; yet in none of them does it appear related in any way to the masculine pronoun (cf. French *histoire*). Yet the world's history is the same for speakers of all languages, generally speaking. This kind of thinking is both ludicrous and totally fallacious, and is discussed at undeserved length here only because the attention it has received has distracted people from thinking of more serious problems. And more recently still, I have read a suggestion that hurricanes be renamed *himicanes,* since the former appellation reflects poorly on women. If this sort of stuff appears in print and in the popular media as often as it does, it becomes increasingly more difficult to persuade men that women are really rational beings.

If we can accept the facts already discussed as generally true, for most people, most of the time, then we can draw from them several conclusions, of interest to readers in any of various fields.

1. People working in the women's liberation movement, and other social reformers, can see that there *is* a discrepancy between English as used by men and by women; and that the social discrepancy in the positions of men and women in our society is reflected in linguistic disparities. The linguist, through linguistic analysis, can help to pinpoint where these disparities lie, and can suggest ways of telling when improvements have been made. But it should be recognized that social change creates language change, not the reverse; or at best, language change influences changes in attitudes slowly and indirectly, and these changes in attitudes will not be reflected in social change unless society is receptive already. Further, the linguist can suggest which linguistic disparities reflect real and serious social inequalities; which are changeable, which will resist change; and can thus help the workers in the real world to channel their energies most constructively and avoid ridicule.

2. For the teacher of second languages, it is important to realize that social context is relevant in learning to speak a second language fluently. It is also important for a teacher to be aware of the kind of language he or she is speaking: if a woman teacher unconsciously teaches "women's language" to her male students, they may be in difficulties when they try to function in another country; if a female anthropologist learns the "men's language" of an area, she may not be able to get anywhere with the inhabitants because she seems unfeminine, and they will not know

how to react to her. Language learning thus goes beyond phonology, syntax, and semantics, but it takes a perceptive teacher to notice the pitfalls and identify them correctly for students.

3. And finally, we have something for the theoretical linguist to consider. We have been talking about the use of language: what can be more germane than this in formulating a theory of language?[22] We have shown that language use changes depending on the position in society of the language user, that a sentence that is "acceptable" when uttered by a woman is "unacceptable" when uttered by a man, or that one sentence may be "acceptable" under one set of assumptions in the subject matter, "unacceptable" under another. That is, it is a mistake to hope (as earlier linguistic theories have sometimes done) that the acceptability of a sentence is a yes-no or *\/non* decision: rather we must think in terms of hierarchies of grammaticality, in which the acceptability of a sentence is determined through the combination of many factors: not only the phonology, the syntax, and the semantics, but also the social context in which the utterance is expressed, and the assumptions about the world made by all the participants in the discourse. It is sometimes objected that this is the realm of "pragmatics," not "linguistics," that it reflects "performance," not "competence." My feeling is that language use by any other name is still linguistics, and it is the business of the linguist to tell why and where a sentence is acceptable, and to leave the name-calling to the lexicographers. If a linguist encounters an example like *The way prices are rising is horrendous, isn't it?* and feels indecisive about its acceptability in various situations, it is his duty to tell exactly where his doubts lie, and why. It is as important for him to catalog the contextual situations under which a tag question like this (or tag questions in general) may be used as to determine the syntactic environment in which the tag question formation rule may apply. To stop with the latter (as is done, for example, in standard transformational grammar) is to tell half the story.

Or to take another instance: we have discussed a wide variety of problematical cases. Why can't you say: *\*John is Mary's widower?* (And this sentence is bad under *any* conditions, and hence is not a question of "performance.") Why have the meanings of *master* and *mistress* changed in a nonparallel fashion over time? Why does *He's a professional* have different implications than *She's a professional?* Suppose a linguist wishes to avoid making reference to social context in his grammar. How can he deal with such cases? First, there is the problem of the nonparallelism in the use of *widow* and *widower*. He might mark the latter in his lexicon as [−NPgenitive——] or a similar ad hoc device. Or one might say that

73

*widow* had underlying it a 2-place predicate, while there was a 1-place predicate underlying *widower.* That this is ludicrous, in that it distorts the meaning of the latter sentence, is evident. In the case of *professional,* the theorist who excludes social context would have a slightly different problem. He has to indicate in the lexicon that there are two words *professional,* presumably accidental homonyms. One is restricted to women, like *pregnant;* the other is restricted to men, like *virile.* (Of course, there are obvious semantic reasons, going back to facts in the real world, in the cases of *pregnant* and *virile* that make their gender restrictions non-ad hoc. Since this is not the case with *professional,* he has already introduced arbitrariness into this lexical item.) Then one sense of *professional,* the one restricted to women, is defined as: "lit. or fig., a prostitute." The other sense, specific to men, is defined: "engaging in certain business activities . . ." or whatever. And similarly, he would in the case of *master* and *mistress* have to construct a very strange theory of historical change in order to allow these words to diverge in sense in the way in which they have.

This is not to say that these facts cannot be handled in some ad hoc fashion; my point here is merely that to take such a course is to violate the principles of valid linguistic description. First, the linguist taking this position has been forced to resort to numerous ad hoc devices purely in order to avoid generating impossible sentences while generating those that are grammatical. Second, and perhaps more seriously, he would be overlooking the real point of what is going on. Each of the nonparallelisms that have been discussed here (as well, of course, as the many others I have mentioned elsewhere, and still others the reader can no doubt supply himself) would in such treatment be nonparallel for a different reason from each of the others. Yet the speaker of English who has not been raised in a vacuum *knows* that all of these disparities exist in English for the same reason: *each reflects in its pattern of usage the difference between the role of women in our society and that of men.* If there were tomorrow, say by an act of God, a total restructuring of society as we know it so that women were in fact equal to men, we would make certain predictions about the future behavior of the language. One prediction we might make is that *all* these words, together, would cease to be nonparallel. If the curious behavior of each of these forms were idiosyncratic, we would not expect them to behave this way en masse. If their peculiarity had nothing to do with the way society was organized, we would not expect their behavior to change as a result of social change. Now of course, one cannot prove points by invoking a cataclysmic change that has not occurred and, in all probability, will not. But I do think an appeal is possible to the reader's intuition: this seems a likely way for these forms to behave. In any event, I think this much is clear: that there is a generalization that can be made regarding the aberrant behavior of all these lexical items, but this generalization can be made only by reference, in the grammar of the language, to social mores. The linguist must involve himself, professionally, with sociology:[23]

first, because he is able to isolate the data that the sociologist can use in determining the weaknesses and strengths of a culture (as we have done, to some extent, here); and then because if he does not examine the society of the speakers of the language along with the so-called purely linguistic data, he will be unable to make the relevant generalizations, will be unable to understand why the language works the way it does. He will, in short, be unable to do linguistics.*

---

*This is not the only known situation in which the linguist must work with the concepts of sociology. To give another example, in his paper "Anaphoric Islands" in Binnick et al., eds., *Papers from the Fifth Regional Meeting of the Chicago Linguistic Society*, May 1969, Postal discusses the distribution of terms like *dogmeat, wombatmeat, pigmeat* (as opposed to *dog, chicken, pork*). He suggests that *-meat* must appear if the item is not regularly eaten by the speakers of the language. This is another example in which reference must be made to purely cultural, extralinguistic facts about a society in order to judge the well-formedness of lexical items.

# PART II: WHY WOMEN ARE LADIES

## 1 ::

## Introduction

In the preceding discussion, I talked at some length about the linguistic uses that characterize traditional "women's language," as well as the ways in which we speak differently of women than of men. I tried to give evidence that the discrepancies that appear to exist are harmful to women's self-image and to the image people in general form of women's character and abilities.

One of the problems I have run into in presenting these ideas is that often, while everyone acknowledges the existence of nonparallel usages such as the ones I described, people also feel that no inequity exists; men and women are "separate but equal," and no redress need be made; *vive*, in fact, *la différence*.[24] In addition, people very often feel affronted at my criticisms — this is true of both men and women — because they have been taught that the discrepancies actually favor women, and here I am trying to change them; I am striking a blow against womankind and maybe even mankind, since it benefits women and everyone else to have these distinctions. The argument most often revolves around the notions of "politeness" we were all taught as children: women's speech differs from men's in that women are more polite, which is precisely as it should be, since women are the preservers of morality and civility; and we speak around women in an especially "polite" way in return, eschewing the coarseness of ruffianly men's language: no slang, no swear words, no off-color remarks. Further, many of the ways we choose to speak of women reflect our higher estimate of them than of men, and exalt and flatter, rather than humiliate. So, the argument runs, my position, that women should be aware of these discrepancies in language and do what they can to demolish them, is the one that denigrates and degrades women.

I appreciate the superficial force of that argument; and certainly, if a woman feels she has no other strength or status in the real world than as "lady," arbiter of morality, judge of manners, she might well be affronted by the comments I make. My hope is that women will recognize that such a role is insufficient for a human being and will then realize that using this language, having it used of them, and thus being placed implicitly in this role, is degrading in that it is constraining. There's nothing wrong, obviously, with having a natural sense of rhythm; but to impute this quality, sight unseen, to *all* blacks and thus to each black in turn that one encounters is insulting. Similarly, if some women want to be arbiters of morality, that's fine with me; but I don't like the idea that, because I came into the world with two X chromosomes, I have no choice but to be an arbiter of morality, and will automatically be treated as though I were.

Hence this discussion. What I want to talk about is precisely the relationship between women's language, language referring to women, and politeness and to reflect on the reasons behind this relationship. The question is complicated by the fact that politeness is many-faceted, just as there are many forms of women's language and many distinctions among the uses so identified in the preceding part of this book. For instance, almost no one I know of my age and general educational status would be caught dead saying "divine," and some even claim not to be able to identify "magenta," while knowing what a universal joint is (in their car, rather than their roach clip).[25] But question intonation in declarative-requiring situations is very common among us still, and much as we feel the need to extirpate it, it flourishes as long as we don't have perfect self-confidence. Using "divine" is not a mark of feelings of inferiority, but rather a mere badge of class—female class. Using question intonation inappropriately is both. The latter dies harder than the former.

Similarly, as I shall discuss at length, there are many types of behavior that can be called "polite." Some forms of politeness are linguistic, some purely nonlinguistic, and many mixed; some are polite in some settings, neutral or downright rude in others; some are polite in some societies, rude in others; and finally some are polite in some societies at one stage of a relationship, but rude in another society at a parallel stage, perhaps polite in the latter society at a different stage. What I will propose are some tentative "working rules" for the types of politeness that are found and an attempt to describe the situations in which each is appropriate. I will then talk about the relationship between women's language and language about women, and these rules of politeness, as compared to and contrasted with what one finds in men's and in neutral language. Finally I will offer some rather tentative speculations on what is possibly going on: why the discrepancies exist, and why they are deleterious to society in general as well as to women in particular, and are not the innocent flattery they are thought of as being.

Let me summarize here for convenience the forms that I see as comprising "women's language," most of which have already been discussed at length.

1. Women have a large stock of words related to their specific interests, generally relegated to them as "woman's work": magenta, shirr, dart (in sewing), and so on. If men use these words at all, it tends to be tongue-in-cheek.
2. "Empty" adjectives like *divine, charming, cute.* . . .
3. Question intonation where we might expect declaratives: for instance tag questions ("It's so hot, isn't it?") and rising intonation in statement contexts ("What's your name, dear?" "Mary Smith?").

4. The use of hedges of various kinds. Women's speech seems in general to contain more instances of "well," "y'know," "kinda," and so forth: words that convey the sense that the speaker is uncertain about what he (or she) is saying, or cannot vouch for the accuracy of the statement. These words are fully legitimate when, in fact, this is the case (for example, if one says, "John is sorta tall," meaning he's neither really impressively tall nor actually short, but rather middling, though toward the tall side: 5 feet 9 rather than 6 feet 5, say). There is another justifiable use in which the hedge mitigates the possible unfriendliness or unkindness of a statement—that is, where it's used for the sake of politeness. Thus, "John is sorta short," where I mean: He's 5 feet 2 and you're 5 feet 8, Mary, so how will it look if you go out with him? Here, I know exactly how short he is, and it is very short, but I blunt the force of a rather painful assertion by using the hedge. What I mean is the class of cases in which neither of these facts pertains, and a hedge shows up anyway: the speaker is perfectly certain of the truth of the assertion, and there's no danger of offense, but the tag appears anyway as an apology for making an assertion at all. Anyone may do this if he lacks self-confidence, as everyone does in some situations; but my impression is that women do it more, precisely because they are socialized to believe that asserting themselves strongly isn't nice or ladylike, or even feminine. Another manifestation of the same thing is the use of "I guess" and "I think" prefacing declarations or "I wonder" prefacing questions, which themselves are hedges on the speech-acts of saying and asking. "I guess" means something like: I would like to say . . . to you, but I'm not sure I can (because I don't know if it's right, because I don't know if I have the right, because I don't know how you'd take it, and so on), so I'll merely put it forth as a suggestion. Thus, if I say, "It will rain this afternoon," and it doesn't, you can later take me to task for a misleading or inaccurate prediction. But if I say, "I guess it will rain this afternoon," then I am far less vulnerable to such an attack. So these hedges do have their uses when one really has legitimate need for protection, or for deference (if we are afraid that by making a certain statement we are overstepping our rights), but used to excess, hedges, like question intonation, give the impression that the speaker lacks authority or doesn't know what he's talking about. Again, these are familiar misogynistic criticisms, but the use of these hedges arises out of a fear of seeming too masculine by being assertive and saying things directly.

5. Related to this is the use of the intensive "so." Again, this is more frequent in women's than men's language, though cer-

tainly men can use it. Here we have an attempt to hedge on one's strong feelings, as though to say: I feel strongly about this— but I dare not make it clear *how* strong. To say, "I like him very much," would be to say precisely that you like him to a great extent. To say, "I like him *so* much" weasels on that intensity: again, a device you'd use if you felt it unseemly to show you had strong emotions, or to make strong assertions, but felt you had to say something along those lines anyway.

6. Hypercorrect grammar: women are not supposed to talk rough. It has been found that, from a very young age, little boys "drop" their g's much more than do little girls: boys say "singin'," "goin'," and so on, while girls are less apt to. Similarly little boys are less apt than little girls to be scolded for saying "ain't" or at least they are scolded less severely, because "ain't" is more apt to remain in their vocabularies than in their sisters'. Generally women are viewed as being the preservers of literacy and cul- ture, at least in Middle America, where literacy and culture are viewed as being somewhat suspect in a male. (That is, in cul- tures where learning is valued for itself, men are apt to be the guardians of culture and the preservers of grammar; in cultures where book larnin' is the schoolmarm's domain, this job will be relegated to the women. Jespersen remarks somewhere that women are more prone to neologism than men and hence more likely to be the originators of linguistic change; but I think he was thinking in terms of European society of the last century, where indeed the men were virtually always more highly edu- cated than the women, and education a mark of status.)[26]

7. Superpolite forms. This is the point alluded to earlier: women are supposed to speak more politely than men. This is related to their hypercorrectness in grammar, of course, since it's consid- ered more mannerly in middle-class society to speak "properly." But it goes deeper: women don't use off-color or indelicate ex- pressions; women are the experts at euphemism; more positively, women are the repositories of tact and know the right things to say to other people, while men carelessly blurt out whatever they are thinking. Women are supposed to be particularly care- ful to say "please" and "thank you" and to uphold the other so- cial conventions; certainly a woman who fails at these tasks is apt to be in more trouble than a man who does so: in a man it's "just like a man," and indulgently overlooked unless his behav- ior is really boorish. In a woman, it's social death in conven- tional circles to refuse to go by the rules.

8. Women don't tell jokes. As we shall see in a while, this point is just an elaboration of the two immediately preceding. But it is axiomatic in middle-class American society that, first, women

can't tell jokes — they are bound to ruin the punchline, they mix up the order of things, and so on. Moreover, they don't "get" jokes. In short, women have no sense of humor.

9. Women speak in italics, and the more ladylike and feminine you are, the more in italics you are supposed to speak. This is another way of expressing uncertainty with your own self-expression, though this statement may appear contradictory: italics, if anything, seem to *strengthen* (note those italics) an utterance. But actually they say something like: Here are directions telling you how to react, since my saying something by itself is not likely to convince you: I'd better use double force, to make sure you see what I mean. It is well known, for instance, that beginning students in English composition tend to use italics far more than do established and confident writers of prose, precisely because the former are afraid, even as they write, that they are not being listened to, that their words are apt to have no effect.

There are doubtless other devices that are parts of women's language. Some can't be described in writing because there is no easy way to give examples: this is true of specifically female intonation patterns. Certainly it can be said that women have at their disposal a wider range of intonation patterns than do men, both within sentences and among full-sentence patterns. I am not sure why this is so. Possibly extra intonational variety is used as a sort of secondary signal, in case the first was not received. That is, if you have reason to be afraid you're not being listened to, or not being taken seriously, you will throw in extra ways for the hearer to figure out what you've said — you'll try every means to ensure that your message is received and responded to. (Thus, if you're speaking to someone you are afraid doesn't understand English very well, you'll be more prone to resort to gestures than you would be if there was no language problem.) Perhaps women realize that they are often not being listened to, because obviously they couldn't be saying anything that really mattered, and therefore, more or less consciously, use voice patterns that have a dual effect: first, of being very attention-catching in the hope that if what you have to say won't be perceived, at least the addressee will hear how you're saying it; and then, since pitch and stress carry some semantic force, the speaker may hope that some of the message will percolate through by that means, though it might be lost if stated only once, by words alone. It may be for this reason as well that women are more prone to gesture as they speak than are men. All this is speculation, though I think interesting speculation.

A first objection that might occur to these points is that men *can* use virtually every item on this list; some men, surely, use none, some use some, and some maybe even use all. The latter is very often the case with academic men; and I think that the decisive factor is less purely gender than power in the real world.[27] But it happens that, as a result of natural gender, a woman tends to have, and certainly tends to feel she has, little real-world power compared with a man; so generally a woman will be more apt to have these uses than a man will. It is equally true that different women speak women's language to differing extents; and interestingly enough, it seems that academic women are among the least apt to be speakers of this language. But this may be because women who have succeeded in academe have more power than other women who have no outside roles; and that in determining their real-world power, women use as a basis the power of the men they know. Since the men that women academics are most likely to know are male academics, on this basis of comparison, with the relatively real-world-powerless, they seem to have more power than other women, so they are less apt to have to resort to women's language. And, in my experience, academia is a more egalitarian society than most, in terms of sex roles and expectations.

In any event, it should be clear that I am not talking about hundred-percent correlations, but rather, general tendencies. If you are a woman, it is more likely that you will speak this way than if you are a man, but that is not to say that I predict you do speak this way if you're a woman, or don't if you're a man. Further, you could speak this way to some extent; or could speak it under some circumstances but not others. (For instance, in the office where you're in charge you might avoid it, but might use it habitually at home, perhaps not even realizing you are making the switch.)

It has recently been suggested by Cheris Kramer (in *Psychology Today*, June 1974) that these claims are inaccurate. Her reason is this: that in questionnaires that they filled out, women did not indicate that they used "women's" language nor did men indicate that they necessarily considered these traits peculiar to women. There are several things to be said in reply to this. First, it has never been claimed—as I have said already—that men can't use these forms, or that women must. What I have said is that women use them, or are likely to use them, in a wider range of linguistic, psychological, and social environments—that women typically lack assertiveness, for one thing, in more contexts than men do. (Obviously there will be exceptions.) Second, the device of the interview in these cases is suspect. Asking people how they feel about linguistic forms makes them self-conscious about them; they may feel that if they say "yes," they will be disapproved of, or that you're not a nice person if you don't answer "right," however "right" may be construed in a given instance. This may not even be explicitly realized but can skew the figures all the same. And very often, people simply aren't aware of what they say; it takes a trained linguist to have the "ear" for that. And it is probably true that the more potentially embarrassing the questions are, the more distortion (whether conscious or not) can be expected. And questions raising concern over one's masculinity or femininity, or the proper role for one's sex, are certainly embarrassing. So it's unsafe to take such a questionnaire at face value.

Another problem with many tests that have been made for recognition of "women's language" is that they have depended on written samples (one example I know of used freshman composition themes). Not too surprisingly, these tests tend to show that little or no correlation is found by the subjects between the sex of the actual writer of the piece and the sex ascribed to him or her. This finding, however, is deceptive.

If you look at the list of distinguishing criteria for women's language that I gave earlier, you will note that most of the characteristics are apt to be found only in spoken, or at least highly informal, style. This is because they are *personal* markers: they signal to the addressee how the speaker feels about what she (he, of course, in the analogous cases of men's language) is saying, and how the speaker hopes or expects that the hearer will react. Such commentary is a part of *informal* style—person-to-person friendly speech, and sometimes, though increasingly rarely these days, letters—rather than formal style—lectures and most forms of writing. In particular, freshman composition style is notorious for its awkward formality, owing to uneasiness in writing, and is the last place one would look for personal characterization, indicative of the writer's feeling of comfortable rapport with a potential reader.

Cartoon captions, minus the cartoons of course, which have also been used as a testing device, will also produce suspect results, because they are not part of connected dialogue and because they are contextless. The criteria I listed above were *not* intended as yes-or-no certainties. What I said was that most women would use most of them in a wider range of psychological and social environments than most men would (a very hedgy statement, but what did you expect?), because women tend to feel unwilling to assert themselves in a wider range of circumstances than men do. Hence, one can judge whether something is "women's language," "men's language," or "neutral" only with reference to the real-world context in which it was uttered—a complex and subtle combination of judgments that would be virtually impossible to reproduce in a natural way in an experimental situation.

There's another point, and that is that a stereotypical image may be far more influential than a (mere) statistical correlation. Let's say, for the sake of argument, that *no* real female person in the United States actually speaks any form or dialect of women's language. Yet there are the innumerable women we see on television, who whether we like it or not form role models for young girls. Maybe Edith Bunker is not presented as a wholly believable or admirable figure, but certainly she is presented as a conceivable female type, one that someone might eventually aspire to fit into. Edith Bunker is obviously an extreme case, but almost every woman you see in the media has many traits of women's language built into her speech. And these stereotypical women, I fear, have great influence over the young: I recall, as a child, worrying because I didn't fit the pattern for which women were being ridiculed in jokes I heard on television. I wasn't fuzzy-minded, I didn't care if another girl at a party wore the same dress I did, I wasn't extravagant, and so on. It frightened rather than cheered me to realize this discrepancy between the female stereotype and myself: I feared I'd never make it. True, I didn't (at least I hope I didn't) remake myself to fit the stereotype, but seeing that image there continually in a thousand variations did nothing for my self-image: first, because that was the *best* I, as a girl, could hope to aspire to; second, and maybe worse, because I couldn't even manage *that* role. Maybe I was especially vulnerable, but I feel that the stereotypes we see in the media are far more influential than we like to think they are, and they should be taken very seriously indeed.

Another thing I have sometimes been accused of saying, and would take exception to, is that women have all the problems, that it's easy for men: *they* aren't constrained or bound into roles; their lives are simple. Nothing is further from the truth, or my mind. Larry Josephson has shown, in an unpublished paper discussing men's language, that men are just as constrained in what they are supposed, and not supposed, to say as are women. For instance, men in most occupations and social strata may *not* use empty adjectives or let on that they know the meanings of words like "kick pleat" or "braise." If men are too grammatical or too polite in their speech, they are viewed with suspicion. Men are supposed to be in command of a whole different range of lexical items, and woe betide a man in some circles if he doesn't know the name and function of everything in his car. He generally is expected to know how to swear and how to tell and appreciate the telling of dirty jokes, and certainly must never giggle when he hears them.

Constraining as all this is, I feel it is constraining in a less damaging way than are the confines of women's language on its speakers. The question to ask is: What happens to people who are taught to speak the language, and then speak it? What are the rewards?

If a man learns to speak men's language, and is otherwise unambiguously placed in his society as a man, his is a relatively (and I say only *relatively*) simple position. His rewards, in the traditional culture, are easy to see. He is listened to and taken seriously; he becomes one of the boys and can engage in various kinds of camaraderie, achieving closeness to his buddies by the language all share, the slang and dirty jokes bringing them closer to each other. His learning of his proper language brings purely positive results, in terms of how people react to the way he talks.

Not so for the woman. If she doesn't learn to speak women's language, in traditional society she's dead: she is ostracized as unfeminine by both men and women. So that is not a possible option, unless a young girl is exceedingly brave — in fact, reckless. But what if she opts to do as she ought — learn to talk like a lady? She has some rewards: she is accepted as a suitable female. But she also finds that she is treated — purely because of the way she speaks and, therefore, supposedly thinks — as someone not to be taken seriously, of dim intelligence, frivolous, and incapable of understanding anything important. It is true that some women seem to adapt to this role quite nicely, and indeed it has apparent advantages: if you're not taken seriously, if you can't understand anything, you then have no responsibility for important ideas, you don't have to trouble your pretty little head about deep problems. Maybe this is nice for a while, but surely it's hard to be a child forever. If a woman learns and uses women's language, she is necessarily considered less than a real, full person—she's a bit of fluff.

Now that means, as I said already, that a woman is damned if she does and damned if she doesn't. And this is a form of the paradox that Gregory Bateson has called a double-bind: a double-bind is a situation in which a person, by obeying an order, automatically disobeys it. Further, the order is given in a situation in which it cannot be questioned—it is given by too potent an authority. The classical example is that of the soldier who is ordered to cut the hair of everyone in the regiment except those who cut their own. The dilemma arises when he comes to consider his own hair. Whichever path he chooses—to cut his hair or not to—he disobeys one part of the order. Now the command that society gives to the young of both sexes might be phrased something like: "Gain respect by speaking like other members of your sex." For the boy, as we have seen, that order, constraining as it is, is not paradoxical: if he speaks (and generally behaves) as men in his culture are supposed to, he generally gains people's respect. But whichever course the woman takes—to speak women's language or not to—she will not be respected. So she cannot carry out the order, and the order is transmitted by society at large; there is no way to question it, no one even to direct the question to. Bateson claims that if someone is exposed to a double-bind in childhood, he may become schizophrenic and that, indeed, double-binds are found in many schizophrenogenic families.

Now clearly it would be ridiculous to claim that therefore women are typically schizophrenic in a clinical sense. But certainly it is true that more women than men are institutionalized for mental illness; women form the huge majority of psychiatric patients. It may be that men and women start out with the same psychological equipment, but fighting the paradoxes a woman necessarily faces tends to break down a woman's mental resources; therefore a woman is more apt to run into mental difficulties and, when she faces real stress, to have fewer inner resources left to overcome her problems. So it is just possible that society is putting a far greater strain on its women than on its men, and it is time to ask whether this is true, and if true, how the burden may be equalized.[28]

Finally, it should be noted that the distinction between men's and women's language is a symptom of a problem in our culture, not the problem itself. Basically it reflects the fact that men and women are expected to have different interests and different roles, hold different types of conversations, and react differently to other people. This point is made especially clearly and nicely by Roy Miller in his book *The Japanese Language*. Although he is discussing the situation in Japanese—and in Japanese society the roles of men and women are much more rigidly stratified than they are in ours—nevertheless an analogy between what he is saying and what I have said can easily be drawn. Let me reproduce the relevant passage in full:

> Another important part of the system of speech levels is the distinction between men's and women's speech. Partly these differences operate within the larger system of speech levels. For example, women make more use of the deferential prefix *o-* and of elegant and exalted verb forms than do men, etc., and certain of these aspects have already been touched upon above in our brief summary of the levels system. But sexual differentiation in Japanese also includes different sets of sentence-final particles for men ( . . . *zo,* . . . *yo,* . . . *ze,* etc.) and for women ( . . . *wa,* . . . *no*), as well as different repertories of interjections for each group. Women also favor variant pronunciations of certain forms (gozāmasu for gozaimasu). But in general the differences between men's and women's speech are too far-reaching and too closely interdependent upon content and style to admit of any simple summary. Put most briefly, women in Japanese society traditionally talk about different things than men do, or at the very least, they say different things even when they talk about the same topics. This makes it difficult and even pointless to attempt to give typical equivalent expressions in men's and women's speech, since in most situations the content and topic will differ as much as would the formal verbal expression.
>
> The following brief text is a good example of fairly elegant but otherwise quite run-of-the-mill women's speech:
>
> A. [I am omitting Miller's Japanese dialogue here for convenience, and using only the English translations Miller gives alongside.] My, what a splendid garden you have here—the lawn is so nice and big, it's certainly wonderful, isn't it?
> B. Oh no, not at all, we don't take care of it at all any more, so it simply doesn't always look as nice as we would like it to.
> A. Oh no, I don't think so at all—but since it's such a big garden, of course it must be quite a tremendous task to take care of it all by yourself; but even so, you certainly do manage to make it look nice all the time: it certainly is nice and pretty any time one sees it.
> B. No, I'm afraid not, not at all . . .

This English version, a fairly literal if not word-for-word translation of the Japanese, will make it clear that in every sense this is a very special kind of discourse. What is being said here is not at all important; the only thing of any concern to either speaker is the way in which it is being said, and the number of times the same thing can be repeated. And it is really pointless to ask what the equivalent of all this would be in men's speech, because Japanese men would not carry on in this way about anything, particularly about gardens. A male equivalent text for speaker A would simply be, *ii niwa da na*, "it's a nice garden, isn't it," and that would be the end of it; to this the reply of speaker B, if any, would most likely be a sub-linguistic grunt, as a sign of acknowledgement or of polite denial.*

We will return to this point later: it will be seen to be equally valid, if sometimes less striking, in American dialogue. But I think Miller's major point is unquestionably valid: typical "men's talk" is done for a different purpose than typical "women's talk." The differences between the two arise largely out of this.

# 2 ::

# Forms of Politeness

With these facts in mind, we can return to our original question: Why are women supposed to be more "polite" than men, and why is it considered necessary for men to be more "polite" in the presence of women? And, a related question: If, as is often suggested, politeness is developed by societies in order to reduce friction in personal interaction, why do many feminists feel affronted by these special women-related forms of "politeness," and why do they feel that they must be abolished if true equality between the sexes is ever to be attained?

The fact that different cultures may adjudge the same act in the same circumstances polite or rude indicates that there must be more than one rule of "politeness"—that is, that some cultures will apply one rule preferentially, at a given state in a relationship, where another will apply another. Also we are aware that certain of the ingredients of "politeness" may be combined with one another, or may coexist—others are mutually exclusive. Again, this suggests the existence of several rules, working together

---

*R. A. Miller, *The Japanese Language* (Chicago: University of Chicago Press, 1967), pp. 289–90.

or separately as the case may be. Ideally the Rules of Politeness, when fully and correctly formulated, should be able to predict *why*, in a particular culture, a particular act in a particular circumstance is polite, or not polite; and should also be valid for both linguistic polite behavior (saying "please"; using "formal" pronouns in languages that have such forms) and nonlinguistic politeness (opening doors for others; bringing wine to your dinner host). As a first attempt, I suggest three such rules; I feel that at least these three are needed.[29] Although at first glance it seems possible and attractive to compress them into one, closer examination reveals that by doing so we would lose the ability to make predictions of certain kinds about the types of behavior and judgments that occur.

The rules are as follows:

1. Formality: keep aloof.
2. Deference: give options.
3. Camaraderie: show sympathy.

The first of these rules is perhaps the one most prominent in etiquette books and other considerations of formal politeness. We see it in those languages that differentiate between a formal and an informal *you*: when the formal *you* is in use, the effect is to create distance between speaker and addressee. Legalese and medicalese, for various reasons known best to their speakers, also utilize this rule in their use of technical terminology. This distances speaker both from addressee and from what he is saying, implying that there is no emotive content to his utterance, and thus the participants can remain aloof. In this way, it is wise to talk about *carcinoma* rather than *cancer*, which carries unpleasant emotional connotations. By using these terms, the doctor (or anyone who uses jargon, including of course all of us academics) maintains both distance from and superiority over his addressee. Another example is what might be called the Academic Passive: "In this paper it has been shown. . . ." Neophyte authors are often advised to use active sentences: the reason is that the active voice indicates involvement on the part of the speaker or writer, and thereby invites the participation, or sympathy, of the reader or hearer. But if you want to appear cool and above it all, you use the passive, and this is what academics are prone to do. Another such device is the academic-authorial *we* (in papers by a single author), parallel in function to the plural *vous* (as opposed to *tu*) in French, and to be distinguished from the various other non-first-person plural *we*'s (the editorial and royal *we*; the *we* reserved for talking to children, as in "Now let's tie our shoes, and then we'll take a nice nap").

Hypercorrect forms and avoidance of colloquialism are another means of achieving distance, and the use of titles (Mr., Dr., Sir, and so on) plus last name still another. Nonlinguistically, formal dress, which is always uncomfortable and generally concealing, plays just this role.

One final example of the use of Rule 1 is the impersonal pronoun *one*, particularly when used as a substitute for *you* or *I*. To Americans, the

British seem especially devoted to Rule 1 politeness, and one indication of their addiction to this rule is, in fact, the many ways in which *one* may be used in standard British English, and not in American English at all: "One feels awful about that" seems, if I read novels by British authors correctly, to be the translational equivalent of "I feel awful about that." I think I have also seen in British novels dialogue such as "One shouldn't have done that now, should one?" as an admonition to a second person.

The second rule, that of deference, may be used alone or in combination with either of the other two rules, while Rule 1 and Rule 3 are mutually exclusive. The application of this rule makes it look as though the option as to how to behave, or what to do, is being left up to the addressee. Of course, this is very often mere sham or convention, when the speaker knows very well that he has the power to enforce a decision. Most forms of Rule 1 behavior tend to suggest that the speaker's social status is superior to that of the addressee; generally Rule 2 politeness conveys, whether really or conventionally, the superiority of the addressee over the speaker. Examples of Rule 2: hesitancy in speech and action generally. Question intonation and tag questioning are Rule 2 related devices as long as the speaker is not really uncertain about the truth of his assertion. Hedges, similarly, work this way: they leave the addressee the option of deciding how seriously to take what the speaker is saying. It is for this reason that "John is sorta short" may be, in the right context, a polite way of saying "John is short," rather than a scaled-down comment on John's actual height.

Finally, and parallel to the use of technical terms that was cited above as a Rule 1 device, we find euphemisms used in accordance with Rule 2. They are similar in that both skirt an issue, and thus are ways of discussing a touchy subject while pretending to be doing something else. But technical terms evade the issue by saying, in effect: Well, this would be touchy if we were emotionally involved, but no, we are remote, so touchiness doesn't arise. Euphemisms grant that the subject is touchy, but pretend that *it* is not the matter under discussion. Hence we find academic writing replete with technical terms when it is objectivity and scholarly aloofness that is desired; but we find cocktail party chitchat full of euphemisms, since when we gossip we aren't after remoteness, but we do want to avoid offense by avoiding coming head on with ideas that may not be fully palatable when made explicit. Thus, neither the doctor writing on sexual practices in a learned text nor the hostess talking about the doings of her friends to mutual friends might want to use the straight four-letter word that most directly describes the situation. So the doctor expounds: "*Copulation* may also be enhanced by the use of oleaginous materials," and the hostess gushes, "Selma told me she found Jimmy and Marion *doing it* with mayonnaise!" Euphemisms, then, are Rule 2 related because they allow the addressee the option of seeming not to be hearing what he actually is hearing, although again the pretense is conventional: both speaker and addressee know full well what it is that they are discussing, or else, of course, the discussion would founder, as it occasionally does when the euphemisms become too thick or too arcane for perception.

The third rule is sometimes said not to be part of politeness; but in American society, gestures of friendliness are certainly considered in this category; it is only in (Rule 1 linked) formal etiquette treatises that the two are not connected, and this is as we would expect, since as I said, Rule 1 and Rule 3 are mutually exclusive. You cannot be extending the hand of friendship and stepping back aloofly at once. But you can combine Rule 3 with Rule 2: you can be friendly and deferential, just as you can combine Rules 1 and 2, to be aloof but deferential. As we shall see, how many and which of the rules you apply in a given situation are determined by your subculture as well as by your personal psychological makeup.

The purpose of Rule 3 is to make the addressee feel that the speaker likes him and wants to be friendly with him, is interested in him, and so on. Like the other rules it can be real or conventional. For instance, back-slapping is a well-known nonlinguistic Rule 3 device. And it can be done where real camaraderie is felt, for instance, between friends, one of whom is glad to see the other after a long absence; or it can be done by a salesman to a (male) prospect, concurrent with telling him dirty jokes, another Rule 3 related device, and here conventional again. Colloquial language generally is Rule 3 linked, as is the use of four-letter words, rather than either the technical terms of Rule 1 or the euphemisms of Rule 2. Saying the thing directly conveys to the addressee: We're in this together, we understand each other, we don't have to stand on ceremony with each other. Finally, the use of nicknames and first name alone in some conditions, last name alone in others, is a Rule 3 device. The first two rules tend to occur where inequality between speaker and hearer exists or may exist; the third implies full egalitarianism. Of course, problems may arise, as they often do in a college class where the professor invites the students to call him (or her) by first name. The students sense that this equality is conventional, since the professor clearly has perquisites they do not possess; and further, if they attempt to extend the invitation to include other Rule 3 devices (like backslapping or friendly teasing) they may be in for a big surprise when the friendship suddenly cools.

It should be clear by now that three separate rules are needed to arrive even at a minimal definition of politeness (and clearly there are plenty of residual problems, which I will not worry about here). So a tag question when used for politeness is purely in the realm of Rule 2, but the use of *please* in a request involves both Rule 1 (the speaker is indicating some distance) and Rule 2 (he is acting probably conventionally as though the addressee might refuse). And an injunction like "You wanna screw, baby?" has elements of both Rule 2 and Rule 3. But combining Rules 1 and 3 seems unlikely: we might end up with: "Wanna screw, Professor Jones?" or perhaps: "Wanna copulate, baby?"

It should be evident too that different cultures consider these rules of different priority, or applicable under different conditions. So, for example, let us consider the case of belching after a meal in public. Standard American society frowns on this; classical Chinese society, on the other hand, considers it the polite thing to do. Can our rules account for the way these two cultures behave?

Here we have a situation that might be viewed in either of two ways. You might feel that any internal physical process, made explicit and evident to the outside world, was an intrusion on other people's privacy. So you would attempt to suppress or conceal any such act in public. Not only is belching thought of this way, but so are sneezing and coughing (etiquette manuals warned people to cover their mouths when performing these acts long before the germ theory of disease was known). Thus you don't remove food from your mouth after you've chewed it, or wipe your nose on your sleeve (where the evidence that you did so will remain in full view of others). All these are violations of Rule 1. Of course, you can violate Rule 2 at the same time, and make matters even worse: it's not good manners to spit in your soup at a dinner party, but it's unspeakable to spit in your neighbor's, thus denying him his autonomy.

But there are other ways of viewing a belch. You might think of it as an expression of repletion, indicating satisfaction with the quality and quantity of the feast, the more powerful because it is (supposedly) involuntary. (Of course, in Chinese society, I would not be surprised if the conventionalized artificial belch existed, rather like our artificial yawn.) In this case, belching is viewed as an application of Rule 3—you have said something nice to your host, made him feel appreciated. So how you categorize a particular act may determine whether it is to be considered polite according to one rule, or rude according to another.

Or it may be that there is an order of precedence among the rules, determining which is preferentially applied at various points in a relationship, and this may differ between cultures. I am suggesting here that the rules as stated are universal: in no society, it is my preliminary prediction, will there be *no* reflexes of any of these rules; but one society may apply Rule 1 every chance it gets, to the very advanced stages of intimacy, and another will switch to Rule 3 with unimaginable celerity. When members of these two hypothetical cultures meet, it is analogous to the meeting of matter and antimatter: an explosion takes place. This happens all the time: one speaker says something meant to indicate warmth and friendship; the second speaker backs away, ending the exchange abruptly, muttering, "He has some nerve!" The first speaker wanders off, musing, "Now what's the matter with *him?*"

Consider what happens when an American, a German, and a Japanese meet. Suppose they all want to make a good impression and to be "polite" according to their own standards. Chances are, unless the members of the group are very sophisticated and have had prior exposure to the other cultures, the American will seem to the others overly brash, familiar, and prying; the Japanese will seem cloyingly deferential; the German will seem distant and uninterested in the others to the point of arrogance. So they will part, each thinking the others are thoroughly detestable because of individual personality defects. And if each meets other members of the other cultures chances are these first impressions will be reinforced, until national stereotypes are formed: Americans are "too personal"; Japanese are "too humble"; Germans are "too stiff." Actually, what is happening is that each is conforming to a cultural stereotype of what constitutes polite behavior toward a slight acquaintance. At this stage of a relationship, a German will emphasize Rule 1, a Japanese Rule 2, and an American Rule 3. (These are of course the stereotypical norms; there are plenty of participants in these cultures whose rule application, for various idiosyncratic reasons, is different.) Now as a relationship increases in familiarity, the Japanese will start moving toward the incorporation of Rule 3 along with his Rule 2; so he will always, probably, seem a bit more deferential than an American will, but ultimately he will seem *friendly* and deferential. The German, after a suitable interval of acquaintanceship, will gradually drop the Rule 1 related devices and start acquiring the forms of Rule 3, but it will take him some time. So it is not that the three cultures have three different rules as to how to be polite; it's just that they have different conditions on the applicability of the three rules they share.

As Miller noted in the excerpt given above, conversations in which politeness is a major criterion for acceptability are of a special kind: they don't seek to impart real-world information, but rather are largely engaged in for the purpose of communicating one's own feelings about one's addressee, and garnering some intuition about his feelings toward one. So it isn't important what you say, really, but rather how you say it, and, perhaps, also, why you say it. If I say, "It's cold out," to someone who is hesitating as to which of two coats to put on, I am probably expressing real-world information primarily; but if I say it to someone I have just met at a bus stop, no information is being communicated (since he knows it's cold as well as I do); rather, I'm trying to interact with him and form a friendship, however short-lived. In the first instance, politeness is not involved; in the second, we might say I was engaged in a Rule 3 type of situation since I was principally expressing a desire for acquaintanceship.

This is an important point, since we shall find it useful to separate the rules by which we structure polite utterances, and decide whether they are appropriate, from the parallel sorts of rules we use for deciding the contextual appropriateness of utterances in circumstances when politeness is not at issue. In the latter cases, we seek to communicate *information*: to apprise an addressee of information we have, but he does not have and needs to know, by the least circuitous route. If we are concerned with the pure transmission of factual knowledge, any communication that does not meet the criteria just listed will be an aberrant or failed communication, while if we are talking for some other purpose, the same utterance may be eminently successful.

A system of rules by which factual information may best be conveyed has been proposed by H. P. Grice in his paper. "The Logic of Conversation." In this work, Grice proposes four basic Rules of Conversation, which we can summarize as follows:

1. Quality. Say only what is true.
2. Quantity. Say only as much, and just as much, as is necessary.
3. Relevance. Be relevant.
4. Manner. Be perspicuous. Don't be ambiguous. Don't be obscure. Be succinct.

Clearly these rules, like the Rules of Politeness proposed earlier, leave much to be desired in terms of specificity: how does one tell if a potential conversational contribution is "relevant"? "Necessary"? But they are useful guidelines. Grice also notices that a great deal of actual conversation is in violation of these rules, yet is not normally considered aberrant, nor is there usually any problem in understanding the force or purpose of such non-conforming contributions. He gives as one example the case of a letter of recommendation for a fellowship that states: "Miss X has nice handwriting." Now at first glance, this is a violation of quantity and/or relevance. It is not necessary to know about a fellowship candidate's handwriting in order to judge if the candidate is worthy of receiving support. What Grice says is that, by its very (apparent) irrelevance, the statement implies something else, approximately: "On a fellowship recommendation one is supposed to say only favorable things about the candidate. Well, this is the only point in Miss X's favor that I know of. *Ergo*, this statement implies another: 'Miss X does not deserve to get the fellowship, since she has no relevant good qualities.' " This is what Grice refers to as a conversational implicature.

The important question for us here is: Why (or when) is it useful to use implicature? Why not always speak logically, directly, and to the point?

Here we have a situation in which the rules of conversation would come into conflict with one or more of the rules of politeness. We have a violation of the third rule of politeness, applied indirectly; that is, to say what we have to say explicitly would be making Miss X look bad, and feel bad, if she knew. There is a colloquial principle that expresses this notion: "If you can't say something nice, don't say anything at all." A clearer illustration of the conflict can be found in cases in which it is the addressee whose feelings would be directly impinged upon. So I might say, "It's cold in here," and mean by it any of the following:

1. Why didn't you close the window?
2. You borrowed my favorite sweater.
3. Let's go into another room.
4. You're going to make me catch cold.

And so on. Now, saying any of 1–4 will violate some rule of politeness, probably 2 or 3 or a combination. Generally, implicature seems to be used as a Rule 2 related device: a means of letting the addressee have the benefit of the doubt, come to his own conclusions (again, often merely by convention, since there is usually only one meaning to be derived from the utterance). So we can say that Grice's Conversational Principles are usable only in case there is no possibility of conflict with the Rules of Politeness, or in situations in which polite conversation is not felt to be required, where pure information is to be transmitted, information about the outside world, rather than about the personal and interpersonal feelings of the speaker and the addressee. And, consequently, the less speaker and addressee wish to communicate about their personal feelings, the more likely it is that the Rules of Conversation will be in effect, permitting the participants in the discourse to say what they need to say, and stop there. So Rule 1 type politeness is consonant with application of the Rules of Conversation; but Rule 2 and 3 politeness situations call for the use of statements whose meaning is derivable by the notion of conversational implicature.

So, to paraphrase Miller again, what you are talking about has a great deal of influence on how you will say it: directly and straight, or indirectly and repetitiously. The former exemplifies the strict use of Grice's principles, the latter of conversational implicature. We may also note that it is among the misogynistic stereotypes in our culture that women cannot follow the rules of conversation: that a woman's discourse is necessarily indirect, repetitious, meandering, unclear, exaggerated — the antithesis of every one of Grice's principles — while of course a man's speech is clear, direct, precise, and to the point. Now obviously to hold this belief literally is idiotic, since everyone knows plenty of women who habitually speak straighter than plenty of men. But, as I remarked earlier, stereotypes are not to be ignored: first, because for a stereotype to exist, it must be an exaggeration of something that is in fact in existence and able to be recognized; and second, because one measures oneself, for better or worse, according to how well or poorly one conforms to the stereotype one is supposed to conform to.

# 3. ⠶

# Women and Politeness

Another, less value-laden way of looking at things is to say that the stereotyped image of men's speech is that it functions in accord with the rules of conversation, and of women's speech, that it tends to make wider use of the properties of implicature. There is no particular reason to suppose that there is extra virtue inherent in the men's way: if people think so, it is because men in this culture tend to impose their value judgments on everyone, so that the men's way of doing things becomes the "good way," and the women's way the bad way.[30] It would be better to think of the situation in these terms: there are two possible conversational styles (with, of course, infinite possibilities for mixtures and intersections); one style tends to predominate in men's speech, another in women's. This might be true in either of two ways: more men might habitually adopt one style usually, more women the other; or, men in general would tend to use more of one style, though sometimes falling into the other; and the same with women. The latter seems to be the truth that underlies the stereotype. In general and in traditional American culture (we are not talking about academia here, for reasons already noted) women will tend to speak with reference to the rules of politeness, conversational implicature, and inter-personal exploration; men will tend to speak with reference to the rules of conversation and straight factual communication. It seems to be true of both men and women, however, that when the crunch comes, the rules of politeness will supersede the rules of conversation: better be unclear than rude.

If this is a viable hypothesis, there is a relationship among several things that are stated to be generally true of women: they are more inter-ested in interpersonal discovery than in discussion of external things; and women are ladies, more polite than men are. The first creates the second, and the second no doubt expedites the first in turn.

Again, it is important to remember that neither of these two styles is good or bad: each is valuable in its own context. But men and women both err if they cannot switch readily from one style to the other as the situation warrants. It may be that the traditional woman could not easily switch styles when necessary, and the stereotype is true in that sense; but it is equally true that the traditional man cannot switch out of his straight-from-the-shoulder pose; and this is just as damaging. But, as with jokes as we shall see below, men make up the stereotypes, and groups typically don't invent stereotypes about themselves, but about other groups. Hence it is the dominant group in a society that establishes stereotypes of the other groups, and decides which groups, on the basis of these stereotypes, are "good" and "bad." The job of people who find themselves, as members of nondominant groups, being stereotyped is not necessarily to decide that there is no truth underlying the stereotype and that therefore the stereotype is bad and must be destroyed (though this may sometimes be true); but it may also be worthwhile to assume that there is some truth behind the stereotype, but that what it represents is a good trait rather than the bad one it had been assumed by the dominant group to be. Women sometimes realize this: thus, it had been axiomatic in our culture for some time that women lacked aggressiveness and that this was a bad thing about women, a reason why they'd never make it in the real world, and never had. Women had two possible options for dealing with this stereotype: to deny it, proving they were just as pugnacious as men, or to reaffirm it and take nonaggressiveness to be a virtue. Different groups have done different things in this regard, but certainly the latter position is a strong one. We must not continue to be brainwashed.

We may ask how these two styles establish themselves as sex-linked traits. Is it inherent, and thus inevitable? Or is it learned at an early age? Evidence for the latter is that some women don't learn the predominant female style; this is a hopeful augury, since we might eventually learn how to educate all children to be equally fluent in both speech types. The distinction appears at a very early age: psychologists studying children in nursery school have found that little boys already tend to communicate about external things—building garages, having battles, and so on—while little girls are more apt to talk about their own and other people's feelings, about each other, and about their socialization patterns (who is best friends with whom, and so on). As mentioned previously, other studies have shown that little girls are "politer" in speech than boys of the same age, so we may assume that these two styles of behavior are learned together, as we would expect.

Another question raised at the outset of this discussion has not yet been answered: Not only are women more polite, but men are supposed to be more polite around women than they are with each other; further, this sort of politeness is problematic: if the purpose of politeness is to decrease friction and promote friendship, why does men-to-women politeness so often seem offensive or constraining? If politeness is supposed to bring people closer together, allowing them to interact more easily with one another, why does this special kind of politeness seem so exclusive—why do women resent the sudden hush that sweeps over a roomful of men when it is realized that "there are ladies present"?[31]

I think that the feeling of exclusiveness produced by men-to-women politeness is not imaginary, and I think that examining it will lead us to some interesting conclusions. We might note, first off, that there is no comparable exclusive female tactic: there's no conversational style you are supposed to drop when a man enters the room. (There are tabooed *topics*, of course, mostly sexual, or rather, gynecological: women go along with men's assumption that female sexual anatomy is particularly revolting.)

On the basis of ethological studies on primates, a theory has been proposed that, while unattractive in many ways and certainly open to criticism in several of its aspects, nevertheless if taken not totally literally offers a means of understanding some of the strange and rather paradoxical things that seem to be going on. This is the notion of male bonding, as proposed by such anthropologists as Lionel Tiger, in his book *Men in Groups*. Tiger says that in primates the males often seem to have the task of hunting together in groups for food, while the females stay behind, functioning as individuals, caring for the young. He hypothesizes that this general situation necessarily pertained in groups of primitive human beings, at least until the advent of agriculture: the men hunted together in packs, while the women stayed behind, caring for their individual living sites and raising the children. Now in order to hunt successfully—particularly since man had only primitive weapons, and was not very strong or swift in comparison with his prey—the male members of the tribe had to work together, develop effective techniques of cooperation, and learn to enjoy one another's company and minimize interpersonal friction. The women, since they worked largely alone—or, if they chose to work together, they did not cooperate at one single task as the men did, but rather each did her individual job in the company of others—did not need to develop techniques of working as a group. Now obviously, within the male group, some members might be singled out as, say, the best archers or the fleetest runners; so that within the general atmosphere of cooperation you might find competition; but basically the males directed their efforts toward a common goal; among the females, each had her own goal and succeeded as an individual. Of course, having no records of human life in those primitive times, we have no means of knowing whether this theory is correct; but Tiger discusses some characteristics of modern life that might be viewed as stemming from those habits inculcated in the species millennia ago. In this view, it is the present-day reflexes of male bonding that enable men to work together in industry, politics, religion, the military—any powerful group, to retain its power, must have some sort of cohesive force underlying it, inducing its members to work as a team. And indeed, in virtually every culture we look at, we see that men are in control of all the major institutions. (Margaret Mead and others have discussed a few isolated societies in which women seem to be in charge, but these are small in size and few in number—and indeed, we may even have reason to believe that the lack of success of these societies is in part due to the fact that women are in control. Certainly such cultures represent aberrations from the norm.) Tiger suggests that these groups work by relying on male bonding and that this is in fact why women find it so hard to be accepted as members, why in fact often they opt out entirely: they feel they are out of place. Further, this is why men like to go on "stag" hunting and fishing trips and generally congregate in all-male groups. There are occasional exceptions, and of course the more a society is able to divest itself of millennia-old habits, the more women will be integrated into the formerly all-male groups. If people can become vegetarians, or avoid war, they presumably can compensate for the reflexes of male bonding; but none of these departures from the age-old norms is very widespread in society as yet.

This thesis is viewed with alarm by many feminists, principally because it seems to suggest that things are hopeless: "This is an ingrained habit," such a theory suggests, "and you'll never change it, because it goes deeper than the roots of the human race." Certainly that is the position Tiger holds. But it is not necessary to accept such a pessimistic point of view. One can, as a feminist, agree that there is something going on in the overwhelming majority of cultures today that can be described as "male bonding," and may want to agree, too, that this goes back as far into re-corded history as we can see, and, from primate evidence, perhaps back to the very dawn of mankind. But man has changed much about himself: from (probably) an original fruit eater, he has become an omnivore; from a tree dweller, a ground animal; and so on. We might work toward either of two goals: to reduce the necessity for bonding among men, or to en-courage it among women, and among all people. Or we might try all these options, mitigating men's desire to bond, and strengthening women's. Con-sidering the changes that have occurred only in the past decade in our views on, say, sexual normality, it doesn't seem too far-fetched that our views on the ways, necessity, and pleasures of bonding might be similarly altered, if people set their minds to it, before too long. Never underestimate the influence of the media.

We would like, that is, not only for men to accept women as integral parts of their groups, but for women to be able to group with other women as men do with men. As Phyllis Chesler points out, this is not at present normally the case:

> Women, although similar to each other in many ways, are more isolated from each other *in terms of groups* [italics hers] than men are. Women are not consolidated into either public or powerful groups. Women as mothers are "grouped" with their children (who grow up and leave them), and only tem-porarily, and superficially with other women: for example, in parks, at women's auxiliary functions, and at heterosexual par-ties,*

I think that a start is being made, in women's groups, to overcome this tendency of women not to bond. The women's movement, in referring to and addressing women universally as "sisters," is working to establish a sense of female camaraderie, though it is still a camaraderie of the under-dog, just as a WASP male doesn't think of himself as a "brother" of other WASP males, but a black male will consider himself a "brother" of other black males. "Sister" really means something like: "You who are one with me in our oppression," rather than merely being an expression of pure unity.[32] It is in any case a good beginning. But perhaps even more impor-tant, for women and for the human race generally, is establishing patterns of bonding between both sexes, so that women, with their special abilities, sensitivities, and talents, may be integrated into the "real world"; and men, with theirs, may learn to function more smoothly in the home.

The notion of bonding, if we can accept the fact that something of the sort occurs in present-day American traditional society, can also serve to explain some of our findings about politeness. We can see that Rule 1

---

*Phyllis Chesler, *Women and Madness* (New York: Doubleday & Co., 1972), p. 270.

acts as a kind of discourager of bonding, saying as it does: Keep away. Rule 3, on the other hand, encourages bonding relationships. (Rule 2 would seem to be able to reinforce the effect of either Rule 1 or Rule 3.) We have noted that women's politeness is principally of the Rule 1 plus Rule 2 type, establishing and reinforcing distance: deferential mannerisms coupled with euphemism and hypercorrect and superpolite usage. Women's language avoids the markers of camaraderie: backslapping, joke telling, nicknaming, slang, and so forth. In all-female groups, we find devices that recall male intimacy-creating gestures: embraces for backslapping, discussion of personal things. But in mixed groups, *all* manifestations of camaraderie disappear: this is really the principal problem: why in mixed groups there is nothing identifiable as Rule 3 behavior. (Again I am talking about traditional society.) And even in all-women groups, my impression is that typically there is less show of camaraderie than in all-men groups. Perhaps more interestingly, the women's type of camaraderie seems less able to be used conventionally: men can tell dirty jokes and slap each other's backs even when they can't stand each other; this is presumably how a great deal of the world's work gets done. But women embrace and share confidences only when there are real feelings of sympathy between them.

One counterexample that has been suggested to me is the use of words like "dear," "honey," "luv," and so forth between people who are not sexually or emotionally intimate. Interestingly, both sexes may engage in it, between or within sex lines. But it still seems that women use these expressions under different conditions than men do. Women who are socially subordinate may use it to either men or women: saleswomen and waitresses are particularly apt to do this. But men (heterosexual males, that is) don't use it to other men at all; and when they use it to women, the woman is definitely in an inferior position. I have known male professors who habitually addressed their female students as "dear," but I have never heard of a female professor addressing her male students thus. (It is barely conceivable that an elderly female professor might so address favorite female students, though I know of no such instances; I can't imagine her addressing a male student that way, though.) Doctors and dentists (male) and especially, I am told, gynecologists are prone to address their female (never male) patients this way; patients may never respond in kind. This is probably related to the fact that men generally feel free to address women by first name alone or nickname much sooner in a relationship than a woman will feel free to so address a male. This is sometimes justified by the user on grounds of "friendship"; but if first name alone is not mutual, we have a relationship not of Rule 3 solidarity but rather one of Rule 1 class distinction, in which the person who is addressed by first name is considered inferior to the one who is not. Compare, for example, the forms of normal address between adults and children, particularly primary school children and their teachers.

Since "dear" and its cohorts are not mutually exchanged, we must assume that a nonparallel relationship exists—as it always does between doctor and patient anyway, but the more markedly when the patient is female.

Then this aspect of the "ladyship" of women may be explained through the concept of male bonding: male politeness is different from female and mixed politeness, in that male politeness makes use of Rule 3 to encourage bonding relationships, and the others do not, and thus discourage them. It is for this reason that women feel excluded by male-type "polite" behavior toward them. Men, in effect, say: "Stay away: our friendship doesn't include you."

A particularly striking instance of the way this principle operates may be seen in joke-telling behavior. A joke is generally considered "tasteful" when it will not offend anyone who is likely to hear it. It is the definition of "anyone" which has changed of late and could use some more changing. Usually we mean "anyone who counts." The reason we tell jokes is to become part of a (Rule 3 governed) bonding relationship. Really or conventionally, joke telling brings the teller and the hearers together. You are nervous to some extent while a joke is being told: as the teller, for fear you'll get it wrong; as the hearer, for fear you won't get it. Both of these possible responses are dangerous because they would inhibit the formation of the bond, making it difficult or impossible for hearer and teller to relate satisfactorily to each other. But if the joke is offensive to someone in the audience, it is guaranteed that the teller will fail in his intention to establish a bond, at least for that person. And when a teller is confronting a huge audience, in the media, then of course he can't tell how many members of the insultable groups might be out there listening: he can't jeopardize his chances of establishing bonding relationships by telling jokes that might offend a sizable portion of his audience.

In the past, it was implicitly assumed that members of various outside groups were not available for bonding with members of other groups. So if you were a WASP, it was all right to tell anti-anybody else jokes; if you were Jewish, you could tell anti-Irish or anti-black jokes, and so on. But lately we have become more sensitive: we have included, at least for the purpose of conventional bond establishing (as opposed to real camaraderie) all ethnic groups among the "anybody" who cannot be offended, at the risk of ruining the effect of the joke.

There is, however, one group that does not comprise part of the "anybody," from all available evidence. This is not a minority, but is usually about half of any audience. That group is, of course, women. There is a whole genre of antiwomen jokes, based on sexual stereotypes as antiethnic jokes were (and are) based on ethnic stereotypes: women as a group and any woman because of belonging to that group are vain, fuzzy-minded, extravagant, imprecise, long-winded . . . and numerous variants on those themes, concerning jealousy of other women, hat buying, driving, and so on. There are to my knowledge no parallel joke types based on stereotypes of men in general. Even female comediennes don't tell such jokes, probably because men make up the jokes, or at least men seem to establish what constitutes acceptable topics for joking about.

A comedian may be very sensitive to ethnic slurs, never be caught dead telling Polish jokes, anti-Semitic jokes, or any of the other no-no's, but he will include lots of antiwomen (these days, anti-"women's lib") jokes in his repertoire. No one (with the exception of a few of those chronic female malcontents who obviously have no sense of humor) will be offended, and generally the women in the audience will laugh as loud as the men. (They'd better, or they'll be accused of typical female humorlessness or stupidity because they "don't get it.") I think considerable damage is done to malleable young female egos in this way: jokes are not harmless, as ethnic minorities are fully aware. This sort of reaction to antiwomen jokes shows that women are not expected, by men or by themselves, to be among the possible people to participate in the bonding induced by joke telling. And it is related to this that women are notorious for not being able to tell jokes well: this is often ascribed to their illogical habits of mind, but probably has at least as much to do with the fact that women don't, can't, gain from telling jokes: in fact, in many circles it's considered a dangerous sign of nonfemininity if a woman *can* tell a real joke (not merely recount an anecdote) without lousing up.

At first glance, there may seem to be a paradox implicit in the claims I have made, namely:

1. That women are person-oriented, interested in their own and each other's mental states and respective status; men are object-oriented, interested in things in the outside world.
2. That men enter into bonding relationships and form relationships of camaraderie, in a way that they do not with women, nor do women really with one another.

But actually there is no paradox. In looking at each other's psyches, and reactions to one another, women retain their individuality; they are not fused into a group. There is not necessarily a sense of cooperation in this process, but rather a sense that each individual is keeping track of the other individuals. In this sense, women's greater ability to express and share emotions is less to be ascribed to camaraderie than to separateness, one individual getting and giving impressions from and to other individuals, and as a means whereby individuals can come to work together when needed.

Men, on the other hand, are not so much concerned about what's going on in one another's minds, but rather on how the group can work as a whole to get something done. This leads to the submerging of everyone's feelings and some gruffness of reaction, of course, which the rules producing camaraderie are expressly set up to help gloss over.

Again, there should be no sense on reading this that one style is

101

*better*, more logical, or more socially useful than another; both, and mixtures of both, are needed in different circumstances. Women must be more flexible—and so must men.

# 4 ::

# Conclusion

This, then, is finally the point for the reader to ponder: I have given reason to believe that the kinds of "politeness" used by and of and to women do not arise by accident; that they are, indeed, stifling, exclusive, and oppressive. But I don't feel that we must maintain the kinds of social relationships we have always assumed. If we are aware of what we're doing, why we're doing it, and the effects our actions have on ourselves and everyone else, we will have the power to change. I hope this book will be one small first step in the direction of a wider option of life styles, for men and women.

::

# Bibliography

Bateson, G. *Steps to an Ecology of Mind*, Part III: "Form and Pathology in Relationship." New York: Ballantine, 1972.

Chesler, Phyllis. *Women and Madness*. New York: Doubleday & Co., 1972; Avon paperback, 1973.

Grice, H. P. "The Logic of Conversation." Unpublished manuscript, Department of Philosophy, University of California, Berkeley, 1968.

Haas, M. R. "Men's and Women's Speech in Koasati," in D. Hymes, ed., *Language in Culture and Society*. New York: Harper & Row, 1964.

Lakoff, R. "Language in Context." *Language* 48 (1972): 907–27.

Miller, R. A. *The Japanese Language*. Chicago: University of Chicago Press, 1967.

Postal, P. "Anaphoric Islands." In *Papers from the Fifth Regional Meeting of the Chicago Linguistic Society*, edited by R. Binnick et al. Chicago: Chicago Linguistic Society, 1969.

Tiger, Lionel. *Men in Groups*. London: Thomas Nelson & Sons, Ltd., and New York: Random House, 1969; Vintage paperback, 1970.

1. "Andy" is my son, now in his midthirties. While my wish may have been overly optimistic, it is true that people his age seem to have resolved at least some of the issues discussed in the text in a highly satisfactory way. As I could hardly have envisioned then, women today occupy roughly a third of all university and college faculty positions as well as positions in law and in medicine and are an increasing presence in politics. As a result, locutions like *She's a professional* have lost their former presuppositions, and the most pernicious forms of linguistic sexism I discuss here have vanished or lost much of their edge. I applaud the obsolescence of my observations as a sign of progress. So the issues have not exactly been "transcended," but they have been significantly mitigated.

2. *He.* If I were writing these words today, I would find a way to evade the "neutral" masculine pronoun. Some thirty years after both the publication of this monograph and the incorporation of gender into the concerns of linguistics, we have had ample time to experiment with many such options and to get used to them and find them nondistracting. When I wrote *LWP* (I wrote the original version of the first part in 1971–72), the problems of, and solutions to, the neutral-masculine pronoun were just beginning to be discussed. There was a wealth of candidates: not only those that are still in use (*he or she, s/he,* syntactic circumlocutions like passivization, *they*), but many others now ancient history: *ve, te, hse, hirm,* and many more. My objections to these had two bases: first, that change in grammatical, rather than semantic, lexical items was highly unlikely; and second, that the adoption of these forms would distract readers' attention from content and force it onto style, alienating many people who might otherwise be persuaded by my arguments. Since the "neutral" masculine was still the norm, I elected to use it—especially since I felt that the cause of pronoun reform was futile.

That is not to say that I thought this option was without problems. In fact, I see the choices for a woman writing in the early 1970s as yet another example of the double bind I discuss at length: adopting the neologisms would have made my writing awkward and irritating to other than committed feminists; but for the choice I made, I was excoriated by many I had considered allies, who were eager to construct me as an antifeminist, antiwoman enemy of the cause, proponent of a female-relevant "deficit theory."

Today, the extant choices (like pluralization, passivization, and *he or she*) are the norm; writers who choose the "neutral" *he* are the ones who have explaining to do. But the more florid suggestions have vanished, as I thought they would, without a trace.

I am by nature a pessimist, and here I was, characteristically, unduly pessimistic. I was right to suggest that neologisms like *ve* and its colleagues would never survive. But I was wrong in thinking that speakers of English would find it impossible to substitute one extant form for another. We are apparently more flexible, and more well-intentioned, than I believed back then. I still heave a sigh in the privacy of my own mind for a time when a writer was not constrained to resort to the awkwardnesses the new world has forced on us. Aesthetically, *he* is at least sometimes preferable to any of the options currently open to us. Progress, like penicillin, has side effects.

3. This statement ("Language uses us . . .") reflects, if indirectly, many of the implicit assumptions of generative semantics. I am, for instance, assuming a direct and rule-governed connection between linguistic form, social circumstance, and psychological attitude of speakers, and that one task of linguistics is to account for and accurately describe these interconnections.

What did I mean, exactly, by that opening sentence? I could paraphrase my intention in this way. Speakers use language to accomplish their goals, but they are not entirely in control of their expression (as Humpty Dumpty and prescriptive grammarians might wish us to be). Linguistic choices, based on speakers' judgments of who they and their interlocutors are, where they are, what they want to accomplish, and what they are talking about, in turn create human self-perceptions. Linguistic options construct their users even as those users construct them.

Thus, in the "declensional" pattern in the next paragraph, speakers choose a descriptive adjective based on their relationship with the person being described. We tend to see ourselves ("I") in the most favorable light; to describe addressees' ("you") behavior of which we disapprove in euphemistically indirect terms; but to be brutally direct in discussing nonpresent third persons. In this simple case social and psychological context governs linguistic options rather obviously. Moreover, by the choice of adjective, speakers also manage to convince themselves (and maybe their interlocutors) of the correctness of their vision. Thus language gets a hammer hold on us and makes it hard for us to see the world unobstructed.

This statement is an elaboration of the Sapir-Whorf hypothesis, which states that users of language cannot experience "reality" except through the mediation of language: the forms and structures of the language they are speaking put blinders on them, or offer them a distorting lens through which to see their universe.

In framing the statement as I did, I am suggesting that language is a kind of sentient creature with a will of its own. In a literal sense this is a pathetic fallacy—language is of course an abstraction, not a creature. But I couldn't resist the chance to open with something shocking, and metaphorically language *does* keep its users imprisoned in the possibilities it offers—and does not offer.

4. Language as a diagnostic. I am trying to articulate a rationale and a methodology, both in opposition to then-current fashion. First, I am arguing for the use of language, rather than more concrete and validable forms of human behavior. Language isn't "just words," it reveals our selves to the world: it is, as Chomsky famously put it, a window into the mind. Moreover, language has the advantage of being able to be recorded and transcribed unambiguously, unlike physical movement. At least this is true of the *verbal* part of communication. What we were much less aware of then than we are now are the accompaniments of the verbal message: motion (gestures, stance); facial expression; intonation, pitch, and other paralinguistic concerns; and the relation between language and other expressions of personal style (dress, makeup or its absence, hairstyle). Even with these caveats, however, linguistic data is still less ambiguous and more fully accessible than almost any other kind.

5. Here I discuss my method, which might be described as informal observation and introspection. Since this has been at the root of some of the more virulent attacks, let me say a few words about it.

In the first place, my critics never seem to notice that I did not claim that introspection is the *best* way to get linguistic data, much less the only way. Nor is it the only method I use, although that claim has often been made: many of my arguments are based on evidence from contemporary popular writing, for instance. (This, too, was heretical at the time, when spoken language was very strongly privileged over written as a basis of linguistic analysis. We have learned better since then.) Another point is that other methods of data collection did not yet exist in linguistics in 1971–72: conversation analysis (CA) was not introduced into linguistics until 1974. The best we can do is to use what we have at our disposal and do the best we can with it, being careful to mention its drawbacks as we do so.

Another problem here is that the critiques assume a dichotomy between "empirical" and "mentalistic" discovery procedures, with the first being infinitely preferable to the second. But just about all linguistic research has a significant mentalistic component. Either the investigator uses her or his mental apparatus (the "language acquisition device") to evaluate the data (as with CA), or the subject uses mental evaluation to produce the data (as with questionnaires). Rather than seeing the choice as a value-laden dichotomy ("good" empiricism vs. "bad" mentalism), we should imagine our options as points on a value-free continuum, from methods that are wholly empirical (e.g., statistical analysis of independently produced naturalistic data) to those that are wholly mentalistic (unchecked judgments based on assumptions about one's own linguistic behavior, produced in response to one's own theoretical bias—the typical approach of formal syntacticians). Most investigations make use of intermediate points on the continuum. The only value judgment that makes sense, it seems to me, is the assessment of the appropriateness of the procedure to the data investigated and the questions posed in the research.

Even the most dogged empiricism must see that some linguistic truths cannot be discovered by CA or other largely empirical means. The forms I discuss do not occur regularly in conversation, but only when certain topics arise, and in certain contexts. The virtue of CA lies in discovering and analyzing *regularities* in conversational structure—overlaps, pauses, sequencing, and the like. Furthermore, questionnaires and other means of direct elicitation of data are of dubious worth in exploring actual language use, of which speakers are often not fully conscious. This is especially the case with stigmatized usages like sexist language. Honestly or not, respondents will often deny doing what they can be observed doing. So empirical methods, though often of great value, may not work in many kinds of research. The intelligent researcher must be versatile and aware of the advantages and shortcomings of all methods of data collection and analysis. Dismissing all but a single personal favorite as "unscientific" or invalid prevents linguists from studying a wide range of important phenomena, forcing them to adopt inappropriate methods and reach dubious conclusions, or prevents linguists from studying a great deal of what is especially important and intriguing about language.

6. "Women's language." One sometimes encounters complaints from men that we concentrate on "women's language" to the exclusion of "men's language." There are a couple of rejoinders to this criticism:

    1. There has been some work on male language per se (as opposed to "language" in general, arguably the semantic equivalent of "men's language": see (3) below. But it is very scanty.

2. Since the great preponderance of work in this area has been done by women (most men seem not to be interested in it as a research area), it is natural that it has concentrated on women's communicative roles. If men feel excluded, they are encouraged to enter the field.

3. But (2) may be too glib a response. There is a reason why scholars have found "women's language" but not "men's language" a productive field of study. When we study women's language we are—explicitly or implicitly—comparing and contrasting a marked case to the norm or prototype, whether that goes by the name of "men's language" or simply "language." Women are, in linguistics as elsewhere, the "other" or the marked group. What norm would we contrast with "men's language"? Until and unless this question can be given a meaningful answer, it is hard to see how "men's language" can be the subject of study.

7. " 'Women's language' . . . submerges a woman's personal identity." This is a crucial point, with reference not only to language, but to any other aspect of behavior or demeanor that is required of a person on the basis of their gender (or race, class, or any other group identification). In such cases, a speaker doesn't have the opportunity to discover or use authentic forms of self-expression, and others are forced to respond to a stereotype, rather than a spontaneous self. We can argue about whether people ever get to represent themselves as their "real" selves, or whether there is such a thing. But as long as a culture has expressions like *a credit to his race* or *just like a woman*, members of nondominant groups are forced to play unnatural roles. While male expression is also constrained (men have historically been discouraged from showing tenderness, expressing interest in others, or asking for directions), the constraints do not diminish men's humanness, individuality, and worth—they do not demean and trivialize. (Indeed, the behaviors from which men are traditionally discouraged are themselves often considered unworthy, while the behaviors forbidden to women are often among the ones humans value most: expressing strong and clear intellectual opinions, for instance.)

Statements such as this form the basis of the charge that I am a deficit theorist, seeing women's ways of speaking (presumably, if this term has any meaning at all and is being used parallel to William Labov's [1969] use of it in his critique of the Black English theories of educators such as Carl Bereiter and Siegfried Engelmann) as logically and expressively inferior to the standard, i.e., men's. Of course I am not saying that; I am instead saying that if women make use of traditional female traits, they will have attributed to them all the old stereotypes. Many critics pointed out that these traits have positive functions, and indeed they may, in certain contexts at least, and among women. But then, even more than now, men were the ones it was necessary to convince that women could and did make sense, could achieve and use influence appropriately. Because the traditional women's forms were so encrusted in negative stereotyping, they had to be abandoned—at least in public discourse.

Much of the criticism has, to me, the odor of the self-esteem movement. There is a clear analogy between those feminist arguments that attack any research that shows anything women do to be negative and certain forms of discourse within African American educational research—for instance, the doctrine of Afrogenesis. The argument is made that even if the claims made (e.g., in the latter case, that Cleopatra was black) are unprovable at best, and most likely untrue, the self-esteem gained by students exposed to these ideas is worth the falsification of history. These arguments, whether made for women or for African Americans, strike me as paternalistic and demeaning, as if we were incapable of tolerating the truth, or that our self-esteem could only be derived from falsehoods.

I now see the public/private distinction much more clearly than I did (at the time, I don't think I was aware of it at all). Back then no one was talking about it with the sophistication and complexity that we now have at our disposal. If I were writing the book now, I might stress that these traditional traits have value but nonetheless are dangerously apt to be misunderstood—by both women and men, it turns out. And since their use makes sense largely in private, intimate contexts—what makes them positive is their ability to express subtle shades of feeling—when women move into the public sphere they should be very careful: private language doesn't usually translate well into public discourse.

8. "Women are systematically denied access to power." Certainly things have started to change, although the change is far from complete. In the early 1970s, there were only a very few women in the U.S. House of Representatives, no women in the Senate or on the Supreme Court, and no female governors. The idea of a female president was risible if it was even possible. It was extraordinarily difficult for women to gain admission to first-rank medical or law schools, and for those who graduated from them, there were barriers, formal and informal, to practicing their professions. Nepotism rules and other exclusionary devices, explicit and implicit, were severe obstacles to women seeking tenure-track positions at major research universities. Often their stereotypically expected styles of communication were used as arguments against them: people who talked irrationally must think that way, and people who thought irrationally shouldn't be trusted with anything important.

Happily, things are different now. Yet something odd has happened, and I don't know how to account for it: just as women started to gain admission into law, medicine, politics, and academe, those professions have been demoted in dignity—partly due to other changes (the rise of HMOs, in the case of medicine), but partly for reasons that seem mysterious. The effect is that women now can reach positions that used to invest their holders in power—but now these positions carry much less clout.

The relationship between indirect language, gender, and power also turns out to be more complex than I suggest here. William M. O'Barr (1982) argues that powerlessness, rather than gender per se, leads people to speak indirectly. This is partly true; but while men can be direct without penalty when they feel powerful, if women do that they are still too often assigned the opprobrious *b*-word epithet. And directness is not necessarily linked to power: the powerful may be indirect when it suits their purposes. The difference is that the powerful can choose indirectness (to preserve credible deniability) or directness (to assure compliance). The powerless have no choice.

9. Remediation of linguistic disadvantage. This comment raises the whole issue of what is sometimes called, disparagingly, "language hygiene": if certain uses of language by and about women deny them their due, should steps be taken to change them? And if so, what steps? The question that must be answered first (and which has not yet been answered satisfactorily) is: Can linguistic change,

however desirable, be imposed from above? Or should we wait for social change to bring language change automatically in its wake?

Even if we decide that language change is unlikely to effect social change, making an issue of language discrepancy can be persuasive. Language is the form of behavior of which we are most explicitly aware, and language discrepancy makes manifest social inequality. So even if a change fails (as with radical pronoun reform), or doesn't work as thoroughly or in the way in which it was intended (as with Ms.), talking about the need for change, and the way in which existing usage reflects inequality, can be powerful. It can also make feminist argument the butt of jokes (as with both of the cases cited) but even that, over time, can have positive effects—it gets noticed.

I was talking here about a particular kind of disparity between the sexes, semantic rather than pragmatic: a difference between female and male access to precise color terminology. In such cases (as opposed to pronouns, occupational terminology [*policeman*], or titles of respect), legislation would be ineffectual if it were even possible. In such cases, we have to wait for real-world change to create a context in which linguistic change can occur. In the pragmatic cases, I think the two are more likely to occur together.

10. Academic males as effete. My male colleagues didn't like this passage much then, and they probably still don't. Some of them affect hypermasculine forms as if to deny the imputation, dropping g's and using multiple negatives and cusswords in lectures to demonstrate their machismo. But I'm not convinced (sorry, guys). By the same token, academic women are less stereotypically "feminine" than women in traditional roles. I wonder why academic men are more apt to take umbrage at the former statement than academic women are at the latter. On second thought, no, I don't.

11. This discussion of tags is what a remarkable number of critics concentrated on to the exclusion of everything else, as if by disproving this single claim they could disprove everything else I said (or, by ranting about the stupidity of this claim, they could avoid dealing with anything else I said—with some of which they *must* have been in agreement).

One criticism that was made was that tags were not necessarily markers of uncertainty and weakness. They have a whole range of other uses, in both female and male speech, from pugnacious to polite. This is certainly true. But at the time I wrote this, linguists were really not aware of the potential for ambiguity that exists in language, beyond a very narrow set of cases. Transformational grammarians (who were the only people discussing ambiguity in any detail) said that while there were a few cases of ambiguity in language, most utterances (what they called "sentences") were unambiguous. The pragmatic ambiguity of tags was not recognized in the early 1970s, nor did we have any theory of such cases. Today I would say that most utterances, taken out of context, are pragmatically ambiguous, and tags are one striking case.

A second criticism was that my claim was not empirically based, but rather derived from my own informal observations of my own speech and that of others. This is quite true but by itself doesn't vitiate the observation. I continue to worry about the theoretical and methodological intransigence of many of my valued colleagues: with them it often seems like "it's my way or the highway." But some linguistic phenomena lend themselves to successful empirical study; others do not. Some of the attempts to argue against my claim have the paradoxical effect of showing the limits of empiricism—especially CA.

Still, I should have been clearer, should have said more explicitly that I was talking about informal spontaneous daily talk, rather than more formal discourse (like faculty meetings and business discussions). I should also have been more aware of the relationship between power and tag usage. Many counterarguments involved examples in which either neither gender used tags, or they were used in equal numbers by women and men. But most of those cases contained no close analysis of the tags (since functional analysis is forbidden in strict CA). When women and men use similar numbers of tags, are they understood similarly? Are tags used differently by women in formal and informal contexts? These are legitimate questions, but they have not been asked or answered, to my knowledge.

Tag usage is sometimes correlated with power, sometimes with the desire to be perceived as not powerful, and sometimes with being powerless (cf. Lakoff 1985). Sometimes women (and men) use tags as a way to achieve conversational collaboration, to encourage the participation of others; sometimes as a way of forcing an interlocutor to speak. The very syntactic complexity of the English tag sentence indicates its pragmatic complexity, the diversity of its uses. In the early 1970s, when pragmatics was just coming into linguistics, we were much less aware of any of this.

12. Rising intonation in declaratives. This phenomenon has recently been recognized in the popular press, associated with adolescent speech, under the name "uptalk." In both cases—traditional women and modern teens—the reasons for this usage, as often for tags, seem similar: either a feeling of real powerlessness or a desire not to appear assertive (because it isn't "nice").

13. Euphemism as a diagnostic of embarrassment, and its relationship to *woman* and woman-related terms. While the need to avoid *lady* and *girl* may not be as strong as it was when I wrote this passage, the euphemization of female-related concepts is not entirely a thing of the past. Since then *gentleman* seems to have greatly extended its domain of usage, apparently replacing *man* even when referring to persons who are not, in any traditional sense, "gentlemen." I have often heard it used, for instance by talk-show participants, in reference to convicted criminals. If in fact *gentleman* were coming to replace *man*, I would have no objection to *lady* replacing *woman*. The problem is that there is a lack of parallel reference to parallel entities. Despite the increasing range of usage of *gentleman*, *garbage gentleman* (parallel to *cleaning lady*) is still nonexistent as an occupational title. And artists still don't have *one-lady* shows, so *lady* has not yet been fully established as equivalent in dignity to *woman*. One question with no satisfactory resolution as yet, especially in public discourse, is how to refer to women who are not employed outside the home. Most common is *stay-at-home mom*, which to my ears is a little condescending. It's an improvement over the older "I don't work/My wife doesn't work" (as though a mother of small children spends the day lying on a divan inhaling chocolate cherries). But here too, the awkwardness we feel in finding a suitable name for women in this status tells us that it is the status itself that is problematic. Why do we never hear about "go-to-work moms"?

Stay-at-home moms often blame either "feminism" or women who work outside the home (how come we never hear of "men who work outside the home"?) for demeaning their status, as if prior to the movement they were treated and talked about with dignity. It's part of the unfortunate tendency of women not to support one another and to see other women as villains, when their adversaries are elsewhere (sometimes inside themselves). Just as younger African Americans—another group whose name keeps undergoing continuous euphemistic substitution (from *black* to *African American* in the late 1980s)—have, to the distress of many of their elders, reclaimed *nigger*, so younger feminists (sometimes to the consternation of their elders) have reclaimed *girl*, often in the form *grrl*. Both of these are healthy signs.

Nonetheless, demeaning or trivializing terms for women are still part of the popular American lexicon. While *girl* might have gained respectability through reclamation, we still encounter the belittling *chick*, particularly annoying in the form *chick flick*, a movie that no serious person would willingly see. A chick flick is a movie that deals with emotions, with relationships among women, with family and domestic life—trivial concerns, apparently, of interest only to "stay-at-home moms." There is no equally condescending term for shoot-'em-ups based on garish special effects and uncontrolled violence that appeal largely to eighteen-to-thirty-five-year-old males, just as there is no trivializing term for males parallel to *chick*.

14. Women "forced to exist only as a reflection in the eyes of others." In the early 1970s, it was a simple and incontrovertible truth that women had no identity of their own, that they existed purely as objects (approved or disapproved) of the male "gaze." By now, that presumption, while not quite vanished, has become more controversial. Certainly women now exist in their own right and have an increasing ability to dress themselves according to their own perceptions of their own identities, to create their identities for themselves and only secondarily for others (including men). Yet a woman who seems to insist too aggressively on self-identity can become the object of virulent hatred: Hillary Rodham Clinton is the paradigmatic example. But a sign of progress is the *possibility* of a Hillary Rodham Clinton. Had a novelist created such a character in 1971 (no such actual person existed then in the world—that is, the 1993–2001 first lady), the novelist would have been criticized for creating an unbelievable character. There has been a good deal of sympathetic discussion in the media of women's issues seen from women's perspectives, from the open discussion of breast cancer, menstruation, menopause, and other formerly taboo female conditions to explorations of the evils of ageism, sizeism, and other-isms that, back then, along with "sexism" had no name—they were unmarked and unremarkable.

Concomitantly with women's liberation from the gaze, men are becoming more obsessed with *their* looks. While plastic surgery has become increasingly de rigueur for women in some social milieux, thirty years ago it was almost unheard of for men (and unmentionable by them), but it is now increasingly common and openly discussed—along with expensive "salon" haircuts and hair dyeing.

15. *Stud* vs. *mistress*. A better contrast (though one that was unavailable in the early 1970s) is *stud* vs. *slut* as casual terms of admiration/opprobrium in the teenage vocabulary. Despite the sexual revolution, despite claims of equality, despite arguments by antifeminists that men are now the oppressed gender, the double standard is still very much with us. *Stud* and *slut* are semantically very close: both refer to human beings who enjoy sex and appear to get a lot of it. The first refers exclusively to men, the second largely (outside the gay community) to women. As a result of the double standard, the connotations of the terms

are not parallel: while *stud* is a term of admiration, *slut*, whether used by females or males of a female, never is.

Some objections have been raised to my example of *mistress*, on the grounds that it represents a frozen survival of an earlier usage, from an olden time when there was true gender inequality. Certainly the usage is old. But if current reality did not support the *master/mistress* distinction via the continuing double standard, the uses I cite would have vanished with the social realities they had represented. The fact that a form has a history in a language does not mean it has no contemporary relevance.

16. Thankfully, this seems no longer to be the case—a true instance of form following function, language changing in response to changing times. Likewise, today, the question "What does your wife/girlfriend do?" is as frequent as "What does your husband/boyfriend do?" and is understood in the same way.

While there has not been much discussion of the figures, bathing beauty or otherwise, of current female Supreme Court justices, and while the insistence I discuss on mentioning the dress and physical attributes of prominent women more often than their male counterparts has notably diminished, the discrepancy has not entirely disappeared. It is still much more common to make an issue of a female candidate's family circumstances than a man's. Most newspapers have adopted last-name-alone reference for both women and men; the *New York Times* almost uniquely adheres to the old custom of using titles of respect (except for convicted felons). That sometimes creates odd discrepancies: some prominent married women (often Republicans) are called *Mrs.*, while others (often Democrats) are *Ms.* Dianne Feinstein (now a senator) is *Feinstein* in the *San Francisco Chronicle*, but *Ms. Feinstein* in the *Times*. The use of *Ms.* is itself an improvement, resisted by most publications for many years. (In the 1984 presidential election, the Democratic vice-presidential candidate was often referred to as *Mrs. Ferraro* despite protests that there was no such person: *Ferraro* was her birth name, not her husband's last name.)

Another discrepancy, not discussed in the text, still remains: the tendency to first-name women much more readily than men. Thus, even in formal discourse (e.g., television news panel shows) Feinstein is very often called *Dianne*, while Governor Davis was seldom called *Gray*, even though that name is uncommon and therefore not apt to create confusion. Women often say they don't mind being first-named by strangers because it's "friendly." But then, why aren't we equally eager to be "friendly" to men in similar positions? In this usage first-naming isn't "friendliness," but forced intimacy—another instance of blurring the line between private and public for women in public life. One of the very few men in an analogous situation that I can think of who is both regularly first-named and whose private and public selves have been blurred is former president Bill Clinton, for reasons I have discussed in *The Language War* (2000): he (and Hillary) have exchanged or at least obscured their genders. Another is the current governor of California, Arnold Schwarzenegger. During his 2003 campaign, he was referred to in the media, and referred to himself, very often as "Arnold," despite being a Republican and a prototypical he-man. Perhaps because of these facts, the usage was not publicly commented on. One reason for it might be the unwieldiness (and foreignness) of the last name; another, Arnold's Hollywood celebrity status.

17. *Widow* and *widower.* Happily, this discrepancy no longer exists: I have en-

countered numerous instances over the last several years of forms like *Mary Smith's widower*, where Mary Smith is prominent. Here is still another example of language reflecting culture.

18. When is a nonparallel case a counterexample, and when is it simply an interesting anomaly? If *man and wife* exemplifies the sexism of English and its speakers, is the French equivalent *mari et femme*, literally "husband and woman," proof that the French are nonsexist, or disproof that speakers of English are sexist? Neither, I would say: no language makes use of *all* possible opportunities for sexist expression; languages choose some options and not others. Therefore it is necessary to look at the total field in order to make (or refute) a claim that a culture is (or is not) sexist on linguistic grounds. Another analogue: Chinese women typically do not take their husbands' names (a fact so shocking to mid-twentieth-century Americans that they created quasi-titles for them: *Madame Chiang, Madame Mao*). But this fact in isolation hardly gives us a reason to suppose that Chinese society was, or is, nonsexist (as its use of selective abortion, abandonment, and infanticide of female babies should make clear).

A similar problem arises in many cases that were true in the English-speaking world when I wrote *LWP* but are less so now or no longer so at all. Does this change indicate that English-speaking society has abandoned sexism? To a degree, yes: some of the changes are certainly due to social changes, improvements in the social and political status of women. But even as the phenomena I examine here have gotten better, linguists' greater sophistication and range today, compared with what we could think about in the 1970s, permit us to see types of linguistic sexism that, while certainly present a quarter-century ago, were beyond the range of the theories and methods of analysis available to us back then.

For instance, conversation and discourse analysis can be used as diagnostics: when speakers of different genders have different options in conversation, sexism may be (but is not necessarily) the cause. A great deal of work during the late 1970s and through the 1980s suggested strongly that women and men of apparently equal social status had very different possibilities in informal conversation with respect to the right to interrupt, to determine choice of topic, to hold the floor, and more. While some of these claims have been questioned (cf. James & Clarke 1993; James & Drakich 1993), an astonishing statistic first cited by Dale Spender (1989) still appears to be true: that in an informal conversation, men occupy 80 percent of the conversational floor. When this figure drops to 70 percent, both women and men say that women are "monopolizing" the conversation. A complete analysis would investigate why this is true: Is it "sexism" or is it due to the different preferences of women and men as to their roles in conversation? It has been suggested that women are often happy to simply support the contributions of others, while men prefer to make the contributions. So an 80-20 distribution of conversational time might not be the result of the suppression of women; it might reflect the preferences of both sexes. (Or it might not: the jury is still very much out here, as often.)

19. On *Ms.* and other possible new titles of respect. Nowadays *Ms.* is not infrequently used in informal conversation, and in written formal discourse, it is in many cases the norm (cf. my remarks in note 16). But the nonparallelism still exists: while there is still only one title for men, *Mr.*, women frequently are offered a three-way choice among *Miss, Mrs.*, and *Ms.* That suggests that marital

status is still more relevant for women than for men, though to a lesser degree than was true a generation ago.

20. On professional titles and last name alone. The first of these has changed significantly, at least in the areas of academia with which I am familiar. In professional written discourse, both sexes are cited by last name alone (except sometimes when a first name or initial is necessary to avoid confusion). In the semiformal speech of academics acting like academics, last name alone is also typical, though not invariable: the current rule seems to be that if you know the referent personally, you can use a first name. (First names have taken over a broad swath of territory between the 1970s and the present. In the San Francisco Bay Area, at any rate, it sometimes seems as if having a last name is like having a loathsome disease: you may have one, but neither you nor polite interlocutors would ever mention it.)

21. The question has not yet been answered to my satisfaction why the black civil rights movement continues to get more respect than feminism. (Some might say because it deserves it, but I don't agree.) Possibly white, middle-class males are less threatened by the former than the latter; the gains of African Americans relative to whites have much less impact on white men's (and women's) daily intercourse in both private and public spheres than do the changes in the role of women over the last generation. Gender is and has always been the great divide; racial differences are not nearly as deep or polarizing in human societies. Changes that seem to minimize that divide, or equalize roles, are threatening to women and men alike who are insecure in their own psyches, even as racism is the last resort of losers (in both the literal and figurative senses of that word).

22. On the role of sociolinguistic concerns (like gender and language) in the development of "core" linguistic theories. As Labov (1972a) has suggested, it is puzzling why decontextualized theories of linguistics (phonology and syntax principally) are called "core" linguistics, with all that that implies about necessity, "basicness," and importance, while areas that are concerned with the relationship between language and its users (e.g., sociolinguistics and psycholinguistics) are marginalized through the ponderousness of their names, the implication often being that someone can easily be a "linguist" with little knowledge of these fields, while no one could be a "linguist" and not know syntax! The dominant figure in the field, Noam Chomsky, has remarked on several occasions, orally and in writing, that "sociolinguistics is uninteresting." But what is linguistics *about?* Why do we study it? I would bet that in most instances what piques our interest is the human interface, the uses we make of language and the abuses we subject others to through its misuse. The use of linguistic data to illustrate social structure seems to me the most important thing linguists can do. Even if you dismiss that argument as subjective or nonintellectual, consider this: many of the artifacts of syntax are wholly or in part based on human interactive needs. Why have complex constructions like passives or tag questions, except that they get speakers something they need—authority or credible deniability, for instance? To study such constructions without bringing to bear the social and psychological reasons for their existence is to render the study of language arid and meaningless.

Then why is it still acceptable, even fashionable, in many circles to deride these areas? A clue may lie in demographics: "core" linguistics is much more heavily male than are the outlying areas. Is there a connection between masculinity and respectability? Is the Pope Catholic? (Cf. the discussion in note 8.)

23. I refer here to sociology, but I should have included anthropology and psychology as well as sociology. This is a continuation of the argument I started in note 22: a linguist who works with decontextualized data is not doing linguistics.

24. "Separate but equal." Are the differences between female and male language forms merely innocent diversity—or even favorable to women? This was one of the arguments against my position often heard from both women and men. If women are treated more "politely" (as in "Not in mixed company"), isn't that a sign that women are *more*, not less, valued and respected than men?

My response borrows from *Brown v. Board of Education*. Whenever one group is treated differently from another, malignant inequality exists: "Separate but equal" is a fiction. This is especially obvious when (as in *Brown*) the "separate" treatment is clearly worse. But it is even true for women, where a case might be made that someone who is treated with superficial deference, and who doesn't *have* to work outside the home, is getting a better deal and should keep her mouth shut. But we have to understand that politeness has a dark side—the denial of full, rough-and-tumble humanity and with it, the privilege and necessity of making choices.

The issue of choice—about what, who has it, and how to evaluate it—has become increasingly fraught since the early 1970s. When I wrote the words here, the ink on *Roe v. Wade* was barely dry, and the controversies surrounding the question of "choice" had not yet reached a head. The idea that women could make many choices—to marry or not, to divorce, to have children, to attend professional school, to work outside the home when it wasn't economically essential, to enter politics at high levels, just to name a few—was not in wide circulation. The women's movement that began in the late 1960s raised the spectre of women's autonomy and access to power—a spectre that has in the interim acquired flesh and blood.

This is a shocking change, probably the greatest change that has happened in the lives of human beings through all our history. "Ladies," like "girls," cannot take part in that change—ladies because they are socioeconomically insulated from the consequences of their decisions, which therefore become empty; girls because they are too young to be responsible for their decisions. But when a woman becomes a woman, she assumes maturity and with it responsibility—the right and obligation to make choices and bear the consequences of those choices.

When you find yourself having to make life-changing choices for the first time, it often proves less than an unambiguous blessing. You can choose wrong—and have no one but yourself to blame! But you cannot be an adult human being without running this risk.

Women and men both found—and often still find—the new rules painful: men, because they had to share adulthood and power (with choice comes power, and vice versa); women, because—brought up as many had been with low opinions of themselves and their abilities—they felt terrified at the exposure and longed for the safety of the doll's house. Anecdotes were common in the media about how women, seduced by the dulcet songs of feminism, got jobs and divorces—and found life tough. (While life had been tough before, that toughness had been kept a secret in the public discourse.) These scary arguments against feminism are still with us, framed in more sophisticated ways. Women, we have recently been told (Hewlett 2002), can't have it all: e.g., they can't postpone childbearing past forty in order to establish their careers. It is extraordinary how much media attention has been showered on this rather obvious revelation, since any rational adult knows that a meaningful life entails tough choices. Nor is the new world as bleak as the brave new scenario suggests: most of the time it is possible to work out a reasonable compromise.

I interpret the opposition to reproductive rights not—as we have let the so-called pro-lifers frame it—as a battle between baby murderers and baby lovers, but between those who want women to have access to choices of *all* kinds and those who find the idea of the autonomous woman repugnant. Being treated politely (that is, being excluded from a wide range of communicative options), being discouraged from making important decisions—these are infantilizing, and the language that encodes them is dangerous to women's full humanity. *Choice* has often been criticized as a wishy-washy alternative to the wallop-packing *life*. But if you think of the wider sense implied by *choice*, that may not be true.

25. "Universal joint." For better or worse, the world of thirty years ago was different from today. The "War on Drugs" was relatively quiescent, allowing me to have my harmless little joke—one I would not dare to make today. (For the very young, the reference is to marijuana.)

26. Are women grammatical innovators or conservatives? As stated in the text, both claims were made and disputed over the twentieth century (cf. Jespersen 1922; Eckert 1989; Labov 1972b, 1990; Moonwomon 1989). Both are true. Women may be ahead of the curve, using nonstandard forms that are not fully accepted in middle-class society when they have less education and are less literate than men. Since education and literacy are powerful forces in favor of the standard language, those who do not have them are more apt to use nonstandard forms—which sometimes become the standard forms of the future.

Many cultures, however, believe (and often incorporate in proverb and folklore) the myth that deeds count more than words. So language is devalued and marginalized, often becoming an object of value only to those to whom autonomous action is forbidden: women, slaves, despised minorities, or colonial peoples. Very often, these groups become the makers and transmitters of vigorous linguistic traditions: the Irish, African Americans, and Jews.

In some cultures women—as mothers and schoolteachers—get the role of guardian of linguistic authority and keeper of the prescriptive grammar. This role allows its bearer a modicum of authority, even though in the adult male world it is despised (a real man talks tough: "Winston tastes good like a cigarette should"). Under these conditions, women are forces for linguistic conservatism.

Although the two positions seem antithetical, they really represent two sides of the same coin. Both arise when some groups are excluded from serious or valuable business.

27. Power vs. gender as the determinant of linguistic difference. As note 8 points out, this dichotomization was offered by O'Barr (1982). It is a valid point—these differences in use and function are not based *purely* on gender; but neither do they depend purely on power.

A male graduate student, facing his committee during doctoral orals, may display many of the traits identified here as "women's language" (of course he's an academic-to-be, so this example may not be completely persuasive). A female trial lawyer may be just as pugnacious in cross-examination as her male counterpart (think of Marcia Clark and Johnnie Cochran! Or better, don't). But women's relation to "powerful" ways of talking is complex: the double bind is apt to manifest itself. (How often was Clark called a bitch during and after the Simpson trial? And think about the media treatment of Hillary Rodham Clinton.) Women may have power, but they are still (even today) expected to conceal it beneath a ladylike demeanor (think of Elizabeth Dole), though less than was true a generation ago.

28. Women and mental illness. Women are still diagnosed with depression far more often than men, and it still isn't clear why. Some argue that men express the same pathology through violence and other forms of acting out; others, that the pressures on women predispose them to depression; others, that women's hormones make them crazy; still others, that women are diagnosed more often because they are more willing to acknowledge distress and seek treatment for it. It is certainly still true that women are allowed more liberty to speak of their feelings, especially feelings of sadness and distress, as well as warmth and caring (expressions that are still ridiculed by the male population as "touchy-feely"—the stuff you encounter in chick flicks and on *Oprah*). One might think, then, that this would immunize women against depression. Why doesn't it?

29. On politeness. This system has undergone many changes in the intervening years, and other systems have been proposed as well (especially those of Brown & Levinson 1987 and Leech 1980). For some discussion of why I was interested in politeness, how I devised this system, and how I view politeness currently, see the introduction to Lakoff and Ide (forthcoming). (Although I say here that formality has the effect of *creating* distance between interlocutors, it is probably better to say that it *acknowledges* or *expresses* it.)

30. On our propensity to judge behavior ascribed to women as inferior. Often, feminists criticize writings like this on the grounds that even acknowledging, or suggesting, the existence of differences between the sexes will have the effect of putting women in a worse position: it is best to deny the existence of any differences except those created by stereotyping and environmental biases.

But there *are* differences between the sexes, and in the last quarter century many of these have been amply documented (including a great many in the linguistic arena). We are still undecided on whether these differences are due to nature (genetics) or nurture (environment). Those taking the strongest position often denigrate *any* claims of difference that cannot be unambiguously ascribed to societal sexism as "essentialism," the belief that the sexes are genetically, intrinsically, and inherently different (and in its strongest version, that therefore they should receive different treatment and have different options). But this absolute position distorts reality. The probability is (there is no incontrovertible evidence for any of these positions) that there are genetic differences between women and men beyond the biologically obvious ones, differences that encourage different perceptions of the world, interactive needs, psychologies, and so on. But these differences are reinforced from birth (if not, these days, conception) by the environment: girls and boys are encouraged to maximize their inherent differences. Gender is organized on a continuum: there is no specific set of behaviors that all girls, or all boys, necessarily display; and individual females and males may display more or less "girlish" or "boyish" behavior depending on context.

This question of "difference" is important, and I wish we understood it better. But the insistence of many people on minimizing (or, in the case of evolutionary psychology) maximizing it is unfortunate: the discussion has become polarized and politicized. The problem is that behavior considered "feminine" is seen as inferior, and therefore many feminists are rightly wary of this kind of language. (This is not atypical for derogated minorities.) If feminists were convinced of the equality of women, they would worry a lot less about whether certain claims were "essentialist."

31. "Ladies present." We understand better now that this gesture was less polite than exclusional. I think here of Katharine Graham's (1997) boast that she "integrated" Washington dinner parties. Back in the mid–twentieth century, at high-society dinner parties the sexes parted after the meal: the men to smoke cigars and talk about weighty (and interesting) affairs of state; the women to remain at the table, chat about family, and trade (trivial) gossip.

We might ask why affairs of state are classified as important and their discussants intelligent, while discussion of family and human interaction (what we disparagingly call "gossip") is dismissed as idle chatter. But since much of the world, including many women, feel this way, postprandial segregation had consequences for women's self-esteem. Therefore Graham's ending of the practice was an important advance.

Let us segue into the discussion of male bonding, of which the situation to which Graham brought an end was a clear case. Here evolutionary psychologists (or sociobiologists, as they were called then) are making fascinating fictions in the guise of objective science. Nobody knows (or ever will know absent a time machine) how our remote ancestors behaved. Drawing conclusions from chimpanzees and gorillas overlooks an important point: at some moment back then, *we* got language (and all that goes with it) and *they* did not. It seems irrational to argue that *in all other respects, including gender relations,* we are just like them; only when it comes to language, religion, literacy, culture, and so on do they differ. I find it intriguing that these investigators always end up arguing in favor of the status quo—and since they are disproportionately white and male, arguing that their supremacy is not merely inevitable, but morally right.

32. "Sister." I recall this usage and wonder why it vanished. Perhaps it became an embarrassment when female solidarity fragmented once the going got tough: as homemaker was pitted against outside worker, childrearer against childless woman, middle class against working class, black against white, feminist against feminist, and so on. When will we ever learn?

REFERENCES

Brown, Penelope, & Stephen C. Levinson (1987). *Politeness.* Cambridge: Cambridge University Press.

Eckert, Penelope (1989). The whole woman: Sex and gender differences in variation. *Language Variation and Change* 1:245–267.

Graham, Katharine (1997). *Personal history.* New York: Knopf.

Hewlett, Sylvia (2002). *Creating a life: Professional women and the quest for children.* New York: Talk Miramax.

James, Deborah, & Sandra Clarke (1993). Women, men, and interruptions: A critical review. In Deborah Tannen (ed.), *Gender and conversational interaction*. Oxford: Oxford University Press. 231–280.

James, Deborah, & Janice Drakich (1993). Understanding gender differences in amount of talk. In Deborah Tannen (ed.), *Gender and conversational interaction*. Oxford: Oxford University Press. 281–312.

Jespersen, Otto (1922). The woman. In *Language: Its nature, development, and origins*. London: Allen & Unwin. 237–254.

Labov, William (1969). The logic of nonstandard English. *Georgetown Monographs on Language and Linguistics* 22:1–31.

——— (1972a). The study of language in its social context. In *Sociolinguistic patterns*. Philadelphia: University of Pennsylvania Press. 183–259.

——— (1972b). The social setting of linguistic change. In *Sociolinguistic patterns*. Philadelphia: University of Pennsylvania Press. 260–325.

——— (1990). The intersection of sex and social class in the course of language change. *Language Variation and Change* 2:205–254.

Lakoff, Robin Tolmach (1985). The politics of language. *CATESOL Occasional Papers* (Fall):1–15.

——— (2000). *The language war*. Berkeley: University of California Press.

Lakoff, Robin, & Sachiko Ide (eds.) (forthcoming). *New perspectives on linguistic politeness: Papers from ISLP 1999*. Amsterdam: John Benjamins.

Leech, Geoffrey (1980). *Language and tact*. Amsterdam: John Benjamins.

Moonwomon, Birch (1989). Another look at the role of female speakers in sound change. In *Proceedings of the fifteenth annual meeting of the Berkeley Linguistics Society*. Berkeley: Berkeley Linguistics Society. 238–247.

O'Barr, William M. (1982). *Linguistic evidence: Language, power, and strategy in the courtroom*. New York: Academic Press.

Spender, Dale (1989). *Invisible woman:The schooling scandal*. London: Woman's Press.

# COMMENTARIES

Note: All citations of *LWP* in the commentaries refer to the page numbers of the text as it appears in this volume.

# PART I: CONTEXTS

# 1 ::

# Changing Places

Language and Woman's Place *in Context*

MARY BUCHOLTZ

Commentators on Robin Tolmach Lakoff's work on language and gender, and particularly her critics, often seem to believe that her ideas about women, language, and feminism stopped in 1975, the year when *Language and Woman's Place* (*LWP*) was published in book form. Yet Lakoff explicitly stated in the text that she considered that work an initial foray into language and gender issues, not a definitive statement of the ways in which language reproduces an asymmetrical gender system: "I present what follows less as the final word on the subject of sexism in language — anything but that! — than as a goad to further research" (*LWP* 40). In her later writings on gender, which are much less widely cited than *LWP*, Lakoff's ideas on these issues continued to develop, and she built on, refined, and revised her earlier discussion. In keeping with the present volume's goal of reassessing the position of *LWP* in language and gender scholarship, in this essay I enlarge the scope of this project to include a wider range of Lakoff's work on gender. This survey, albeit brief and partial, is intended to encourage readers to explore all of Lakoff's rich writings on gender, rather than limiting their acquaintance with Lakoff's work to her most sensationalized and misunderstood text, *LWP*. By situating *LWP* within the context of the ongoing development of Lakoff's thought, I argue, we are better able to appreciate her continuing contributions not just to feminist linguistics but to feminism more generally.

## Lakoff's Feminist Practice

Even a cursory glance at Lakoff's extensive bibliography of publications on gender makes clear that all of her work in this area demonstrates a fundamental orientation to both feminism and linguistics as bodies of knowledge that should not be restricted to the domain of academic theory. Instead, as she shows through example, both endeavors must be recognized as central to the concerns of daily life. Her efforts to make these ideas accessible to a wide audience are thus simultaneously political and theoretical—a feminist challenge to structures of inequity that restrict access in order to perpetuate the power of a select few. It is no accident, for example, that with the exception of her dissertation work on Latin syntax, all of her scholarship is written to be accessible to a lay readership without sacrificing conceptual or analytic sophistication. Even in her earliest research, Lakoff was writing against the grain of linguistic fashion by eschewing the unwieldy technical apparatus of linguistic theory that often obscured more than it revealed. Moreover, her publications appear in newspapers and magazines as well as academic venues. One of the reasons that Lakoff's work is readily understood by the general public is that for her, feminist theory is closely tied to feminist practice. Thus in addition to publishing a detailed feminist analysis of Freud's abuse of one of his most celebrated patients, a young woman he called Dora (Lakoff & Coyne 1993), Lakoff has also produced a client's guide to selecting an effective psychotherapist (Aftel & Lakoff 1985); both are feminist interventions into the power imbalance of the psychotherapeutic relationship, long an intellectual interest for Lakoff.

There are other reasons why Lakoff's books after *LWP* deserve greater notice within feminist linguistics. First, it is noteworthy that many of them are collaborations with scholars in other fields. Lakoff's commitment to interdisciplinary scholarship has acted as an important counterpoint to the entrenchment of linguistics as an autonomous discipline that too often stands aloof from developments in adjacent fields. While some may object that Lakoff's interdisciplinary work isn't "real linguistics," as with much innovative research, it has been a harbinger of larger intellectual trends that redefine the scope of the discipline. Psychotherapy, for example, is a practice constructed almost entirely through talk, and in recent years many scholars have come to recognize that understanding such talk is well within the domain of linguistic inquiry. Similarly, Lakoff's attention to discourses of beauty in American culture (Lakoff & Scherr 1984) is a contribution both to feminism and to linguistics that anticipates interest in bodies and embodiment within studies of language. And in forging new intellectual directions, Lakoff has not worked alone. Her commitment to sustained collaborative research and writing has long been a hallmark of feminist scholarship both within linguistics and in other fields. Viewing scholarship as a social and interactive endeavor rather than the solitary work of a heroic lone researcher, many feminists advocate dialogical methods throughout the research process. Lakoff puts these principles into practice in her own scholarship by entering into intellectual partnerships with researchers from her own and other disciplines.

Yet perhaps the most important reason why language and gender scholars should be more aware of Lakoff's complete oeuvre is that many of her writings, and especially *LWP*, are unmistakable illustrations of the first principle of feminism: the personal is political. This slogan of 1970s radical feminism calls attention to the ways in which individual women's everyday encounters with sexism cumulatively create social structures that enforce the subordination of all women. Thus for women to speak out to other women about their own experiences of gender oppression is a revolutionary act of resistance against patriarchy. From this perspective, one of the most controversial aspects of *LWP* for later scholars, its use of an introspective methodology, may be seen as an instantiation of the same feminist tenet. Elsewhere, Kira Hall and I argue that Lakoff's methodology was influenced by the data-collection practices that predominated within linguistics in the 1970s (Bucholtz & Hall 1995). In addition, it is important to examine the role of feminist theory in Lakoff's approach. Thus, for example, Lakoff writes of her own ambivalent relationship toward stereotypes of gender as represented in the popular media:

> I recall, as a child, worrying because I didn't fit the pattern
> for which women were being ridiculed in jokes I heard on
> television. . . . It frightened rather than cheered me to realize
> this discrepancy between the female stereotype and myself: I
> feared I'd never make it. True, I didn't (at least I hope I
> didn't) remake myself to fit the stereotype, but seeing that im-
> age there continually in a thousand variations did nothing for
> my self-image: first, because that was the *best* I, as a girl,
> could hope to aspire to; second, and maybe worse, because I
> couldn't even manage *that* role. (*LWP* 83–84)

Lakoff's invocation of her childhood memories in a scholarly text is a deliberate violation of academic discourse conventions. Like feminist consciousness-raising groups of the 1970s, it is a political challenge to norms of silence about uncomfortably intimate matters.[1]

In using her own experiences as a source of data, Lakoff—like many feminists in a variety of fields—was attacked as unempirical, unobjective, unscientific. If to speak out as a feminist was a risky move in the academy of three decades ago, to speak out as a woman was riskier still. In very few of the linguistic writings on gender at that time or afterward did an author locate herself so squarely within her text; other feminist scholars adopted an equally impassioned stance but one that was far more impersonal. Although personal experience undoubtedly informed these texts, it was not explicitly acknowledged, and for good reason. At that time, to reveal one's interest in gender as personal as well as professional could call into question one's legitimacy as a scholar. In such an environment, open acknowledgment of the force of gender ideologies in one's own life was nothing less than a quiet act of defiance of mainstream male-dominated intellectual practice.

Moreover, Lakoff's willingness to acknowledge her presence in the text, controversial at the time, participates in one of the most important transformations of the human and social sciences in the last quarter century. Feminist, multiculturalist, and postmodernist scholars have all made the case for knowledge claims as partial and perspectival and hence for the necessity of scholarly self-reflection on the research process. From this vantage point, Lakoff's approach to the study of language and gender anticipated the shift toward reflexivity in scholarship in the academy as a whole.

In the same way that Lakoff's concern with sexism in language arose from her own experiences, so too did her inquiry into other cultural systems that control women: beauty as a sexist ideal and psychotherapy as a sexist institution. Her coauthored book on the politics of beauty opens with reflections by both authors on their individual confrontations with the ideology of beauty in American culture. Likewise, her scholarly interest in therapy arose in part from her own experience as a client. Lakoff's decision to expose her own vulnerabilities is a courageous one, designed not to put herself at the center of her analysis but to help others in similar situations to question structures of power. This explicit demonstration that the personal truly is political must certainly be seen as a feminist act.

## Lakoff's Feminist Theory

In her later research, Lakoff continued the work she began in *LWP* of identifying cultural ideologies of femininity and the practices of gender inequality that result from them. Yet many readers misunderstood Lakoff's discussion of "women's language" to be a straightforward description of women's linguistic practice rather than a characterization of ideological expectations of women's speech — expectations to which many speakers conform. Although this point was made in *LWP*, Lakoff's concern was the close connection between gender ideology and gender practice, and hence these concepts were often treated as equivalent in her early analysis. In her later work, however, "women's language" is more explicitly framed as ideology as well as practice; she writes, for example, that features of women's language represent "behavior supposedly typical of women across the majority of cultures: alleged illogic, submissiveness, sexual utility to men, secondary status" (1990: 202–203). In this and other passages, Lakoff documents the cultural power of "women's language" as ideology even as she expresses skepticism of the stereotypes that assign it exclusively to women and endow it with negative social meanings. An early theorist of the relationship between gender ideology and linguistic practice, Lakoff continues to develop her ideas about this fundamental issue.

To be sure, as she herself acknowledges, Lakoff's initial hypotheses about language and gender have in some cases been found to be incorrect by later researchers. Yet such analytic errors should be viewed with an eye toward the fact that language and gender did not yet exist as a field of scholarship: especially in the early stages of a field, the development of testable hypotheses can help advance disciplinary knowledge. Lakoff's formulation of one possible relationship between language and gender gave necessary shape to the research that was later conducted; without the laying of such groundwork, linguistic research on gender would have continued as a set of disparate studies and would not have converged into a coherent field (compare the field of language and sexuality, which remained diffuse until the recent emergence of theoretical statements; see Bucholtz & Hall 2004). Thus the counterexamples of later research should be recognized as the necessary work of refining the ideas proposed in earlier scholarship. As Lakoff notes, such revision furthered not only the study of language and gender but linguistic theory more generally:

> Until well into the 1970's we were unable to comprehend
> the prevalence of ambiguity in language, and if we talked
> about the functions of tags at all, we tried to assign all of
> them a single function. For example, I suggested in the early
> 1970's that tags represented a strategy of the conversationally
> less powerful. . . . But it was soon apparent, as we started to
> develop functional theories of grammar, that ambiguity was
> much more common in language than had been assumed.
> (2000: 135)

Scholars who object to Lakoff's early speculations about tag questions or other linguistic structures ideologically associated with women's speech tend to overlook such evidence that Lakoff continues to rethink her own earlier ideas in the light of later research.[2]

Perhaps the most dramatic and complex way in which Lakoff's ideas about language and gender have shifted is not with respect to particular claims but more generally in relation to feminist theory itself. Always an iconoclast, Lakoff has never explicitly aligned herself with a particular feminist camp. Yet it is possible to categorize specific statements that Lakoff has made about gender as characteristic of particular forms of feminism. An exercise of this kind yields both insights and perils; my discussion of Lakoff's feminism is intended to demonstrate the richness of her thought rather than to fix her within a single feminist perspective (see also McElhinny, this volume).

Lakoff's analysis of women's language use has been characterized by some of its critics as a "deficit" approach to language and gender, a term that continues to have a remarkably wide circulation. Yet the now-familiar alliterative taxonomy that is often used to organize language and gender scholarship—*deficit, dominance, difference,* and now *discourse*—does not only oversimplify, as those who use it readily acknowledge; it also misses an opportunity to link language and gender research to larger trends within academic feminism and thus to demonstrate the intellectual underpinnings of such work. In *LWP,* Lakoff's theorizing of "women's language" as symbolic powerlessness and her proposed remedy, to move toward a more an-

125

drogynous or gender-neutral style, participates in the project of liberal feminism, which seeks to bring women into institutions dominated by men in part by eradicating gender differences in social practice. At the same time, her emphasis on male hegemony in that text and others makes it necessary to include her work within the "dominance" framework as well (in fact, before the label *deficit* was assigned to her research, Lakoff was cited as an example of a "dominance" theorist). Such a viewpoint is compatible with the radical feminist perspective, and indeed McElhinny (this volume) offers a possible argument for classifying Lakoff in this way.

Less recognized is Lakoff's ongoing use of concepts usually ascribed to the "difference" approach, which, in emphasizing women's distinctive practices as rooted in a distinctive culture, is characteristic of cultural feminism (see Tannen, this volume, for other links between Lakoff's work and a cultural model of language and gender). Yet unlike the liberal form of cultural feminism, which espouses a "different but equal" interpretation of language use by each gender, Lakoff's own approach is more in keeping with radical cultural feminism in that it highlights male power and celebrates women's special linguistic abilities: "Women's special contributions to discourse (as to everything else) are ignored, disparaged, or—if their value is conclusively demonstrated—co-opted and credited to men. . . . Women over the millennia have learned to use with skill what is left to them" (1990: 199). And in opposition to liberal cultural feminism, she suggests that gender difference is not rooted in different cultures, but in cultural ideologies that insist on dichotomous gender roles: "Gender differences in language use arise not because male and female speakers are isolated from each other, but precisely because they live in close contiguity, which constantly causes comparisons and reinforces the need for polarization—linguistic and otherwise" (1990: 202).

Finally, the "discourse" approach to feminism can be seen in Lakoff's work as well. This model, heavily influenced by postmodern feminism, severs any necessary connection between gender (or sex) and social practice; all gender is performance, whether normative or not (see Barrett, Kiesling, both this volume). Yet violations of cultural norms of gender are of special interest in this framework because they vividly demonstrate that gender is a social construct rather than a natural essence. Because *LWP* has often been criticized as normative, it is usually overlooked that Lakoff's work has long attended to gender transgression in language use, from her discussion of nonnormative male speech styles in *LWP* (Hall, this volume) to her more recent consideration of public figures as "gender-transgressive." Thus her observation that during his presidency, George H. W. Bush was a user of "women's language" (1990: 271–273) is in keeping with her assertion in *LWP* that upper-class men may use features of "women's language" to symbolize their deliberate withdrawal from the aggressively competitive style culturally required of less powerful men (*LWP* 47). In later research, she comments that President Bill Clinton and First Lady

Hillary Rodham Clinton were often seen by the public as having swapped gender styles and explains why (1995: 36; 2000: 172). Such analyses demonstrate that for Lakoff, as for postmodern feminists, the association between gender and specific linguistic features is far from inevitable, but neither is it immune from cultural challenge; as she shows, violations of ideologically normative gender practice are harshly sanctioned.

These disparate theoretical threads in Lakoff's scholarship are worth tracing in order to demonstrate that Lakoff is not a failed feminist thinker, as some of her critics have alleged, but a serious scholar of gender whose theoretical position defies neat classification. As Lakoff showed so powerfully with the publication of *LWP*, it is in challenging rather than conforming to intellectual fashion that scholarship can make the most profound impact.

## Conclusion

Given its foundational role and ongoing importance for language and gender research, it is no surprise that scholars have continued to cite *LWP* heavily over the years. But it is more surprising, in light of Lakoff's continuing publications in this field, that many commentators, and especially its harshest critics, have treated the book ahistorically, not as a text written in response to a specific sociohistorical context, but as a timeless characterization of the relationship between language and gender.

Although commentators have sought, determinedly but unsuccessfully, to relegate *LWP* and Lakoff herself to the margins of language and gender research, the relevance of her work has not abated. Indeed, as feminism has entered the mainstream of the academy and language and gender is increasingly legitimated within linguistics, Lakoff's long-standing concern that feminist linguistics should be directed outward, to the women and men who most need its insights, becomes ever more important. In her writings since *LWP*, Lakoff has expressed worry that feminist scholarship that adheres too closely to dominant norms, whether in linguistics or in other fields, can have little political effect (e.g., 1990: 209; 1995: 48). As she continues to contribute to both scholarly and public discussions of language, gender, and power, Lakoff's work will continue to act as a "goad" not only to research but to feminist thought and action.

NOTES

1. Lakoff's shift in focus over the years from the private everyday speech of women and men in *LWP* to the public discourse of political and media figures in her later research is thus not as dramatic as it may seem. Now as before, Lakoff's focus is the relationship between the personal and the political, in how

women may speak and how they are spoken of within male-dominated structures of power—and how they have begun to challenge both of these aspects of "women's language" (e.g., Lakoff 1995).

2. Although a vast number of studies have sought to test Lakoff's assertions regarding tag questions and hedges, other characteristics of "women's language" that Lakoff delineated, such as women's detailed differentiation of color terms, have received very little attention. It is worth noting that the single study on this topic (Frank 1990) supports Lakoff's hypothesis.

REFERENCES

Aftel, Mandy, & Robin Tolmach Lakoff (1985). *When talk is not cheap; or, How to find the right therapist when you don't know where to begin.* New York: Warner.

Bucholtz, Mary, & Kira Hall (1995). Introduction: Twenty years after *Language and Woman's Place.* In Kira Hall & Mary Bucholtz (eds.), *Gender articulated: Language and the socially constructed self.* New York: Routledge. 1–22.

———— (2004). Theorizing identity in language and sexuality. *Language in Society* 33(4).

Frank, Jane (1990). Gender differences in color naming: Direct mail order advertisements. *American Speech* 65:114–126.

Lakoff, Robin (1975). *Language and woman's place.* New York: Harper & Row.

———— (1990). *Talking power.* New York: Basic Books.

———— (1995). Cries and whispers: The shattering of the silence. In Kira Hall & Mary Bucholtz (eds.), *Gender articulated: Language and the socially constructed self.* New York: Routledge. 25–50.

———— (2000). *The language war.* Berkeley: University of California Press.

Lakoff, Robin Tolmach, & James C. Coyne (1993). *Father knows best: The use and abuse of power in Freud's case of Dora.* New York: Teachers College Press.

Lakoff, Robin Tolmach, & Raquel L. Scherr (1984). *Face value: The politics of beauty.* Boston: Routledge & Kegan Paul.

# 2 ::

# "Radical Feminist" as Label, Libel, and Laudatory Chant

*The Politics of Theoretical Taxonomies in Feminist Linguistics*

BONNIE MCELHINNY

Robin Lakoff's book *Language and Woman's Place* (*LWP*) (1975) is one of the earliest, most influential, and most widely discussed contributions to feminist linguistics, but the question of how to place it within the larger context of feminist theory is far from straightforward. A decade ago I set out to compare existing feminist work in sociolinguistics with feminist work done in other related disciplines, using a modified form of philosopher Alison Jaggar's (1983) influential taxonomy of liberal, Marxist, radical, and socialist feminism (McElhinny 1993). Jaggar's taxonomy has served as the structuring framework for many introductory textbooks in women's studies. I argued then that Lakoff's work could be labelled *radical feminist*. In this essay, I briefly review how I made this argument and how Lakoff's work converges with radical feminist work in other disciplines. A decade later, I have some second thoughts about the use of Jaggar's taxonomy, and so I will also use this essay to reflect on the uses and limits of taxonomies in labelling and classifying feminist work. Indeed, feminist analyses of sexist language, like that conducted by Lakoff, can be said to have pioneered linguistic work on labelling that suggests how categories are constructed as normative. Conflicts over category content may present themselves as debates over what labels "really" mean, but the real issue is judgements about the normativity or deviance of particular practices (Eckert and McConnell-Ginet 1995: 479). Taxonomic approaches to feminist theory do not simply describe existing variation, but imply a unilinear evolutionary progress in ways that attempt to place certain approaches firmly in the past and thus actively obscure the rich diversity of approaches extant in the field. In the end, rather than taking the definition of *radical feminist* for granted, I ask about the political uses for which that notion can be mobilized in evaluations of work like Lakoff's.

## Claiming Lakoff for Radical Feminism

I begin with a quick summary of Lakoff's influential argument. For Lakoff, women's language has three characteristics: (1) it lacks resources for women to express themselves strongly, (2) it encourages women to talk about trivial subjects, and (3) it requires women to speak tentatively. Lakoff argues that a female speaker faces a double bind. If she does not learn to speak like a lady, she will be criticized or ostracized. If she does learn to speak like a lady, she will be systematically denied access to power on the ground that she is not capable of holding it, with her linguistic behavior as partial evidence for that claim.

Not all commentators have seen Lakoff's argument as feminist. She has been understood by some as accepting sexist notions of women as deficient (see Bucholtz & Hall 1995 and Freeman & McElhinny 1996 for reviews of the reception of Lakoff's work). Lakoff has thus became a useful target for those interested in countering what they took to be a concise statement of patriarchal norms. This use of Lakoff was possible in part because her study was based largely on introspection and intuition. There is a remarkable similarity between Lakoff's description of women's language and prescriptions for women's speech in post–World War II women's magazines (compare Norgate 1997). In recent years, some scholars have found Lakoff's work more helpful as a description of a particular ideology of femininity rather than an empirical description of it (Barrett 1997; Bucholtz & Hall 1995; Hall 1995).

In part, however, to blame Lakoff for having negative and conservative views is to conflate the messenger's views with her message. One response is to assume that the label *feminist* masks an enormous amount of variety in epistemological focus and political strategy and to consider whether labelling Lakoff's work as antifeminist is one way of dismissing a particular approach to feminism. The taxonomy of theories of gender in Jaggar 1983 was helpful to me and has been helpful to students to whom I have taught it, both in showing how wide the range of political strategies in feminism is and in forcing us to ask precisely what we mean by *feminist*.

By the lights of Jaggar's taxonomy, I argued in 1993 that Lakoff would probably be labelled a radical feminist. Although in popular usage *feminism* is often modified by *radical*, in academic usage *radical feminism* describes a particular approach to feminism. Radical feminism grew out of the disaffection of women (mostly white) with sexism in the social movements of the 1960s (especially the civil rights movement and the antiwar movement). While liberal theorists divide social life into a public sphere where the state can operate legitimately and a private sphere where citizens operate without fear of state interference, radical feminists argue that "the personal is political." Liberal feminists tend to call for reforms that allow women's equal participation in the public sphere (in education, workplaces, and political organizations), while radical feminists focus on women's oppression through their gender and sexuality. Like socialist feminists, radical feminists call for more radical transformations of political systems; unlike them they focus on patriarchy, rather than capitalism, as the primary source of women's oppression. Radical feminists often emphasize the commonalities of women's experience, arguing that women are universally oppressed by a ruling class called "the patriarchy" and that because sexism, unlike other forms of oppression, is evident in every culture and every period of history, gender oppression is the original and fundamental (or root, thus *radical*) form of oppression.

In order to understand women's "universal subordination" in the face of vast cultural variation in the arrangement between the sexes, many radical feminists have focused on sexuality, childbearing, and childrearing as the elements of women's oppression. Other radical feminists explore the ways that women are subordinated by direct physical coercion (e.g., rape, incest, domestic abuse) and by indirect physical and psychological coercion (e.g., pornography and narrow notions of beauty).

Perhaps where radical feminist thought is most relevant for linguistics is in its portrayal of the psychology of women. The radical feminist notion of false consciousness suggests that "women's minds as well as women's bodies are under constant attack" and "women's perceptions of reality are systematically distorted or denied" (Jaggar 1983: 114) in ways that cause them to believe that they benefit from prevailing cultural structures. In Mary Daly's widely read radical feminist manifesto *Gyn/Ecology*, for example, she argues that men control women's thought and that women are therefore unable to express their experience: "The words simply do not exist. . . . Women struggling for words feel haunted by false feelings of personal inadequacy, by anger, frustration, and a kind of sadness/bereavement. For it is, after all, our 'mother tongue' that has been turned against us by the tongue-twisters" (Daly 1978: 330, cited in Jaggar 1983: 114). Daly's work has deeply influenced such feminist linguists as Dale Spender (1980) and Julia Penelope (1990). Spender argues that "the English language has been literally man made and that it is still primarily under male control" (1980: 12). Likewise, Penelope argues that "the experiences described by English are those of men, who have controlled the development and grammatical explanations of English" (1990: xxxv) and that "the language itself is hostile to women's perceptions and thinking" (1990: xiv).

Lakoff's argument is similar to these early radical feminist studies. All tend to portray women as helpless victims of a patriarchy that forces them to act in passive, irrational, ineffective ways or evaluates their actions as passive, irrational, or ineffective (see McConnell-Ginet, this volume). By portraying women as victims, such studies attempt to save them from being blamed for their behavior. Some of what is now understood as the rhetorical excess of radical feminist work can be much more readily understood if one considers how small the numbers of women in such key institutions as law, medicine, and business were in the early 1970s (Blum 1991: 204).

Nonetheless, even if women's exclusion from powerful institutions has affected the shape of institutional discourse, control over ordinary speech cannot be and has not been nearly so complete (Cameron 1985: 111). By overemphasizing the power that men have over women, and by failing to acknowledge that women have any source of resistance, this style of feminist argument accords existing patriarchal institutions more power than they already have. This strategy depreciates the amount of power that women have succeeded in winning and minimizes the chances of further resistance (Jaggar 1983: 115). It also fails to see the ways that some women benefit from the power of hegemonic men and the ways that some subordinate men are disadvantaged by hegemonic masculine norms.

The label of *radical feminist* may always be a rather uneasy fit for Lakoff, in significant part because she has not, to my knowledge, ever described herself as such. Labelling Lakoff's work as *radical feminist* was and is a frankly political move. It attempts to reunite linguistic work with larger currents in feminist thought. It makes it possible to understand the influence of her work on feminists, to see it as political and critical in response to accounts that questioned this in the light of ongoing, heated debates in linguistics and elsewhere about which intellectual and political strategies feminists should adopt.

## Chronopolitics and Conflicts in Feminism: Taxonomy as Teleology

In the 1980s, radical feminism became associated in the eyes of many with a universalizing, theoretically naïve antiporn activism and was increasingly portrayed as the politics of white women. One failed attempt to rehabilitate radical feminism carefully distinguished it from cultural feminism (Echols 1989), a distinction reprised in sociolinguistics as the dominance-versus-difference debate (see Talbot 1998 for a summary). Echols (1989) suggested that after 1975 radical feminism was eclipsed by cultural feminism, just as social transformation was replaced by a kind of personal transformation easily coopted by consumer capitalism (see Bell and Klein 1996 for critiques). Other key works willing to recognize the contributions of radical feminism, but eager to consign it to feminism's past, also appeared in the 1980s. The best-known and most carefully developed of these was the taxonomy I still found useful in 1993: Jaggar's *Feminist Politics and Human Nature* (1983).

As late as the early 1990s, it was possible to conclude that a slightly watered-down version of radical feminism was the prevailing feminist paradigm in sociolinguistics. Or at least, so I concluded. Although I am about to critique the use of feminist taxonomies, I will offer a few words in their (and perhaps my younger self's) defense. Taxonomies can be useful in processing the ever-burgeoning literature in feminist and gender studies, especially for relative newcomers to feminist theory, like students and many sociolinguists. They also can serve a helpful comparative role, in highlighting disparate emphases in different disciplines. However artificial the boundaries between feminist theories might be, however much they leave out the novel approaches that do not fit their categorizing criteria, it was and is still striking to me how different feminist work in sociolinguistics seems from other feminist disciplines in which Jaggar's taxonomy has been applied. Even using fairly generous criteria for inclusion, I found virtually no liberal feminist studies and only a few socialist feminist studies in 1993. In the past decade, this has changed very little. In 1993, I also concluded that there were few published sociolinguistic studies influenced by postmodernism. In the past decade, this has changed quite a lot. Many publications influenced by postmodern social theorists have appeared in the past decade (see McElhinny 2003 for a review). The comparative approach that a taxonomy allows forces us to ask what it is about either the study of language as object or the institutional structures of linguistic enquiry that pulls us toward certain kinds of theoretical frameworks.

A decade ago I perceived labelling the work of Lakoff and others as *radical feminist* as a way of trying to determine what kind of feminist work was and was not being done in sociolinguistics in order to decide what needed to be done next. Indeed, one effect of a taxonomic approach is to suggest that each subsequent theory is proposed in order to remedy apparent deficiencies in earlier theories. If one adopts the objective stance of some forms of science and social science, this progress is seen as unproblematic — it mimics the orderly march of science (see, e.g., Jaggar 1983).

In anthropology, however, there is a long-standing discussion about the ideological uses of cultural taxonomies. One of the distinctive devices of much anthropological discourse was and to some extent is the *denial of coevalness*, "a persistent and systematic tendency to place the referent(s) of anthropology in a Time other than the present of the producer of anthropological discourse" (Fabian 1983: 31). Fabian calls this phenomenon *chronopolitics*. In such a context, cultural taxonomies cannot be neutral; they are immediately yoked to evolutionary schemata. Alhough they seem to be constructed as mere classificatory devices, the taxonomist in fact takes a position on a temporal slope. Her position is generally construed as the more progressive, innovative, or appropriate one.

More recently, a discussion about taxonomies has sprung up in feminist thought. King (1994: 59) argues that "feminist taxonomies work as little machines that produce political identities." She points out that although Jaggar claims that her taxonomy reflects the historical development of feminist theory, it actually does so only roughly. Radical feminist thought is constructed by Jaggar as preceding, and being eclipsed by, socialist feminist thought, which is thus constructed as a remedy for the deficiencies of that theoretical approach rather than competing with it. Further, King argues that Jaggar's book is intended to reduce and conquer diversity by organizing feminist theories into mutually exclusive, fundamentally incompatible genera. But Jaggar herself is forced to admit, at least implicitly, that sometimes the boundary between different theories is hard to draw, as can be seen with Lakoff. What is more to the point than trying to label Lakoff's work is the attempt to try to contain it and permanently fix its position in sociolinguistic history (see also Bucholtz, this volume). The effect is to lose some of its richness. A label can highlight certain similarities with other work; it also inevitably paints over or ignores certain differences. A label is thus best understood not as inaccurate but as always incomplete.

## Pigeonholing Lakoff: Making Birds of a Feather Flock Together

The use of a taxonomy is politics in the guise of objectivity. Knowledge production in capitalist economies, like other kinds of production, is driven by the attempt to establish new developments and new markets. Labelling Lakoff's work as *radical feminist* was, in part, a way to try to demarcate academic generations and to mark work associated with socialist and perhaps especially postmodern thought as newer. In the rush to innovate, there is always a danger in seeing continuing problems as outdated. In a focus on difference we can overlook what we owe to earlier approaches.

If we cannot use taxonomies, then what can we resort to? Anthropologist Ann Stoler (2002: 206) advocates using *working concepts*, that is, concepts that we *work with* to track variation in their use and usefulness and that *work* to destabilize received historical narratives. What this means in practice is not completely clear, but perhaps a model lies in recent work on how meaning is negotiated in and through keywords, in works such as Charles Briggs and Clara Mantini Briggs's (1997) analysis of *genocide* and Penelope Eckert and Sally McConnell-Ginet's (1995) analysis of *jock*. In each of these analyses, the meanings and uses of certain terms are carefully linked with certain groups and social formations.

Our own scholarly practices must be subjected to the same political and critical attention and analysis as other practices are. The place that anyone, including Lakoff, holds in feminist theory will depend on the theoretical position, empirical interests, and social networks of the researcher using others' work.

REFERENCES

Barrett, Rusty (1997). The "homo-genius" speech community. In Anna Livia & Kira Hall (eds.), *Queerly phrased: Language, gender, and sexuality*. Oxford: Oxford University Press. 181–201.

Bell, Diane, & Renate Klein (eds.) (1996). *Radically speaking: Feminism reclaimed.* North Melbourne, Australia: Spinifex.

Blum, Linda (1991). *Between feminism and labor: The significance of the comparable worth movement.* Berkeley: University of California Press.

Briggs, Charles, & Clara Mantini Briggs (1997). "The Indians accept death as a normal, natural event": Institutional authority, cultural reasoning, and discourses of genocide in a Venezuelan cholera epidemic. *Social Identities* 3: 439–469.

Bucholtz, Mary, & Kira Hall (1995). Introduction: Twenty years after *Language and Woman's Place.* In Kira Hall & Mary Bucholtz (eds.), *Gender articulated: Language and the socially constructed self.* New York: Routledge. 1–24.

Cameron, Deborah (1985). *Feminism and linguistic theory.* London: Macmillan.

Echols, Alice (1989). *Daring to be bad: Radical feminism in America, 1967–1975.* Minneapolis: University of Minnesota Press.

Eckert, Penelope, & Sally McConnell-Ginet (1995). Constructing meaning, constructing selves: Snapshots of language, gender, and class from Belten High. In Kira Hall & Mary Bucholtz (eds.), *Gender articulated: Language and the socially constructed self.* New York: Routledge. 469–507.

Fabian, Johannes (1983). *Time and the other: How anthropology makes its object.* New York: Columbia University Press.

Freeman, Rebecca, & Bonnie McElhinny (1996). Language and gender. In Sandra Lee McKay & Nancy Hornberger (eds.), *Sociolinguistics and language teaching.* Cambridge: Cambridge University Press. 218–280.

Hall, Kira (1995). Lip service on the fantasy lines. In Kira Hall & Mary Bucholtz (eds.), *Gender articulated: Language and the socially constructed self.* New York: Routledge. 183–216.

Jaggar, Alison (1983). *Feminist politics and human nature.* Totowa, NJ: Rowman & Allanheld.

King, Katie (1994). *Theory in its feminist travels: Conversations in U.S. women's movements.* Bloomington: Indiana University Press.

Lakoff, Robin (1975). *Language and woman's place.* New York: Harper & Row.

McElhinny, Bonnie (1993). We all wear the blue: Language, gender, and police work. PhD diss., Stanford University.

—— (2003). Theorizing gender in sociolinguistics and linguistic anthropology. In Janet Holmes & Miriam Meyerhoff (eds.), *The handbook of language and gender.* Oxford: Blackwell. 21–42.

Norgate, Sheila (1997). *Storm clouds over party shoes: Etiquette problems for the ill-bred woman.* Vancouver: Press Gang Publishers.

Penelope, Julia (1990). *Speaking freely: Unlearning the lies of our fathers' tongues.* New York: Pergamon.

Spender, Dale (1980). *Man made language.* London: Routledge.

Stoler, Ann Laura (2002). *Carnal knowledge and imperial power: Race and the intimate in colonial rule.* Berkeley: University of California Press.

Talbot, Mary (1998). *Language and gender: An introduction.* Cambridge: Polity Press.

# 3 ::

# Positioning Ideas and Gendered Subjects

*"Women's Language" Revisited*

SALLY McCONNELL-GINET

In 1973, as I was planning my first course on language and gender ("Language and the Sexes"), I read Robin Lakoff's "Language and Woman's Place" (1973). I was infuriated. I interpreted her as claiming that women in general were wimps, unwilling and unable to take a stand, vague and imprecise, deferential to men, and reduced to saying silly euphemisms, such as *fudge*, when things got really bad. In 1975 when the book, *Language and Woman's Place* (LWP), containing that article and "Why Women Are Ladies" appeared, I wrote an essay (McConnell-Ginet 1975) that expressed my dismay at what I saw as Lakoff's devaluation of women and their capacities, linguistic and otherwise. I still have the copy of the book that I scribbled on in preparing that review. It is full of exclamation points, "Nonsense," and many "Yes, but..." entries. Although Lakoff clearly shared my own goal of promoting gender equity, she seemed to me to ignore not only many women but also successful strategic uses of language by women on whom she did focus (upper-middle-class Americans of European descent).

It is undoubtedly relevant that I allied myself with the interpretive semanticists against the challenge of the generative semanticists, a group of influential young linguists that included Lakoff. This group was drawing attention to ways in which social and communicative contexts affected the linguistic forms people used, and there was a rush to include all sorts of contextual factors in grammatical rules. I thought then (and still do) that although contextual factors are fundamental to understanding how language is used, their role in the grammar is sharply constrained. Most important generalizations about how language functions, I contend, are not grammatical but arise from putting grammar together with distinct theories of social life and human communication. I part company, however, from those who hold grammar to be the only appropriate subject matter for linguistics. In my view, theories of how language works in society and culture are also appropriate grist for the linguist's mill. I suspect I came to that view in part through engagement with work like *LWP*. I agreed with many of the general claims Lakoff made about ways in which language could contribute to women's social disadvantage. Nonetheless, I was unhappy with many specific claims and with what I understood as her explanatory framework, for both linguistic and, as noted above, feminist reasons.

In the intervening years, I have come to realize that my first reaction to Lakoff misjudged her enterprise. Like many others, I had seen her as engaged in an empirical characterization of the speech of actual women and of gendered restrictions on the use of particular linguistic resources. In this way of construing her work, there certainly were major problems. It was by no means clear, for example, that most women used the various features she had tagged as part of "women's language" (WL) or that men who employed those features were viewed as speaking "as women." But as Mary Bucholtz and Kira Hall (1995) made clear, such a flat-footed interpretation of Lakoff's work misses the point. Lakoff was trying to explore language ideology and its connections to gender ideology and gender arrangements. Her WL includes a range of linguistic resources that language users draw on in presenting themselves as women or, although this point was only implicit in *LWP*, in hearing others as women. Crucially, she was also drawing attention to some ways in which women's apparently problematic status as speakers contributed to their overall social disadvantage, including their subordination to men.

Lakoff's proposals had the immediate effect of prompting others to explore ways in which gender identities and relations interacted with language. Many began by looking at the array of linguistic forms that *LWP* had associated with WL. In addition to richly elaborated color vocabularies (*magenta, puce*), diminutives (*panties*), euphemisms (substitutes for profanities like *piffle* or *heck* and expressions like *go to the bathroom* instead of "vulgar" or tabooed expressions such as *pee* or *piss*), and a generally superpolite style of speech, Lakoff saw WL as characterized by such resources as the following:

- tag questions (*This talk about war in Iraq is frightening, isn't it?*)
- "uptalk" or rising intonation on declaratives (A: *When will dinner be ready?* B: *Six o'clock?*)
- various kinds of hedges (*That's kinda sad* or *It's probably dinnertime*)
- "empty" boosters (*I'm so glad you're here*)
- "speaking in italics" (frequent tonal accents)
- indirection (saying, e.g., *Well, I don't really understand it* to convey dislike of a film)

All of these can be used to express some aspect of the speaker's position on or stance toward the basic content conveyed, what is called *idea positioning* in Eckert and McConnell-Ginet 2003, chap. 5. Idea positioning can involve the speaker's degree of commitment to or confidence in the propositional content conveyed, the speaker's degree of interest or involvement in what is said, or the degree to which the speaker is serious or playful or whatever about the content. WL, according to Lakoff, had the effect of undercutting the positions that women might be trying to take. Even features such as euphemisms and politeness particles, while not obviously markers of idea positioning, could often be interpreted as diminishing the force of what was said, rendering it powerless. At the same time, Lakoff argued, to eschew WL was hard for women who wanted to be judged as acceptably feminine.

I read *LWP* as implying that WL itself was inherently problematic, unable to launch ideas and projects with any degree of success, and that women using it did so because of psychological hang-ups, most notably their putative insecurity. (Lakoff spoke of women's apparent "unwillingness to assert an opinion" [*LWP* 50] but saw the explanation as lying in learning the lessons of "femininity" too well.) Many later discussions (e.g., Crawford 1995) associate *LWP* with a "deficit" view of women's speech, in which both the language used and the women using it are seen as deficient. Although Lakoff tries at points to indicate that she does not see women themselves as deficient, such readings of *LWP* are not unwarranted. There is talk of "empty" adjectives in WL (e.g., *That's a fabulous dress you're wearing*) but no attention to the possibility that such "neutral" forms as *terrific* might be equally empty. The "feminine" domain of color and its associated terminology are characterized as "trivial" and "unimportant" but sports and its jargon, quintessentially "masculine," go unexamined. Such asymmetries suggested to me and other readers that Lakoff was uncritically buying into evaluations of WL and its users that had more to do with the sexist assumptions of a male-dominated society than with any actual appraisal of the effects of the use of particular components of WL or the motives of those using those components, what they might be trying to do. (The possibility that a woman and a man might be judged differently when using the same form is relevant here, but this possibility is not explored in *LWP*.)

The very idea of WL seemed to me to assume that the various features Lakoff pointed to would co-occur as elements of a single "language" or system, ignoring the fact that speakers might draw on some but not all of these resources and that different women might avail themselves of different components of WL. Furthermore, talk of WL arguably obscured the fact that the use of such resources was by no means constant across situations and settings even for speakers who did indeed draw on them. Nonetheless, there was something powerful in the "language" metaphor, the idea that women might learn at a young age ways of speaking distinctively different from those that their male peers were acquiring. Certainly, women beginning to move into positions of authority in workplaces were often struck by the conflict between modes of talk needed there and those they and their mothers might employ at home or at dinner parties. And they often encountered hostility and resistance from coworkers, not only men but also other women, if they spoke (and acted) as if entitled to exercise authority. Lakoff put it eloquently:

> So a girl is damned if she does, damned if she doesn't. If she refuses to talk like a lady, she is ridiculed and subjected to criticism as unfeminine; if she does learn, she is ridiculed as unable to think clearly, unable to take part in a serious discussion: in some sense, as less than fully human. These two choices which a woman has—to be less than a woman or less than a person—are highly painful. (*LWP* 41)

Lakoff goes on to offer a plausible analogy between women's linguistic double binds and the forced bilingualism of many other subordinated groups. For both women and these other groups, the language associated with their most fundamental sense of identity is looked down on by dominant groups (compare the situation of Spanish speakers in much of the United States or, even more dramatically, of speakers of African American Vernacular English; see Mendoza-Denton's and Morgan's essays in this volume). Lakoff's picture of women as forced to struggle with a new language in order to succeed resonated with many women's experience.

Much subsequent research on language and gender explored use of the various features Lakoff had assigned to WL. One strand investigated the extent to which these features signaled gender identity. Dubois and Crouch (1975), for example, found that male conference attendees used more tag questions in their comments than female participants. And William M. O'Barr and Bowman K. Atkins (1980) report a study in which WL features were statistically more strongly associated with the "powerless" (as defined by status in the courtroom setting they studied) than with women as such. Although they did not look at the effects of individual features of WL, O'Barr and Atkins also report experimental work that suggests, as Lakoff had hypothesized, that speech with many WL features did seem to weaken the force or credibility of what was said (at least for speakers giving testimony in a courtroom).

But idea positioning is not all that the WL features might do. One of the major claims of *LWP* was that these features not only reduce the force of their users' discourse contributions but at the same time position those users as women (or perhaps, as nonmasculine men; see also Hall, this volume). In other words, they enter into what is called *subject positioning* in Eckert and McConnell-Ginet 2003, chap. 5. As we talk with one another, we are always adopting particular subject positions, such as teacher or pupil or friend or supplicant or benefactor. And we are also assigning positions to the others with whom we are talking: we may condescend or defer to them, express solidarity with them or claim distance from them, and so on. Although she did not put it this way, Lakoff's most original insight may be that idea positioning is a major component of subject positioning. The fundamental mechanism through which WL was said to feminize its users was by positioning the ideas and projects advanced as only tenuously held. A woman speaking WL was positioning herself directly as only half-heartedly pushing her ideas and thereby indirectly helping position herself as a woman. The idea of what Elinor Ochs (1991) dubbed the "indirect indexing" of gender is already there in *LWP*. At several points, Lakoff makes clear that she sees most WL forms as having as their primary function something other than marking gender. For example, she says that "these words aren't, basically, 'feminine'; rather, they signal 'uninvolved,' or 'out of power' " and "they are often considered 'feminine,' 'unmasculine,' because women are the 'uninvolved,' 'out of power' group *par excellence*" (*LWP* 47). The term *woman's language*, however, obscured the indirectness of the link to gender identity. O'Barr and Atkins, for example, imply that WL would have to be either "women's" or "powerless" language, without considering that it might be both—that is, it might index gender in part through indexing lack of power. As the quoted passages make clear, Lakoff did indeed see that WL could be both.

Another research strand that arose in response to *LWP* looked at alternative functions for the components of WL. In particular, a number of investigators suggested that these forms could also be used to good effect for social positioning that was not explicitly gendered. Tags, for example, might be used to invite another's participation in the interaction or to mark social solidarity with other interlocutors. Drawing on naturally occurring data, Janet Holmes (1982) and Deborah Cameron, Fiona McAlinden, and Kathy O'Leary (1988) showed that many uses of tags were best explained in these ways. (Their studies also found men more likely than women to use tags to express uncertainty.) I pointed to similar positioning functions for "uptalk" and "speaking in italics" (McConnell-Ginet 1978, 1983). These and many other studies stressed the importance of investigating which functions particular forms serve in particular contexts, noting that there is not a one-to-one mapping between linguistic forms and their functions.

The form-function problem in the study of language and gender went even deeper. As Deborah Tannen (1994) and others note, many linguistic resources relevant for constructing gendered identities can serve multiple functions in a single utterance. For example, *sir* may express both (genuine) respect and socially required deference. Alternatively, the speaker may have one function in mind but those interpreting may assign another: I use rising intonation to invite you to express your opinion (or to inquire indirectly about motives for your earlier contribution), but you interpret me as deferring to your thinking on the matter we're discussing (or as so lacking in confidence that you feel justified in insisting on having your views prevail).

Even where the focus was on idea positioning, there were many challenges to Lakoff's implied claim that WL components consistently undermined their users' effectiveness. Pamela Fishman (1980) argues that many WL features arise as strategies for coping with conversational problems created by uninterested or otherwise dismissive male interlocutors. Penelope Brown (1980), though dealing with a very different population, explores how polite language is called on strategically, to help speakers accomplish their ends, given their place in the social hierarchy. My own work, especially that already cited, has always emphasized speakers' strategizing and ways in which choices from the WL repertoire can advance speakers' goals. And Holmes (1995) demonstrates the efficacy of various WL components for enabling women to accomplish important things in their communities. At the same time, many of these authors explicitly acknowledge that women are handicapped if strategies that serve them well in one kind of context are imported into a different setting, which is certainly part of what prompted Lakoff's analysis of the double bind some women face. Women are also sometimes handicapped by being heard through distorting gender and language ideologies that, for example, may misinterpret open-mindedness as insecurity or lack of conviction.

There is no question that *LWP* started much productive exploration of language and gender issues. I have focused on WL in connection to speakers' gendered identity, ignoring Lakoff's important discussion of sexist talk about women. I've done this because it was the idea of women as weak and ineffective speakers that annoyed me so thirty years ago. I now, however, appreciate some of the insights that underlay Lakoff's talk of WL: that idea positioning is central to gendered subject positioning and that our talk indexes gender indirectly. With hindsight (including three decades of research on language and gender), it is easy to see some of what Lakoff overlooked. But *LWP* was and continues to be a work of paramount importance to language and gender studies in particular and to the wider field of language in social life.

REFERENCES

Brown, Penelope (1980). How and why are women more polite: Some evidence from a Mayan community. In Sally McConnell-Ginet, Ruth Borker, & Nelly Furman (eds.), *Women and language in literature and society*. New York: Praeger. 111–136.

Bucholtz, Mary, & Kira Hall (1995). Introduction: Twenty years after *Language and Woman's Place*. In Kira Hall & Mary Bucholtz (eds.), *Gender articulated: Language and the socially constructed self*. New York: Routledge. 1–22.

Cameron, Deborah, Fiona McAlinden, & Kathy O'Leary (1988). Lakoff in context: The social and linguistic functions of tag questions. In Jennifer Coates & Deborah Cameron (eds.), *Women in their speech communities*. London: Longman. 74–93.

Crawford, Mary (1995). *Talking difference: On gender and language*. London: Sage.

Dubois, Betty Lou, & Isabel Crouch (1975). The question of tag questions in women's speech: They don't really use more of them, do they? *Language in Society* 4:289–294.

Eckert, Penelope, & Sally McConnell-Ginet (2003). *Language and gender*. Cambridge: Cambridge University Press.

Fishman, Pamela (1980). Conversational insecurity. In Howard Giles, W. P. Robinson, & Philip Smith (eds.), *Language: Social psychological perspectives*. Oxford: Pergamon. 127–132.

Holmes, Janet (1982). The functions of tag questions. *English Language Research Journal* 3:40–65.

———. (1995). *Women, men, and politeness*. London: Longman.

Lakoff, Robin (1973). Language and woman's place. *Language in Society* 2:45–79.

———. (1975). *Language and woman's place*. New York: Harper & Row.

McConnell-Ginet, Sally (1975). Our father tongue: Essays in linguistic politics. *Diacritics* 5:44–50.

———. (1978). Intonation in a man's world. *Signs: Journal of Women in Culture and Society* 3:541–559.

———. (1983). Intonation in a man's world. In Barrie Thorne, Cheris Kramarae, & Nancy Henley (eds.), *Language, gender, and society*. Rowley, MA: Newbury House. 69–88. (Revised version of McConnell-Ginet 1978.)

O'Barr, William M., & Bowman K. Atkins (1980). "Women's language" or "powerless language"? In Sally McConnell-Ginet, Ruth Borker, & Nelly Furman (eds.), *Women and language in literature and society*. New York: Praeger. 93–110.

Ochs, Elinor (1991). Indexing gender. In Alessandro Duranti & Charles Goodwin (eds.), *Rethinking context*. Cambridge: Cambridge University Press. 335–358.

Tannen, Deborah (1994). The relativity of linguistic strategies: Rethinking power and solidarity in gender and dominance. In Deborah Tannen (ed.), *Gender and discourse*. Oxford: Oxford University Press. 19–52.

# 4 ::

## *Language and Woman's Place*

### *Picking Up the Gauntlet*

ANNA LIVIA

## Robin and Dianne

I read Robin Lakoff's *Language and Woman's Place* (LWP) in 1975. I was nineteen years old, studying French at University College London. Before the end of the year, I had formed the London Women and Language Group with fellow linguists Linda Shockey, Trista Selous, and Eva Eberhardt. We were inspired and infuriated by Lakoff's insights into women's conversational practices, which seemed destined only to make us appear powerless and airheaded. We began to scrutinize our own language for traces of such weak speech as "What a divine idea!" and "What a lovely steel mill!" We expunged the word *lady* from our vocabulary, and we learned to tell jokes. At the time, Lakoff's most important insights concerned the way women spoke and the disparate way women and men were referred to.

Fifteen years later, I arrived in Berkeley, California, to start a graduate degree in French and met the illustrious Dr. Lakoff, teaching two floors below in the linguistics department. I became her student, we became friends, and she became Robin. The world had changed too. Lakoff recalls, "In the 1971 mayoral campaign in San Francisco, the sole woman candidate was repeatedly referred to as Mrs. Feinstein, never Feinstein, when her opponents were regularly referred to by first and last names or last names alone: Joseph Alioto or Alioto, not Mr. Alioto" (*LWP* 61).

Well, Feinstein and Alioto are still very much on the political scene. Feinstein is the better known of the two, as a U.S. senator, while Alioto is merely a former mayor. Both Feinstein and Alioto are frequently referred to by first name. Indeed, Feinstein's Web site encourages us to "breakfast with Dianne." There is no hint of a lowering in status in this invitation to meet the senator: it is, rather, an illusion of equality offered to the California voter, to let us imagine for a second that we might share her status and be allowed to call her *Dianne*, as she calls us *Anna* or *Robin*.

143

## Transsexuals and the Cast of *Friends*

These are changes predicted in *LWP*. In this essay I examine some of the less-well-studied insights contained in Lakoff's early analysis of gender and language. Many of the issues that linguists and cultural critics are grappling with in the second millennium were previewed in some way in her book, including phenomena like transsexual speech, cross-expressing (men talking like women and vice versa), media representations of gender, and whether language can be changed by feminist will.

As Lakoff remarked back in 1975, "Social change must precede lexical change" (*LWP* 68). It is, Lakoff argued, fruitless to try to correct a social inequity by changing linguistic disparities (*LWP* 39). Instead, she advised us to view language as a clue to the external situation (69). Any type of language is fair game for this type of analysis, not only the attested speech prized by sociolinguists like William Labov. As Labov (1984: 29) states in an article on sociolinguistic methodology: "We place a very high value on records of vernacular speech which show a minimum shift or accommodation of the presence of an outside observer." However, as Lakoff observes, valuable information is also contained in literary and media representations of speech, albeit of a different kind: "The speech heard in commercials or situation comedies mirrors the speech of the television-watching community: if it did not, it would not succeed" (*LWP* 40). This constructed speech provides clues to sociolinguistic phenomena like insecurity and prestige and can give insights into the linguistic attitudes of viewers.

Lakoff develops this point further when discussing the influence of the media, arguing that stereotypical images are often more influential than statistics (*LWP* 83). Women seen on the media have many traits of women's language built into their speech, which has of course been constructed for them by a team of writers. Female viewers pick up on these traits and seek to emulate the characters in their turn. This circuit of influence and re-action is difficult to analyze without close scrutiny of media images.

Indeed, this insight has been utilized by some speech pathologists involved in training male-to-female transsexuals to speak like women. Joan Erickson of the Department of Speech and Hearing Science at the University of Illinois (personal communication) advises the transsexuals who consult her to study the language of the women on the popular TV series *Friends*. Although this language is highly exaggerated, scripted to avoid (or play up) many naturally occurring linguistic features like interruptions and overlaps, it can serve as a blueprint for the kind of vocal traits transsexuals may wish to emulate. Alison Laing, who runs classes for male-to-female transsexuals, uses many of the examples of stereotypical women's speech discussed in *LWP*. Her training video, *Speaking as a Woman with Alison Laing* (1992), shows her demonstrating the correct, feminine use of tag questions like *isn't it?*

As Lakoff so aptly put it back in 1975, stereotypes are important "first, because, for a stereotype to exist, it must be an exaggeration of something that is in fact in existence and able to be recognized; and second, because one measures oneself . . . according to how well or poorly one conforms to the stereotype one is supposed to conform to" (*LWP* 94). Evaluating not only the persuasive power of the stereotype but also its use as an analytical tool is one of the less recognized insights of *LWP*. It is, however, an insight that has been extremely useful in my own work on literary linguistics.

Literary and linguistic analyses have traditionally been considered two separate, even incompatible fields. The constructed, nonspontaneous dialogue of a film script tells us little of the way people really talk, but it often represents an ideal to which speakers aspire. It allows us to see what expectations different speech communities have, and what patterns are deemed appropriate for each sex. Whether or not particular individuals respect the stereotypes, they are familiar with them as competent users of the language, and the ways in which people flout the conventions provide rich material for analysis.

If we take two examples from novels for children aged eight to fourteen, we will see that even children as young as eight years old are expected to be familiar enough with the stereotypes that when they are not followed, these young readers know what to expect. In Nina Bawden's *Granny the Pag*, eleven-year-old Cat's grandmother scolds the school bully in the following words: "If you bully my granddaughter, I will not only inform the authorities, your parents and your teachers, but I will myself personally throw you *so hard* into the middle of next week that you may never come back" (1996: 30; original emphasis). The promise to tell the bully's parents and teachers is an unexceptional, entirely orthodox warning, but the threat of physical violence moves the remark into a more masculine frame, reinforced by its unhedged, unequivocal phrasing.

Cat's grandmother's *so* is not the feminine, intensive *so* cited by Lakoff, the *so* of "I like him *so* much" (*LWP* 80), where the hearer is left wondering exactly how much fondness is being expressed, but a fully finished equation: *so hard . . . that you may never come back*. This is not how a grandmother is supposed to speak to a child, even a bully, and it marks this character as unfeminine and socially aberrant. The reader is being prepared for a challenge to the grandmother's status as Cat's guardian: women who speak this way are unfit to look after children. It is no surprise to learn that this same immodest grandmother rides a Harley-Davidson motorcycle through the middle of London.

A rather different example is to be found in Diana Wynne Jones's fantasy *Castle in the Air* (1990), which tells the story of a young carpet seller named Abdullah who sets out to rescue a group of enchanted princesses. Abdullah consistently uses flowery, feminine speech. When addressing his magic carpet, Abdullah exclaims, "O most excellent of carpets, o brightest-colored and most delicately woven, whose lovely textile is so cunningly enhanced with magic, I fear I have not treated you hitherto with proper respect" (1990: 54). If we look at Lakoff's nine-item checklist of traits of women's language (*LWP* 78–81), we see that Abdullah uses at least four of them: superpolite forms (*O most excellent of carpets*); exaggeratedly correct grammar (*I fear I have not treated you hitherto*); empty adjectives (*most excellent, brightest-colored*); hedges (*I fear*). Given these manifold and overt signs of femininity, the reader is not surprised when it is Abdullah's beloved, the princess Flower-in-the-Night, who hatches the plot that will ultimately save the imprisoned princesses.

What is particularly significant about these examples is that they come from books for children. Although Lakoff was the first to articulate the most common traits of "women's language," they are in fact conventions that every competent speaker of English may be assumed to have absorbed. If this was not the case, both Abdullah and Cat's grandmother would be incomprehensible as characters.

## Lakoff's Gauntlet

Lakoff insists on the futility of expending too much energy on changing language rather than the society from which it comes. The battle to create and popularize a neutral pronoun to replace generic *he* is a case in point. She goes so far as to say that, unlike other linguistic disparities that discriminate in favor of men and against women, this issue is both less in need of change and less open to change. Indeed, as she puts it, "an attempt to change pronominal usage will be futile" (*LWP* 71). However, I believe we should consider Lakoff's prediction of the ultimate outcome of the pronominal battle as a gauntlet thrown down before us rather than as a dismissal of the battle's validity. Lakoff mentions in passing the important option of singular *they* but pays it scant attention, remarking only that it is "a usage frowned on by most authorities as inconsistent or illogical" (*LWP* 70). She recognizes that the problem itself is not trivial, as it has caused too much anguish to too many women, but advises her readers to attempt to change only what can be changed.

In fact, singular *they* has made great headway in the last quarter century, as Dennis Baron reports (1986: 194). (See Livia 2001a for a book-length consideration of pronominal experiments.) It is hard to know what will prove futile and what can be changed. If we believe that in order to eliminate generic *he*, we need to create and circulate an entirely new pronoun, we may indeed renounce the attempt. What we have found instead, in the twenty-first century, is that *they* will do, and does do, the trick quite nicely. It turns out to be a question of expanding popular usage into more formal speech, a phenomenon that accounts for much language change through the ages.

Nowadays, no one gibbers much at the sight of *someone . . . they*. In fact, the August 15, 2002, edition of the *Berkeleyan*, official staff newsletter

of the University of California at Berkeley, features four different strategies
for avoiding generic *he:*

(i)   *Staff* choose the program *they* want to attend. (1)
(ii)  The ombudspersons hope to expand *staffers'* ability to
      prevent or deal with difficult situations on *their* own. (5)
(iii) Another advantage offered by electronic publishing is in-
      terjournal linking whereby *a reader* can navigate via hy-
      perlinks to any journal article cited by the authors of the
      research *he or she* is reviewing. (6)
(iv)  "To see the look of appreciation on *someone's* face when
      you return *their* stolen wallet was very gratifying." (8)

Example (i) uses *they* to anaphorize a grammatically singular noun with
plural meaning (*staff*), while (ii) pluralizes that noun (*staffers*) to justify the
use of the plural pronoun *they*. In (iii), the antecedent noun is singular
(*the reader*) and is anaphorized by a choice of masculine or feminine singular (*he or she*); while (iv) offers the now classic *someone . . . they*. One
must conclude that singular *they* is no longer frowned on, even in academic contexts. Feminists have picked up Lakoff's gauntlet and provided
a panoply of responses to the supremacy of generic *he.* The attempt has
proven far from futile, but the strategies that have been most successful
have involved using the already existing resources of the language rather
than creating an entirely new pronoun.

## Raising Doubts about Masculinity

Although Lakoff addresses the specific question of women's speech, she
leaves enough clues in the text about men's speech and the consequent
societal positioning of men for us to be able to reconstruct some of her
ideas on that topic. In her references to men's speech, Lakoff always demonstrates how their conversational style reflects their class position. She
observes, for example, that upper-class British men are allowed to use a
typically feminine vocabulary, to be finicky about nuances of color in the
way that women are, "without raising doubts as to their masculinity" (*LWP*
47). This implies that among other social classes, men who are articulate
about color tones are marked out as homosexual.

Lakoff hypothesizes that upper-class British men are not required to
demonstrate any commitment to the work ethic. As gentlemen of leisure,
they have the economic wherewithal to pursue any interests, even the most
trivial (like interior decorating) and need not demonstrate any aptitude for
money-making tasks like business or politics (*LWP* 47). In fact, their in-
ability to pursue these more material goals is offered as proof of their leisure
status. We could in fact turn this around and say that men of leisure as a
group are perceived as nonmasculine. As the working-class hood Pat re-

marks in Mehdi Charef's novel *Le Thé au Harem d'Archi Ahmed* (Tea in the Harem of Archimedes), "C'est tous des peds, les bourgeois" (All middle-class men are faggots) (1983: 178). We might disagree with this statement, but we can also use it to infer a number of things about Pat's social class, attitude to society, and personality. The fact that the remark is meaningful to us shows that it refers to a recognized stereotype.

Lakoff also comments on the enactment of masculinity in middle America. Here it is literacy and culture that are seen as suspect in a man (*LWP* 80). Suspicion is also triggered if men are too grammatical or polite in their speech (*LWP* 84). In contrast, masculine men are required to know how to swear, tell dirty jokes, and speak familiarly of the workings of their car engine. In America, it seems, real men must play down their schooling and play up their blue-collar associations.

Lakoff throws out these insights without much elaboration, in her usual unassuming manner. Her speculations about gender and class turn out to be astonishingly accurate. My research on collocations of class and masculinity in French discourses of sexuality shows that we cannot understand the workings of gender if we consider it on its own, removed from other essential demographics like class, race, and age (see Livia 2001a, 2001b, 2002). Speech conventions are different for upper-class and middle-class men, as Lakoff suggested. On one end of the class scale, upper-class masculinity is so similar to femininity as to be indistinguishable from it to all but its closest adherents. The politeness, good grammar, and interest in nonprofitable pursuits that are coded feminine are all coded upper-class too. These social signifiers are so familiar that they may be used by members of liminal communities (as well as by writers of fiction) as common currency in the construction of identity.

In the summers of 2000 and 2001, I conducted field research in Paris and in the city of Lille in northern France. I was specifically looking into representations of masculinity among lesbians and their interpretation by in-group members. The starting point for this research was the descriptions of desirable characteristics featured in the personal ads in *Lesbia* magazine, the French lesbian monthly. While many ads ended with the exclusionary coda "lesbiennes masculines s'abstenir" (masculine lesbians need not apply) or variations on this wording, on closer analysis it was evident that the exclusion applied only to lesbians who affected working-class masculinity. Thus lexical items connoting working-class masculine status, like *camion-neuses* (truck drivers), *catcheuses* (wrestlers), and *armoires* (wardrobes — implying that the person is built like a heavy piece of furniture) were used as descriptions of lesbian undesirables, whereas lexical items connoting upper-class masculine status, like *dandies, Romaine Brooke lookalike, garçonnes* (tomboys), described highly prized lesbians.

When I asked what characteristics were associated with masculine lesbians, my respondents mentioned swilling beer, speaking ungrammatically, using slang, having bad manners, and having low educational status.

To be masculine was to be working-class. Upper-class masculinity, then, was not recognized as masculinity. Since the representations of masculinity cited by this liminal community were quite orthodox and corresponded closely to Lakoff's descriptions, it may be assumed that for the wider community, too, masculinity implies working-class masculinity. Expanding on this finding to look at other social demographics such as race, I found that blackness is typically interpreted as masculine and whiteness and Asianness as feminine (Livia 2002).

It is part of the extraordinary prescience of *LWP* that its impact has been felt far beyond the confines of women's language in calling into question all naturalizing discourse, be it about gender, race, or class (see also Morgan, this volume). The many theoreticians who have picked up Lakoff's gauntlet over the years and answered her soft-spoken challenge to normative values attest to the enduring importance of *LWP*.

REFERENCES

Baron, Dennis (1986). *Grammar and gender.* New Haven, CT: Yale University Press.

Bawden, Nina (1996). *Granny the pag.* New York: Houghton Mifflin.

Charef, Mehdi (1983). *Le thé au harem d'Archi Ahmed* (Tea in the harem of Archimedes). Paris: Mercure de France.

Jones, Diana Wynne (1990). *Castle in the air.* New York: Greenwillow Books.

Labov, William (1984). Field methods of the project on linguistic change and variation. In John Baugh & Joel Sherzer (eds.), *Language in use: Readings in sociolinguistics.* Englewood Cliffs, NJ: Prentice-Hall. 28–53.

Lakoff, Robin (1975). *Language and woman's place.* New York: Harper & Row.

Laing, Alison (1992). *Speaking as a woman with Alison Laing.* CDS Premium Videos.

Livia, Anna (2001a). *Pronoun envy: Literary uses of linguistic gender.* New York: Oxford University Press.

Livia, Anna (2001b). Les camionneuses et les dandies: Sexualité, genre et classe (Truckies and dandies: Sexuality, gender and class). In Christine Lemoine & Ingrid Renard (eds.), *Attirances: Lesbiennes fem, lesbiennes butchs* (Attractions: Butch and femme lesbians). Paris: Presses Lesbiennes et Gaies. 122–137.

Livia, Anna (2002). Camionneuses s'abstenir: Community creation through the personals. In Kathryn Campbell-Kibler, Robert J. Podesva, Sarah J. Roberts, & Andrew Wong (eds.), *Language and sexuality.* Stanford, CA: CSLI Publications. 191–206.

# 5 ::

# Power, *Lady*, and Linguistic Politeness in *Language and Woman's Place*

JANET HOLMES

Robin Lakoff is undoubtedly the linguist who has most profoundly influenced the direction of language and gender research worldwide—most especially perhaps in its infancy, with her groundbreaking article (1973) and book *Language and Woman's Place* (*LWP*) (1975). But even thirty years later, as this volume testifies, she continues to contribute insightfully and incisively to the field. *LWP* addressed two fundamental dimensions of the interaction of language and gender, namely the language used *by* and *about* women, dimensions which have continued to attract the attention of researchers and which have increasingly been regarded as simply different facets of one issue—the role of language in the construction of gender identity (see Holmes 2001).

Lakoff's provocative claims about the ways in which American women spoke compared to men generated a huge amount of quantitative research in the late 1970s and early 1980s—for the most part, interestingly, by nonlinguists. Sociologists, psychologists, and researchers in communication and many related areas of social science embraced with enthusiasm Lakoff's hypotheses (which she offered as a "goad to further research" [*LWP* 40], little realizing how successfully they would serve this function). These researchers diligently counted women's and men's uses of a range of specific linguistic forms, some of which Lakoff had provided as examples, but many of which she had never mentioned.

When the dust settled, a number of sociolinguists and discourse analysts stepped in and identified a number of misunderstandings about the nature of language which underlay and invalidated much of the bean-counting research (see, e.g., Aries 1996; Crawford 1995; Holmes 1984, 1995; Talbot 1998). Most important, they pointed out that Lakoff's hypotheses about a range of superficially distinct linguistic forms (such as stress, tag questions, and modal adverbs) were unified by an underlying analysis of two basic pragmatic functions (namely, hedging and boosting), while by contrast the disparate linguistic forms that became the focus of quantification (typically lexical items easily identified by a computer program that ignored their different meanings) had no such claims to coherence. Moreover, Lakoff's comments on the relevance of social context were honored more in the breach than the observance. Indeed, many early researchers completely overlooked the fact that the underlying coherence of *LWP* as a whole was grounded in a fundamental political argument about power and politeness.

Lakoff's reflections on politeness were published several years before those of Brown and Levinson (1978, 1987), and she anticipated their influential theory of politeness in a number of interesting ways. First, Lakoff posed the crucial question facing those interested in analyzing meaning in contexts of use (pragmatics) as opposed to meaning in the abstract (semantics)—namely, in everyday real interaction, why don't people follow Grice's (1975) "Rules of Conversation"? "Why not always speak logically, directly, and to the point?" (*LWP* 93). One reason, she proposed, was concern for the rules of politeness. Lakoff's three rules of politeness have obvious parallels with Brown and Levinson's concepts of negative and positive politeness:

1. Formality: keep aloof.
2. Deference: give options.
3. Camaraderie: show sympathy. (*LWP* 88)

While rules 1 and 2 are clearly aspects of negative politeness, recognizing a person's need for autonomy or "space," rule 3 refers to positive politeness needs—individuals' need for approval from others, their need to be liked, their need to express shared values and attitudes, and so on. In this area, then, Lakoff anticipated the most influential theory of politeness in the last thirty years, and her reflections on the implications of these three politeness rules for gendered interaction provoked an astonishingly fruitful spate of research (for one example, see Davies, this volume).

## Sexist Language

Turning to language used about women, *LWP* provides a number of equally stimulating and challenging suggestions. Lakoff identified some of the more subtle aspects of the ways in which women are constructed as inferior, second-class human beings through the categories and association of specific English words available to name women as a group: "Throughout English one finds evidence of many sorts that women are viewed (by women as well as men) as secondary beings: as having an existence only when defined by a man" (*LWP* 57).

In other words, one way in which women's inferior social identity is constructed in English is through the semantic distinctions encoded in the lexicon and grammar of the language and the ways in which in everyday

usage those distinctions are both unavoidable on the one hand and ex-
ploited on the other. English frequently forces a choice between forms that
are loaded against women. When a title is required, for instance, as Lakoff
noted (*LWP* 64–65), English presents a choice between *Mrs., Miss, Ms.*
for women, with no equivalent choice for men, an indication that marital
status and currently, in some varieties at least, feminist alignment are components of the social construction of female gender (see Chiles 2003; Pauwels 1987, 1998). The choice between *Chair, Chairperson, Chairman*, and
*Chairwoman* is equally no neutral selection (Ehrlich & King 1994). Such
usages reflect societal attitudes toward gender roles, and underlying ideological influences are clearly identifiable in the choices people make. As
Deborah Cameron (1994) notes, when speakers are faced with a range of
variants, there is no neutral or unmarked choice. Rather, "every alternative
is politically loaded, because the meaning of each is now defined by contrast with all other possibilities" (1994: 26). Lakoff made this point most
extensively in her discussion of the choice English speakers face between
the terms *lady* and *woman*. In what follows I illustrate how her intuitive
comments about the meanings of these terms in the American usage of
the 1970s proved prophetic in relation to a corpus analysis of New Zealand
usage in the 1990s.

## Ladies *and* Women

In 1975, Lakoff suggested that the term *lady* was replacing *woman* "in a
great many contexts" (*LWP* 52, 56) for two related reasons. First, she argued, *lady* had become a "euphemism" for *woman* (*LWP* 51–54). The term
*woman*, she suggested, had become "marked" over time, like the term
*nigger*, and the use of *lady* as a euphemism was "a signal that something
is wrong" (*LWP* 53). The term *woman*, like *broad* and *mistress*—terms with
respectable origins in the distant past—was becoming tainted with the embarrassing sexual connotations that ultimately seem unavoidable for terms
referring to women. As other feminists have also argued, society appears to
regard women's sexuality as their main distinguishing feature and as a major threat to societal order; euphemistic expressions are one means of attempting to keep women's sexuality out of sight and under control.

A second reason for the use of the term *lady*, Lakoff suggested, is its
"polite" use, to add or attribute status to the referent: "Most people who
are asked why they have chosen to use *lady* where *woman* would be as
appropriate will reply that *lady* seemed more polite" (*LWP* 55). This, she
suggested, is especially apparent in its attributive use in relation to "demeaning" jobs, such as *cleaning lady* and *tea lady*, as opposed to, say,
*woman doctor* and *woman judge* (*LWP* 54).

In some of my recent research, I thought it would be interesting to
explore to what extent Lakoff's predictions about the direction of change

(i.e., that *lady* was replacing *woman*), and her comments on the meanings and uses of the terms *lady* and *woman* were supported by evidence from corpus analysis, one of the few available means of collecting reliable information on relatively low-frequency lexical items. I looked first at evidence of change over time in the relative frequency of the terms in a number of corpora of English usage, and then I examined New Zealand usage in particular in more detail in order to identify the meanings of these terms in current usage (Holmes 2000). The results showed that while Lakoff's predictions do not seem to have been sustained in relation to the disappearance of the term *woman,* her comments about the politeness function of the term *lady* are well supported by the New Zealand data (see also Livia's discussion of changes in gendered lexicon and grammar in this volume).

Women *Rules*

A simple check on the relative frequency of the terms *woman, women, lady,* and *ladies* in six comparable corpora of written English, two collected in the 1960s and four in the late 1980s and early 1990s, indicated that in American, British, and New Zealand usage alike, the terms *woman* and especially *women* dramatically increased in frequency, while the terms *lady* and *ladies* remained at a relatively low frequency in written usage over the past thirty years. So, for example, in the American corpora the term *women* occurred 197 times in the 1961 Brown Corpus, but 817 times in the similarly constructed 1991 FROWN Corpus. *Ladies* by comparison occurred only 36 times in the 1961 data and 28 times in the 1991 data (Holmes 2000). Overall, while references to female adults in the texts more than doubled over the period (from 531 to 1,371), an indication of the change in women's status in American society during this period, the number of occurrences of *lady* and *ladies* barely altered. The forms *woman* and *women* have clearly become the unmarked ways of referring to female adults in American usage over the last thirty years, at least in written material.

Examining the 1961 LOB Corpus for British usage and the 1986–1990 Wellington Corpora of New Zealand English for New Zealand usage revealed a similar pattern, with almost no change in the frequency with which the terms *lady* and *ladies* occurred, while occurrences of the term *women* more than doubled. Indeed, in the New Zealand data, the term *ladies* is outnumbered almost twentyfold by instances of *women.* The term *ladies* has undoubtedly gone into a decline. Since the reason is almost certainly an increase in the status of women in public social life, Lakoff is no doubt pleased that her prediction in this area does not hold, at least in written usage. Feminism of the 1970s clearly changed societal trends, as indicated by this change in linguistic usage.[1]

It is possible that Lakoff's prediction that *lady* would displace *woman* holds for spoken rather than written English. The fact that comparable speech data for the 1960s is unavailable makes this possibility difficult to explore. However, data from current British usage suggests that, while the terms *woman* and *women* are spread across both written and spoken texts, they may be avoided in British speech (Holmes 2000; Romaine 1999). In other words, perhaps people find, as Lakoff suggested, that it feels impolite to refer to female adults as *women* in speech, but it is acceptable in writing. It certainly seems plausible that politeness factors affecting such a choice would carry greater weight in face-to-face interaction than in writing. And while there is little evidence that the terms *lady* and *ladies* are replacing *woman* and *women* in speech, it is possible that other avoidance strategies are being adopted.

## Women and *Politeness*

Turning to the issue of the current meanings of the terms *woman* and *lady*, data in the International Corpus of English from Great Britain (1992) and New Zealand (1998) provide interesting support for Lakoff's early observations. Analysis of the forms *lady* and *ladies* in context indicates that they have increasingly acquired the features <+patronizing>, <+conservative>, and <+dated> over the last twenty-five years or so. The most obvious context in which these terms are marked as <+polite> and <+respectful> is in the formulaic phrase *ladies and gentlemen*. Indeed, the majority of instances of *ladies* in the spoken corpora occur in this politeness formula, used as an address term in formal contexts such as a courtroom or a formal discussion or debate.

Second, there were a number of instances of *lady/ladies* in the corpora in which the discussion had a decidedly dated flavor. In the British corpus, for instance, in a broadcast discussion of whether women should be allowed into men's clubs, female adults were consistently referred to as *ladies*, and the underlying patronizing attitude sometimes became quite explicit: "I've nothing against them the ladies except that it's very pleasant to go into a man's club and don't have to worry about . . ." A parallel example from New Zealand referred to the practice in a previous century of courting the *local ladies*.

A third group of instances highlighted the patronizing or trivializing component of the meaning of the terms *lady* and *ladies*. This was obvious in examples such as *little old lady*, *grey-haired old lady*, *deaf old lady*, and *spinster ladies*. A similar meaning was evident in references to a *lady editor*, a *lady film star*, a *ladies rugby team*, and even *my good lady wife* (see Holmes 2000 for details). Serious occupations, such as judge and doctor, were modified by the term *woman* rather than *lady*. These examples clearly support Lakoff's suggestions that use of the terms *lady* and *ladies* serves to undermine the seriousness of the referent. The terms trivialize the referent in a phrase in the same way as the suffixes -*ess* and -*ette* function in relation to a root.

In sum, a detailed examination of the contexts in which the terms *lady* and *ladies* occurred in British and New Zealand corpora suggests that the choice of these terms rather than *woman* or *women* is always marked. And while these terms may still be used in formal contexts as markers of politeness, in less formal contexts they increasingly suggest that the speaker or writer does not take the female referent(s) seriously. In other words, as Lakoff predicted (*LWP* 54), *lady/ladies* is now marked not only as <+polite>, but also as <+trivializing> and <+patronizing> in many contexts.

## Conclusion

Research in politeness generally, and on the relationship between gender and politeness in particular, has burgeoned since *LWP* was published. It is a tribute to Lakoff's acumen in reflecting on this topic in the early 1970s that the seeds of many subsequent theoretical developments can be identified in her early book. It is also noteworthy that many of her predictions and insights have been validated. Her comments on the meaning of the term *lady* provide a case in point, as I have demonstrated.

The corpus analysis summarized above suggests that over the last thirty years, the social significance of the choice between *woman* and *lady* has altered in an interesting way. Whereas at one point, as Lakoff indicated in *LWP*, the term *woman* was socially marked as impolite, with connotations of social inferiority and possibly even impropriety, this is no longer the case. The high frequency of its use to refer to female adults in the corpora that I reviewed provides ample evidence that *woman* can now be used as an unmarked term in this way. As Lakoff noted, pointing to the decline of euphemisms for Jews in American usage, "Euphemisms vanish as they are no longer needed" (*LWP* 53). Similarly, *lady* is now rarely used in English as a euphemism for *woman*.

As Lakoff pointed out, choosing between alternative vocabulary items is rarely a matter of selecting from among stylistically neutral synonyms. In the same vein, current approaches to language and gender emphasize that a specific lexical choice may constitute a component in the construction of or resistance to established power relations in a male-dominated society. In other words, linguistic choices are often enactments of the more extensive political struggles over "who is to be master," in Humpty Dumpty's famous words in *Through the Looking Glass*. As *LWP* suggested in the 1970s, the issue is basically one of power, that is, of whose values will prevail. While "men are in control of all the major institutions" (*LWP* 97), language is likely to continue to be one of the few weapons easily available to challenge the status quo.

NOTE

1. For complete details regarding the corpora used and the results of the analysis, see Holmes 2000.


REFERENCES

Aries, Elizabeth (1996). *Men and women in interaction*. Oxford: Oxford University Press.

Brown, Penelope, & Stephen Levinson (1978). Universals in language usage: Politeness phenomena. In Esther N. Goody (ed.), *Questions and politeness*. Cambridge: Cambridge University Press. 56–289.

—— (1987). *Politeness: Some universals in language usage*. Cambridge: Cambridge University Press.

Cameron, Deborah (1994). Problems of sexist and non-sexist language. In Jane Sunderland (ed.), *Exploring gender: Questions for English language education*. London: Prentice-Hall. 26–33.

Chiles, Tina (2003). Titles and surnames in the linguistic construction of women's identities. *New Zealand Studies in Applied Linguistics* 9:87–97.

Crawford, Mary (1995). *Talking difference: On gender and language*. London: Sage.

Ehrlich, Susan, & Ruth King (1994). Feminist meanings and the (de-)politicization of the lexicon. *Language in Society* 23:59–76.

Grice, H. Paul (1975). Logic and conversation. In Peter Cole & Jerry Morgan (eds.), *Syntax and semantics 3: Speech acts*. New York: Academic Press. 41–58.

Holmes, Janet (1984). "Women's language": A functional approach. *General Linguistics* 24(3):149–178.

—— (1995). *Women, men and politeness*. London: Longman.

—— (2000). *Ladies* and *gentlemen*: Corpus analysis and linguistic sexism. In Christian Mair & Marianne Hundt (eds.); *Corpus linguistics and linguistic theory: Papers from the 20th International Conference on English Language Research on Computerized Corpora (ICAME 20), Freiburg im Breisgau 1999*. Amsterdam: Atlanta/Rodopi. 141–155.

Holmes, Janet (2001). A corpus-based view of gender in New Zealand. In Marlis Hellinger & Hadumod Bussman (eds.), *Gender across languages: The linguistic representation of women and men*. Vol. 1. Amsterdam: John Benjamins. 137–155.

Lakoff, Robin (1973). Language and woman's place. *Language in Society* 2:45–80.

—— (1975). *Language and woman's place*. New York: Harper & Row.

Pauwels, Anne (1987). Language in transition: A study of the title "Ms." in contemporary Australian society. In Anne Pauwels (ed.), *Women and language in Australian and New Zealand society*. Sydney: Australian Professional Publications. 129–154.

—— (1998). *Women changing language*. London: Longman.

Romaine, Suzanne (1999). *Communicating gender*. Mahwah, NJ: Lawrence Erlbaum.

Talbot, Mary M. (1998). *Language and gender: An introduction*. Oxford: Polity Press.

# 6 ::

## Cultural Patterning in *Language and Woman's Place*

DEBORAH TANNEN

I ambled into the sphere of Robin Lakoff—and of linguistics—in the summer of 1973. A teacher of remedial writing named Debby Paterakis, I knew nothing of linguistics except that it was a way of studying language—and language had always been my passion. Nearly everything I have written about conversational style—and about language and gender, which to me is a subcategory of conversational style—was seeded by the course I took with Lakoff at the 1973 Linguistic Institute at the University of Michigan. My decision to abandon a secure faculty position in the academic skills department at CUNY's Lehman College, and my native New York City, for a distant territory out west and an indeterminate future as a linguistics PhD can also be traced to that summer, that course, and that professor.

Several years before, while working on my master's degree in English literature, I had looked longingly at a poster advertising the upcoming Linguistic Institute at SUNY–Buffalo. The topics listed on the poster were intriguing and inviting but completely out of the range of possibility, since I was married to a man from the island of Crete whose idea of marriage did not include his wife going away for the summer to take courses because they interested her. (It wasn't that he needed to keep me near: he offered that if I wanted to go away for a couple of months, I could spend the summer in Crete with his parents.) When in 1973 George Paterakis decided to return to Greece and I decided not to go with him, I knew immediately where I would go instead: to that summer's Linguistic Institute in Ann Arbor.

The fates were looking out for me. The summer I found myself free to attend a Linguistic Institute was the summer the institute was devoted to "Language in Context" and the year Robin Lakoff was on the faculty. In addition to "Introduction to Linguistics" (which was taught by A. L. Becker, whose view of language was deeply anthropological), I took Lakoff's class. What captured my imagination most in the course was Lakoff's elegant notion that communicative style resulted from three differentially applied rules, each associated with a different sense of politeness (see

Holmes, this volume). I saw in this system an explanation for the crazy-making frustrations I had experienced and been helpless to understand or explain in seven years living with a man born and raised in a different culture. In the term paper I wrote for that course, which I titled "Communication Mix and Mixup: How Linguistics Can Ruin a Marriage," I worked out how Lakoff's schema illuminated the causes of those frustrations. Her rules of politeness allowed me to reframe many of my husband's and my grievances as conversational misunderstandings.

A year later, in 1974, I began graduate study at the University of California at Berkeley—not as Debby Paterakis, but as Deborah Tannen. The paper I had written for Lakoff's class became the first paper I delivered at a linguistics conference: a regional meeting held at San Jose State University. (It also became my first linguistics publication, in the mimeographed, staple-bound *San Jose State Occasional Papers in Linguistics* [Tannen 1975]). In that paper, I recast myself as "Wife," George Paterakis as "Husband," and the two of us as "the couple." Here's how Lakoff's rules of politeness accounted for our repeated arguments, reframed as examples in my academic paper: "Husband" was applying Rule 1 of politeness, *Don't impose*, when he dropped hints rather than telling "Wife" directly what he wanted; "Wife" was applying Rule 3, *Maintain camaraderie*, when she missed those hints, assuming "Husband" would tell her directly what he wanted. He was angered because his clearly expressed preferences were continually ignored, and she was angered because her clearly demonstrated efforts to accommodate were continually unacknowledged; instead of gratitude, she got grief.

That early paper said nothing about how Wife and Husband had come by their contrasting notions of politeness. It did not address whether their differing applications of rules of politeness reflected their cultural differences. Nor did it say anything about gender-linked patterns. I assumed, however, that our contrasting notions of politeness reflected not our genders but rather our cultural backgrounds: Greek and American, respectively.

The year of that crucial institute, 1973, was also the year Lakoff published two influential essays: "Language and Woman's Place" and "The Logic of Politeness" (Lakoff 1973a, 1973b). Scholars in English departments refer to "the linguistic turn" whereby some literary theorists began to borrow terms, concepts, and perspectives from our field. In the 1960s and early 1970s, a different kind of "turn" was taking place in linguistics—a turn of attention by some to the language of everyday conversation. And Lakoff's work, as reflected in these two essays and in her 1975 book *Language and Woman's Place* (*LWP*), played an enormous role in accomplishing that turn. Furthermore, just as an understanding of phonology, morphology, syntax, and semantics is enhanced by comparing those elements in vastly different languages, so also is an understanding of the pragmatics

159

of politeness enhanced by cross-language comparison (see Ide, this volume). In *LWP*, Lakoff uses cross-cultural encounters to explain her rules of politeness:

> Consider what happens when an American, a German, and a Japanese meet. Suppose they all want to make a good impression and to be "polite" according to their own standards. Chances are, unless the members of the group are very sophisticated and have had prior exposure to the other cultures, the American will seem to the others overly brash, familiar, and prying; the Japanese will seem cloyingly deferential; the German will seem distant and uninterested in the others to the point of arrogance. (*LWP* 91–92)

Lakoff goes on to explain that the impressions made by individuals can become the basis for national stereotypes when generalized to the entire group of which the individuals are members:

> Americans are "too personal"; Japanese are "too humble"; Germans are "too stiff." Actually, what is happening is that each is conforming to a cultural stereotype of what constitutes polite behavior toward a slight acquaintance. At this stage of a relationship, a German will emphasize Rule 1, a Japanese Rule 2, and an American Rule 3. (These are of course the stereotypical norms; there are plenty of participants in these cultures whose rule application, for various idiosyncratic reasons, is different.) (*LWP* 92)

This is the sense in which Lakoff's rules of politeness, and her related notion of communicative style, were revelatory to me: their explanatory power to shed light on everyday interaction, especially interactions that could be called cross-cultural. No doubt, part of my visceral response was my personal experience in a cross-cultural marriage as well as the more general experience of having lived in Greece and taught English as a second language there. (Our personal experiences often — perhaps always — play a role in our choice of research topics, although we rarely acknowledge this in our academic writing).

I enrolled in graduate school at the University of California at Berkeley, because that's where Lakoff taught. But once there, I discovered other faculty members whose perspectives shaped my thinking about language. One whose work dovetailed particularly elegantly with Lakoff's was John Gumperz. During those key years, the early 1970s, Gumperz was developing his theory of conversational inference based on the analysis of everyday conversations among speakers of British English and speakers of Indian English in London. Gumperz focused on how culturally variable contextualization cues signal the speech activity to which utterances contribute. Lakoff's theory of communicative style provided a way to characterize the interactional goals (distance, deference, and camaraderie) that motivate patterns of contextualization cues. Drawing on both these conceptual frameworks, I focused my own research on "the processes and consequences of conversational style" (as my dissertation was titled) in everyday conversations, especially those among friends and intimates.

Thus my interest in conversational style focused not on gender but on regional differences. Again I had a personal motivation: as a native of Brooklyn, New York, of East European Jewish background, I was experiencing culture shock in northern California. In New York City I had been regarded as so diffident, polite, and indirect that one friend habitually referred to me as a WASP. In California I was surprised and hurt to realize that I was sometimes perceived as aggressive and even rude. For example, in New York City if you are in a department store and you want to ask a quick question such as "Where is the ladies' room?" it is perfectly acceptable — indeed, unmarked — to interrupt an ongoing service encounter to do so. It would be unacceptably rude for a salesperson to expect you to wait while she finishes a lengthy interchange, when you only need a brief moment of her time to answer a question. But in Berkeley, my ever-so-polite, deferentially high-pitched "Excuse me, could I just interrupt to ask where the ladies' room is, please?" was met with an obviously annoyed "I'll help you when I'm finished with this customer." Clearly, the ladies'-room query, which in New York City came under Rule 3, *Maintain camaraderie*, was regarded in California as governed by Rule 1, *Don't impose*.

I figured out these contrasts, reassured myself that I was still a good person, and developed my notion of conversational style in writing my dissertation. I investigated the conversational style differences among six friends at a Thanksgiving dinner: three natives of New York City of Eastern European Jewish background (I was one); two southern California natives of Christian background; and one woman who had grown up in London, England. I found that three speakers (the New Yorkers) shared what I called a "high-involvement style" characterized by such Rule 3 (*Maintain camaraderie*) strategies as overlapping another speaker's talk to show enthusiasm, which was often interpreted as interruption by the three who shared what I called a "high-considerateness style," governed by Rule 1 (*Don't impose*). In other words, one style shows good intentions by emphasizing interpersonal involvement, whereas the other shows good intentions by emphasizing social distance. In doing the analysis for this study, I tried to explain how conversational style accounts for what goes on in all conversations, as well as to explain cross-cultural differences based on ethnic and regional background. I did not focus my analysis on the gender of the speakers (although I did take into account their sexual orientation, as three of the four men at the dinner were gay).

When I joined the faculty of the linguistics department at Georgetown University in 1979, my colleague Muriel Saville-Troike suggested I offer a course on gender and language. I unhesitatingly rejected the idea on the grounds that neither my expertise nor my interests prepared me to teach such a course. I was in fact slightly offended, certain that she would never have asked this question had I been male. (At the time—and continuing for more than a decade—I was one of only two women in the eighteen–member department). In contrast, when Saville-Troike left Georgetown the next year, I eagerly assumed responsibility for a new course she had proposed but had not yet taught: "Cross-Cultural Communication." That course, which I came to regard as my signature course, led to my first general-audience book, *That's Not What I Meant!* (Tannen 1986).

In that book I mention five social categories that affect conversational style, which I still think of as the "Big Five": geographic or regional background, ethnicity, age, class, and gender. (There are, of course, many others, including sexual orientation and profession.) In order to cover these areas as best I could, and to reflect my abiding interest in how ways of talking affect close relationships, I included a chapter entitled "Talk in the Intimate Relationship: His and Hers," in which I combined the framework Lakoff had laid out in *LWP* with the perspective of a paper by anthropologists Daniel Maltz and Ruth Borker (1982) titled "A Cultural Approach to Male-Female Miscommunication." Maltz and Borker drew on Gumperz's framework of cross-culturally variable contextualization cues to integrate and explain a broad range of findings in the field of language and gender. They used the term *cultural* as a metaphorical way to represent the pattern they had discerned in the seemingly unrelated findings reported by such researchers as Marjorie Harness Goodwin (1980a, 1980b), Candace West (1979; West & Zimmerman 1977), Pamela Fishman (1978), and Lynette Hirschman ([1973] 1994). That pattern, Maltz and Borker showed, could be traced to ways of using language that girls and boys learn as children at play in sex-separate groups (see Cook-Gumperz, this volume)—this is the sense in which women and men grow up in "different cultures."

My own contribution (Tannen 1982) to the volume in which Maltz and Borker's article appeared, based on my master's thesis, addressed the issue of cultural patterning in the use of directness and indirectness. Once again I presented a conversation between Wife and Husband but did not examine the speakers' verbalizations in relation to their gender. I did, however, home in on the cultural patterning, comparing the responses of Greeks, Americans, and Greek Americans.

I have presented this personal account to show why I believe that Lakoff's work on language and gender is grounded in her notion of communicative style, which is inseparable from the notion that rules of politeness are learned in cultural context. I would like to make one more point about why I believe the influence of culture is embedded in *LWP*. Lakoff's work on language and gender grew out of a concern for social justice that was so much a part of the zeitgeist that accompanied and inspired the turn in linguistics and related fields to the language of everyday conversation. For example, William Labov's *Language in the Inner City* (1972) was grounded in and grew out of a concern for the civil—and linguistic—rights of speakers of Black English Vernacular (now called African American Vernacular English). Similarly, Gumperz's (1977) studies of mismatched contextualization cues between speakers of Indian English and British English were fundamentally aimed at addressing pervasive discrimination against South Asians living in London. A similar concern can be seen in Erickson's (1975) analyses of culturally relative patterns of listener response to explain why counseling interviews produced better results for students who shared a cultural background with their school counselors. In all these and many other studies of language and language use in the late 1960s and early 1970s, the revolution in linguistics that turned attention to the language of everyday conversation, of which Lakoff was both a part and an inspiration, was inseparable from the drive to right social wrongs and empower members of socially disadvantaged groups.

In this spirit, Lakoff's pioneering attention to the topic of language and gender was very much motivated by the women's movement, which was beginning to make visible the many ways that women were relegated to second-class citizenship. *LWP*, as Lakoff makes explicit in her introduction, "is an attempt to provide diagnostic evidence from language use for one type of inequity that has been claimed to exist in our society: that between the roles of men and women" (*LWP* 39). She closes the book, moreover, by concluding that "the kinds of 'politeness' used by and of and to women do not arise by accident; that they are, indeed, stifling, exclusive, and oppressive." Finally, she expresses her hope that "this book will be one small first step in the direction of a wider option of life styles, for men and women" (*LWP* 102).

Remembering that Lakoff's examination of gender and language was part of the activist 1960s and 1970s, an era in which many of us tried to do our part in seeking social justice, is inextricable from locating the notion of culture in *LWP*. Remembering this is also essential to understanding why so many, myself included, found the book so necessary, so motivating, so inspiring to our own work.

REFERENCES

Erickson, Frederick (1975). Gatekeeping and the melting pot: Interaction in counseling encounters. *Harvard Educational Review* 45:44–70.
Fishman, Pamela M. (1978). Interaction: The work women do. *Social Problems* 25:397–406.
Goodwin, Marjorie Harness (1980a). Directive-response speech sequences in girls' and boys' task activities. In Sally McConnell-Ginet, Ruth Borker, &

Nelly Furman (eds.), *Women and language in literature and society.* New York: Praeger. 157–173.

—— (1980b). He-said-she-said: Formal cultural procedures for the construction of a gossip dispute activity. *American Ethnologist* 7:674–695.

Gumperz, John (1977). Sociocultural knowledge in conversational inference. In Muriel Saville-Troike (ed.), *Linguistics and anthropology: Georgetown University Round Table on Languages and Linguistics 1977.* Washington, DC: Georgetown University Press. 191–211.

Hirschman, Lynette ([1973] 1994). Female-male differences in conversational interaction. *Language in Society* 23:427–442.

Labov, William (1972). *Language in the inner city: Studies in the Black English Vernacular.* Philadelphia: University of Pennsylvania Press.

Lakoff, Robin (1973a). Language and woman's place. *Language in Society* 2:45–80.

—— (1973b). The logic of politeness, or minding your p's and q's. In Claudia Corum, T. Cedric Smith-Stark, & Ann Weiser (eds.), *Papers from the Ninth Regional Meeting of the Chicago Linguistics Society.* Chicago: University of Chicago Department of Linguistics. 292–305.

Lakoff, Robin (1975). *Language and woman's place.* New York: Harper & Row.

Maltz, Daniel N., & Ruth A. Borker (1982). A cultural approach to male-female miscommunication. In John J. Gumperz (ed.), *Language and social identity.* Cambridge: Cambridge University Press. 196–216.

Tannen, Deborah (1975). Communication mix and mixup, or how linguistics can ruin a marriage. Michael Noonan (ed.), *San Jose State Occasional Papers in Linguistics.* Vol. 1. San Jose, CA: San Jose State University Department of Linguistics. 205–211.

—— (1982). Ethnic style in male-female conversation. In John J. Gumperz (ed.), *Language and social identity.* Cambridge: Cambridge University Press. 217–231.

—— (1986). *That's not what I meant! How conversational style makes or breaks relationships.* New York: Ballantine.

West, Candace (1979). Against our will: Male interruption of females in cross-sex conversation. In Judith Orasanu, Mariam Slater, & Leonore Loeb Adler (eds.), *Language, sex and gender. Annals of the New York Academy of Science* 327:81–100.

West, Candace, & Don H. Zimmerman (1977). Women's place in everyday talk: Reflections on parent-child interaction. *Social Problems* 24:521–529.

# 7 ⠶

# The Good Woman

PENELOPE ECKERT

So who is this woman who inhabits the pages of *Language and Woman's Place*? Is she me? Is she women? Clearly not. She is an ideological artifact—a stereotype. And what makes the book important is that this stereotype is there to invoke. It is not a stereotype of women, but of a particular kind of woman—a woman who strives to be refined and superpolite, who mitigates her stances and exaggerates positive affect. The simple existence of that kind of woman at one end of the array of kinds of woman one can be is definitional—it is the main thing that makes women different from men.

The years following the publication of Robin Lakoff's *Language and Women's Place* (LWP) (1975) saw an energetic search for differences in speech between women as a group and men as a group. And on a good day, these differences were viewed as emerging from the power relations that constitute the gender order. In recent years, as the status of the gender binary itself has taken center stage, an emphasis has moved from homogeneity to diversity. Attention has moved from the opposition created by the binary to its territories—to the borders and to the insides of the two categories. Gender is viewed as performed and sought in differences not between women as a group and men as a group, but in the differences among women and among men. What are the constraints on being a woman or a man? What kinds of women and men are there, and what can each get away with? Lakoff's woman dominates the female array. She is the target of our socialization (that is, of others' socialization of us), as she is the target presented on Melanie Phillips's (2003) transgender support Web site. Lakoff's female speaker is the quintessential "good woman"—the "good girl" grown up and wearing a hat. Those of us who aren't that woman (indeed, most of us) are aware of her. She dominates with all the power of the hegemonic. We comment on her. We joke about her. And as girls, we anticipate being her (see also Cook-Gumperz, this volume).

When I was a child, I didn't want to grow up because I thought I'd have to dress up, take care of children, and be offended by dirty jokes. I didn't think I would be able to succeed at becoming a "good woman."

Indeed, I never did succeed for lack of trying. Early in my recent fieldwork in a northern California elementary school, I saw this girlhood misgiving about adulthood from the other side. One of the girls in a group of fifth graders I was hanging out with interrupted a dirty joke to tell me not to listen: "Married women don't like dirty jokes." Fancy that—excluded from one of my favorite speech activities because my civil status has transformed me into a prude. When I asked her how she knew, she wasn't sure. And she was glad to learn that it wasn't true—that she would still be able to enjoy dirty jokes as an adult even if she got married. We didn't discuss how she felt about taking care of children.

And speaking of children, while public humor is full of jokes about men and babies (e.g., the recent Volkswagen ad in which a father furtively uses his baby's diapered bottom to wipe a drop of water off his treasured Passat), I have seen none about women. The same ad but with a mother hasn't made it onto the screen, although I'm sure it would get a laugh from a lot of women. You don't frequently hear jokes about women being bored or annoyed with baby care, finding clever shortcuts or diversions, or maybe parking their babies in clever ways so they can head out to hang with the girls. One might expect to hear it from a female comedian, most likely in a predominantly female audience. Not a very common speech situation. Come to think of it, another ad in the same series depicts a man in a car dealership lot standing by the vehicle of his choice and watching a salesman with two clients moving toward it with the apparent intention of making a deal. In a canine move, the man leans over and licks the door handle. Could this ad have featured a woman licking the door handle? Certainly the good woman in a hat wouldn't lick a door handle. Which woman would? Do women not covet automobiles? Or perhaps they simply can't make territorial moves with impunity—and certainly not *silly* territorial moves.

It may appear that I have digressed, but I don't think I have. However silly we may find the good woman, she certainly does not *act* silly. In my ethnography following kids from childhood to adolescence (Eckert 1996), I've seen girls learning not to act silly. Little girls and boys run around, play games, roll in the dirt, act silly, look for excitement. But something happens as they move toward adolescence. Silliness, along with serious sports, open competition, and roughhousing, becomes boys' prerogative. Sixth-grade boys can run and tumble, have funny walks, make funny faces. They can wiggle their butts while at the pencil sharpener, they can wave their hands wildly and shout "I know! I know!" when the teacher asks a question. And once called on, they can grin mischievously and say "I forget." And when they do, they may enhance their status. Sixth-grade girls who do these things are branded as immature. Girls can't be class clowns. If girls want to do fun things, they can try on cosmetics, false fingernails, and sexy clothes. When the class sits on the floor so the teacher can read to them, they can do each other's hair. If they want excitement, they can't whiz around on their bikes or roughhouse without being tomboys—which they're too old for. But they can engineer relationships and create social drama. This is not a temporary condition. I have been told on good authority that undergraduate women at Stanford also feel constrained to leave joke making in the classroom to the men. The good woman is not a jokester. She does not bend meaning. A female stand-up comic is odd. She may get away with catty humor or with aping "good-woman" traits. Very few women have made it being raunchy or doing social commentary.

The key idea in *LWP* is not in the details of how women as a whole speak but in the elaboration of the relation between language use and hegemonic womanhood (see also Mendoza-Denton, this volume). Central to this relationship is the claim that how women speak matters a hell of a lot: "A woman's reputation and position in society depend *almost wholly* on the impression she makes upon others" (*LWP* 57; emphasis added). A man's value on the market is based on what he does and what he has, while a woman's value is based on what she is. In other words, women's influence depends primarily on the accumulation of symbolic capital (Bourdieu 1977), the painstaking creation and elaboration of a worthy self. While men can justify and define their status on the basis of their accomplishments, possessions, or institutional roles, women must justify and define theirs on the basis of their overall character and the kinds of relations they can maintain with others. I have said elsewhere (Eckert 1990a) that as a result, women, unlike men, are inclined to be preoccupied with being the perfect teacher, the perfect parent, the perfect spouse. Men *do* things; women *be* things. Women are expected to be a particular kind of person—to perfect not their skills or their actions, but their *selves*.

It seems perfectly natural, then, that women also *are* symbolic capital. The trophy wife and the first lady serve to enhance the images of their husbands. And however much they may accomplish this work, they will be viewed as "pretenders" for working purely in the symbolic. They will be seen as concerned with status itself rather than with the content of status. Consider the traditional stay-at-home wife of a professional, ambitious for her husband's advancement. Unable to do the actual work that will win his advancement (unless she's doing it behind the scenes), she can focus only on her support role—on the domestic trappings of advancement and on the goal of advancement itself. Her husband, however, can appear to be primarily engaged in "real things"—in the work itself, of which status is merely a byproduct.

This role follows many women into the workplace, where their job success depends to a great extent on enhancing the images of their companies—the elegant secretary, the friendly and efficient flight attendant,[1] the inviting receptionist. Women commonly occupy jobs whose primary function is to serve as the firm's face to the public. And even in situations in which women are expected to show the same skills as men, they are expected to do it differently. Qing Zhang's (2001) study of Beijing yuppies is a case in point. Managers in foreign-owned financial businesses are expected to project a sophisticated, cosmopolitan image. But women and men do so quite differently. Men tend to use a style that has a tinge of the "wheeler-dealer" in it, using a few Beijing phonological features that give their speech what is commonly referred to as an "oily" style. Women, in contrast, use a crisp deterritorialized style, eschewing stereotypical Beijing features and adopting a tone feature characteristic of nonmainland dialects of Chinese. A female wheeler-dealer will not do, but a worldly and efficient woman will. Similarly, Bonnie McElhinny (1992) found female police officers constructing an acceptably gendered police persona that emphasizes administrative competence. In other words, not only is the decorative woman standard-speaking, so is the competent woman.

There is indeed plenty of evidence that on the whole, women's grammar (but not their phonology) is more standard than men's. Probably the most consistent demonstration of this is in Walt Wolfram's (1969) study of Detroit speakers. Peter Trudgill (1972) was the first variationist sociolinguist to attribute women's standardness to lack of access to the marketplace, arguing that women's relative lack of access to advancement through actions in the marketplace constrains them to seek advancement through symbolic means. If we consider the kinds of jobs that are available to women and the importance of the good woman in our cultural discourse, this makes perfect sense. But it is not the whole story. Not all women are proper. And the nature of their lack of propriety is crucial. In my study of a Detroit suburban high school (Eckert 2000), the individuals who used the most negative concord (multiple negation, as in *I didn't do nothing*) in their entire age cohort were girls. But they weren't just any girls—they were wild girls. Bad girls. Girls who prided themselves on being the "biggest burnouts." Take any linguistic resource for doing "urban" or "tough," and these girls used it more than anyone else in their cohort, female or male. We find other such crossovers in comparisons of women and men of similar status (e.g., Labov 1991). At the upper end of the status hierarchy, women use more standard grammar than men; at the lower end, women use more nonstandard grammar than men. While my colleagues are all pretty comfortable with the former observation, some tend to ignore the latter, or at least to consider it problematic. If we have an across-the-board assumption that women as a group are essentially proper, the data face us with a paradox. But if we assume, like Lakoff, that the primary difference is that women are scrutinized on the basis of appearances, we have only to ask what appearances women are trying to achieve. Sally McConnell-Ginet and I have argued elsewhere (Eckert and McConnell-Ginet 1995) that women are continually called on to establish their authenticity. If a girl wants to be bad, she has to do Very Bad. If a woman wants to show that she is a loyal working-class woman, she has to do Very Working-Class. And if she wants to show that she is a competent administrator, she has to do

Very Competent Administrator. The linguistic resources she exaggerates in these performances will depend on the nature of the performances.

Arguments about whether the gender differences implied by Lakoff's portrayal of the good woman actually exist are almost beside the point. I have been quite happy to argue that women's speech is not as conservative as is commonly thought (Eckert 1990b). But the fact that many women speak "badder" than men is perfectly consistent—even superconsistent— with the good-woman construct. The good woman is a white, middle-class, feminine ideal, and however particular women speak, they do it against the backdrop of this ideal.

NOTE

1. See, for example, Hochschild 1983 for a discussion of the extent to which flight attendants' lives are dominated by the need to manage affect for the sake of the airline's image as safe.

REFERENCES

Bourdieu, Pierre (1977). The economics of linguistic exchanges. *Social Science Information* 16:645–668.
Eckert, Penelope (1990a). Cooperative competition in adolescent girl talk. *Discourse Processes* 13:92–122.
——— (1990b). The whole woman: Sex and gender differences in variation. *Language Variation and Change* 1:245–267.
——— (1996). Vowels and nailpolish: The emergence of linguistic style in the preadolescent heterosexual marketplace. In Jocelyn Ahlers, Natasha Warner, Leela Bilmes, Monica Oliver, Suzanne Wertheim, and Melinda Chen (eds.), *Gender and belief systems: Proceedings of the fourth Berkeley Women and Language Conference.* Berkeley, CA: Berkeley Women and Language Group. 183–190.
——— (2000). *Linguistic variation as social practice.* Oxford: Blackwell.
Eckert, Penelope, and Sally McConnell-Ginet (1995). Constructing meaning, constructing selves: Snapshots of language, gender, and class from Belten High. In Kira Hall & Mary Bucholtz (eds.), *Gender articulated: Language and the culturally constructed self.* London: Routledge. 469–507.
Hochschild, Arlie (1983). *The managed heart: Commercialization of human feeling.* Berkeley: University of California Press.
Labov, William (1991). The intersection of sex and social class in the course of linguistic change. *Language Variation and Change* 2:205–251.
Lakoff, Robin (1975). *Language and woman's place.* New York: Harper & Row.
McElhinny, Bonnie S. (1992). "I don't smile much anymore": Affect, gender, and the discourse of Pittsburgh police officers. In Kira Hall, Mary Bucholtz, & Birch Moonwomon (eds.), *Locating power: Proceedings of the sec-*

*ond Berkeley women and language conference.* Berkeley, CA: Berkeley Women and Language Group. 386–403.

Phillips, Melanie Anne (2003). How to develop a female voice. Transgender Support Site, http://www.heartcorps.com/journeys/voice.htm (accessed March 5, 2004).

Trudgill, Peter (1972). Sex, covert prestige, and linguistic change in the urban British English of Norwich. *Language in Society* 1:179–195.

Wolfram, Walt (1969). *A sociolinguistic description of Detroit Negro speech.* Washington, DC: Center for Applied Linguistics.

Zhang, Qing (2001). Changing economics, changing markets: A sociolinguistic study of Chinese yuppies. PhD diss., Stanford University.

# 8 ::

# Language and Marginalized Places

KIRA HALL

In the early 1990s, the field of language and gender began to shift to what many scholars now identify as an ideological understanding of linguistic gender. This perspective views the "women's language" and "men's language" of previous generations not as indexically bound to the sex of the speaker, but as culturally and socially produced beliefs that are available for consumption, negotiation, and contestation (Gal 1991). Just when feminist linguistics had declared the death of Robin Lakoff's (1975) "women's language" — construing it as an inherently essentialist entity that could be neither verified empirically nor observed interactively — it suddenly sprang back to life with new vitality. When reread through the lens of ideology, Lakoffian "women's language" was liberated from the taint of essentialist thinking. With "women's language" redefined as the patterns of speaking ideologically associated with women and hence femininity, the field moved its focus from sex differentiation to gender negotiation, observing how speakers incorporate the complex interplay of global and local understandings of gendered talk into everyday identity positioning.

Certainly, Lakoff did not have the benefit of the term *ideology* when she was writing *Language and Woman's Place* (LWP); it was only when American sociologists began to engage more directly with Marxist theory in the 1980s that the term began to gain widespread currency in the social sciences. But Lakoff's repeated characterization of "women's language" throughout her text as a stereotype — perpetuated in the media, differentially marketed to women and men, and available for consumption by both — in many ways predicts, if not predates, the poststructuralist focus on the symbolic nature of discourse. In several senses, her writings provide a gendered counterpoint to Pierre Bourdieu's (1991) work on symbolic domination, for she fleshes out the ways in which women, as a subjugated class, come to accept the inferiority of a discursively produced "women's language." This nonstandard variety — the representation of which, according to Lakoff, reached its pinnacle in the 1970s through television portrayals of characters like the self-deprecating housewife Edith Bunker — becomes symbolic of women's everyday marginalization from male workplaces and hence potentially emblematic of women's social and economic insecurity. Socialized into the double bind of a society that expects women to use certain patterns of speaking while at the same time deeming those very patterns inferior, women are kept in their place, as it were, segregated both physically and linguistically from institutionalized power structures.

Thus, Lakoff's "women's language" is ultimately about power, not gender. Reworking for linguistics the gendered-division-of-labor arguments that became prominent in feminism and anthropology, Lakoff offers an explanation for how certain styles of speaking, through their association with institutionalized masculinity, come to be associated with power. This is undoubtedly why the political style of President George H. W. Bush caught her attention in the late 1980s. Lakoff (1990) suggests that Bush, in order to win the respect and confidence of his American audience, went through a linguistic "sex change" during his campaign for the presidency. While Bush's speech patterns at the beginning of his public career were consistent with the linguistic stereotype of women's language (replete with incomplete sentences and speech acts, lexical hedges, and even the occasional giggle), by the time of his election he had learned to project a masculine, and hence more powerful, gender. After months of training by speech writers and image consultants, Bush was finally able to turn into the nation's quintessential male, catering to cultural expectations of gender-appropriate speech and performing a linguistic masculinity. It is certainly no coincidence that the early 1990s "Drag-King-for-a-Day" workshop in New York City adopted the new President Bush as its transgendered hero (Bell 1993). Lakoff's notion of "women's language" and "men's language" as construed within relations of power also had application for my work on transgendered *hijras* in northern India. In their self-identification as neither man nor woman, *hijras* exploit ideologies of feminine and masculine speech in establishing egalitarian and hierarchical relations, respectively (Hall & O'Donovan 1996).

One of my purposes in writing this essay, then, is to question the way in which scholars have essentialized the writings of various pioneers in the field in order to pattern a neat delineation of theoretical perspectives, from "deficit" to "dominance" to "difference" to "discourse." While such categorizations are no doubt useful to an understanding of the development of a scholarly field (not to mention an indispensable teaching tool), they also work to canonize inaccurate representations of earlier scholarship, particularly when bits and pieces of much larger works are used in the service of distinguishing mutually exclusive standpoints. Deborah Cameron, for instance, who has provided us with some of the most provocative and insightful reviews of the field, has also represented Lakoff's work in a way that is not borne out by the text: "Both [Lakoff and Tannen] assume that 'women's language' is, in essence, the language characteristically used by women. A presupposition here is that the 'women' pre-exist the 'language'. 'Women's language' is the language of subjects who are already, definitively, women" (1997: 27). But this is not the assumption that guides Lakoff's work. It is easy to misinterpret Lakoff's text in today's academic climate, rooted as it is in discourses of the early 1970s feminist movement as well as in the prevailing political and theoretical perspectives of the time (see also Bucholtz and McElhinny, both this volume). While Lakoff suggests that women, as a result of their socialization into normative femininity, are perhaps more likely to use the indirect forms of speech that have come to index powerlessness, she is quick to point out that such forms can also be appropriated by men, particularly those who wish to index disenfranchise-ment from male realms of power. She presents these acts of linguistic defiance together with the situation by which certain men, as a result of class positioning or other societal considerations (read: George H. W. Bush), are socialized along with women into using linguistic features consistent with "women's language." Moreover, Lakoff acknowledges not only that many women do not use stereotyped "women's language" (e.g., "It is equally true that different women speak women's language to differing extents; and interestingly enough, it seems that academic women are among the least apt to be speakers of this language" [*LWP* 82]), but also that the employment of this variety is entirely dependent on diverse contextual factors and thus cannot be tested experimentally (e.g., "one can judge whether something is 'women's language,' 'men's language,' or 'neutral' only with reference to the real-world context in which it was uttered — a complex and subtle combination of judgments that would be virtually impossible to reproduce in a natural way in an experimental situation" [*LWP* 83]).

It is the piecemeal representation of Lakoff's work by subsequent critics, reiterated and canonized for academic consumption in anthologies and field reviews, that turned *LWP* into old-school essentialism, not the text itself. In contrast to early anthropology's exoticizing representations of "women's languages" and "men's languages" as mutually exclusive entities (Trechter 1999; Hall 2003), Lakoff allowed for much more linguistic variability with respect to the relationship between the biological and social worlds, establishing a new way of conceptualizing gender, language, and marginality. Scholars who have read her work as being concerned only with women's patterns of speaking continue to ignore her rather extensive discussions of a variety of other social groups who also make use of "women's language," among them the effeminate homosexual, the anti-capitalist hippie, and the effete male professor. Because Lakoff is interested in the socializing forces that produce an asymmetry in the way women and men speak, she tests her theoretical argument with reference to the speakers who are in some way tangential to this socialization. For Lakoff, women have much in common with homosexuals, hippies, and academics: specifically, all of these identities share a marginality determined by their exclusion from institutionalized male power.

Central to Lakoff's explanation for this shared marginality is the gendered division of labor, and more specifically, the divergent ways of speaking brought about by this division. This concern prompts her to devote several pages of her discussion to Lionel Tiger's *Men in Groups* (1969). Like many physical anthropologists of his era, Tiger supports the explanatory power of a "man-the-hunter" model of human evolution, which holds that the evolution of male-dominant human societies was initiated by cooperative male hunting, a sex-based behavior observed in primates and supposed to have existed in primitive human communities. For Tiger, this evolutionary argument is the key to understanding the concept for which he is most well known: male bonding in human societies. While primitive females stayed behind with their young and made decisions primarily in an individual capacity, males were forced by the circumstances of labor to develop a group mentality. Because the hunt would be successful only if hunters found ways to cooperate with one another, primitive males, unlike their female counterparts, began to develop interactive techniques to enhance group enjoyment and minimize personal friction. These interactive techniques, according to Tiger, find their modern-day realization in human male-bonding rituals.

Scores of articles written by feminist anthropologists subsequently challenged the man-the-hunter model of human evolution, including a female-focused model of human evolution often referred to as the "woman-the-gatherer" challenge (see overview in di Leonardo 1991), a perspective that allows for the possibility of some kind of group mentality for women as well. But Lakoff did not have the benefit of these critiques, writing as she was in the early 1970s, and she embraces Tiger's evolutionary discussion of male bonding as one way of explaining women's and men's differential orientations to politeness. Women, excluded from a male workplace built on "present-day reflexes of male bonding" (*LWP* 97) tend to orient themselves to politeness forms that discourage bonding, gravitating toward the first two rules of Lakoff's politeness paradigm: Formality (*Keep aloof*) and Deference (*Give options*). Men, however, as a result of their socialization within workplace situations that require them to develop techniques of working together as a group, are more likely to embrace Lakoff's third rule of politeness: Camaraderie (*Show sympathy*). The latter rule would be essential in, for example, a male-dominated corporate workplace, as group members must develop interactive measures to gloss over emotional reactions and disagreements that might hinder progress toward a common goal. These are measures women have generally not needed to develop, Lakoff suggests, since they have historically been excluded from such group-oriented work environments.

The notion of a masculine workplace, then, is fundamental to Lakoff's theoretical explanation for women's and men's differential use of linguistic phenomena. This explains why hippies, academic men, and homosexuals are central figures of Lakoff's text as problematized gender identities (*LWP* 44–47). Like women, these groups are in some way excluded from a social history of male bonding in the labor force, and as with women, this exclusion leads to language patterns disassociated from what Lakoff terms "real-world power" (*LWP* 82). Male hippies, male academics, and male homosexuals are all in some sense gender deviants— social groups who have forsaken a capitalistic power structure built on masculine ideals for pursuits considered trivial in the "real world." This would explain, suggests Lakoff, why the language patterns of hippie, academic, or homosexual so often appear to resemble those of the American middle-class housewife. That these disenfranchised groups are likely to use some of the same specialized lexical items as American middle-class women, she argues, points to a more general conclusion: "These words aren't, basically, 'feminine'; rather, they signal 'uninvolved,' or 'out of power'" (*LWP* 47). While certain patterns of speech may be considered feminine because women are, in her own terms, the "'uninvolved,' 'out of power' group *par excellence*" (*LWP* 47), Lakoff is careful to note that any group in society may presumably use patterns associated with "women's language" (an observation that best explains her regular use of scare quotes around the term). For Lakoff, then, it is the feminine-sounding man, marginal to the world of institutionalized masculinity, who ultimately enables her to formulate the crux of her argument: "The decisive factor is less purely gender than power in the real world" (*LWP* 81).

In spite of their centrality to Lakoff's theory, these marginal figures have been frequently, if not entirely, overlooked in subsequent discussions of her work. The majority of her critics, swept up in an imperative to test her argument quantitatively, interpreted Lakoffian "women's language" to be only about women, developing study upon study to determine whether or not female speakers actually use "women's language" more than their male counterparts (e.g., Crosby & Nyquist 1977; O'Barr & Atkins 1980). What is amusing, in retrospect, is that a great number of these studies analyze the speech patterns of the very academics that Lakoff identifies as linguistically divergent (e.g., Dubois & Crouch 1975; cf. Newcombe & Arnkoff 1979). The continued misreading of Lakoff's work undoubtedly stems from her decision to name this speech variety the scare-quoted "women's language" instead of "powerless language"—the term William O'Barr and Bowman K. Atkins (1980) suggest as an alternative. But this decision, in tune with the radical feminist ideas of the time, was clearly as academically provocative as it was politically savvy, spawning three decades of impassioned uptake.

The ideological approach to language and gender has been said to offer a new understanding of the relationship between biological sex and social gender, whereby gender is not bound to sex in any precise and predictable way. As in Judith Butler's (1990) theory of gender performativity, it is in fact social gender that creates biological sex and not the other way around, for societal discourses about gender make certain aspects of biology salient in the service of differentiation and hierarchy. While Lakoff is often held up as the naïve precursor to this perspective who blindly assumes a direct mapping of gender onto biological sex, her writings reveal something altogether different. The marginalized characters in Lakoff's book use "women's language" not so that they can be heard as women (as might be the case, for instance, with some male-to-female transsexuals whose goal is to "pass" as the other sex), but to signal various kinds of disengagement from institutionalized masculinity. Lakoff's understanding of marginality is contingent on what Elinor Ochs (1992) calls the "constitutive relation" between language and gender. For both authors, the relation between linguistic form and social meaning is not a simple or straightforward mapping; rather, linguistic forms index a variety of social meanings (disenfranchisement, formality, deference, powerlessness) which in turn constitute gender positions (e.g., femininity).

Indeed, in attending to the ways in which institutions of power promote certain types of discourse while demoting others, Lakoff predicts many of the concerns of queer linguistics (Barrett 1997; Bucholtz & Hall 2004; Livia & Hall 1997) — a field that explicitly questions the assumption that gendered ways of talking are indexically derived from the sex of the speaker (see also Barrett, this volume). In this related and still evolving field, the power-laden institution under primary examination is not masculinity but heterosexuality — an institution that maintains its integrity by excluding (and hence "queering") social subjects whose lives are not authorized by state-sanctioned structures of kinship, marriage, and family. But because heterosexuality is dependent on normative conceptualizations of both femininity and masculinity for its articulation, ideologies of "women's speech" and "men's speech" are very much at issue in both in-group and out-group expressions of queer subjectivity. Lakoff's definition of "women's language," unabashedly bound up with a variety of social groups rarely discussed in linguistic literature, set into motion a fervor of academic interest in language, power, and marginality. It is a testament to Lakoff's work that the social groups she once identified as linguistically marginalized are now being studied ethnographically in their own right, as members of localized communities whose "place" is continuously negotiated through language practice.

NOTE

Some of the ideas expressed in this essay appear in slightly different form in Hall 2003 as part of a more comprehensive discussion of the concept of marginality in language and gender research. I am grateful to Mary Bucholtz for helping me recontextualize that discussion for the current volume. I would also like to express my gratitude to my advisor and mentor Robin Lakoff, who inspired my own work in ways I can only hint at here.

REFERENCES

Barrett, Rusty (1997). The "homo-genius" speech community. In Anna Livia & Kira Hall (eds.), *Queerly phrased: Language, gender, and sexuality*. New York: Oxford University Press. 181–201.

Bell, Shannon (1993). Finding the male within and taking him cruising: Drag-king-for-a-day at the Sprinkle Salon. In Arthur & Marilouise Kroker (eds.), *The last sex: Feminism and outlaw bodies*. New York: St. Martin's. 91–97.

Bourdieu, Pierre (1991). *Language and symbolic power*. Cambridge, MA: Harvard University Press.

Bucholtz, Mary, & Kira Hall (2004). Theorizing identity in language and sexuality research. *Language in Society* 33.

Butler, Judith (1990). *Gender trouble*. New York: Routledge.

Crosby, Faye, & Linda Nyquist (1977). The female register: An empirical study of Lakoff's hypotheses. *Language in Society* 6:313–322.

di Leonardo, Micaela (1991). Introduction: Gender, culture, and political economy: Feminist anthropology in historical perspective. In Micaela di Leonardo (ed.), *Gender at the crossroads of knowledge: Feminist anthropology in the modern era*. Berkeley: University of California Press. 1–48.

Dubois, Betty Lou, & Isabel Crouch (1975). The question of tag questions in women's speech: They don't really use more of them, do they? *Language in Society* 4:289–294.

Gal, Susan (1991). Between speech and silence: The problematic of research on language and gender. In Micaela di Leonardo (ed.), *Gender at the crossroads of knowledge: Feminist anthropology in the modern era*. Berkeley: University of California Press. 175–203.

Hall, Kira (2003). Exceptional speakers: Contested and problematized gender identities. In Miriam Meyerhoff & Janet Holmes (eds.), *Handbook of language and gender*. Malden, MA: Blackwell. 353–380.

Hall, Kira, & Veronica O'Donovan (1996). Shifting gender positions among Hindi-speaking hijras. In Victoria L. Bergvall, Janet M. Bing, & Alice F. Freed (eds.), *Rethinking language and gender research: Theory and practice*. London: Longman. 228–266.

Lakoff, Robin (1975). *Language and woman's place*. New York: Harper & Row.

―――― (1990). *Talking power: The politics of language*. San Francisco: Basic Books.

Livia, Anna, & Kira Hall (eds.), *Queerly phrased: Language, gender, and sexuality*. New York: Oxford University Press.

Newcombe, Nora, & Diane B. Arnkoff (1979). Effects of speech style and sex of speaker on person perception. *Journal of Personality and Social Psychology* 37:1293–1303.

O'Barr, William, & Bowman K. Atkins (1980). "Women's language" or "powerless language"? In Sally McConnell-Ginet, Ruth Borker, & Nelly Furman (eds.), *Women and language in literature and society*. New York: Praeger. 93–110.

Ochs, Elinor (1992). Indexing gender. In Barbara Diane Miller (ed.), *Sex and gender hierarchies*. New York: Cambridge University Press. 146–169.

Tiger, Lionel (1969). *Men in groups*. New York: Random House.

Trechter, Sara (1999). Contextualizing the exotic few. In Mary Bucholtz, A. C. Liang, & Laurel Sutton (eds.), *Reinventing identities: The gendered self in discourse*. New York: Oxford University Press. 101–119.

# 9 ::

# Exploring Women's Language in Japanese

SACHIKO IDE

## The Awakening of a Female Sociolinguist

It was not until I read Robin Lakoff's article "Language and Woman's Place" in *Language in Society* (1973) in the mid-1970s that I awakened to the realization that a woman could be a full-fledged scholar. Lakoff keenly analyzed the mechanisms handicapping female students, who have to be "bilingual" in order to be perceived as appropriately serious in class and when talking to professors. As she noted, "It may be that the extra energy that must be (subconsciously or otherwise) expended in this game is energy sapped from more creative work, and hinders women from expressing themselves as well as they might otherwise, or as fully or freely as they might otherwise" (1973: 48, n. 2; cf. *LWP* 41–42). When I read this passage, I could not agree more. As a beginning linguist I had believed that to be a scholar meant to abandon my femaleness and think and talk in a male way, that any other way was unacceptable. Having been brought up as the daughter of a medical professor, I took as a compliment my father's words to me: "Sachiko, you're so smart that you could even be a secretary."

Without Lakoff's work in "Language and Woman's Place" (and in *Language and Woman's Place* [LWP], the 1975 book that grew out of the article), I could not have established myself as a sociolinguist. This work inspired me to think about language in relation to social reality. It also made clear to me that the world was governed by men who were in the mainstream and that women were usually pushed into a marginal position. It was then that I realized that as a woman in a non-Western culture I am doubly marginal (see also Morgan, this volume). This recognition led me to create ideas from a nonmainstream perspective.

## The Acceptance of *Language and Woman's Place* in Japan

While I was in the United States during the academic year of 1974–75, I was much influenced by the women's movement. Having read Lakoff's work on women's language several times, I was convinced by her arguments and was determined to introduce them when I returned to Japan. I wrote such articles as "Women's Liberation and the Study of Women's Language" (1975) and "Language and Women's Consciousness in the Contemporary United States" (1976) for a Japanese audience, trying to advocate this new movement to liberate women in Japan by changing sexism in language. Meanwhile, Katsue Akiba Reynolds translated LWP into Japanese in 1986 and provided an accompanying and articulate explanation of the text.

Teaching at a women's university, I felt a mission to liberate my female students through lectures and seminars. Contrary to my expectation, however, I was to be faced with an unwelcoming reaction. The reality in Japan was quite different from what I had presumed based on my experience in the United States. I learned from my students that they did not feel that they were oppressed or marginalized; instead, they were content as they were. Even if they did elevate men and chose to put themselves in subordinate positions, they enjoyed relationships in which women and men took different roles. They were polite enough not to challenge my ideas outright, but they clearly showed that they weren't buying my newly imported ideas on language and woman's place. (The translated version of LWP, incidentally, did not seem to circulate as widely as the original did.) What went wrong? It took me all of the 1980s and 1990s to explore the reasons behind my failure.

## Not Gender Difference but Role Difference: A Survey Result

In the early 1980s I was offered a Japanese Education Ministry research grant to investigate the use of women's language in Japan. Takesi Sibata, a leading sociolinguist who was the general director of the Special Research Project on Language Standardization in the Age of Information Technology, told me that unless I did a thorough survey of women's language, one couldn't be sure that what I had written about Japanese women's language was true. He was reluctant to accept my articles on women's language written under the influence of American feminism. The grant made it possible for me to form a research group and conduct a survey with more than five hundred subjects. The research focused on the use of honorifics, linguistic devices that mark varying levels of politeness. The research question posed in this project was how and why women speak more politely in Japanese. It was assumed from the outset that women do speak more politely than men, but this question was tested as well.

Our survey of the use of honorifics by women and men asked subjects which honorific forms for the verb *iku* (to go) they would use when asking the question "When do you go?" in a variety of hypothetical contexts, such as when addressing a workplace superior, a neighbor, a spouse, and so on. It was found, as expected, that women did use more polite honorific forms than men. However, the major finding was that this tendency was due not to gender difference per se but to the different roles in which women and men engage in their everyday lives. That is, women, who usually work inside the home, are more frequently engaged in more private, socially oriented activities, whereas men are more frequently engaged in public, efficiency-oriented activities. Since it is a general tendency to use more polite speech in social interaction than in workplace interaction, it is natural for both women and men to use polite speech in ways that reflect this general distinction. It became clear that the women's use of more polite language was not due to their subordinate position in society. Instead, it was because most female subjects were housewives whose roles primarily involved social interaction. This was the reason for their use of more polite honorifics (S. Ide et al. 1986; S. Ide 1991).

Consequently, it was predicted that women's language would change as women began to work outside the home and assume roles in the workplace. Two decades after this survey was conducted, we see that women's use of language is now diversified (see Matsumoto, this volume). While women have acquired the variety associated with men's repertoire in the workplace, they still use more polite forms as an index of femaleness in social interaction.

## Group Identity Markers and Molding the Self: Tracing the Origin of Women's Language

Contrary to an almost universal tendency to view women's language negatively, Japanese women's language tends to have been regarded positively—that is, as beautiful and elegant. It has no tinge of being the language of lower status or lesser position. What makes it appear nonnegative? I will explain from two different angles, first from a historical perspective.

The issues of feminism certainly reached Japanese scholarship and triggered a number of studies of women's language. However, interest in studies of Japanese women's language goes as far back as 1929, when Toshio Kikuzawa wrote an article entitled "On the Features of Women's Language." Subsequently, a number of descriptive studies of women's language were published. The approach taken in these studies reflects traditional Japanese linguistics (*kokugogaku*), in which the study of language focuses exclusively on Japanese. Interestingly, these works do not deal with women's language in contrast to men's but view it as a "section" of language called an *isoo*. None of the roughly equivalent English terms such as *register* or *dialect* really reflect the concept of *isoo*. This linguistic-pragmatic category is an example of the traditional Japanese way of looking at language: the variety of language used is an identification marker of the professional or social role of the speaker. In the Japanese view, speakers shape themselves into representatives of their profession. Molding oneself in this way is seen as an integral part of personality formation. During the Edo Period (1603–1867) when Japan closed itself off from the rest of the world (except for interaction with China and Holland) for almost three centuries, an indigenous philosophy was established in which Confucianism was revised to match the closed society. The teaching of this philosophy was that in order for society to work harmoniously, everybody must fulfill a specific role. Role fulfillment has been one of the moral ideals underlying the working of Japanese society up to this day (S. Ide & Peng 1996).

If one disassembles language into various kinds of speech based on the group to which the speakers belong, the result will be *isoo* languages (*isoo go*). These languages differ according to age, generation, and social, regional, and professional background, as well as class and gender. In other words, people are viewed as speaking different languages according to the groups to which they belong. Among the many *isoo* languages associated with professional roles are the languages of monks, merchants, scholars, samurai, and craftsmen. In the traditional Japanese linguistic literature, the field of women's language has secured its own position as one of the differentiated *isoo* languages.

Every person belongs to several groups and therefore has learned several *isoo* or group languages (e.g., women's language, teachers' language, Tokyo language, and mothers' language). But the group languages taken together do not make up the whole of the Japanese language like mosaic stones, with each one having a border and form distinct from all others. Instead, the group languages overlap like colored oil drops heated on a projector slide, so that women's language and Tokyo language and teachers' language, for example, all play a role in determining how a female teacher from Tokyo will express what she has to say, since her language will reflect her identity as a member of all these groups.

Looking back in history, women's language can be shown to have existed since the eighth century, the time of *Mannyooshuu*, the earliest existing collection of Japanese poems. The poems show that women and men were speaking slightly differently at that time, but there have been no studies done on this aspect of the language. Women's languages in women's social worlds throughout history have had an impact on women's language today but not because contemporary Japanese women's language has simply incorporated these languages. The impact of earlier women's languages can be seen in the following three areas. First, they established the domain of women's language as a group language. There are literatures describing the language of court ladies in the fourteenth century and the language of courtesans in the seventeenth century. The languages of court ladies and courtesans are not direct predecessors of present-day women's language; rather, they were the first recorded instance of gendered language (S. Ide 2003; R. Ide & Terada 1998).

Another impact of women's languages is their function as markers of role identities. By using the special languages of special social worlds, court ladies and courtesans (1) created a feeling of group solidarity, (2) identified themselves as members of these groups, and (3) molded themselves into people suitable for membership in each group.

A third impact of earlier women's languages involves the value placed on them. There are many lexical items in present-day Japanese that stem from such languages. The dissemination of women's languages from women's worlds to Japanese society more generally should be interpreted as an indication of how positively they were regarded. This addition of expressions is felt to have enriched contemporary Japanese, especially because expressions from women's worlds are felt to be more sophisticated and to carry more elegant connotations. Women's language was viewed as something of value.


## Signifying Elegance or Dignity: The Reflexive Function of Women's Language

Another approach to explaining the positive aspect of Japanese women's language may be in order. Here, I examine the reflexive function of natural language use in context and discuss the mechanism whereby elegance or dignity can be signified by higher linguistic forms. (For more details, see S. Ide forthcoming.)

Research on the language of women working in Japanese corporations presents evidence worth noting in this regard (S. Ide & Inoue 1992). It is generally believed that women of lower status use more polite forms to superiors in order to acknowledge the difference in status. Contrary to such expectations, it was found that women with higher positions in the workplace use more polite expressions than those with lower positions. How can we explain this seeming contradiction? These executives use more polite expressions as a tool or even a weapon to express a dignified demeanor in keeping with their status, not to show deference to those they address. Why is it that linguistic forms can function to signify elegance or dignity?

The use of polite forms expresses or, more precisely, indexes context: the appropriate relationship between the speaker and the hearer and the formality of the situation. But polite forms do more than this: they can index the speaker's attributes. While polite forms that index context are geared to politeness toward others, their usage to index the speaker's attributes is quite different in nature. Polite forms index the speaker's identity through the metapragmatic function of language use. Listening to the kind of forms speakers employ, we get a metapragmatic message about what kind of people speakers are.

How can we account for this phenomenon? Even though talking

about varieties of language in terms of social class is somewhat taboo in a democratic society, it is a fact that there are dialects that differ on the basis of social class. Female executives are one case in point, since they are indexing their high status by the use of more elaborate linguistic forms.

Geographical dialects are a familiar occurrence the world over, so let us look at an example from Japanese geographical dialects. People in Kyoto speak in what is called Kyoto dialect. If we listen to somebody speaking Kyoto dialect, we understand the meaning of the propositional content, but we also get the metapragmatic information that the speaker is from Kyoto. That is, the speaker's accent signifies an attribute of the speaker, in this case, that of being from Kyoto.

Parallel to geographical dialects, people tend to have different dialects according to their social class. The higher the social status of the speaker, the more elaborate and formal linguistic forms they are likely to use. Regardless of an individual's ability to employ the elaborate linguistic forms, people in a speech community share as common knowledge at least passive communicative competence concerning their use. Just as we know that people are from Kyoto by their accent, we are able to categorize the social status of speakers by the speech forms they use.

There are varieties of language that differ on the basis of geographical, social, gender, and generational differences in a society. To the extent that a society is complex, the same propositional content can be expressed in a range of linguistic forms. And it is by their choice of form that speakers index their attributes. If you use forms that signal the Kyoto dialect, women's dialect, middle-class dialect, and young people's dialect, you index with great precision where you belong in the society. Listeners who share common knowledge concerning the structure and configuration of the paradigmatic variety of linguistic forms in the speaking context will in return understand the metapragmatic message about what is meant by the very choice of linguistic form.

It is very often the case that high-status people, such as executives in large corporations, use elevated linguistic forms appropriately and with a relaxed tone. In the minds of the members of a speech community, the correlation between type of speech and type of person is widely recognized. It is because of the reflexive nature of language use that the linguistic forms chosen by the speaker, together with contextual knowledge of the speech community, is negotiated to yield metapragmatic meaning. Since speakers who choose elevated linguistic forms are very often those who hold high status, those who belong to the group of sophisticated women, and those whose behavior exhibits dignity or elegance, we connect this information with the user of such speech. In this way, the use of polite linguistic forms signifies elegance or dignitiy.

## Everything Started with Lakoff

It was Lakoff's groundbreaking article "Language and Woman's Place" that inspired me to believe that it is acceptable to speak out from my own perspective. It became the foundation of my scholarship. The article also awakened me to the realization that language could be insightfully analyzed in relation to social reality. At first glance, I thought Lakoff's analysis could be applied in parallel fashion to women's language in Japanese society. However, the reality was not so simple. While Lakoff argues that "linguistic imbalances" between women and men should be corrected (1973: 73; cf. *LWP* 69), the parallel argument was not successful in the case of Japanese women and language, as I have illustrated in this essay. I eventually realized that the underlying assumption of Lakoff's argument about linguistic imbalance came from the egalitarian idealism of an individualistic society. Japanese society, on the contrary, assumes role differences, as stated above. If one is subordinate to the other, it may be called imbalance under egalitarian idealism. However, if one has a different role from the other, it is a matter of difference that may work complementarily. Thus, Lakoff's keen look at language and society and her articulate writings not only led me to think about the interaction of language and Japanese women's place but also led me to investigate the workings of language and social phenomena from my own perspective, as a woman and a scholar claiming her place in Japanese society.

REFERENCES

Ide, Risako, & Tomomi Terada (1998). The historical origins of Japanese women's speech: From the secluded worlds of "court ladies" and "play ladies." *International Journal of the Sociology of Language* 129:139–156.
Ide, Sachiko (1975). Wuumanribu to jyoseigo kenkyuu (Women's liberation and the study of women's language). *Eigobunngakusekai* (The World of English Literature) 10:14–17.
——— (1976). Gendai amerika shakai ni okeru kotoba to seibetu ishiki (Language and women's consciousness in the contemporary United States). *Bulletin of Faculty of the Arts* (Japan Women's University) 25:13–26.
——— (1991). How and why do women speak more politely in Japanese? In Sachiko Ide & Naomi MacGloin (eds.), *Aspects of Japanese women's language*. Tokyo: Kurosio. 63–79.
——— (2003). Women's language as a group identity marker. In Marlis Hellinger & Hadumod Bussmann (eds.), *Gender across languages: The linguistic representation of women and men*. Vol. 3. Amsterdam: John Benjamins. 227–238.
——— (forthcoming). How and why honorifics can signify dignity or elegance: The indexicality and reflexivity of linguistic rituals. In Robin Tolmach Lakoff & Sachiko Ide (eds.), *New perspectives on linguistic politeness*. Amsterdam: John Benjamins.

Ide, Sachiko, Motoko Hori, Akiko Kawasaki, Shoko Ikuta, & Hitomi Haga
(1986). Sex difference and politeness in Japanese. *International Journal of
the Sociology of Language* 58:25–36.
Ide, Sachiko, & Miyako Inoue (1992). Onna kotoba ni miru aidentiti (Identity in
women's language). *Gekkan Gengo* (Monthly Journal on Language) 11:46–
48.
Ide, Sachiko, & Guoyue Peng (1996). Linguistic politeness in Chinese, Japanese,
and English from a sociolinguistic perspective. In *Festschrift in celebration
of Dr. Takesi Sibata's 77th birthday.* Tokyo: Sanseidoo. 971–983.
Kikuzawa, Toshio (1929). Fujin no kotoba no tokuchou ni tuite (On the features
of women's language). *Kokugo Kyouiku* (Language Education) 3:66–75.
Lakoff, Robin (1973). Language and woman's place. *Language in Society* 2:45–
80.
———— (1975). *Language and woman's place.* New York: Harper & Row.
———— (1986). *Gengo to sei* (Language and woman's place). Trans. Katsue Akiba
Reynolds. Tokyo: Yuuseidou.

# 10 ::

## "Women's Language" and Martha Stewart

*From a Room of One's Own to a Home of One's Own to a*

*Corporation of One's Own*

CATHERINE EVANS DAVIES

Whereas recent research on gender and language has typically abstracted away from the gendered individual to attempt to generalize about the linguistic behavior of the social category, especially about the occurrence of selected linguistic features, a more comprehensive treatment of gendered style, inspired by Robin Lakoff's work in *Language and Woman's Place* (*LWP*) (1975), also exists within the tradition of interactional sociolinguistics (e.g., Tannen 1996). Meanwhile, Barbara Johnstone (1996, 1999) has drawn our attention to the linguistic individual (see also Bean & Johnstone, this volume). My own work on the lifestyle entrepreneur Martha Stewart's linguistic presentation of self is in this tradition: the close examination of linguistic individuality as performed in public discourse, especially that of a highly visible person in an apparently traditional gender role, but whose total situation encompasses aspects of both traditional gender roles.

Martha Stewart is a complex figure who has become a powerful corporate executive through representing the traditional woman's role of homemaker and commodifying her vision of upper-middle-class "good taste." In my work to date I have analyzed her linguistic presentation of self on her television show, *Martha Stewart Living*, in terms of three interrelated frames: politeness, credibility, and authenticity (Davies 2002a); I have considered her from an international perspective as representative of "American good taste" (Davies 2003a); and I have begun to explore methodologies for assessing her potential impact as a linguistic role model (Davies 2002b). My work engages with Lakoff's by problematizing the idea that certain ways of speaking are inherently powerful or powerless; Martha Stewart may be using certain features that were identified by Lakoff as typical of "women's language," but she is also perceived to be very powerful. In my analysis I would like to think that I am carrying forward Lakoff's emphasis on the importance of context (Lakoff 1972), by examining these linguistic features in discourse. My findings are also consistent with Lakoff's comments about upper-class speakers' use of women's language (see also Livia, this volume).

Martha Stewart's linguistic presentation of self on her television show is clearly part of a "gendered" persona; in fact, Martha Stewart's speech includes all ten forms Lakoff identifies as characteristic of "women's language" (*LWP* 78–81). I discuss each of these features, noting Lakoff's original commentary and then considering how Stewart may be using these forms in the service of a powerful presentation of self:

1. "Women have a large stock of words related to their specific interests" (*LWP* 78)

The "homemaker" focus of Martha Stewart's show ensures the use of specialized words relating to women's interests (e.g., *mandoline, dollop, rhizome*). Stewart's entrepreneurial skills, however, together with her successful self-presentation as the purveyor of upper-middle-class cultural capital, seem to be a factor in the spread of such lexical items to the male population. I have only a couple of bits of evidence of this phenomenon to date, both from middle-aged white men: one asked for a "mandoline" in a cooking store after viewing Stewart's show on this topic; another explained to female relatives that he had learned all about "dollops" from Stewart's show.

2. "The use of hedges of various kinds" (*LWP* 79)

Stewart uses a variety of hedges, as in the following excerpt from a monologue on the preparation of ginger tea:

> You could add a little bit of fresh lemon if you like
> but I would prefer just letting it cook like this
> and then add the lemon juice
> if you like the taste of lemon
> right before you're gonna drink it

Lakoff analyzes the general use of hedges as part of a pattern in which women are not allowed to express power directly through language. The hedges here are syntactically in the form of conditional clauses and are oriented to politeness considerations as part of deferential "involvement." Such usage could be seen as clever marketing that avoids the potentially overbearing imperative mood.

3. "Hypercorrect grammar" (*LWP* 80)

Stewart's grammar is generally very "correct" and is explicitly judged to be so by my female interviewees from the lower middle class. Certain characteristics of her speech could be seen as hypercorrections or as a symbolic concern with "correctness." For example, she uses the typically British pronunciation of *herb*, with initial [h], and she claims always to have pronounced the word in that way. Stewart and her mother both appear to aspirate intervocalic /t/ in *water* and *little*, but Stewart does so apparently differentially, depending on how much attention she's paying to speech. It is also quite striking that she does not drop her g's. However, Stewart's speech also includes forms that are moving from vernacular into informal standard (e.g., *there's* with plural complement) and some typical American speech reductions (*gonna* for *going to*). In general, the constellation of characteristics of her spoken language, in conjunction with other aspects of her self-presentation, seems to convey both that she has definite ideas about the right way to speak and that she is comfortable with herself linguistically across the whole range of her informal standard variety of American English.

4.    "Superpolite forms" (*LWP* 80)

Extremely polite language forms are typical of Stewart's interaction, as in the following excerpt, in which she performs her characteristic double-thanking of her guests:

MS:  Sebastian, thank you very much
       for the perfect cup . . . of perfect green tea
SB:  you're welcome
       Thank you
MS:  [thank you VERY much

Lakoff noted that "women's politeness is principally . . . [used for] establishing and reinforcing distance: deferential mannerisms coupled with euphemism and hypercorrect and superpolite usage" (*LWP* 99). Stewart's general style of politeness seems to fall clearly within this description. Other aspects of her style, however, seem more consistent with a solidarity politeness system emphasizing involvement and an egalitarian ethos, in which the main principle is to assume similarity and commonality with others. This style is prototypically associated with an American ideology that promotes a fictive equality and solidarity. The segments in which she demonstrates how to do something are presented in a personal way, consistent with a solidarity politeness system. She presents things personally to the audience, using *I*, and addresses the audience as *you*, as illustrated both in the example in (2) above and in the following example: "You could boil them / but roasting them keeps in all those flavors / . . . / some people put a little olive oil inside / even a little bit of water / but I don't think you need to do any of that."

5.    "Women don't tell jokes" (*LWP* 80)

Martha Stewart does not express a sense of humor as part of her crafted persona on the show. In the data I have collected, I have found only one instance of joking that she initiated. In this case she and her employee are talking about a kitchen tool; the joint joking involves intertextuality with a different sort of promotional discourse that sells a similar kitchen tool directly via television.

```
01   MS:   now if you like to make french fries
            this is the tool to have too
            because
02   SS:   yeah
03   MS:   you can make shoestring french fries
            you can make waffle french fries
            you can do everything
04   SS:   OK
05   MS:   with a mandoline
            we sound like an advertisement on television
06   SS:   ah hahahaha
            we do
            it slices
            it dices
07   MS:   wonderful
08   SS:   huhuhuh
            and it does all that
            it's true but it really is a great helper in the kitchen
```

In contrast with stereotypical male joking of the ritual insult type, this joking creates a footing that is initiated with the utterance of the pronoun *we*, inviting the other woman to play along within the intersubjective fantasy world of the joking footing (Davies 1984, 2003b; Kotthoff 1999). The other woman acknowledges the initiation of the joking footing with laughter at turn 06, repeats the pronoun *we* to agree in the next line, and then continues the joking footing by imitating the rhyming discourse of the well-known commercial (*it slices, it dices*). Stewart then comments at turn 07 (*wonderful*) within the joking footing, signaling the conclusion of the joint joking. The other woman responds with more laughter, marking both Stewart's contribution and the end of the footing, and then shifts back into the original footing of the television show with *and it does all that* . . . —the antecedent of *it* being the kitchen tool that they've been talking about. The argument could be made that this style of joking is actually deferential (unlike joke telling) in the sense that it invites the other person to contribute.

6.   "Women speak in italics" (*LWP* 81)

7.   "The use of the intensive 'so'" (*LWP* 79)

8.   " 'Empty' adjectives like *divine, charming, cute*" (*LWP* 78)

9.    "Women have at their disposal a wider range of intonation patterns
      than do men" (*LWP* 81)

Several of the features that Lakoff observes together create a stylistic constellation that is exemplified in the following excerpt. Lakoff's evocative
comment that women "speak in italics" is very clearly true of Stewart. She
makes liberal use of emphatic stress, indicated in the following excerpt
through capitalization. In this sample of her speech we also see the use of
the intensive *so* and a wide intonational range. She also uses adjectives
that could be classified as "empty," a set of words that Lakoff analyzes as
usually indicating that the speaker is "out of power" (*LWP* 47):

> and my mom's recipe is utterly fantastic / . . . / I love borscht /
> . . . / I LOVE celery leaves/ . . . / oh that looks SO GOOD /
> . . . / um gorgeous/ / . . . / so that looks good / . . . / so that'll
> thicken the soup beautifully / . . . / how pretty / . . . / oh I
> LOVE it with boiled potatoes / . . . / now that is the perfect
> soup/ . . . / it's really good

The effect of this constellation of features seems to be not that Stewart is
dismissed as powerless, however, but rather that she is evaluated favorably
for her strong feelings and is awarded credibility for the knowledge that it
is assumed that she has acquired as a result of her passion and perfection-
ism. Interestingly, the combination of intensifying modifiers and emphatic
stress has been identified as characteristic of American upper-class speech,
conveying confidence, self-assurance, and the expectation of agreement
from the interlocutor (Kroch 1996; Nunberg 1980), a finding consistent
with Lakoff's observations regarding upper-class use of "women's language."

10.   "Question intonation where we might expect declaratives"
      (*LWP* 78)

One of the most controversial features identified by Lakoff as characteristic
of women's language is the heavy use of tag questions and question intonation in statements, interpretable as indicating uncertainty and insecurity.
Given that an important dimension of Stewart's presentation of self is oriented to credibility, we might expect to see few such usages. However,
given the demands of her role as facilitator with her guests, we might expect
to find question intonation in statements and tag questions used as interactional devices to move her guests along and make the most efficient use
of precious television air time. In the following excerpt we see a tag question, *right*, which may appear to signal that Stewart is not sure about the
accuracy of what she has just said:

> MS:   so Ralph's been going around my property
>       and feeding the trees with this fabulous food
>       and it is all organic, right?

> Man: all natural absolutely
> MS: [nonchemical
> Man: yup

In fact, however, we can see from the combination of the response, Stewart's follow-up, and the subsequent response that the illocutionary force of the tag question is to elicit strong confirmation of the truth of Stewart's statement about the tree food. The ultimate perlocutionary effect of the tag question, analyzed within the discourse context, is to affirm Stewart's knowledge and credibility.

I hope to have demonstrated that the forms identified by Lakoff as characteristic of "women's language" serve Martha Stewart's commodified presentation of self in complex ways. It is striking that all ten of the forms can be found in her speech; if we assume that Lakoff identified aspects of a linguistic prototype or stereotype associated with the female gender role in American (white middle-class) society, then Stewart's use of these forms may serve to convey a strongly feminine gender role. Such a social meaning associated with her linguistic presentation of self would be important and effective in her role as homemaker lifestyle entrepreneur. As I have discussed above in relation to each form, Stewart uses the forms in discourse context in ways that convey her confidence, credibility, agency, and interpersonal effectiveness. This linguistic presentation of self matches Stewart's complex public persona, combining traditional gender roles of both women (homemaker) and men (corporate executive). Lakoff was concerned that women's language

> submerges a woman's personal identity, by denying her the means of expressing herself strongly, on the one hand, and encouraging expressions that suggest triviality in subject matter and uncertainty about it. . . . The ultimate effect . . . is that women are systematically denied access to power, on the grounds that they are not capable of holding it as demonstrated by their linguistic behavior along with other aspects of their behavior. (*LWP* 42)

It would appear, then, that Martha Stewart's linguistic presentation of self is potentially transformative.

The main critique of Martha Stewart seems to be that she represents an extreme form of hypocritical inauthenticity: an upper-middle-class fantasy world based on vast unacknowledged resources. In striking contrast to this view, Joan Didion (2000) suggests that Martha Stewart is rather an important symbol of women's power, that she is not "Superwoman" but "Everywoman." Didion refers to Stewart's "protean competence" and proposes that the underlying message of the Martha Stewart phenomenon is that competence in the home can translate into competence outside the home. According to Didion (2002: 279), "The dreams and fears into which

Martha Stewart taps are not of feminine domesticity but of female power, of the woman who sits down at the table with the men and, still in her apron, walks away with the chips." What seems significant about the Martha Stewart phenomenon from the point of view of "women's language" is that this gendered individual in public discourse is speaking from a position of power and agency. Didion (2000: 279) quotes a contributor to an unofficial Martha Stewart Web site who defines Martha Stewart as "a good role model. . . . she's a strong woman who's in charge, and she has indeed changed the way our country, if not the world, views what used to be called 'women's work.' " One of my interviewees likewise commented that Martha Stewart was "very powerful. . . . She's like the family matriarch who is smiling so you don't realize that she's controlling what you do."

A popular sociolinguistics text (Wolfram & Schilling-Estes 1998: 198) discusses and critiques LWP in relation to the "female deficit" approach to understanding the relationship between gender and language. Whereas certain aspects of Lakoff's analysis appear to be consistent with this approach, it seems to me that such a categorization is overly simplistic. It is clear that Lakoff's protean work also contained the seeds of the "difference" and "dominance" approaches discussed in their chapter (Cameron 1996), as well as seeds of an approach to understanding socially organized language use based in the notion of style. I believe that the significance of Lakoff's work is that it continues to point us in new directions of greater insight and potential transformation. In her conclusion, she stated her aims very clearly: "If we are aware of what we're doing, why we're doing it, and the effects our actions have on ourselves and everyone else, we will have the power to change. I hope this book will be one small first step in the direction of a wider option of life styles, for men and women" (LWP 102). As a lifestyle entrepreneur, Martha Stewart is an exemplar of one such option, combining traditional "women's language" and female roles with new forms of female power, agency, and economic and cultural capital.

REFERENCES

Cameron, Deborah (1996). The language-gender interface: Challenging co-optation. In Victoria L. Bergvall, Janet M. Bing, & Alice F. Freed (eds.), *Rethinking language and gender research: Theory and practice.* New York: Longman. 31–53.
Davies, Catherine Evans (1984). Joint joking: Improvisational humorous episodes in conversation. In Claudia Brugman and Monica Macaulay with Amy Dahlstrom, Michele Emanatian, Birch Moonwomon, & Catherine O'Connor (eds.), *Proceedings of the 10th annual meeting of the Berkeley Linguistics Society.* Berkeley, CA: Berkeley Linguistics Society. 360–371.
———— (2002a). Martha Stewart's linguistic presentation of self. *Texas Linguistic Forum* 44:73–89.
———— (2002b). Assessing the effects of language in the media on linguistic vari-

ation. Paper presented at the 31st meeting of the Conference on New Ways of Analyzing Variation, Stanford University, October.

———— (2003a). Martha Stewart and American "good taste." In Jean Aitchison & Diana Lewis (eds.), *New media language.* London: Routledge. 146–155.

———— (2003b). How English-learners joke with native speakers: An interactional sociolinguistic perspective on humor as collaborative discourse across cultures. *Journal of Pragmatics* 35:1361–1385.

Didion, Joan (2000). Everywoman.com: Getting out of the house with Martha Stewart. *New Yorker* (February 21): 270–280.

Johnstone, Barbara. (1996). *The linguistic individual: Self-expression in language and linguistics.* New York: Oxford University Press.

———— (1999). Uses of Southern-sounding speech by contemporary Texas women. *Journal of Sociolinguistics* 3:505–522.

Kotthoff, Helga (1999). Coherent keying in conversational humour: Contextualizing joint fictionalisation. In Wolfram Bublitz, Uta Lenk, & Eija Ventola (eds.), *Coherence in spoken and written discourse.* Amsterdam: John Benjamins. 125–150.

Kroch, Anthony (1996). Dialect and style in the speech of upper class Philadelphia. In Gregory R. Guy, Crawford Feagin, Deborah Schiffrin, & John Baugh (eds.), *Towards a social science of language: Papers in honor of William Labov.* Vol. 1: *Variation and change in language and society.* Amsterdam: John Benjamins. 23–45.

Lakoff, Robin (1972). Language in context. *Language* 48:907–927.

———— (1975). *Language and woman's place.* New York: Harper & Row.

Nunberg, Geoffrey (1980). The speech of the New York City upper class. In Timothy Shopen & Joseph M. Williams (eds.), *Standards and dialects in English.* Cambridge, MA: Winthrop. 150–173.

Tannen, Deborah (1996). *Gender and discourse.* New York: Oxford University Press.

Wolfram, Walt, & Natalie Schilling-Estes (1998). *American English: Dialects and variation.* Oxford: Blackwell.

# 11 ::

# Public Discourse and the Private Life of Little Girls

## Language and Woman's Place *and Language Socialization*

JENNY COOK-GUMPERZ

"When you grow up and I grow up we'll be the bosses."
— Two four-year-old girls playing "Mothers"

"I think I should understand that better," said Alice very politely,
"if I had it written down: but I can't quite follow it as you say it."
— Lewis Carroll, *Alice's Adventures in Wonderland*

In *Language and Woman's Place* (LWP) (1975), Robin Lakoff opens up new pragmatic perspectives on politeness by proposing that talking politely is an essential part of being a woman. Lakoff's proposition answers a critical question in language socialization: how children create a gendered self through their own language practices. Women recognize the importance of relations with others, and as Penelope Brown and Stephen Levinson (1987) point out, politeness provides the essential social mechanism for establishing positive bonds within a group. Politeness thus provides a blueprint for exploring the ways in which children's early understanding of relations with others leads to an awareness of a gendered self. Children's spontaneous talk shows how they differentiate life within the intimate relationships of the family from life in the more public domain of their peers and unfamiliar others outside of the home.

Child development theory has generally assumed that until middle childhood, gender does not play a significant part in the lives of young children. Children are treated as passive recipients of their parents' views of gender. While parents are said to create a differentiated world of activities, names, clothing, and playthings that map their expectations about gender-appropriate behavior onto their children's lives, their ways of talking also model their expectations of gender. And the discourse of politeness is an essential part of these gender expectations, although children's politeness has been studied as merely the routine repetition of parental models (Berko

Gleason 1987). Recent detailed studies of children's language socialization have changed this view. We now know that through their play children create gendered scenarios and that they talk in ways that reflect their awareness of a gendered self. That is, children are active agents of their own sociocultural understanding. Moreover, we have also come to realize that for children nursery-school classrooms are public places, presenting interactive experiences different from those of the home. Children experience the making of friends and alliances through activities of their own choosing, activities that are not brokered by parents (Cook-Gumperz 2001; Kyratzis 2004).

## Gender and the Paradox of Language Socialization

In light of these claims, I look at how young girls from two to four years old begin to acquire a sense of their own gender identity as they move from a family-focused life into the more public domain of nursery school. Using examples from some of my own work, I explore how girls learn to "talk politely." I also show how in their own peer talk, girls can experiment with the possibility of constructing opposition to their compliant, polite, and conciliatory selves by rejecting what seems to be predetermined in their gendered life.

The first stage of children's gender theory at work can be seen in games they play at home, often involving domestic plots that have mummies and babies and sometimes fathers and siblings, yet where the mother role remains primary, whatever the family configuration. Later in the developmental cycle as the young child enters into the world outside of the home, there is a shift toward accommodating to new social demands that provide another aspect of a gendered self. Through a later set of examples of play in nursery school, I show how a second stage to the child's gender theory is developed through peer interaction. In the peer exchanges of this stage, girls face a very different set of discourse demands from what they encounter in the home.

My argument is that young girls must to a large extent rely on the conventional images and symbols of womanhood and motherhood as they grow up observing them firsthand, in order to explore their own future womanhood. Nancy Chodorow (1978), building on psychoanalytic insights, describes how girls come to understand their gender future as dependent on becoming mothers in their turn. As young children, girls construct a socially embedded concept of the woman by identifying directly with their mothers; they see their own future as determined through the needs of children and families. Through their awareness of the mother's ability to control the resources of the home and the activities of its residents—in short, to be one of "the bosses," as the above quotation from two four-year-olds shows—little girls see their mothers as powerful and controlling. As *LWP* tells us so directly, they please their powerful mothers by "being polite," and so at the same time they begin to use the pragmatic strategies that outside of the power arrangements of the home will soon be taken as evidence of a more deferential or compliant position. To paraphrase Lakoff, they will be seen as "talking like ladies," albeit very young ones. They also hear and learn to use the language of persuasion from their own mothers, who, in many familial contexts, as Elinor Ochs and Carolyn Taylor (1995) show, construct interactions in which the mother plays a subsidiary role in family discussions, so that the father can be seen as the family decision maker (cf. Kendall, this volume).

In their play talk, little girls demonstrate that they see the role of the woman as one of power and dominance in the family; research has shown they use unmitigated directives and issue orders to other players (Andersen 1992; Sachs 1987). However, these same girls are also likely to conduct their interactions with peers and adults in situations other than family play in a verbal style that is marked by negotiative skills, hedges, justifications, and above all politeness markers. All of these are verbal strategies that may later be interpreted as reflecting the abdication of power in both familial and other social relations, as Lakoff suggested in *LWP*. The distinction between verbal strategies and social action becomes the crux of the paradox of language socialization.

## Reproducing the Discourse of Mothering

Elsewhere, I suggest that in play activity children discover some of their own gender possibilities and so begin to construct a theory of gender by enacting the possibility of womanhood through the activities of the powerful and controlling mother (Cook-Gumperz 1995). Exploring the spontaneous play of two three-and-a-half-year-old girls, Lucy and Suzy, as they enact a frequently played game of "Mothers and Babies," I argue that the girls employ three markedly different "voice tones"—that is, intonationally distinctive rhythmic styles that enact game talk and distinguish whether they are (a) speaking as mothers to mothers or (b) as mothers to their babies or (c) providing game plot and commentary. At no time during the game do the girls make the babies themselves speak. Babies are talked at and about, they are scolded, cajoled, fussed over, and comforted by the mothers. The mother characters give directives or direct requests to each other, such as "Sandra [the name of one girl's mother character], your baby wants you" or "Sandra, do you have pins?" However, when the two little girls speak to each other in their ordinary voices, it is to further negotiate details of activities, and when this happens they are likely to mitigate or hedge their requests. Such requests usually carry a politeness tag, such as "Can I borrow this *if you mind?*" Or they carry a tag question: "And my baby sits there, *don't she?*" In game commentary talk the two girls use conditionals and justifications such as *because* to provide explanations: "And . . . this is my baby . . . the littler (one) . . . I have to have this *cause* . . . *cause* . . . she has to have the little cup." Or: "Not that babe . . . I'll give her some tea . . . *cause* she wants tea, don't she." In short, through play the two little girls construct the voices of mothering.

The girls demonstrate an understanding of the activities of women as mothers beyond their conscious awareness. Their characterizations and pragmatic strategies in their activities as mothers and family managers create a compromised power, one whose individual freedom is limited by having children for whom they are responsible and who must be scolded and cajoled. While to her children the mother is powerful, that power is limited. Young girls observe and note the cultural politics of gender first-hand in the family, but it is through interaction with their peers in the public domain outside of the family that they learn to subvert the consequences of this limited power through their talk.

### The Rhetoric of Persuasion

In their peer interaction in nonplay contexts, Lucy and Suzy use different verbal strategies. While having an afternoon snack, Lucy tries to persuade Suzy to take some of her unwanted apple slices. In the following, Lucy moves from an offer to a demand for a politeness token to the presentation of an extensive argument about how Suzy should talk to her.

> Lucy: Want another apple/ yes// say yes
> Suzy: No // no thank you
> Lucy: Want another apple/ that's you—ou (sing-song) No I don't
>     want it you can have it/ Do you want it/ say yes and I'll give
>     it to you
> Suzy: No
> Lucy: No //say yes/ what did I say /yes/
>     Yes/ Say yes (louder)
> Suzy: if I don't want to say yes I don't want to / cause my sister
>     says
>     if you don't want to say yes// you don't have to/ my sister . . .
> Lucy: no/ you *do* want to say yes/ you don't say you don't *want* to/
>     you say I don't need to talk like that
> Suzy: I don't need to talk like that
> Lucy: no/ it's too late/you can't say it again// too late and goodbye
>     and that's for nothing.

In this example, the insistence on saying yes—giving a politeness token as conditional on receiving some apple—is a strategy that the children must often have experienced. Lucy puts this strategy to her own rhetorical use, to construct the first stage in her argument to persuade Suzy to take Lucy's unwanted apple. At this point, the argument about saying yes takes over from the initial request. Both Lucy's and Suzy's long speeches are set up as rhetorical sequences with stylistic contrasts that use direct and indirect speech as a way of voicing the different sections of their own argument. Suzy uses her big sister's opinion as a way of voicing opposition to Lucy's demands. Both girls recognize the need to negotiate and persuade — that is, both use the power of words to achieve their ends.

## Gender as a Group Interactional Accomplishment

Moving into the public world of the nursery school presents further challenges. In their talk with other peers and adults, young girls reveal their understanding of the nature of gender-based power distinctions. These distinctions are at the heart of the interactional accomplishment of gender, as the following episode shows.

Three four-year-old girls, Jenny, Emily, and Alicia, are playing with small blocks and miniature animals in a carpeted area of the nursery classroom. They construct a house into which animal characters are introduced. The play scenario involves making food, tending and feeding pets, and tidying the area. Alicia introduces a topic: "Sweep our roads, everybody . . . sweep here." Jenny follows with making rice and other food. Shortly afterward, James comes to play nearby with the blocks. His presence seems to bother the girls. He keeps making noises and looking in their direction as if wanting to join in their play, until Jenny speaks to him:

Jenny: If you will not please, don't bother us!
James: I'm not bothering you.
Jenny: OK — well then don't trip the horses or the dogs or the zebras.
James: I wasn't doing that.
Jenny: What?
James: I wasn't doing that.
Jenny: Oh good — good. [Turning to talk to the other girls] He's just being a next door neighbor or something because we have a house. [James continues to play by himself without making any sounds.]

On the surface this sequence appears as a stereotypically gendered scenario of domestic play in which the girls as "animal minders" take care of the animals. The interruption by a lone boy is quickly negotiated by Jenny, who issues a polite request — "not please, don't bother us" — which seems successful in persuading James to be quiet and so to be treated as nonthreatening (*He's just being a next door neighbor*). James becomes a warranted part of the girls' play, remaining nearby as just a "neighbor," who does not have a specifically gendered character. However, with the arrival of a group of three boys, the play changes.

The newcomers encamp on the other side of the rug from the girls. The boys sing loudly as they walk back and forth — "We're walking . . . we're working" — all the while watching the girls play. After a while Jenny asks her friends how to deal with this intrusion, trying out politeness strategies: "And we should say to be quiet, we should say you should be quiet, we should say be quiet, we should say you should be quiet." But the boys go on singing while they walk back and forth carrying large blocks to make a structure. At first the girls play on, then Jenny tries out a polite request with her friends to find the right degree of authority mitigated by politeness, but she says nothing to the group of boys. Confronted by a group situation, she is less successful in her attempts at control. The boys' group seems to become more powerful and dominant; all the girls can do is keep watch on them and then change their own game into one where the animals are threatened, cry out, and fall off the cliffs. Finally, Emily leaves the play to be nearer the boys' group, and after that Alicia and Jenny walk away. In other words, the boys acting as a group dominate the girls while a single boy alone could not. The group of boys succeeds in introducing gender into the play as an underlying dynamic to the ensuing action, through the threat from one group to another that did not arise with the individual intruder. That is, since the arrivals are a group of boys, the three original players can no longer be seen as a gender-unspecified group of "animal minders"; rather, they become a group of girls. As the two groups evolve into gendered and oppositional groups their gender becomes the salient element solidifying the group and helping it to develop into a new kind of socially organized entity that takes on a life of its own for the duration of the activities. From this point onward, any additional members will need to be inducted as gendered members. In both episodes the girls try polite requests for compliance from the other. With a single boy this proves to be a successful strategy that leads to resolution, whereas in the group situation, the opposite happens, and the girls find themselves affected by the others' play. The construction of gender, in other words, becomes a group accomplishment, and politeness as a strategy needs to be redefined.

## Subversive Politeness

*LWP* provides us with guides to the potential of politeness as a pragmatic strategy not only for compliance but also for control. Young women in their lives will learn how to use politeness strategically in ways that subvert its compliant aim. As Lakoff (1994) has shown in her discussion of *Alice in Wonderland*, pragmatics is concerned with such issues as how to use words politely but still get your own way. Alice's adventures are those of a young girl who realizes how to use words to establish her own sense of reality and control. Her emerging awareness is that talk can be powerful, even if your social position, body size, and gender make you seem of lesser importance.

The potential asymmetry that young girls experience between the consequences of womanhood, control of life events, the awareness of the burden of motherhood, and the lesser social power of women outside of the home presents them with a paradoxical situation. Focusing on specific instances in which young girls take an oppositional stance toward the agenda set for women shows how girls develop a conception of "being a woman" that enables them to confront this paradox. The notion of an oppositional stance illustrates a struggle against what can be described as an oversocialized female persona that is the result of verbal strategies of compliance and persuasion. We can see how young girls experiment with constructing opposition to their compliant, polite, and conciliatory selves so as to be able to reject what seems to be predetermined in their gendered lives.

## REFERENCES

Andersen, Elaine S. (1992). *Speaking with style: The sociolinguistic skills of children*. London: Routledge.

Berko Gleason, Jean (1987). Sex difference in parent-child interaction. In Susan Philips, Susan Steele, & Christine Tanz (eds.), *Language, gender, and sex in comparative perspective*. Cambridge: Cambridge University Press. 189–199.

Brown Penelope, & Stephen Levinson (1987). *Politeness: Some universals in language usage*. Cambridge: Cambridge University Press.

Chodorow, Nancy (1988). *Reproduction of mothering: Psychoanalysis and the sociology of gender*. Berkeley: University of California Press.

Cook-Gumperz, Jenny (1995). Reproducing the discourse of mothering: How gendered talk makes gendered lives. In Kira Hall & Mary Bucholtz (eds.), *Gender articulated: Language and the socially constructed self*. London: Routledge. 401–420.

——— (2001). Girls' oppositional stances: The interactional accomplishment of gender in nursery school and family life. In Bettina Baron & Helga Kotthoff (eds.), *Gender in interaction*. Amsterdam: John Benjamins. 21–50.

Kyratzis, Amy (2004). Talk and interaction among children. *Annual Review of Anthropology* 33.

Lakoff, Robin (1975). *Language and woman's place*. New York: Harper & Row.

——— (1994). Lewis Carroll: Subversive pragmaticist. *Pragmatics* 3:376–386.

Ochs Elinor, & Carolyn Taylor (1995). The "Father knows best" dynamic in dinnertime narratives. In Kira Hall & Mary Bucholtz (eds.), *Gender articulated: Language and the socially constructed self*. London: Routledge. 97–120.

Sachs, Jacqueline (1987). Preschool boys' and girls' language use in pretend play. In Susan Philips, Susan Steele, & Christine Tanz (eds.), *Language, gender, and sex in comparative perspective*. Cambridge: Cambridge University Press. 178–188.

# 12 ::

## Mother's Place in *Language and Woman's Place*

SHARI KENDALL

At seven years old in Utah, I asked my mother why all the cooks I knew were women but the chefs at the restaurants were men, why the church choir was stocked with sopranos but the voices I heard on the records my parents played were male. I was deeply unsatisfied when she replied that this was the way it was supposed to be. Granted, there were even then well-known female chefs and vocalists, the latter well represented on now defunct records and eight-track tapes, but I was overwhelmed by a pattern of women working at home unrecognized and men doing similar work with public approbation. Thirteen years later I found myself a mother at age twenty, attempting to create a marriage based on equality and shared parental and professional goals. Despite the admonition of my elders to support my husband through school, I clung to my seemingly absurd desire to become a university professor and selfishly, as it was seen, to pursue this goal without delay. Largely isolated from the women's movement and its cultural effects, I discovered like-minded women in early feminist work outside academia. Simone de Beauvoir, Marilyn French, Gertrude Stein, and others articulated my turmoil and provided direction for my personal life.

After a divorce in which I retained custody of my son, I pursued a degree in a linguistics department devoted to the formal linguistic theory of Noam Chomsky and the variationist sociolinguistic methods of William Labov, but I took courses in literary and women's studies as well. It was there—not in linguistics—that I encountered Robin Lakoff's *Language and Woman's Place* (*LWP*) (1975). Her descriptions of language used by and about women illuminated and named social and linguistic patterns true to my experiences in that time and place. It was not until I read the work of her student Deborah Tannen in a course entitled "Discourse Analysis," taught by a professor in the English department, that I learned that I could unite my major interests in linguistics and gender. With this purpose in mind, I packed up my seven-year-old son and moved to Washington, DC, to pursue a PhD at Georgetown University. My interest in the language of mothers increased as I noticed the lack of research in the area and the fact that, as far as I knew, I was the only female graduate student in the department who had a young child.

## Where Did All the Mothers Go?

I offer this personal narrative as an initial basis for the continuing relevance of *LWP* to the study of language and gender and to make a place for the study of mothers within it. An obvious absence within the plethora of studies that followed the publication of *LWP* were those involving mothers (and fathers as well). Studies of mothers' language were conducted in the context of child language acquisition rather than gender. However, I believe the role of mother is an integral part of Lakoff's framework, so integral that she may not have deemed it necessary to make this explicit at the time that the work was published. Lakoff identifies the goal of the book as "an attempt to provide diagnostic evidence from language use for one type of inequity that has been claimed to exist in our society: that between the roles of men and women" (*LWP* 39). The role most expected of women in the early 1970s would undoubtedly have been that of mother. Lakoff explicitly mentions mothers only once, when claiming that girls and boys under the age of five are socialized to use "women's language" by mothers and other women because of their central role in children's lives (*LWP* 41). She also alludes to the role of mothers when she addresses potential opposition to her argument. She notes that some might argue that women should be more polite (one component of "women's language") because they are "the preservers of morality and civility" (*LWP* 77). In response, Lakoff notes that although being polite is not intrinsically negative, women are expected to assume this role, and even those who do not choose to be such mavens of morality "will automatically be treated as though [they] were" (*LWP* 78). Who, at this time, was expected to polish children until they gleamed of civilization? Mothers.

    I suspect that one reason for the lack of research on mothers following the publication of *LWP* was the vehement criticism leveled at the use of a sex-based division of labor—particularly in terms of a public/private dichotomy—as an explanation for gendered patterns of behavior (e.g., Ortner 1974; Rosaldo 1974). Linguistic anthropologists and others who identified such patterns were condemned as essentializing women and men by positing sex-based universals (see discussion in Philips 2003). The essentialist condemnation, with its corollary of determinism—the view that gender determines or predicts language behavior—was leveled at *LWP* as well. Yet a close examination reveals that Lakoff's paradigm is neither essentialist nor deterministic. Lakoff does not attribute the use of "women's language" to the essence of the speaker, but to power or, rather, the lack thereof: "The decisive factor is less purely gender than power in the real world" (*LWP* 81). Thus, other groups excluded from institutional power in some sense may use "women's language" (she names hippies, academic men, and homosexuals; see also Hall, this volume). The centrality of women to "women's language" stems from their status as the " 'uninvolved,' 'out of power' group *par excellence*" (*LWP* 47). Similarly, Lakoff's view of "women's language" is not deterministic. She claims that "if you are a woman, it is more likely that you will speak this way than if you are a man, but that is not to say that I predict you do speak this way if you're a woman, or don't if you're a man. Further, you could speak this way to some extent; or could speak it under some circumstances but not others" (*LWP* 82).

A second reason for the lack of research on mothers is a reflex of the women's movement of the 1970s. In a sense, women were demanding choices besides marriage and motherhood. The focus was on getting women out of the home, not back into it. For this reason, there have been many studies (my own included) on the language women use in occupations traditionally restricted to men, de facto if not de jure (e.g., Ainsworth-Vaughn 1998; Case 1988; Fisher 1993; Kendall & Tannen 1997; Kotthoff 1997; McElhinny 1993; West 1990). *LWP* reflects this concern with expanding the possible social roles of women, particularly into roles of power. Lakoff describes a cycle that begins with the unequal role of women and men in society, resulting in differential gender socialization. Girls learn to use a "nonforceful style" because unassertiveness is a social norm of womanhood, given men's role in establishing norms. The use of "women's language," in turn, denies women access to power, thus keeping them "in their place" (*LWP* 42). Lakoff concludes her treatise by expressing hope that "this book will be one small first step in the direction of a wider option of life styles, for men and women" (*LWP* 102). Women have made many advances over the past decades; however, I believe that mothering is a more central concern to more women than the literature on language and gender would suggest. There is, in fact, a place for mothers in gender and language research, and *LWP* can show us the way.

## The Language of Mothers

The link between gender and language in *LWP* stems from the differential social roles of women and men in general and from the specific roles expected of women in particular. The need to consider gender in relation to other social roles and identities is currently recognized. For example, Bonnie McElhinny (1997: 107–108) calls for investigations of the links "between occupations (including mothering) and gendered styles." As I have noted elsewhere (Kendall 2003), women and men do not generally choose linguistic options for the purpose of creating feminine or masculine identities; instead, they draw on gendered linguistic strategies to perform pragmatic and interactional functions of language and thus constitute roles in a gendered way. It is the manner in which people constitute their identities when acting within a social role that is linked with gender—that is, being a "good mother," being a "good manager."

This approach stems, in part, from an influential study of gender and familial roles by Elinor Ochs and Carolyn Taylor (1995). In an analysis of narrative roles at dinnertime, the authors demonstrate that some of the roles mothers and fathers take up at dinnertime reproduce gendered relations that are linked with power and authority. They theorize the relationship between language and gender much as Lakoff does, as a cycle that begins with the unequal roles of women and men in society, which results in differential gender socialization. The mothers tend to introduce narratives and to select fathers as primary recipients (e.g., *Tell Daddy what you did in karate today*). The fathers take up the role of problematizer, which positions them as family judge. Ochs and Taylor conclude that the patterns of mothers' and fathers' narrative roles contribute to a traditional arrangement of "Father knows best," which, they observe, is a configuration of power that is generally thought to be extinct in middle-class families.

Drawing on a framework for gender-related discourse inspired by Lakoff's rules of politeness as outlined in *LWP* (see Tannen, this volume), Tannen (2003: 187) argues that phenomena observed in family interaction in prior research can be explained by gender-related patterns of discourse, which involve negotiations of both power and solidarity. For example, Susan Ervin-Tripp, Catherine O'Connor, and Jarrett Rosenberg (1984: 134–135) found that children used nondeferential imperatives to mothers but not to fathers, "suggesting that the children expect compliance and believed their desires to be justification enough." Tannen observes that it is possible that children use more bald imperatives when speaking to their mothers either because they have less respect for them (the power dimension) or because they feel closer to them (the solidarity dimension), or both. In relation to Ochs and Taylor (1995), Tannen notes that when a mother asks her children to tell Daddy about their day, she may be initiating the "Father knows best" dynamic, but her likely goal is to "involve the father in the family, bring him into the circle of intimacy she feels is established by such talk" (2003: 186). Such mothers put into practice a verbal ritual observed to characterize women's friendships: exchanging details of daily life (Coates 1996; Tannen 1990). More specifically, they are sharing difficulties through the ritual of "troubles talk." Since this ritual is not as common among men, fathers may think they are being asked to solve the problem and, when they try to do so, it results in an apparent power imbalance.

My own work on the language of mothers extends the work of Ochs and Taylor (1995) and Tannen (1994, 2003) to consider the gendered distribution of discursive roles as discursive positions (Davies & Harré 1990) within a model of linguistic politeness and face. In the domestic component of a study of one woman at work and at home (Kendall 1999), I demonstrate that the mother and father in the family take up gendered positions vis-à-vis each other and their ten-year-old daughter at dinnertime. Although both parents work full-time outside the home, the positions the mother takes up—and the father does not—reflect both a gendered division of labor and the quintessence of "women's language": talking "like a lady" (*LWP* 84). The mother assumes positions associated with (1) the domestic sphere (as Head Chef she directs the preparation and service of food); (2) caregiving (as Caregiver she assists her daughter, as Teacher she teaches her dinnertime skills, and as Manager she gets her ready for after-dinner activities); and (3) she acts as the "judge of manners" (*LWP* 77) in the position of Civilizer, in which she monitors her daughter's dinnertime etiquette, behavior, and appearance. The father primarily takes up positions based on humor, particularly those that counter the mother's efforts to maintain the family face: as Playmate he teases and jokes with his daughter, and as Rebel he jokes about "taboo" topics. Although the mother and father presumably share the working role, they maintain a traditional division of labor in the domestic sphere. Furthermore, the position of Civilizer reflects the "superpolite" component of "women's language": the absence of "off-color or indelicate expressions" and the enforcement of conventional etiquette (*LWP* 80). In addition, the mother uses directive forms identified in *LWP* as sounding more "polite" (those phrased as requests rather than commands) because she assumes positions characterized by these directives (*LWP* 50). Thus, *LWP* provides a basis for understanding the interactional patterns in this family at dinnertime, and we see the continuing relevance of "domesticity": a gender system of beliefs and structures that supports a sex-based division of labor (Williams 2000). By considering how family members constitute gendered identities through positioning within a situated activity, it is possible to relate linguistic phenomena to the social institutions and processes that produce gender.

Some of the issues Lakoff identifies regarding language that is used about, rather than by, women are also relevant to mothers. She argues that women's practice of taking their husbands' surname is part of a broader pattern in which women have "an existence only when defined by a man" (*LWP* 57). As a result of a greater awareness of the underlying meanings of this practice, many women now retain their last names. However, a perhaps unforeseen complication arises when they become mothers. Many families use the paternal surname for their children, with the result that women are nominally segregated from the rest of their family. Considering the role of mothers within our investigations of language and gender reveals hidden ways in which many women's choices are still limited.

The increasing awareness of social roles in gender and language research indicates that it may be time to make a place for mothers in our investigations. The pioneering role of Lakoff in *LWP* can be embraced as a directional beacon in exploring the role of mothers, which, through its very pervasiveness, has often been too easy to overlook.

REFERENCES

Ainsworth-Vaughn, Nancy (1998). *Claiming power in doctor-patient talk.* New York: Oxford University Press.

Case, Susan Schick (1988). Cultural differences, not deficiencies: An analysis of managerial women's language. In Laurie Larwood & Suzanne Rose (eds.), *Women's careers: Pathways and pitfalls.* New York: Praeger. 41–63.

Coates, Jennifer (1996). *Women talk: Conversation between women friends.* Oxford: Blackwell.

Davies, Bronwyn, & Rom Harré (1990). Positioning: Conversation and the production of selves. *Journal for the Theory of Social Behavior* 20:43–63.

Ervin-Tripp, Susan, Catherine O'Connor, & Jarrett Rosenberg (1984). Language and power in the family. In Cheris Kramarae, Muriel Schulz, & William M. O'Barr (eds.), *Language and power.* Beverly Hills, CA: Sage. 116–135.

Fisher, Sue (1993). Gender, power, resistance: Is care the remedy? In Sue Fisher & Kathy Davis (eds.), *Negotiating at the margins: The gendered discourse of power and resistance.* New Brunswick, NJ: Rutgers University Press. 87–121.

Kendall, Shari (1999). The interpenetration of (gendered) spheres: A sociolinguistic analysis of mothers and fathers at work and at home. PhD diss., Georgetown University.

——— (2003). Creating gendered demeanors of authority at work and at home. In Janet Holmes & Miriam Meyerhoff (eds.), *The handbook of language and gender.* Oxford: Blackwell. 600–623.

Kendall, Shari, & Deborah Tannen (1997). Gender and language in the workplace. In Ruth Wodak (ed.), *Gender and discourse.* London: Sage. 81–105.

Kotthoff, Helga (1997). The interactional achievement of expert status: Creating asymmetries by "teaching conversational lecture" in TV discussions. In Helga Kotthoff & Ruth Wodak (eds.), *Communicating gender in context.* Amsterdam: John Benjamins. 139–178.

Lakoff, Robin (1975). *Language and woman's place.* New York: Harper & Row.

McElhinny, Bonnie S. (1993). We all wear the blue: Language, gender and police work. PhD diss., Stanford University.

——— (1997). Ideologies of public and private language in sociolinguistics. In Ruth Wodak (ed.), *Gender and discourse.* London: Sage. 106–139.

Ochs, Elinor, & Carolyn Taylor (1995). The "Father knows best" dynamic in dinnertime narratives. In Kira Hall & Mary Bucholtz (eds.), *Gender articulated: Language and the socially constructed self.* New York: Routledge. 97–120.

Ortner, Sherry (1974). Is female to male as nature is to culture? In Michelle Rosaldo & Louise Lamphere (eds.), *Woman, culture, and society.* Stanford, CA: Stanford University Press. 67–87.

Philips, Susan U. (2003). The power of gender ideologies in discourse. In Janet Holmes & Miriam Meyerhoff (eds.), *The handbook of language and gender.* Oxford: Blackwell. 252–276.

Rosaldo, Michelle Zimbalist (1974). Woman, culture, and society: A theoretical overview. In Michelle Zimbalist Rosaldo & Louise Lamphere (eds.), *Woman, culture, and society.* Stanford, CA: Stanford University Press. 17–42.

Tannen, Deborah (1990). *You just don't understand: Women and men in conversation.* New York: William Morrow.

———— (1994). The relativity of linguistic strategies: Rethinking power and solidarity in gender and dominance. In *Gender and discourse.* Oxford: Oxford University Press. 19–52.

———— (2003). Gender and family interaction. In Janet Holmes & Miriam Meyerhoff (eds.), *The handbook of language and gender.* Oxford: Blackwell. 179–201.

West, Candace (1990). Not just doctor's orders: Directive-response sequences in patients' visits to women and men physicians. *Discourse and Society* 1:85–11.

Williams, Joan (2000). *Unbending gender: Why family and work conflict and what to do about it.* New York: Oxford University Press.

## 13 ::

# Doing and Saying

*Some Words on Women's Silence*

MIRIAM MEYERHOFF

To a linguist, whenever a person is silent it is always superficially the same—silence is, after all, by definition, the absence of speech or phonetic content—but that hardly means all silence is the same. In *Language and Woman's Place* (*LWP*) (1975), Robin Lakoff brought many aspects of talk by and about women to our attention (see also Holmes, this volume). Linguists have understandably focused mainly on the overt, spoken-aloud aspects of talk discussed in *LWP*, but it is worth remembering that Lakoff was interested not only in what was said of and by women but also in the constraints or restrictions on what might be said. Indeed, since *LWP* was published she has often returned to explore the realm of what is not said (Lakoff 1996, 2003).

This essay provides me, a sociolinguist, with the chance to think a bit more about silence, a feature of communication that is technically extralinguistic, but one that sociolinguists nevertheless often find themselves having to deal with. This is perhaps increasingly true as sociolinguistics and language and gender studies so often have to bridge many domains of experience, from the spoken to the unspoken, and this is one of the things that people find attractive about the field. So it is worth having a look at what kind of role silence plays in understanding women's place in language: it is an appropriate tribute to both the dynamism and interdisciplinarity of Lakoff's original work and the field of language and gender studies as a whole.

## What Is Silence?

There are many ways in which a person can be silenced, and many writers deal with the extent to which women's voices or perspectives are systematically silenced by the sexism of society as a whole (e.g., Cameron 1998; Elgin 2000; Spender 1989). Obviously, as individuals, everyone has had the experience of wanting to say something but of being prevented from doing so—maybe there is no time, or it would be unkind to say it. In these cases, the silence is a simple and perfect one: the utterance that will express your desires, or intentions, or beliefs is never born. But sometimes silence is more complicated. You might actually say something—utter words you think express your intentions or desires—but the person you are talking to seems to hear you say something different. Or you might speak up and utter your idea but it only seems to be heard when it is appropriated and restated by someone else (often by someone with more status than you), and a lot of people would want to consider these to be examples of silencing, too.

In *LWP*, Lakoff argued that women are sometimes silenced in the most perfect way; that is, they are constrained or prohibited from uttering the same words or phrases that men can use. But she also argued that women's ideas and intentions can't always be fully realized because they aren't given the same kind of weight that men's ideas and intentions are, and women get silenced in this way, too (*LWP* 42, 45). Sometimes people try to make a qualitative distinction between the two kinds of silencing. People want to say that when no words are allowed to be uttered (the first case) then the would-be speaker has really been silenced, but that in the other cases—where intents or desires are misinterpreted or misappropriated—this is not "really" silencing; we just call it silencing because of some metaphorical extension of the notion of "real" silence. However, it can be argued that where women's ability to express their experiences and intentions are systematically thwarted, this is just as real a form of silencing as any sexist proscriptions on a woman's right to utter certain words or phrases.

This, at any rate, is the argument made by the feminist philosopher Rae Langton (1993), and it is an important and useful argument to explore in a bit more detail because it has the potential to greatly enrich our understanding of the silencing of women.[1] It is important for linguists for two reasons. First, Langton's argument takes seriously the different levels of meaning in J. L. Austin's (1962) theory of speech acts. Austin's distinction between locutionary and illocutionary acts may seem arcane, but Langton shows that we can find significant social reflexes of these different levels of meaning in day-to-day linguistic practices. Second, Langton's claim that the locutionary and illocutionary force of women's speech can be silenced connects some of Lakoff's insights on silencing with work on silence in other disciplines in the social sciences. Here I introduce Langton's arguments about the silencing of women's speech acts and then touch on how I think her arguments reverberate further in understanding how language and attitudes toward women and men interact, and how this interaction constructs women and men as different (and contrastive) social groups.

Langton (1993) makes a distinction between *locutionary silencing* and *illocutionary silencing*, and it is this distinction that is of most relevance to us. She takes the distinction from Austin's notion of *locutionary* and *illocutionary acts*. Austin argued that it was important to differentiate between what we *say*, that is, our locutionary acts, and what we *do* when we say something, that is, the illocutionary act performed by saying something. Here's a simple example: suppose I say, "It's cold in here"; depending on the situation, saying these words does rather different things. They might simply describe the room, in which case they're a declarative, or they might tell you to turn on a heater, in which case they're an order or imperative. Of course, they can only *do* an order if other conditions are met. I can give you an order if the social distance between us is low or if the power difference between us is high. These are examples of the kinds of *felicity conditions* that have to be met in order for me to *do* the illocutionary act of giving an order.

Langton argues that in a post-Austinian world, we should be sensitive to both the locutionary and illocutionary levels of an utterance. Certainly, it is true that if you gag a person or forbid them to speak in a particular social context, then you have silenced them. If you do this, you have silenced their locutionary act.

Clearly, this kind of silencing is intimately tied up with conventionalized power relations in any society: a judge is empowered to prohibit others from speaking in court, parents are empowered to prohibit a child from speaking while they are talking to another adult, and so on. But equally clearly, it is not the context alone that provides the empowerment, because if I try to prohibit the judge from speaking in court, I am at best a fool and at worst in contempt of court. Similarly, not everyone in a family has to respect one another's rights to talk; parents can prohibit children from interrupting their conversations, but children have much less authority to stop parents from interrupting their games.

There are numerous ways in which locutionary silencing intersects with the gendering of society. For example, it can be argued that because the larger social construction of femininity and masculinity is very deeply intertwined with rites and rituals of heterosexual attraction, the self-silencing of same-sex desires actively contributes to the construction of what it means to be a successful woman or man.[2] Locutionary silence has generally been the focus for linguists, sociologists, and social psychologists.[3] However, Langton tries to convince us that illocutionary silence is just as real.

Although Lakoff doesn't make use of the same terminology as Langton, there are some deep similarities to their claims. Lakoff suggests that even when women do speak, society is structured in such a way that their intentions and desires are not recognized or heard as consistently as men's are (*LWP* 45). And even if women's contributions to social, artistic, or scientific thought are heard, they are more consistently forgotten than men's contributions are (Spender 1989).[4]

Langton, too, sees the silencing of women as arising from their disempowerment and subordination to men, and like Lakoff she attributes this subordination to the way society is structured. But Langton tries to pin down exactly what enables this subordination. Her thesis is essentially that some speech acts are gendered—that is, the social conventions associated with them mean that women simply can't satisfy the felicity conditions necessary for someone to perform those speech acts. Hence, she argues, women suffer illocutionary silencing over and above the perfect silencing of their locutionary acts.

Langton gives the example of the felicity conditions required to perform a divorce under Islamic law. If a man says "Divorced" (or some conventional equivalent, e.g., "You're to me like my mother") between one and three times, he performs the illocutionary act of divorcing his wife: saying the word once or twice performs a "revocable divorce"; three times performs an "irrevocable divorce" (incidentally, only the former is discussed in the Qur'an; the latter is an innovation). In performing the locutionary act, the man does something that has social content. There is nothing to prevent a woman from saying those same words, but if she does, she doesn't *do* the same thing that the man does.[5] That is, the locutionary act is not silenced, but the illocutionary effect is, because she fails to satisfy the felicity conditions required to do the performative. Langton argues that this is illocutionary silencing and that it is as real as prohibiting a woman from speaking at all, because as Austin showed, it is in our illocutionary acts that we actually *do* things with words.

The notion of illocutionary silencing becomes even more interesting and perhaps more contentious when Langton explores it in her analysis of what happens when a woman's intended illocutionary act fails to be picked up or accurately identified by an interlocutor. What happens during sexual activity when a woman says "no" or utters some other form of refusal, asks Langton, and her partner fails to stop? Obviously, she has not been silenced from making a locutionary act because she has actually said something, but if her refusal is not recognized as a refusal, then her illocutionary act has misfired. Why is this similar to the example of Islamic divorce above? Langton argues that in this case, too, the woman fails to *do* a refusal—her illocutionary act is thwarted—because socially constructed conventions about who has the power or authority to refuse sex in our society are part of the felicity conditions for refusing sex, and so for some men women simply cannot satisfy those felicity conditions. Particularly if society eroticizes women's resistance and eroticizes men's force, then a woman will, *by definition for some men*, fail to satisfy the felicity conditions required for the illocutionary act of a refusal. This argument is independently taken up in Susan Ehrlich's (2001, this volume) discourse analysis of how ideologies of agency and responsibility play out in sexual-assault trials. Lakoff's point that talk about a woman often "treat[s] her as an object—sexual or otherwise—but never a serious person with individual views" (*LWP* 42) foreshadows Langton's arguments about illocutionary silencing. You have to be a serious person with your own views to satisfy the felicity conditions for most speech acts, and if women are socially and discursively constructed in roles that preclude having serious views, then as far as some speech acts go, their attempts to act are silenced. Lakoff identifies the social preconditions for women's silencing; Langton identifies the linguistic dimensions on which this semantic silencing occurs.

This analysis, of course, raises its own questions. It would be nice to have some idea about why so much creative energy is put into the silencing of women, and I think it is in answering this question that Lakoff's and Langton's arguments begin to offer connections with work in areas outside of linguistics, specifically, the work of social psychologists on group identities and intergroup distinctiveness. Elsewhere (Meyerhoff 2001), I have discussed the deep parallels or connections between sociolinguistics and the social psychology of language, and I have tried to show that a number of very useful principles about interpersonal and intergroup behavior have made their way into sociolinguistics (or sometimes been reinvented there). Intergroup theory has been criticized for being essentialist, but I think that to the extent that this is true, it is a consequence of the methodological constraints that researchers inherited from psychology rather than a tenet of the theory itself. Henri Tajfel's own writing on intergroup theory is more in tune with approaches to identity that stress interpersonal negotiation and the subjective interaction between multiple identities than some of the implementations of intergroup theory in the experimental literature would suggest or than characterizations of it in the secondary literature would lead you to believe (see, e.g., Oakes, Haslam, & Turner 1998: 77; Tajfel 1978: 39; and the discussion of mobility and creativity in Tajfel & Turner 1986).

One of the points made in intergroup theory is that there is a tendency for people to accentuate differences between people they identify with and people who they see as members of some out-group. At the same time, they tend to perceive differences within their own groups as smaller or less significant than they might actually be. The effects of these principles can be seen at many levels of engagement: there are conventions that police the kinds of clothes women and men wear, there are conventions that restrict women (still) to a much narrower range of occupations than men or encourage women and men to participate in different social activities.

One implication of this discussion of silencing is that it reminds us how deep and unseen some of the conventionalized restrictions on women's behavior are. If, as Lakoff points out, one of the intergroup differences that gets accentuated between women and men is that women are not seen as fully competent agents, able to express and form strong opinions, and if, as Langton points out, this means that women, as opposed to men, may consistently fail to satisfy the felicity conditions for certain speech acts, then we are starting to get a fuller picture of silence as a social, intentional, and cognitive act. I have tried here to draw a picture that links the phenomenon of silencing, the mechanisms by which silencing occurs, and the cognitive motivations underpinning those mechanisms. But in the end, what I hope emerges most clearly is the sound of silence, calling out directions for its further study.

NOTES

1. My thanks to Dharshi Santhakumaran for insightful discussions of this work.

2. There is an ever-burgeoning literature on this subject that is well beyond the scope of this essay to explore (e.g., Cameron & Kulick 2003; Eckert 2003; Livia & Hall 1997; McIlvenny 2002).

3. See, for example, Billig 1999; Foucault 1981; Goffman 1971; Kurzon 1998. Cf. chapter 4 in Jaworski 1993, which does deal with silencing along the lines discussed here.

4. There is, of course, an extensive literature exploring alternative modes of expression as a corrective to this, some beyond our world (Elgin 2000) and some within it (Daly 1978).

5. In fact, under Islamic law, a woman can reserve in her marriage contract the right to divorce with the same locutionary acts, but in practice few if any women do reserve this right. Stipulating this right in her marriage contract is a necessary felicity condition for a woman to be able to enact the performative. My thanks to Atiqa Hachimi for explaining the performatives involved in Islamic divorce to me. She is not responsible for any misunderstandings I may yet have.

REFERENCES

Austin, J. L. (1962). *How to do things with words*. Oxford: Oxford University Press.

Billig, Michael (1999). *Freudian repression: Conversation creating the unconscious*. Cambridge: Cambridge University Press.

Cameron, Deborah (ed.) (1998). *The feminist critique of language*. 2nd ed. London: Routledge.

Cameron, Deborah, & Don Kulick (eds.) (2003). Language and desire. Special issue, *Language and Communication* 23(2).

Daly, Mary (1978). *Gyn/ecology: The metaethics of radical feminism*. Boston: Beacon Press.

Eckert, Penelope (2003). Language and gender in adolescence. In Janet Holmes & Miriam Meyerhoff (eds.), *The handbook of language and gender*. Oxford: Blackwell. 381–400.

Ehrlich, Susan (2001). *Representing rape: Language and sexual consent*. London: Routledge.

Elgin, Suzette Haden (2000). *Native tongue*. New York: Feminist Press.

Foucault, Michel (1981). *The history of sexuality*. Vol. 1. London: Pelican Books.

Goffman, Erving (1971). *Relations in public: Microstudies of the public order*. New York: Basic Books.

Jaworski, Adam (1993). *The power of silence: Social and pragmatic perspectives.* Newbury Park, CA: Sage.

Kulick, Don (2003). Language and desire. In Janet Holmes & Miriam Meyerhoff (eds.), *The handbook of language and gender.* Oxford: Blackwell. 119–141.

Kurzon, Dennis (1998). *Discourse of silence.* Amsterdam: John Benjamins.

Lakoff, Robin (1975). *Language and woman's place.* New York: Harper & Row.

——— (1996). The (rise and fall and)[n] of Hillary Rodham Clinton. In Jocelyn Ahlers, Natasha Warner, Leela Bilmes, Monica Oliver, Suzanne Wertheim, and Melinda Chen (eds.), *Gender and belief systems: Proceedings of the fourth Berkeley Women and Language Conference.* Berkeley, CA: Berkeley Women and Language Group. 387–402.

——— (2003). Language, gender, and politics: Putting "women" and "power" in the same sentence. In Janet Holmes & Miriam Meyerhoff (eds.), *The handbook of language and gender.* Oxford: Blackwell. 161–178.

Langton, Rae (1993). Speech acts and unspeakable acts. *Philosophy and Public Affairs* 22:293–330.

Livia, Anna, & Kira Hall (eds.) (1997). *Queerly phrased: Language, gender, and sexuality.* Oxford: Oxford University Press.

McIlvenny, Paul (ed.) (2002). *Talking gender and sexuality.* Amsterdam: John Benjamins.

Meyerhoff, Miriam (2001). Dynamic of differentiation: On social psychology and cases of language variation. In Nikolas Coupland, Srikant Sarangi, & Christopher N. Candlin (eds.), *Sociolinguistics and social theory.* Harlow: Pearson. 61–87.

Oakes, Penelope, Alexander S. Haslam, & John C. Turner (1998). The role of prototypicality in group influence and cohesion: Contextual variation in the graded structure of social categories. In Stephen Worchel, J. Francisco Morales, Darío Páez, & Jean-Claude Deschamps (eds.), *Social identity: International perspectives.* London: Sage. 75–92.

Spender, Dale (1989). *Invisible women: The schooling scandal.* London: Women's Press.

Tajfel, Henri (1978). Interindividual behaviour and intergroup behaviour. In Henri Tajfel (ed.), *Differentiation between social groups: Studies in the social psychology of intergroup behaviour.* London: Academic Press. 27–60.

Tajfel, Henri, & John Turner (1986). The social identity theory of intergroup behavior. In Stephen Worchel & William G. Austin (eds.), *Psychology of intergroup relations.* Chicago: Nelson Hall. 7–24.

# 14 ::

# Computer-Mediated Communication
# and Woman's Place

SUSAN C. HERRING

The world is no longer as it was when Robin Lakoff first published *Language and Woman's Place* (*LWP*) (1975) nearly thirty years ago. The activist feminism of the 1970s, predicated on the premise of women's subordination through patriarchal social, political, and economic systems, has been replaced by generations X and Y, pro-sex feminism, antivictim feminism, antifeminist feminism, and the deconstruction of gender as a meaningful category. Meanwhile, technology in the form of the Internet has cast its web of communication networks across the globe, shrinking distances already reduced by earlier teletechnologies and enabling members of out-of-power groups to seek individual and political empowerment across geographical boundaries. In the current postgender "Internet Age" (as some would have it), Lakoff's classic observation that language used by and about women reflects their subordinate status may seem outmoded, even quaint. After all, although they admittedly got off to a somewhat slow start, aren't women and girls now claiming an equal place in cyberspace alongside men and boys, bonding, debating in computer-mediated chatrooms, and self-publishing on the Web, unconstrained by patriarchy and gender?

So the popular wisdom goes. But popular wisdom, especially when it concerns the Internet, is often wrong. Whether traditional patriarchal gender arrangements have ceased to be relevant on the Internet is an empirical question, one best approached with an open mind and evaluated on the basis of systematic observation. As Lakoff pointed out in 1975, spoken language constitutes an object through which feelings and values can be nailed down and examined. The Internet goes further yet: computer-mediated text is not only observable, it is persistent and self-preserving, an ideal medium in which to mine language for the insights it can provide into social structures and mental states. What, then, does computer-mediated communication (CMC) reveal about language and woman's place?

I have spent the past twelve years investigating this question, bringing methods of linguistic discourse analysis to bear on the interactions that take place in public discussion groups, chatrooms, educational Web forums, and the like. My research and observations of many online contexts have led me to conclude that gender—and gender hierarchy—is alive and well on the Internet and that indeed a number of Lakoff's observations about informal speech apply remarkably well to computer-mediated discourse. At the same time, there are differences, and it behooves us to understand their nature. Has society changed, or does the electronic medium affect gender communication in novel ways? It is also possible that where Lakoff's observations and my own agree, we are both wrong. In what follows, I consider each of these possibilities in turn.

I should state first that my research was not modeled on *LWP* nor initially motivated by it. It is possible that I had not even read Lakoff's book at the time I undertook my first study of gender and CMC, although I cannot be certain of this. Thus I approached the analysis of gender and CMC, in some respects, as a neophyte, with a lack of training but also with fresh eyes. What my eyes saw surprised me and sent me scrambling to the language and gender literature, including to Lakoff's book. But that was later.

Initially, what drew me to study online communication was my increasing dissatisfaction with the popular hype about the invisibility of gender on the Internet—"On the Internet, nobody knows you're a dog," a New Yorker cartoon famously proclaimed in the early 1990s—which was belied by my personal experience and powers of direct observation. Not only could I tell perfectly well the gender of most of the contributors to the academic discussion lists to which I subscribed, but I could also see that women were participating less than men, and less than their proportional representation on the lists. I was puzzled, and troubled, by this. I noted my own reactions to certain kinds of behaviors favored by men on the lists—challenging, assertive, often ridiculing behaviors—and formulated a hypothesis that women would be less likely to engage in such behaviors and more likely to find them off-putting. I tested this hypothesis by analyzing the discourse features of female and male participants in an extended discussion on a list for academic linguists and by distributing an electronic questionnaire in which I asked list members about the discussion in question and their reactions to it.

The results of this study were positively Lakoffian. Not only did it turn out that men used measurably more assertive and less polite language than women, but women also expressed more aversion to such language, withdrawing from the discussion or observing it from the margins as a result. Moreover, they displayed features of "women's language" (in Lakoff's terms) and were sometimes trivialized and patronized when they did interact with men. They also received fewer responses to their messages overall (Herring 1992, 1993). Here were academic women and men, communicating in a supposedly gender-blind medium, displaying the genderlects and gender asymmetries we thought we as a society had left behind years, if not decades, earlier. I concluded that societal sexism runs deep and that technology in and of itself was unlikely to change it. Lakoff said much the same thing in 1975, with reference not to technology but to language. She was reacting to the linguistic determinism favored by some feminists of the time, who maintained that by changing language, one could engineer less-sexist attitudes in speakers. Similarly, Internet studies in the early 1990s were characterized by technological determinism, the belief that technology could change what and how people communicated, leading to positive (including more gender-equitable) social outcomes. The more things change, the more they stay the same.

Or do they? Not all Internet discourse involves women standing politely on the sidelines while men hold forth; diverse contexts of CMC exist. Consider, for example, synchronous chat, typically recreational and typically populated by eighteen-to-twenty-somethings with raging hormones, or so the evidence superficially suggests. Women in chat environments, as my later research revealed, are not particularly polite, although they support one another and "laugh" more than men. Nor are they marginal; rather, they garner considerable attention, typically from men, and typically of a sexual nature (Herring 1998). While some women appear to enjoy this attention, others seek to avoid it by taking on gender-neutral or male pseudonyms in public chatrooms; conversely, men take on female pseudonyms in order to attract sexual attention (Bruckman 1993). For some feminist theorists, such "play" with gender demonstrates that gender has been effectively deconstructed in chat environments and that the playing field has been leveled. Lakoff would, I suspect, have a different interpretation, as do I. As Lakoff points out with respect to women's and men's language more generally, the rewards of choosing to take on a different gender (or "cross-expressing"; Hall 1996: 151) in an online chat are different for women and for men: women avoid unwanted attention (a negative reward), while men gain wanted attention (a positive reward). The fact that many women perceive online sexual attention as undesirable has less to do with a lack of interest in sex than with the demeaning connotations of male heterosexual come-ons in the larger societal context: when targeted indiscriminately at anyone with a female-sounding name or pseudonym, such come-ons communicate that women are only good for sex. No such connotations inhere in sexual come-ons directed toward men. Moreover, the fact that men "become" women in order to have sex and women "become" men in order to avoid it reifies the association of sexuality with women. Thus the seemingly exotic discourse of chatrooms in fact reinforces a rather traditional notion of woman's place as sexual object (see also Herring 2003).

I noted above that women in chatrooms tend to support one another and laugh more than men. That is, they display camaraderie, a feature considered by Lakoff to be more typical of male groups. Although males sometimes show camaraderie (especially in banding together to harass "outsiders," including women; see, e.g., Herring 1999a), my research has identified a more common axis of gender differentiation involving linguistic politeness. According to this pattern, women preferentially show support and appreciation, or positive politeness (Brown & Levinson 1987), and men violate politeness of both the positive and negative varieties, favoring distancing strategies. That is, a man in a discussion list or a chatroom is more likely than a woman to set himself off from everyone else ("All of you are wrong; I'm right"), while a woman is more likely to align herself with other participants in the discussion ("I agree with X") (Herring 1994, 1996a). These patterns differ from Lakoff's observations about politeness, which associate distancing and formality with women and camaraderie with men (but see Herring 1999b and Herring & Paolillo 2001 for women's use of formal and distancing strategies).

Another difference between my observations and Lakoff's concerns "men's language." Lakoff writes that men tend to speak directly and factually, in observance of Grice's (1991) rules of conversation; women's language is represented as marked or divergent with respect to men's language. In Internet discussion groups, in contrast, women are often more informative and conversationally cooperative than men (Herring 1996b), particularly when men engage in boastfulness, sarcasm, and "flaming" (the exchange of hostile message content). This latter style is in fact highly marked in that it involves violations both of the Gricean maxims of quality, quantity, relevance, and manner and of conventional norms of politeness. Elsewhere, Lakoff refers to the "rough talk" of men and boys, from which girls and women are excluded: "Women are allowed to fuss and complain, but only a man can bellow in rage" (*LWP* 45). This, it seems to me, is a more apt parallel to online "men's language" than the characterization of men's speech as direct and cooperative, although of course many men are direct and cooperative online, as are many women. It is important not to naturalize "rough" male CMC as conversationally normative, for it is often used to intimidate and harass, and women are often the targets of such intimidation and harassment. This occurs, in most of the cases I have observed, not because women are using "trivial" women's language, but rather in contexts in which women are communicating straightforwardly and assertively, or among themselves (rather than orienting to men), or in a way that could be construed as critical of men (Herring, 1999a, 2002). This, of course, points back to Lakoff: women are damned if they don't (use women's language), and certain men enforce use of women's language by punishing deviance from it through harassment. However, the enforcing mechanism (men's language) is hardly linguistically or ideologically neutral.

It would seem, then, that compared to the characterization presented in *LWP*, women on the Internet today are more solidary and more assertive, and men are "rougher," in their typical communication styles. To what might these differences, if in fact they exist, be attributed? One possible explanation is a technologically deterministic one: the Internet made them do it. More than a few Internet scholars have speculated that the text-based electronic medium reduces gender cues and thereby empowers users to speak out without fear of being interrupted (or silenced with a withering look): this might explain greater assertiveness in women. Moreover, these and other scholars have observed that CMC seems to make users more disinhibited and aggressive: this could be taken as an explanation of men's "roughness." What technological determinism does not explain, however, is how (if the medium reduces gender cues) women and men recognize one another's gender, which is necessary in order for women to show same-sex solidarity and men to harass women. Furthermore, a strong technolog-ically deterministic position would predict that women and men would communicate similarly, yet gender differences persist. For these reasons, the properties of the electronic medium do not entirely account for the discrepancy between Lakoff's observations and the findings of research on gender and CMC.

Could it be, then, that society has changed? Thirty years of feminist consciousness raising (including, not insignificantly, *LWP* itself) could have fostered a greater shared awareness of women's subordinate status, account-ing for an increase in solidary uses of language. Generations of girls raised in the 1970s and 1980s have inherited a world in which women can be assertive and succeed, at least some of the time. Generation X and Gen-eration Y women, although they often shy away from the word *feminist*, may nonetheless carry less "women's language" baggage than their parents' generation into their online communication. For the sake of the present discussion, let us assume that this is indeed the case. But what of the men? Is flaming a form of antifeminist backlash? Or does the "roughness" of much male CMC simply reflect the influence of a particularly populous Internet demographic: young white males? Whatever the explanation, it appears that as women and girls have advanced into traditionally male territory, men and boys have advanced further (some might say, regressed) into a hypermasculinity characterized by ever more violent acts of linguistic aggression (see also Gilboa 1996).

In the process, however, gender difference in language use is main-tained. We still find "men's language" and "women's language" on the Internet, even if the manifestations of each are not identical to those posited by Lakoff for face-to-face speech thirty years ago. Gender differentiation emerges from this historical and cross-medium comparison as a powerful social force, one that leads to the active reproduction of gendered patterns of behavior even under conditions of "bodylessness" and potential neutral-ity. This is a point of profound significance: the more things change, the more they stay the same. Whereas the surface manifestations of gender differentiation vary across media, the language that reproduces the differ-entiation still employs politeness to symbolize femininity, and assertiveness to symbolize masculinity, as Lakoff found. More profoundly yet, the same underlying social hierarchy remains in evidence: women occupy second place in relation to men. We may hope that the surface changes signal the beginning of a move toward a more equal sharing of power and prestige between women and men and that the Internet might help to bring this about, although for now this is mostly speculation. In the meantime, Lakoff's fundamental observation — that linguistic differences reflect and reproduce gender-based status differences — stands affirmed by public CMC on the Internet.

It is also possible that Lakoff and I, each in our respective domains, are wrong. Some feminists are uncomfortable with research that focuses on gender differences and inequality, criticizing such research as reifying dangerous (and by definition, inaccurate) stereotypes. In *LWP*, Lakoff's response is to distance herself from the stereotypical elements in her observations by attributing pure "women's language" and "men's language" to mass media representations; actual communicative behaviors could, and no doubt would, vary. My response is somewhat different. Actual CMC is at times highly gender-stereotypic (see also Hall 1996); accurate description must take this into account. At the same time, women's and men's behavior is of course not uniformly stereotypical; exceptions abound. These too must be acknowledged and their significance considered. The question, it seems to me, is not "Should feminist researchers describe stereotyped behavior?" but rather, "What is the nature of online behavior, and under what circumstances does it follow or diverge from traditional gender norms?" Only then are we in a position to consider what should and can be done if the answers to those questions displease us.

That said, I do not interpret Lakoff as implying that women's secondary status is in any way natural or justifiable, or that women's language is an essential feature of the female sex that cannot be changed, nor do I subscribe to such views myself. On the contrary, by pointing out patterns of gendered behavior, especially those that make us uncomfortable because they naturalize gender inequality, I aim (as does Lakoff, I suspect) to denaturalize and problematize them, precisely so that they can be changed. It seems to me that in the nearly thirty years since its publication, *LWP* has contributed significantly toward this outcome.

REFERENCES

Brown, Penelope, & Levinson, Stephen (1987). *Politeness*. Cambridge: Cambridge University Press.

Bruckman, Amy S. (1993). Gender swapping on the Internet. *Proceedings of INET '93*. Reston, VA: The Internet Society. http://www.cc.gatech.edu/elc/papers/bruckman/gender-swapping-bruckman.pdf.

Gilboa, Netta "grayarea" (1996). Elites, lamers, narcs, and whores: Exploring the computer underground. In Lynn Cherny & Elizabeth R. Weise (eds.), *Wired women*. Seattle: Seal Press. 98–113.

Grice, H. Paul (1991). Logic and conversation. In Steven Davis (ed.), *Pragmatics: A reader.* New York: Oxford University Press. 305–315.

Hall, Kira (1996). Cyberfeminism. In Susan Herring (ed.), *Computer-mediated communication: Linguistic, social, and cross-cultural perspectives.* Amsterdam: John Benjamins. 147–170.

Herring, Susan C. (1992). Gender and participation in computer-mediated linguistic discourse. Document no. ED345552. Washington, DC: ERIC Clearinghouse on Languages and Linguistics.

———— (1993). Gender and democracy in computer-mediated communication. *Electronic Journal of Communication* 3, http://ella.slis.indiana.edu/~herring/ejc.txt.

———— (1994). Politeness in computer culture: Why women thank and men flame. In Mary Bucholtz, Anita C. Liang, Laurel Sutton, & Caitlin Hines (eds.), *Cultural performances: Proceedings of the third Berkeley women and language conference.* Berkeley, CA: Berkeley Women and Language Group. 278–294.

Herring, Susan C. (1996a). Posting in a different voice: Gender and ethics in computer-mediated communication. In Charles Ess (ed.), *Philosophical perspectives on computer-mediated communication,* Albany: SUNY Press. 115–145.

———— (1996b). Two variants of an electronic message schema. In Susan Herring (ed.), *Computer-mediated communication: Linguistic, social, and cross-cultural perspectives.* Amsterdam: John Benjamins. 81–106.

———— (1998). Virtual gender performances in Internet relay chat. Paper presented at the Linguistics Colloquium Series, Texas A&M University, September 25.

———— (1999a). The rhetorical dynamics of gender harassment online. *The Information Society* 15:151–167.

———— (1999b). Actualization of a counter-change: Contractions on the Internet. Paper presented at the 14th International Conference on Historical Linguistics. Vancouver, Canada, August 13.

———— (2002). Cyber violence: Recognizing and resisting abuse in online environments. *Asian Women* 14:187–212, http://ella.slis.indiana.edu/~herring/violence.html.

———— (2003). Gender and power in online communication. In Janet Holmes & Miriam Meyerhoff (eds.), *The handbook of language and gender.* Oxford: Blackwell. 202–228.

Herring, Susan C., & John C. Paolillo (2001). Homogenization and diversification in English on the Internet. Paper presented at the 15th International Conference on Historical Linguistics, Melbourne, Australia, August 16.

Lakoff, Robin (1975). *Language and woman's place.* New York: Harper & Row.

# 15 ::

# Linguistic Discrimination and Violence against Women

*Discursive Practices and Material Effects*

SUSAN EHRLICH

The introduction to Robin Lakoff's *Language and Woman's Place* (*LWP*) (1975) sets out the book's primary purpose—"to provide diagnostic evidence from language use for one type of inequity that has been claimed to exist in our society: that between the roles of men and women" (*LWP* 39). While much of Lakoff's text describes instances of linguistic discrimination, her goals go beyond a description of discriminatory language use. Indeed, she ultimately poses a question about the relationship between linguistic discrimination and social realities: "Does one correct a social inequity by changing linguistic disparities?" (*LWP* 39). With this and other related comments, Lakoff foreshadows a debate that has figured prominently within the field of language and gender and in feminist studies more generally—that is, does a focus on linguistic inequities and their elimination necessarily have any bearing on the eradication of material inequities between women and men? In a variety of contemporary feminist writings, for example, a focus on discourse or discursive practices has often been counterposed with a focus on material realities. Indeed, Michèle Barrett (1992: 201) points to a central issue evident in feminist scholarship that sets the valuing of "words" against that of "things": "Many feminists have traditionally tended to see things be they low pay, rape or female foeticide as more significant than, for example, the discursive construction of marginality in a text or document." In what follows, I want to suggest that a simple dichotomizing of the discursive versus the material does little to illuminate the intersection of the two: that is, *the way that discursive practices can have material effects* or, in Lakoff's terms, the way that linguistic disparities can influence social inequities.

The idea that sexist linguistic practices can adversely influence the kinds of gendered identities women are able to produce was a major impetus behind nonsexist language reform efforts in the 1970s and 1980s. Early work on sexist language, for example, pointed to the detrimental effects, both practical and symbolic, of masculine generics such as *he* and *man*—forms, it was argued, that render women invisible. Indeed, a substantial body of empirical evidence showed, among other things, that *he/man* generics readily evoke images of males rather than females, have negative effects on individuals' beliefs in women's ability to perform a job, and have a negative impact on women's own feelings of pride, importance, and power (for a review of this work see Henley 1989). While more recent work in feminist linguistics has broadened its conception of sexist linguistic representations beyond single words and expressions to discursive practices (see Cameron 1998a, 1998b for discussion), the negative effects of such representations continue to be of concern to language and gender researchers. Deborah Cameron (1998a) demonstrates how a range of linguistic features, none of which would be deemed problematic by a word-based critique of sexist language, can together function to construct rape in sexist and androcentric ways. And Helen Benedict (1992, 1993) and Kate Clark (1998) demonstrate the pervasiveness of rape reports in the media that portray rapists as crazy, evil sexual deviants and fiends rather than as women's husbands, partners, and family members, in spite of the fact that women are much more likely to be raped by husbands, lovers, and dates than by strangers. As Clark (1998:197) comments, "the intense hyperbole of fiend naming focuses a self-righteous fury on stranger attacks, which are actually a very small area of male/female violence." Indeed, Benedict argues that rape reporting in the mainstream media is socially controlling to the extent that it simultaneously curtails women's freedom by fostering a fear of violence in public spaces and creates a false sense of security around the situations wherein women are most vulnerable.

Focusing on the discursive practices of the legal system rather than the mainstream media, Susan Estrich's (1987) book, *Real Rape*, is suggestive of the social control and regulation exercised by such discourses in relation to perpetrators and victims of male violence against women. (For an extended version of this argument, see Ehrlich 2001, 2002.) The question Estrich explores in her book is why many cases of rape in the United States that meet the statutory definition are not considered as such by police, prosecutors, judges, and juries. That is, Estrich argues that the law differentially prosecutes perpetrators and differentially protects the interests of victims. And paradoxically, it is the cases of rape that are least frequent that the law treats most aggressively. In cases of stranger rape, what Estrich calls "real rape," in which the perpetrator is an armed stranger jumping from behind the bushes and, in particular, a black stranger attacking a white woman, Estrich argues, the law is likely to arrest, prosecute, and convict the perpetrator. By contrast, in cases of what Estrich calls "simple rape"—that is, when a woman is forced to engage in sex with a date, an acquaintance, her boss, or a man she met at a bar, when no weapon is involved and when there is no overt evidence of physical injury—rapes are much less likely to be treated as criminal by the criminal-justice system. Given that stranger rape is considered to be real rape by the criminal-justice system, from the system's point of view rape prosecution is not a problem. First, stranger rape is a relatively infrequent event and second, when it does occur, it tends to be prosecuted more successfully and more frequently than many other violent crimes.

Put in slightly different terms, the discourses that surround the prosecution of real rape versus simple rape cases in the criminal-justice system (e.g., the discourses of police, lawyers, and judges) bring into being definitions and categories of what constitutes a well-founded complaint, a legitimate or believable victim, and a legitimate perpetrator. Legitimate perpetrators, for example, are strangers to their victims, carry a weapon, and inflict physical injury upon their victim beyond the sexual violence; legitimate or believable victims are women raped by precisely these kinds of perpetrators. The discourses of rape that surround the criminal-justice system's treatment of rape, then, construct stranger rape as real rape and render the vast majority of rapes invisible. Consider the difference between the legal system's treatment of real rape versus simple rape in relation to victim disclosure and reporting rates. In a well-cited survey of approximately 1,000 adult women in 1978, Russell (1984: 35) found that 44 percent of her respondents said that at some point in their life they had been a victim of "forced intercourse or intercourse obtained by threat of force." Of these, 82 percent of the rapes involved nonstrangers, yet less than 10 percent of these were reported to the police. On the basis of a number of other studies investigating rape reporting rates, Estrich draws the generalization that the closer the relationship between victim and assailant, the less likely women are to report rape (1987: 11). That is, while rape generally is a vastly underreported crime, real rapes are more likely to be reported than simple rapes. In other words, definitions and categories of real rapes and legitimate or believable victims are socially controlling in the sense that they determine the likelihood of women's disclosing and reporting rape.

In my own work (Ehrlich 2001), I have explored some of the interactional processes by which the institutional discourse of rape trials can radically constrain the kinds of institutional identities complainants are able to construct. Trial discourse is notable for its question/answer format; moreover, given the institutionally sanctioned power accorded to questioners in such contexts (e.g., lawyers and judges), witnesses are "systematically disabled" from asking questions or initiating turns (Hutchby & Wooffitt 1998: 166). In analyzing the presuppositions of questions asked of complainants in sexual-assault trials, I have argued that, when taken together, such presuppositions formed a powerful ideological frame through which the events under investigation were understood and evaluated. This ideological frame is based on the "utmost-resistance standard"—the idea that complainants must resist the accused "to the utmost"—which, though no longer codified in law in the United States or Canada, circulated discursively in the sexual-assault adjudication processes I analyzed. And in response to innumerable questions whose presuppositions embodied the utmost-resistance standard, the complainants involuntarily cast themselves as ineffectual agents: their strategic attempts to resist the perpetrators of sexual assault were transformed into ineffectual acts of resistance within the discourse of the trial. Put another way, the identities performed by the complainants in these contexts — as passive and lacking in appropriate resistance — were structured and constrained by the dominant discourse (i.e., the utmost-resistance standard) that circulated within these trials. And insofar as the complainants were unable to represent their strategic acts of resistance in the context of their perpetrators' sexual aggression, the discursive characteristics of the trials may have had an influence on their outcomes. Thus, it is not only through coercive legal measures (e.g., the enactment of rules and the imposition of punishments) that (some) men's sexual interests and prerogatives are protected at the expense of women's sexual autonomy; it is also through culturally powerful discourses that circulate within the legal system. These discourses achieve their force by the curtailing of women's activities such as disclosing and reporting rape as well as by the curtailing of their identities as strategic agents in the face of men's sexual aggression.

While discursive representations of violence against women (both in media and legal contexts) surely have regulatory (i.e., material) effects, Livia Polanyi (1995) highlights the social control exercised by actual instances of sexual harassment (see also Herring, this volume). In an ethnographic study of American university students in a Russian study-abroad program, Polanyi shows that the routine sexual harassment experienced by the female students created target language interactions (with Russian men) in which they were reduced to silence or made to feel humiliated and degraded (see also Meyerhoff, this volume). In contrast to the silence and degradation experienced by the young women in their encounters with Russian men, Polanyi cites the journal of a young man whose pleasant flirtation with a Russian woman resulted in an evening of increased linguistic fluency: "My Russian felt good, and her ongoing barrage of smiles certainly helped. . . . We joked and chatted. . . . My Russian was smooth and flexible" (Polanyi 1995: 281). Clearly, target-language interactions in which learners are encouraged to speak by, among other things, an "ongoing barrage of smiles" will produce a different kind of output in the target language (i.e., output that is "smooth and flexible") than interactions that involve harassment. In fact, Polanyi makes the point that when "faced with complex interpersonal situations" (1995: 285) the young women in the study-abroad program were acquiring the linguistic skills to cope: some reported learning useful vocabulary for dealing with sexually harassing situations; others reported that their linguistic ability to deal effectively with harassing situations in Russian became a point of pride. In spite of the considerable linguistic and sociolinguistic competence acquired by these women, however, the linguistic skills developed in response to the sexually harassing situations were not the focus of language-proficiency tests. Thus, not surprisingly, Richard Brecht, Dan Davidson, and Ralph Ginsberg (1995: 56), in their long-term study of the predictors of language gain in the same Russian study-abroad programs, found that women made fewer gains than men in listening and speaking skills and that men were more likely to "cross the crucial divide between Intermediate+ to Advanced level" than women. It is important to note that the young women performed as well as the young men on Russian tests before the study-abroad program. The problem, according to Polanyi, is not that the young women were less gifted language learners than the young men. Rather, despite the fact that the women were subject to sexist and androcentric practices in the foreign-language learning situation, the tests that measured their proficiency took as their norm men's linguistic activities and practices — activities and practices that did not involve sexual harassment.

Translated into the terms of this discussion, the linguistic activities and identities performed by these young women and men were regulated — that is, facilitated or constrained — by the gendered ideologies and power relations that characterized the foreign-language learning situation. Indeed, positioned as victims of sexual harassment, the young women developed a linguistic identity in Russian that was not primarily of their own making. Polanyi's work, then, shows how actual instances of (verbal) violence against women, like legal and media representations of violence against women, are socially controlling and regulatory to the extent that they shape and constrain the activities and identities that women are able to perform.

While attention to discriminatory language and discursive practices, at least with respect to violence against women, is no substitute for other approaches to ending such violence — for example, developing counseling services and shelters, attempting to rehabilitate violent men, ensuring that women have the economic ability to leave abusive men, and so on — it is significant insofar as discursive practices are themselves socially controlling and regulatory. Indeed, Lakoff's focus on discriminatory language had as its ultimate goal the elimination of inequities between women and men that she saw reflected and reproduced in language. Thus, if the ultimate goal of feminist approaches to language is social change and, in particular, change to material realities, then we need to avoid the dichotomizing of "words" versus "things" evident in some feminist scholarship. Instead, we must be attentive to the way that the discursive and linguistic intersects with the material.

REFERENCES

Barrett, Michèle (1992). Words and things: Materialism and method in contemporary feminist analysis. In Michèle Barrett & Anne Phillips (eds.), Destabilizing theory. Stanford, CA: Stanford University Press. 201–219.

Benedict, Helen (1992). Virgin or vamp: How the press covers sex crimes. New York: Oxford University Press.

Benedict, Helen (1993). The language of rape. In Emilie Buchwald, Pamela Fletcher, & Martha Roth (eds.), *Transforming a rape culture*. Minneapolis: Milkweed Press. 101–105.

Brecht, Richard, Dan Davidson, & Ralph Ginsberg (1995). Predictors of foreign language gain during study abroad. In Barbara Freed (ed.), *Second language acquisition in a study abroad context*. Amsterdam: John Benjamins. 37–66.

Cameron, Deborah (1998a). Introduction: Why is language a feminist issue? In Deborah Cameron (ed.), *The feminist critique of language: A reader*. London: Routledge. 1–28.

Cameron, Deborah (1998b). Gender, language, and discourse: A review essay. *Signs: Journal of Women in Culture and Society* 23:945–973.

Clark, Kate (1998). The linguistics of blame: Representations of women in *The Sun*'s reporting of crimes of sexual violence. In Deborah Cameron (ed.), *The feminist critique of language: A reader*. London: Routledge. 183–197.

Ehrlich, Susan (2001). *Representing rape*. London: Routledge.

Ehrlich, Susan (2002). Guest editorial: Discourse, gender and sexual violence. *Discourse and Society* 13:5–7.

Estrich, Susan (1987). *Real rape*. Cambridge, MA: Harvard University Press.

Henley, Nancy M. (1989). Molehill or mountain?: What we know and don't know about sex bias in language. In Mary Crawford & Margaret Gentry (eds.), *Gender and thought: Psychological perspectives*. New York: Springer-Verlag. 59–78.

Hutchby, Ian, & Robin Wooffitt (1998). *Conversation analysis*. Oxford: Polity Press.

Lakoff, Robin (1975). *Language and woman's place*. New York: Harper & Row.

Polanyi, Livia (1995). Language learning and living abroad: Stories from the field. In Barbara Freed (ed.), *Second language acquisition in a study abroad context*. Amsterdam: John Benjamins. 271–291.

Russell, Diana (1984). *Sexual exploitation*. Beverly Hills: Sage.

# 16 ::

# What Does a Focus on "Men's Language" Tell Us about *Language and Woman's Place?*

SCOTT FABIUS KIESLING

In an editor's note to the journal article that eventually became Robin Lakoff's *Language and Woman's Place* (*LWP*) (1975), Dell Hymes wrote: "A focus on women brings to light an aspect of language in social life that has its counterpart for men. . . . 'Men's language' needs study too" (Lakoff 1973: 79). While Hymes is right that a focus on men is as important as a focus on women when studying language and gender, the time was not right in 1973 for such a critical focus on men and masculinities in language and gender research, when it was necessary to expose and refute the assumption that female behavior is somehow deficient or deviant from the male norm. However, given the relational nature of gender, any discussion of gender must at least make assumptions about men and masculinity, although these assumptions may be inexplicit. So men and masculinity actually figure prominently in *LWP*.

In this essay I consider how some key themes in research on men and masculinities are addressed in *LWP*. This discussion is organized around three themes: (1) the distinction between masculinity and men, (2) the nature of men's power and the relations between masculinities, and (3) performativity (the notion that identities are performed in interaction rather than static attributes of individuals). These themes provide a starting point from which to consider many of the claims in *LWP*, as well as future directions in language and gender. The consideration of these themes shows that the study of men and masculinities dovetails with Lakoff's insight that differences found between women's and men's language are part of cultural gender Discourses about femininities and masculinities.

## Masculinity versus Men

There has been considerable debate in sociological studies as to whether the object(s) of study should be men or masculinity. *Masculinity* is a col-

229

lection of traits that a culture tends to associate with *men*, a group of actual human beings with describable patterns of practice. The argument against limiting the object of study to men is that this focus limits one to simply describing men's practices, while studying masculinity allows the discussion of idealizations of manhood that no man may actually fulfill, but that nevertheless affect the practices of individual men (see Connell 2000: 16–17). The usefulness of this distinction lies in the possibility that the study of masculinities is not limited to men only; women can be masculine, men can be feminine. It also allows for the study of institutions that are not necessarily made up exclusively of men but may be described as *masculine*.

The parallel distinction can logically be made for women and femininity. This distinction is important to the argument in *LWP*, but it is one area in which Lakoff has often been misunderstood and for which she has been criticized. When Lakoff outlines characteristics of "women's language" in *LWP*, she seems to be talking about feminine language—those idealizations of how a "lady" ought to talk. Lakoff notes early in the book that a girl may be scolded if she "talks rough" (*LWP* 40), which suggests that talking rough is too masculine for a "lady." She implies, therefore, that women and girls are perfectly capable of using masculine language and sometimes do. This observation is about cultural ideals of *femininity* and *masculinity*, how children come to learn these norms and recreate them. The importance of the possibility of decoupling femininity and masculinity from women and men is also shown in a remark that Lakoff makes in her discussion of elaborated color terms: "If [a] man should say ['The wall is mauve'], one might well conclude he was imitating a woman sarcastically or was a homosexual or an interior decorator" (*LWP* 43). The man is still male, but he is also feminine. Here Lakoff is discussing cultural models or Discourses, not actual behavior. (I capitalize *Discourses* to indicate that these are Discourses in the poststructuralist sense of changeable, self-perpetuating cultural ideologies rather than real interactions.) While linguists tend to privilege women's and men's behavior, those behaviors are organized by and interpreted through cultural models and Discourses.

Lakoff is not necessarily always clear about this distinction. In the first chapter she states that one of her foci is "the way [women] are taught to use language" (*LWP* 39). This is logically not the same as the way women do use language, but it is often assumed that the teaching of such social norms is done successfully and without challenge. From this perspective the way women are taught to use language is the same as the way they actually do so. That Lakoff shares this perspective is suggested by her often-quoted assertion that women's language is "both language restricted in use to women and language descriptive of women alone" (*LWP* 42). Thus Lakoff did collapse women's behavior and femininity and, by extension, men's behavior and masculinity. Of course Lakoff was grappling with new ideas, and we are still trying to sort it out: the distinction is difficult to teach to students, and researchers (including myself) often collapse it. Perhaps this continued theoretical mixing of practice and ideology persists because ideology supports practice. The problem is that if women's and men's actual behavior is described, not all women turn out to be "feminine" and not all men turn out to be "masculine" (see Livia, this volume).

Two related research directions are suggested by focusing on practices as related to Discourses or ideologies. First, how do different ways of speaking become associated with femininity and masculinity? For example, is masculine talk associated with other masculine things, like work or sports, or is it simply seen as masculine in itself? Bonnie McElhinny (1992) has investigated how women and men employ masculine styles in a masculine profession, but the constraints and uses of such gender crossing could be explored further, especially by investigating the ways in which women and men create diverse femininities and masculinities. Second, as cultural notions of femininity and masculinity change, to what extent do women and men's ways of speaking change, both in time and across cultures? Do ideologies of equality help lead to similar ways of speaking? What exactly is the relationship between actual linguistic practices and ideologies of femininity and masculinity, and how does each affect the other?

## Power Relationships among Men and Masculinities

A second focus in the recent study of men and masculinities has been to investigate power relationships between men and between masculinities. In one of the most important and most overlooked statements in *LWP*, Lakoff addresses the importance and variable workings of power: "The notion of 'power' for a man is different from that of 'power' for a woman: it is acquired and manifested in different ways" (*LWP* 59). This statement points to the fact that power is not everywhere the same. Lakoff's comment also shows a sensitivity to power relations within gender categories, which could help account for differences in both gender practice and ideology. If we understand how men differentiate themselves from other men (or masculinities), and how this is different from how women differentiate themselves from other women (or femininities), then we can understand what is most valued in femininities and masculinities while still understanding how individual women and men can have different practices.

One of the problems with early work in language and gender, and with masculinity studies as well, is the lack of an accounting for differences among men, especially when talking about men's power. Power is one of the defining characteristics of masculinity in most societies, but it is not something that all men subjectively feel they have. In fact, one of the things that got me interested in language and gender and the study of masculinity was this difference: I had been convinced of the advantages and privileges of the social group I belonged to (white, male, upper middle class, heterosexual), but on a daily subjective level I did not feel this privilege. When I experienced power relations, it was to feel powerless. This is not to say that these advantages weren't present, just that they were not subjectively felt. Thus, even though statistically people of my group have more social power than people of other groups, many individuals in my group at some point feel powerless.

One key to resolving such a paradox is the distinction between men and masculinity discussed above: there is a powerful ideal of masculinity that is not always or completely experienced by individual men. Men have advantages as a class that many individual men do not, but the class of men is nevertheless more powerful than the class of women. These distinctions between the aggregate and the particular and between ideology and practice necessitate an understanding of power relations among men and masculinities. This observation is one of the most important contributions of Robert W. Connell (1995, 2000), who outlines some relationships that can hold between masculinities. Most important is the relationship between the hegemonic form of masculinity—the form a culture most honors—and other forms of masculinity. Connell (2000: 11) points out that "many men live in a state of some tension with, or distance from, the hegemonic masculinity of their culture or community." This is an important point, one that is sometimes lost when a "general" masculinity is simply relabeled as hegemonic masculinity without any distinction among masculinities or explanation of how a particular behavior is related to the hegemonic form in the culture. In other words, just because many men do it doesn't make it hegemonic masculinity.

In my work (Kiesling 1997a, 1997b, 1998, 2001), I have shown how men use language to connect themselves with hegemonic cultural models and to place other men in subordinated or marginalized masculinities. I have found that there can be multiple hegemonic models: an economically powerful white business executive and a physically powerful black basketball player can both be hegemonic. Men may index any of these models with their language use. Lakoff obliquely addresses the fact that within-gender relations are important when she claims that "eccentricity is far more common and far more tolerated in men than in women" (*LWP* 58). I suggest, however, that eccentricity is something that characterizes gender everywhere by defining the boundaries of the categories (see Hall, this volume), and it is therefore essential to understanding the diversity of gender relations. The organization of within-gender diversity in language is still relatively uncharted in language and gender studies, although such research is becoming more common (see, e.g., Bucholtz 1999a, 1999b; Eckert 2001).

## Performativity and Materiality

A third area in which the study of men and masculinity can illuminate *LWP* is the issue of performativity, or the notion that identities are performed in interaction rather than static attributes of individuals. One of the most exciting theoretical debates in gender in the past fifteen years or so is the debate about the relationship of gender to material bodies; that is, the question of whether and how gender is rooted in biological distinctions of sex. This discussion has recently entered research on men and masculinities (see esp. Connell 2000: 69–101; see also Whitehead 2002: 181–204). The debate hinges on the definition of gender as performance and the extent to which physical bodies determine or are determined by gender.

While important to explore, this debate at times loses sight of the importance of cultural Discourses on the one hand and the corporeal reality of bodies on the other. While it can be shown that gender practices are performances in that they can be changed regardless of one's genitalia, it is also the case that these performances draw on symbols and practices that have meaning in cultural Discourses (Butler 1990; Hall and O'Donovan 1996). Performativity is often shown to destabilize gender Discourses, but in fact it also demonstrates how widely shared and strong such Discourses are; they "override" biology, or at least have the potential to do so. This point has an important bearing on one of the strongest criticisms of *LWP*: its introspective methodology. In fact, the strength of the Discourses here suggests that the introspections provided by Lakoff should not be discarded as bad methodology. Rather, such subjectivities will allow us to better explain the pattern of practices we do find "objectively."

Lakoff makes an argument from Discourses. She is saying that there is a particular Discourse surrounding femininity ("being a lady") and that this Discourse structures how women speak and how they are supposed to speak. She argues that "a stereotypical image may be far more influential than a (mere) statistical correlation" (*LWP* 83). As much as linguists argue against this idea, recent research (e.g., Hill 1995; Johnstone, Bhasin, & Wittkofski 2002) shows that these Discourses are important, in that they provide resources on which people draw to make performances, and they therefore have meaning in a speech community.

Gender is thus neither just a performance nor just biology in isolation. Rather, it combines performances and bodies as part of an organized, patterned gender Discourse. This approach allows us to understand the subjectivities that speakers bring to their language, and why they make the linguistic choices they do. Understanding gendered behavior patterns as part of a whole Discourse pattern is a recent approach in studies of men and masculinities (see Petersen 1998; Whitehead 2002) but has been slow to be theorized in language and gender, even though Lakoff suggested this direction in *LWP*. This view of looking at actual behavior and its understanding within complex gender Discourses might be investigated from a perceptual angle, by exploring how indexicalities are affected by the understood identity of the speaker, and by focusing on language acquisition and socialization. For example, do tag questions have the same "powerless" social meaning when uttered by a woman and a man, or does the hearer's knowledge of the person's ascribed social identity (obtained nonlinguistically, through vision or naming cues) affect the interpretation of an index? Based on informal surveys in classes, whether the speaker is a woman or man makes a significant difference, with the woman more likely to receive the powerless interpretation. As linguists, we have tended to focus on the language produced and the effect flowing from it, while not always appreciating that our perceptual system is a unitary whole of all sensory inputs and contexts.

The focus on performativity has arisen largely through the study of "marginal" or "cross"-gender categories. One aspect of research on men and masculinities that has been applied in language and gender research is the view that performativity must be found everywhere if it is a tenable theoretical construct, even among those performing "powerful" identities (see Cameron 1997; Kiesling 1997a, 1997b). Most important, this "mainstream" performativity shows how gender Discourses are reinscribed through "normal" behavior (which speakers do not always think of as performance). Studies of men and masculinities in language and gender have thus furthered what can be read as Lakoff's view that cultural Discourses are part of mainstream identity performances, especially in language.


## Conclusion

There are a number of ways in which Lakoff's early work prefigured later conclusions in the study of language and gender and of men and masculinities. The most important relevance of Lakoff's text today is not the predictions of what is or is not women's and men's language, but the insight that differences that are found between women's and men's language are part of a gender Discourse about femininities and masculinities. The issue is not just behavior—how women and men talk. Rather, the question is: How do expectations about speech affect linguistic practice? How are social categories, expectations, and Discourses attached to language, and how do people use these connections to perform identities? How do expectations of how women and men speak constrain their language? In what ways can these be challenged?

A focus on men contributes to many aspects of the study of language and gender, especially in the realms of cultural Discourses, within-gender relations, and understandings of power. However, we have seen that Lakoff's focus on women over thirty years ago also suggested these questions. In fact, one of the most important things that Lakoff showed was the influence of expectations on behavior, especially how idealizations of femininity create differently valued femininities. This mismatch between the cultural ideal and the subject positions of speakers, as well as the ordering and structuring of femininities and masculinities within these categories, has also been a focus of the study of men and masculinities in recent decades, and thus we find a dovetailing of the focus on women and on men to understand more fully the full range of identities that fall under the rubric of gender.

REFERENCES

Bucholtz, Mary (1999a). "Why be normal?" Language and identity practices in a community of nerd girls. *Language in Society* 28:203–223.

———— (1999b). You da man: Narrating the racial other in the production of white masculinity. *Journal of Sociolinguistics* 3:443–460.

Butler, Judith (1990). *Gender trouble.* New York: Routledge.

Cameron, Deborah (1997). Performing gender identity: Young men's talk and the construction of heterosexual masculinity. In Sally Johnson & Ulrike Hanna Meinhof (eds.), *Language and masculinity.* Oxford: Blackwell. 47–64.

Connell, Robert W. (1995). *Masculinities.* Berkeley: University of California Press.

———— (2000). *The men and the boys.* Berkeley: University of California Press.

Eckert, Penelope (2001). *Linguistic variation as social practice.* Malden, MA: Blackwell.

Hall, Kira, & Veronica O'Donovan (1996). Shifting gender positions among Hindi-speaking hijras. In Victoria L. Bergvall, Janet M. Bing, & Alice F. Freed (eds.), *Rethinking language and gender research: Theory and practice.* New York: Longman. 228–266.

Hill, Jane (1995). Junk Spanish, covert racism, and the (leaky) boundary between public and private spheres. *Pragmatics* 5:197–212.

Johnstone, Barbara, Neeta Bhasin, & Denise Wittkofski (2002). "Dahntahn Pittsburgh": Monophthongal /aw/ and representations of localness in southwestern Pennsylvania. *American Speech* 77:148–166.

Kiesling, Scott F. (1997a). From the "margins" to the "mainstream": Gender identity and fraternity men's discourse. *Women and Language* 20:13–17.

———— (1997b). Power and the language of men. In Sally Johnson & Ulrike Hanna Meinhof (eds.), *Language and masculinity.* Oxford: Blackwell. 65–85.

———— (1998). Variation and men's identity in a fraternity. *Journal of Sociolinguistics* 2:69–100.

———— (2001). Stances of whiteness and hegemony in fraternity men's discourse. *Journal of Linguistic Anthropology* 11:101–115.

Lakoff, Robin (1973). Language and woman's place. *Language in Society* 2:45–80.

———— (1975). *Language and woman's place.* New York: Harper & Row.

McElhinny, Bonnie (1992). "I don't smile much anymore": Affect, gender, and the discourse of Pittsburgh police officers. In Kira Hall, Mary Bucholtz, &

Birch Moonwomon (eds.), *Locating power: Proceedings of the second Berkeley Women and Language Conference*. Berkeley, CA: Berkeley Women and Language Group. 386–403.

Petersen, Alan (1998). *Unmasking the masculine: "Men" and "identity" in a skeptical age*. Thousand Oaks, CA: Sage.

Whitehead, Stephen (2002). *Men and masculinities*. Malden, MA: Blackwell.

# 17 ::

# Gender, Identity, and "Strong Language" in a Professional Woman's Talk

JUDITH MATTSON BEAN AND BARBARA JOHNSTONE

One of the most striking illustrations in *Language and Woman's Place* (*LWP*) (1975) of the potential effect of having to choose a "weaker" way of talking over a "stronger" one is this hypothetical example: "Oh, fudge, my hair is on fire" (44). Lakoff suggests that, in general, "the 'stronger' expletives are reserved for men, and the 'weaker' ones [like *fudge*] for women" (44). In this essay, we explore this suggestion, examining the links between gender and "strong language" as they are represented in how one woman talks about and simultaneously performs her uses of language in professional life. We pay particular attention to how she represents her uses of profanity, using excerpts from her talk to show that she claims profanity and other aspects of strong language as resources associated with professional power and working-class identification, while at the same time weakening the expletives she refers to and mitigating her performance in other gendered ways.

For Lakoff, people who are required to choose euphemisms like *fudge* over stronger forms risk having their identity obscured: " 'Women's language' . . . submerges a woman's personal identity, by denying her the means of expressing herself strongly . . . and encouraging expressions that suggest triviality in subject matter and uncertainty about it" (*LWP* 42). Although Lakoff does not discuss what she means by "personal identity," she seems to be drawing here on one of the two most common ways of thinking of identity in the Western intellectual tradition (Johnstone 1996, 2000, 2002). In this approach, identity is seen from the phenomenological perspective of the individual, experiencing the environment from in a uniquely "emplaced" way in a particular body with a particular set of memories and projecting the uniqueness of that experience into discourse via "self-expression" for various communicative purposes. If having an identity, in the eyes of others, requires self-expression, then any restrictions on the range of a speaker's linguistic resources—including resources associated with "strong language"—could obscure her identity.

If, however, we think of a person's identity from the outside inward rather than from the inside outward, as a set of social roles and expectations, a different hypothesis about the connection between identity and "strong language" emerges. In this view, individuals construct changeable, flexible identities by drawing on linguistic and other semiotic resources that they associate with social categories defined by roles or personas. A particular set of resources can be utilized to different degrees in different situations and for different purposes. In this view (Bergvall, Bing, & Freed 1996; Bucholtz, Liang & Sutton 1999; Butler 1990; Cameron 1996; Hall & Bucholtz 1995), "doing gender" means casting one's talk (and other activity) in such a way as to display characteristics that are associated, in the social world at hand, with one or another gender category. There are competing (or overlapping) ways of "doing" femininity (Coates 1997), however, associated with competing "cultural discourses": the discourse of repression casts women as helpless and identityless, but there are also gendered ways of being professional or being political. Gender norms can also be challenged, resisted, and played with, and gender can sometimes matter and sometimes not. Lakoff sometimes talks this way about identity, too, when she describes men who adopt "women's language" (for example, academics and upper-class Britons; see *LWP* 47) and the increasing tendency for women to adopt "men's language" (44).

Linda Chavez-Thompson is one of nine women who participated in a series of case studies of Texas women who use language in public settings (Johnstone 1995, 1998, 1999, 2002; Johnstone & Bean 1997). The daughter of a Mexican American sharecropper from west Texas, Chavez-Thompson (born in 1945) became a secretary for the American Federation of State, County, and Municipal Employees (AFSCME) in San Antonio in the 1960s and moved up through the ranks. As executive vice president of the AFL-CIO, a federation of labor and trade unions representing over 13 million U.S workers, she is now one of the few women in the top echelon of the U.S. labor movement. Her struggle for acceptance as a professional and a woman, as well as the particular work she pursues, create a complex orientation to dominant ideas of gender and gendered speech, which she expresses both in her talk and in answers to questions we asked her about how she uses language (cf. Davies, this volume). With our colleague Delma McLeod-Porter, we talked to her in her San Antonio AFSCME headquarters in 1993.

In our interviews, we asked women to talk about the sources of their senses of self and interactional styles. At the same time, we tried to elicit a range of speaking styles, so that the transcripts would be rich both ethnographically and linguistically. Here Chavez-Thompson contrasts Southern femininity with her own style. (Excerpts are transcribed for maximum readability. Italic type indicates emphatic stress; material in boldface is the focus of discussion in the text. Double parentheses surround paralinguistic material.)

Delma McLeod-Porter: Do you ever think of yourself as a South-
　　ern woman?
Linda Chavez-Thompson: No. I don't know why. I know I am, but,
　　no, not really.
McLeod-Porter: Do you have a notion of what that means? South-
　　ern woman?
Judith Mattson Bean: Would you know a Southern woman if you
　　met one?
Chavez-Thompson: I- I've got a picture of one: **someone who
　　doesn't cuss** ((laughter)); uh, someone who's not a union
　　leader ((laughter)); uh, **someone who uh, is in the back-
　　ground** and does social events and is interested in in those
　　kind of things. And, and that certainly doesn't fit me. So,
　　even though I am a Southern woman, I've never, I've never
　　really, I've never had time for that.

Chavez-Thompson is aware of linguistic expectations for Southern women
and of her distance from that model. She thinks of the Southern lady as
someone who stays "in the background" and "doesn't cuss," but she dis-
sociates herself from that image, implicitly distancing herself from indirectness and genteel politeness and aligning herself with people who use
language in strong ways.

Chavez-Thompson repeatedly represented her work as crossing
boundaries. In contrast with the conventional "background" role of the
Southern woman, she often describes the realm of her work and political
activism as "out there." In the following passage, Chavez-Thompson elaborates on her sense of having crossed gender boundaries to work actively
in politics and in the union movement, contrasting this with the enforced
passivity she felt as a secretary:

Chavez-Thompson: I always have bumper stickers on my cars for
　　this candidate or that candidate. And I'm always on phone
　　banks. And *I'm always out there*, you know, passing out hand
　　bills, or supporting this or supporting that. And then, of
　　course, once I got into the, to the, to the union business, you
　　know, once, once I started in on that, ah, I mean, hey! I was
　　having a field day, because it was just my line of of of work,
　　because **I *love* to be out there** just, you know, doing this.
　　　And really it started, it started back in 1970, [ . . . ] and
　　maybe before that I, I wasn't as active because I was, a, a sec-
　　retary, for a labor union, and there's only so much you *can*
　　do. And then you have to **keep your mouth shut** and type
　　the letters, and that's it. But in 1970, we had a tornado in
　　Lubbock, and [ . . . ] they needed someone who was bilingual;
　　they needed someone that that knew the community, to do
　　tornado relief work for the Texas AFL-CIO. So they said,

"Well, who'll we put in there?" [ ... ] So I said, "I'll do it,"
you know. *Again,* I've done some things, uh, in, in retrospect
saying, "*Why* did I even volunteer for this, or why did I raise
my hand, or **why did I open my mouth?**" But I said, I think
I can do it. So, **I went out there** and worked in the community [ ... ] getting relief to people, uh making sure that that
insurance companies weren't gouging [ ... ]. And half of the
stuff, I didn't know, what to do, I just knew that it was wrong,
and **I went out there** to try to get it corrected. And so, **once
I was out in the field, for those three months, I just, I
couldn't go back.** I couldn't go back to an 8 to 5 job.

Chavez-Thompson associates being "out there," both in a concrete sense
(the disaster-relief job took her out of the office) and in a symbolic one,
with "opening your mouth": crossing gendered boundaries requires using
stronger language (see also Mendoza-Denton, this volume).

As it is actually displayed in her interaction with us and her reports
of interactions with others, however, Chavez-Thompson's orientation to
"strong language" is complex. In the ways she refers to and uses profanity,
it is clear that gender expectations (that women don't swear) intersect in
complicated ways with her sense of her idiosyncratic desires and drives
(loving to be "out there," being compelled to open her mouth) and with
her rhetorical purposes. In the passage below, she talks about strong language as a strategic resource: "I don't often have to use the strong language
that I . . . am sometimes prone to do." With reference to "cussing," she
makes a point of saying that she "know[s] some words."

Johnstone: Now you were saying this morning . . . that [some men
  she was working with] were thinking that you just would uh
  kind of be their "mom," kind of solve their problems.
Chavez-Thompson: But, but, in fact, in fact, in fact, they st- they
  call me "Mom."
Johnstone: Oh, yeah?
Chavez-Thompson: Yeah. Now they call me "Mom," but every
  once in a se—in a, in a while, I ask them, **"What kind of
  mother are you calling me?"** ((laughter)), uh, because—
  ((laughing)) Honest! They're bad sometimes! But the question here for them—and, and for me—is that *occasionally*, a
  city manager or *occasionally* a department head, ah, that because I'm a woman they're going to be able to walk all over
  me, or because I'm a woman I don't know how to take them
  on. And every once in a while, ah I have to show them, that
  they're going to deal with me at the same level as they would
  a man. And uh **I don't often have to use the strong language that I, I, I am sometimes prone to do, ah, I know**

> some words ((laughter)), but I and, and, and I am prone to
> do that.

The reference to profanity (*mother* is potential shorthand for a familiar curse word) was clear to all of us, as our laughter indicates. Yet Chavez-Thompson's performance of profanity here, both as she represents it to us as having happened for the original audience and in her recounting with us as audience, is indirect, not an instance of cursing but an indirect reference to it. Her use of "some words" to reference profanity is also indirect, a way of pointing at profanity and claiming it as a rhetorical resource without using it or even directly referring to it.

Continuing with the same answer, Chavez-Thompson elaborates by narrating an anecdote involving the firing of workers who protested the firing of a supervisor. In a televised confrontation, she reports having used a (mild) profanity and an abbreviation for another:

> I, when I get excited and angry — it wasn't until I heard the
> tape on radio — because they played that tape, and they had
> me on TV for about three days in a row — **I called one of**
> **the board members a "damned liar."** In public. I was so an-
> gry at the way the people were being treated. I'm, **I *have***
> **gone, to the city manager and told him he was an SOB. I**
> **have gone, to department heads and told them that their**
> **supervisors were SOBs, and I will not, mince the words.**
> Ah, **I try not to make them a part of my everyday language,**
> **uh but th** —, sometimes that has shown: they *mess* with me,
> they *mess* with the union, they *mess* with the folks ((tapping
> table when she says "mess")). And they don't do that any-
> more.

While calling someone a "damned liar" on camera may have been a slip, Chavez-Thompson's conclusion ("they don't do that anymore") indicates that she finds profanity and other forms of strong language effective and necessary in representing her constituents. She recreates (probably in idealized form) the emphatic, assertive speech of the style she is representing via parallelism, repetition, vocal stress, and intonation. But while her forceful linguistic alignment of herself with the union and the working class ("[If] they mess with me, they mess with the union, they mess with the folks") displays rhetorical strength directly, profanity is once again referred to somewhat indirectly: in claiming to illustrate how she doesn't "mince the words," Chavez-Thompson minces *son of a bitch* to a conventional abbreviation (*SOB*) that is hardly profanity at all.

As this excerpt demonstrates, Chavez-Thompson claims to have an assertive, confrontational style she employs for union business. While she does not frame it as a masculine style, she does frame it in contrast to the expected style of a Southern woman, who stays in the background and does not curse. As a public speaker, she acknowledges the need to "be controversial." Power as a speaker, in her account, can be established when the audience recognizes the speaker's authenticity of emotion and commitment to a cause. As Lakoff pointed out (*LWP* 44), profanity serves as a condensed symbol of the expression of emotion in talk, and the right to "cuss" is a sign of the right to express emotion. Chavez-Thompson draws strategically and self-expressively on this association of profanity and emotionality. Her use of profanity in the context of her work in the labor movement, strongly linked to class and masculinity, illustrates Lakoff's claim that "the decisive factor is less purely gender than power in the real world" (*LWP* 81).

Yet she is also clearly constrained by the range of available social identities and the linguistic resources associated with them. Being a woman is one of these (and being a man is not). The constraining influence of expectations associated with "women's language" are also visible in the interview. For one thing, Chavez-Thompson's style is mitigated in the interview, and probably in the interactions she reports on in the interview, by humor. In the one-hour interview there were fifty instances of laughter, most of them initiated by Chavez-Thompson. Most of her laughter is self-deprecating, mitigating her success or acknowledging (and mitigating) the violation of gender standards for the use of profanity. She also draws on traditional gender identity through physical presentation—willingness to smile and the adopting of "feminine" apparel, jewelry, hairstyle, and other aspects of grooming. And, as her actual performances of profanity in our interview suggest, even her "strong language" gets mitigated in gendered ways that reflect how she is socially categorized by others.

Lakoff's sketch, in *LWP*, of the links between gender, identity, and strong language is mirrored in a complex way in Chavez-Thompson's presentation of her professional identity. The expectation that she not use profanity does not, contra Lakoff, appear to "submerge" Chavez-Thompson's identity; she does not seem to have to choose whether to be "less than a woman or less than a person" (*LWP* 41). Rather, this expectation is worked into her self-presentation in two ways. On the one hand, it is a source of rhetorical power and creativity: Chavez-Thompson defines herself against the Southern woman who "doesn't cuss" and is proud of her ability to use "some words" when necessary. Here, newer theories of identity that stress its flexibility and inventiveness seem to provide the best fit. On the other hand, the expectation that women do not swear is also a source of constraint, making it necessary for Chavez-Thompson to work to show that she is still being feminine even when she curses or talks about cursing. Identity here seems more fixed, more a matter of social attribution and less a matter of choice. That gender is one of the less avoidable aspects of identity is the insight on which *LWP* is based, and this insight continues to be relevant.

## REFERENCES

Bergvall, Victoria L., Janet M. Bing, & Alice F. Freed (1996). *Rethinking language and gender research: Theory and practice.* New York: Longman.

Bucholtz, Mary, A. C. Liang, & Laurel A. Sutton (eds.) (1999). *Reinventing identities: The gendered self in discourse.* New York: Oxford University Press.

Butler, Judith (1990). *Gender trouble: Feminism and the subversion of identity.* New York: Routledge.

Cameron, Deborah (1996). The language-gender interface: Challenging co-optation. In Victoria L. Bergvall, Janet M. Bing, & Alice F. Freed (eds.), *Rethinking language and gender research: Theory and practice.* London: Longman. 31–53.

Coates, Jennifer (1997). Competing discourses of femininity. In Helga Kotthoff & Ruth Wodak (eds.), *Communicating gender in context.* Philadelphia: John Benjamins. 285–314.

Hall, Kira, & Mary Bucholtz (eds). (1995). *Gender articulated: Language and the socially constructed self.* New York: Routledge.

Johnstone, Barbara (1995). Sociolinguistic resources, individual identities, and the public speech styles of Texas women. *Journal of Linguistic Anthropology* 5:1–20.

――― (1996). *The linguistic individual: Self-expression in language and linguistics.* New York: Oxford University Press.

――― (1998). "Sounding country" in urbanizing Texas: Private speech in public discourse. *Michigan Discussions in Anthropology* 13:153–164.

――― (1999). Uses of Southern speech by contemporary Texas women. *Journal of Sociolinguistics* 3:505–522.

――― (2000). The individual voice in language. *Annual Review of Anthropology* 29:405–424.

――― (2002). Selfhood, personhood, linguistic stance, and rhetorical ethos: Two case studies. Paper presented at the annual meeting of the American Anthropological Association, New Orleans, November.

Johnstone, Barbara, & Judith Mattson Bean (1997). Self-expression and linguistic variation. *Language in Society* 26:221–246.

Lakoff, Robin (1975). *Language and woman's place.* New York: Harper & Row.

# 18 ::

# The New (and Improved?) Language and Place of Women in Japan

YOSHIKO MATSUMOTO

In Japan recently, I had an encounter that brought into focus for me how *Language and Woman's Place* (*LWP*) (1975) illuminated Japanese women's language. A forty- or fifty-year-old Japanese woman, who had concluded from overhearing my conversation that I was a linguist, suddenly approached me to inquire if she could ask me a question about contrastive linguistics. She expressed the view that women had been discriminated against in Japan on account of the categories of *onna kotoba* (women's speech), *otoko kotoba* (men's speech), and *keigo* (expressions of respect, honorifics), which force speakers to choose a specific register or form of speech. She also thought that Japanese was peculiar in this regard and that this peculiarity was responsible for the sexual harassment and domestic violence that she had suffered. She had confirmed with her American friends that women and men were treated equally in the United States, and she attributed this to the absence of such gender-based linguistic distinctions in English.

In response to my suggestion that she should speak up for herself and state her opinions in the more forceful linguistic forms that she wished to employ, she expressed doubts, believing that such action would provoke even more negative responses from men. She would not dare say, for example, *yamero* (stop it!) in the plain imperative form as men sometimes do, but she hoped that gendered linguistic forms could be abolished to permit social change. Hearing her opinion, and feeling a bit like Mary Poppins, I pulled from my bag a copy of *LWP*, which I happened to be carrying around that day, and recommended that she read it and more recent discussions of language used by Japanese women. Thirty years later, *LWP* can still speak directly to such women's concerns.

This brief encounter made me see the issue of language and women in a new light. First of all, it was clear that, whatever the empirical facts of language use in Japan, the ideology of gendered language is still a potent force that needs to be addressed. Second, from the perspective of *LWP* and

244

from my experiences as a woman living in the United States, I recognize that perceptions of gender relations in the United States may be somewhat overstated and idealized. This realization made me suspect that common observations about the language used by Japanese women may be no more accurate. The difference is simply that perceptions of the United States may be idealizations of equality, while those of Japan may be a model, generally deplored, of gender inequality. (For a different perspective, see Ide, this volume.)

## Exotic Japanese

There has been a frequently expressed perception in American and other foreign media that the speech of Japanese women is distinctive in its high pitch and characteristically feminine vocabulary, expressing an attitude of reserve and self-effacement that reflects women's inferior position in society. A summary of this common perception is found in an article in the *New York Times Magazine* (September 1, 1991) by Ellen Rudolph, an American photographer and film producer who lived in Tokyo. She wrote: "Newspapers and magazines report almost daily on shifting sexual mores in Japan. . . . But the linguistic divide between the sexes endures, even if it is little acknowledged. In Japan, men and women have different ways of speaking."

This description can give the misleading impression that Japanese women and men speak differently at all times, as if they were originally from two different tribes with two different languages. Even language textbooks that have been criticized for exaggerating and essentializing the differences between women's and men's language, such as Mizutani and Mizutani (1987: 150–151), have not gone that far: "In polite or formal speech, there is very little difference between men and women, but in familiar speech, there are some differences between the two." "Women's speech" has been ideologically distinguished from "men's speech" in the choice of sentence-final expressions, referential terms, and honorifics, which indicate softness, nonassertiveness, and politeness (e.g., Ide 1982; Mizutani & Mizutani 1987; Okamoto 1995; Reynolds [1986] 1990; Shibamoto 1985). Such culturally preferred characteristics of women's speech do not seem to be very exotic or specific to Japanese. What is different in Japanese is that differences can be more clearly located in morphology than in languages like English, and speakers can therefore more easily be aware of such differences.

A description of women's and men's speech in Japanese is cited in *LWP* from an observation made in *The Japanese Language* by Roy Andrew Miller (1967). I have reproduced in (1) the conversation cited in *LWP* (86–87), along with the original Japanese text from Miller's book. The italics indicate expressions that Miller referred to as characteristics of women's speech, including "the deferential prefix o–," "elegant and exalted verb forms," "a different set of sentence final particles ( . . . *wa*, . . . *no*)," "a different repertoire of interjections," and "variant pronunciations of certain forms (*gozaamasu* for *gozaimasu*)" (1967: 289).

(1)  A:  *maa*, go-rippa na o-niwa de *gozaamasu wa* nee. shibafu ga hirobiro to shite ite,
kekkoo de *gozaamasu wa* nee.
'My, what a splendid garden you have here—the lawn is so nice and big, it's certainly wonderful, isn't it?'

   B:  iie, nan desu ka, chitto mo teire ga yukitodokimasen mono de gozaimasu kara, moo, nakanaka itsumo kirei shite oku wake ni wa mairimasen no de *gozaamasu yo*.
'Oh no, not at all, we don't take care of it at all any more, so it simply doesn't always look as nice as we would like it to.'

   A:  aa, sai de gozaimashoo nee. kore dake o-hiroin de *gozaamasu* kara, hitotoori o-teire *asobasu* no ni datte taihen de gozaimashoo nee. demo maa, sore de mo, itsumo yoku o-teire ga yukitodoite *irashaimasu wa*. itsumo honto ni o-kirei de kekkoo de *gozaamasu wa*.
'Oh no, I don't think so at all—but since it's such a big garden, of course it must be quite a tremendous task to take care of it all by yourself; but even so, you certainly do manage to make it look nice all the time: it certainly is nice and pretty any time one sees it.'

   B:  iie, chitto mo sonna koto *gozaamasen wa*.
'No, I'm afraid not, not at all . . .' (Miller 1967: 289–290)

Aside from the choice of linguistic forms, which has been the focus of most academic discussions on language and women in Japan, what is remarkable is Miller's explanation that "what is being said [in this conversation] is not at all important" (1967: 290) and that it was pointless to ask for the male equivalent of the italicized expressions, since men would simply say that the garden was nice, and that would be the end of it. As was pointed out in *LWP*, Miller's description reflected the stereotypes of "women's talk" as verbose and without content and of "men's talk" as brief—a stereotype that goes beyond exoticism and could be thought exotic for this reason too, but this cultural expectation could be "seen to be equally valid, if sometimes less striking, in American dialogue" (*LWP* 87).

## Has the Speech of Women Changed? How about the Ideology?

Considering the date of publication, Miller's example and description above are likely to be based on data from the late 1950s, if not earlier. We may ask whether anything has changed since then.

Unlike the time of Miller's observation, adults in current Japanese society have had much less exposure to prewar Confucian ideology and to a rigidly stratified society. Public schools have been coeducational for over half a century. Japan's remarkable economic success followed by the bursting of the economic bubble in the early 1990s seems to have made many Japanese doubt the reliability of long-trusted authority. There are more women than ever before occupying nontraditional positions across all social levels: as government ministers, diplomats, mayors, leaders of political and social groups, CEOs in industry, and intellectuals, as well as parcel deliverers, train station attendants, and taxi drivers. Their activities are sometimes reported in the news simply because they are women, but at other times their gender is not even a topic.

Changes in attitude may also be discerned both in women's increasingly insistent demands for equality and in the response to such demands. Women who have been denied promotions on account of their gender have recently won lawsuits against their employers. Sociological studies of urban homemakers show that they are becoming more regionally active, with increased social participation outside the home through part-time jobs and volunteer activities (e.g., Fujimura-Fanselow & Kameda 1995; Imamura 1987, 1996). A major newspaper recently announced that it would begin to use nondiscriminatory titles and descriptions for women (Asahi Newspaper 2002). There is also a movement to make school textbooks "gender-free" (Kanai 2002).

In addition, not only women but also men who are considered to have passed the most marriageable age are now reportedly put under stress to marry by their relatives and professional associates. The coinage *pawahara* ('power harassment,' by analogy with *sekuhara*, 'sexual harassment'), meaning the imposition by bosses of their social power, is used to describe the experience of male as well as female workers. There are naturally other aspects of society that have undergone changes, but equality is still far from an actuality. But Japan now is a clearly different world than that associated with the traditional gender stereotypes expressed in Miller's account.

With regard to women's use of language, media accounts as well as recent linguistic studies illustrate that speech varieties that do not fit the stereotypical description of "Japanese women's language" are found in abundance among female speakers. Newspaper columns in the 1990s that focused on Tokyo speech, the dialect on which the normative women's language use was based, reported that their interviewees believed that teenagers and young women frequently used coarse and forceful expressions that were conventionally regarded as belonging to the realm of men's language. Several recent studies have presented similar facts, although from a different ideological perspective (Matsumoto 1996; Okamoto 1995; Okamoto & Sato 1992; Shibamoto Smith & Okamoto forthcoming; Uchida 1993). In fact, if one turns on the TV or overhears conversations in public places, one can hardly fail to notice discrepancies between actual speech and the supposed norm.

In the absence of a reliable descriptive record of women's speech in earlier times, it is difficult to measure exactly how different the current practice is from that in the past. The use of particular forms, such as *gozaamasu* in (1), has changed considerably, and forms that were once categorized as belonging to men's speech are now used unselfconsciously by women.

An interesting contrast with Miller's example of a highly formalized exchange of compliments (example 1 above) is provided by the following fragment of a naturally occurring conversation collected in 2002, involving a compliment between two female friends in their seventies, both upper-middle-class homemakers.

(2)   A:   sono sukaato ii zya nai. Niatteru.
            'You have a nice skirt on, don't you? You look nice.'
      B:   e, soo? hometemo nannimo *denai yo.*
            'Oh, yeah? Praise won't get you a thing, you know.'
      A:   shittete itten *da yo.*
            'I know that.'
   [A, B:   Laughter]

In (2), not only do we fail to find any of the expressions that were given as characteristics of female speech in (1), but we find expressions (italicized in the text) that are assertive and conventionally associated with men's speech, or in recent years with younger people's speech. Right after the cited conversation, however, one of the speakers addressed a stranger, a much younger woman, using the expression *Ara, gomenasobase* (Oh, do please excuse me), which is reminiscent of the conventionally "elegant and feminine" style exemplified in (1).

What (2) illustrates is that speakers with an apparently similar background to those of (1), and in a similar context of compliment giving, can exhibit language practice that is different from stereotypes, or at least from older stereotypes, and that such differences are not confined to the expression of an identity as a young woman.

Examining the multitude of varieties that middle-aged, middle-class women with children use even within the same topic and context—a phenomenon observed also among professional women (Takasaki 2002)—I have elsewhere (Matsumoto 2002, forthcoming) illustrated the significant gulf between the ideology of gendered language and language use in actual practice, and I have discussed the ways in which a woman uses various forms to portray the complex stances in her individual persona.

It is probably a fair assumption that the language spoken by women in Japan has shifted to include forms and styles conventionally thought to be within the exclusive province of men while allowing some of the expressions considered "feminine" to fall into disuse. An obvious question to ask in light of *LWP* is whether such a shift in the use of linguistic forms has ameliorated any of the problems that were associated with the ideology of gender difference and women's lack of power. The answer is probably "some but not all." Younger women, married or unmarried, have been reported to use more assertive forms and styles of language. However, such linguistic forms are found not only in contexts of empowerment, but also, for example, in magazine articles and advertisements that portray teenagers concerned with how to dress in a "feminine" or "cute" way. These women are not modeled after Confucian precepts of stern rectitude and self-sacrifice, but they remind us of another old ideology—that of the "weaker sex" (see Matsumoto 1996 for further discussion). As an example of media portrayals of middle-aged women, there is a middle-aged married female character in a newspaper cartoon series who notably does not use expressions traditionally associated with women but instead uses the more assertive varieties and is usually depicted as confident and assertive. In one recent strip, however, we still find a portrayal of women as verbose but concerned with matters of less importance, in that this character displays knowledge of a great deal of trivia concerning Koichi Tanaka, a 2002 Nobel Prize winner, but admits in the final panel that she has no idea what the laureate researched. In short, the shift to linguistic forms that are pragmatically more forceful does not necessarily shift the ideology to one of greater equality of status.

What then can we do, using words, to improve women's place in Japanese society? What can we say to the woman I mentioned at the beginning, who is sincerely looking for an answer to this question but traps herself in the ideology that she suffers from? Complaints by men about *pawahara* (power harassment) show that linguistic desegregation alone is not enough to redress an imbalance in power. What we need first is probably the belief that each one of us can be an agent of change, rather than waiting for someone else to abolish a bad system.

The belief in women's agency for change runs throughout *LWP*—Lakoff argues that "if we are aware of what we're doing, why we're doing it, and the effects our actions have on ourselves and everyone else, we will have the power to change" (102), and this belief is still useful and needed (see also Trechter, this volume). Another important point that can be taken from *LWP* is that we should not be blindly bound by the existence or absence of conventional categories. The recognition of categories of "women's language" and "men's language" in Japanese should not lead us into accepting their reality without question, while the nonexistence of such ready-made categories in English does not mean that there are no distinctions in the use of language between women and men. Accordingly, the ideologies associated with such categories are not simply descriptions of unchanging fact. In the past few years I have often heard Japanese people say that there is much diversity in society these days—ideas, clothing, tastes, jobs, and use of language. This may just be a popular thing to say, but it gives some hope for a movement toward accepting nonorthodox categories and ideas that, if women are persistent, may be heard.

NOTE

My sincere gratitude goes to Mary Bucholtz for her effort and patience in editing. I dedicate this chapter to Robin Lakoff, my mentor, whose insights in linguistics and life are never exhausted.

REFERENCES

Fujimura-Fanselow, Kumiko, & Atsuko Kameda (eds.) (1995). *Japanese women: New feminist perspectives on the past, present, and future.* New York: Feminist Press.
Ide, Sachiko (1982). Japanese sociolinguistics: Politeness and women's language. *Lingua* 57:357–385.
Imamura, Anne E. (1987). *Urban Japanese housewives.* Honolulu: University of Hawaii Press.
——— (ed.) (1996). *Re-imaging Japanese Women.* Berkeley: University of California Press.
Kanai, Keiko (2002). Sono otokonoko ga, sukaato o haku hi no tameni—jendaa hurii kyooiku to kokugo (For the day when that boy wears a skirt—gender-free education and the national language). *Gekkan Gengo* (Language Monthly) 31:62–69.
Lakoff, Robin (1975). *Language and woman's place.* New York: Harper & Row.
Matsumoto, Yoshiko (1996). Does less feminine speech in Japanese mean less femininity? In Natasha Warner, Jocelyn Ahlers, Leela Bilmes, Monica Oliver, Suzanne Wertheim, & Melinda Chen (eds.), *Gender and belief systems: Proceedings of the fourth Berkeley Women and Language Conference.* Berkeley, CA: Berkeley Women and Language Group. 455–467.
——— (2002). Gender identity and the presentation of self in Japanese. In Sarah Benor, Mary Rose, Devyani Sharma, Julie Sweetland, & Qing Zhang (eds.), *Gendered practices in language.* Stanford, CA: CSLI Publications. 339–354.
——— (forthcoming). Alternative femininity: Personae of middle-aged mothers. In Janet Shibamoto Smith & Shigeko Okamoto (eds.), *Japanese language, gender, and ideology.* New York: Oxford University Press.
Miller, Roy Andrew (1967). *The Japanese language.* Chicago: University of Chicago Press.
Mizutani, Osamu, & Nobuko Mizutani (1987). *How to be polite in Japanese.* Tokyo: Japan Times.
Okamoto, Shigeko (1995). "Tasteless" Japanese: Less "feminine" speech among young Japanese women. In Kira Hall & Mary Bucholtz (eds.), *Gender articulated: Language and the socially constructed self.* New York: Routledge. 296–325.
Okamoto, Shigeko, & Shie Sato (1992). Less feminine speech among young Japanese females. In Kira Hall, Mary Bucholtz, & Birch Moonwomon (eds.), *Locating power: Proceedings of the second Berkeley Women and Language Conference.* Berkeley, CA: Berkeley Women and Language Group. 478–488.

Reynolds, Katsue Akiba ( [1986] 1990). Female speakers of Japanese in transition. In Sachiko Ide & Naomi H. McGloin (eds.), *Aspects of Japanese women's language.* Tokyo: Kuroshio Shuppan. 129–146.

Rudolph, Ellen (1991). On language. *New York Times Magazine* (September 1).

Shibamoto, Janet S. (1985). *Japanese women's language.* New York: Academic Press.

Shibamoto Smith, Janet, & Okamoto, Shigeko (eds.) (forthcoming). *Japanese language, gender, and ideology.* New York: Oxford University Press.

Takasaki, Midori (2002). "Onna kotoba" o tukurikaeru josei no tayoona gengo koodoo (Diversity of women's linguistic behavior which will recreate the "women's language"). *Gekkan Gengo* (Language Monthly) 31:40–47.

Uchida, Nobuko (1993). Kaiwa-koodoo ni mirareru seisa (Gender differences in conversation). *Nihongogaku* 12:156–168.

# 19 ::

# "I'm Every Woman"

*Black Women's (Dis)placement in Women's Language Study*

MARCYLIENA MORGAN

I'm every woman
It's all in me
Anything you want done, baby
I do it naturally
—Nickolas Ashford and Valerie Simpson, "I'm Every Woman"

## The Race to Feminism

For nearly three decades, scholars in the humanities and social sciences have participated in the long march to reevaluate, reconstruct, and, in many cases, expose systems of misrepresentation, exclusion, and marginalization regarding the study of gender and language. At the same time, scholarship on women of color has actively asserted that the interrelationship between race, gender, and class is integral to understanding both race and gender. Paradoxically, rather than social science and linguistic canons and paradigms shifting in light of the extensive writings on African American and other nonwhite and working-class women, academic theories of gender have simply shrugged in disregard. True, the emerging scholarship established a brand of feminism that challenged and introduced theoretical arguments; but it also ensured that the body and background of what is considered the "normal" woman remained intact—white and mainly middle-class. In contrast to stereotypes of the dominant, submissive and subversive, emasculating, uncaring black woman, feminist psychology and linguistic theory have stereotyped middle-class white women as indiscriminate "people pleasers," concerned with harmony, being accepted, and so on in life and in conversation.

Unfortunately, many current theories privilege this racialized and class-based concept of woman, making it nearly impossible to locate black women within women's writing at all. Instead, depictions of black women persist that stereotype them as primitive, uncivilized, uncontrolled, immoral, and lascivious and the opposite of the "good" woman who has personal control over her desires and impulses. Rather than disrupting these troubling representations, feminist theories have mostly ignored them as though they in no way spoil or are integral to theories of gender, sexuality, and power. Evelyn Brooks Higginbotham (1992: 5) extends this argument one step further: "Woman studies for so long rested upon the premise of racial (i.e., white) homogeneity and with this presumption proceeded to universalize 'woman's' culture and oppression, while failing to see white women's own investment and complicity in the oppression of other groups of men and women." Overly optimistic predictions that feminist scholarship would expose the mechanisms by which dominant cultures impose their interpretation of others on all members of society quickly disintegrated into occasional and half-hearted inclusion—a big tease that refused to include race, ethnicity, and class while romancing gender and sexuality.

Although the above critique applies today, it must be remembered that the period following the modern women's movement and the Black Power movement was full of hope and excitement. In the 1970s, Robin Lakoff's *Language and the Woman's Place* (*LWP*) (1975) was the singularly most influential and provocative treatise on language and gender in linguistics. *LWP* breathed life into discourse on sexism and gender in linguistics, and many graduate students of that generation eagerly welcomed its appearance. The text was based on Lakoff's observations and intuitions as a middle-class white woman and focused on what she considered to be the two main forms of discrimination in women's language: that women are taught a weaker form of language than men (e.g., tag questions), and that there is inherent sexism in the structure and usage of language itself (e.g., euphemisms for women). Although Lakoff's focus was on her own language and that of her peers, *LWP* is of particular relevance to African American women's discourse in that it demonstrates how the field of linguistics can be changed through the raising of critical questions that are both particular and universal. In this way, it provides a framework from which to move African American women and other women of color to the very center of language and gender studies (see also Mendoza-Denton and Trechter, both this volume).

The preceding critique of language and gender studies is not an isolated phenomenon and is representative of the absence of direct racial and social-class discussions within the field of sociolinguistics at large. Regrettably, the groundbreaking linguistic arguments of the late 1970s that African American English (AAE) is a systematic dialect and should be respected as such did little to improve the representation and inclusion of black women in language and discourse studies. This was in large part because women were originally excluded as subjects of research, and the data presented contained numerous canonical grammatical and phonological examples of AAE with content that regularly supported racist stereotypes of African Americans and instances of profanity and references to drug use, violence, and misogyny (e.g., Folb 1980; Kochman 1981). Yet virtually no folklorist or linguist managed to produce examples, expressions, and terminology associated with racism, white supremacy, and hegemony and injustice in general—of which there are many throughout African American culture. Although Claudia Mitchell-Kernan (1971) and Geneva Smitherman (1977) provided scholarship based on ethnographic research and participant-observation with numerous rich models and instances of language and interaction, their work was treated as subjective largely because it did not include extensive salacious examples. Unfortunately, this state of affairs also served to marginalize the emerging studies of the language of working-class and Native American, African American, Latina, and Asian American and Pacific Islander women in the United States.

As mentioned earlier, the feminist scholarship of the 1970s did not occur in a vacuum but was part of an impressive body of scholarship related to race and the intersections of race and class. Nancy Henley's (1995) comprehensive review of ethnicity and gender issues in linguistics considered the representation of women's language both in the field of linguistics and in society in general and argued that the language of working-class women and women of color has been on the periphery as a unique, marginal, or special case, rather than as one among many examples of language use. Moreover, although there has been a rise in linguistic research on both women and men, there has been little if any research on interactions between black women and black men outside of sexual encounters and conflict—in the linguistic world they simply do not interact unless in relation to explicitly misogynistic conversations. As Patricia Bell Scott argued (1974: 218), "The English language has dealt a 'low blow' to the self-esteem of developing Black womanhood."

This essay argues that omissions of black and other nonwhite women in language and gender research are admissions of how pervasive and significant race remains in framing gender in all aspects of study, including language (see also Livia, this volume). This essay focuses on the problematics of race and gender through the use of arguments from feminist, literary, critical race, and linguistic theory. It goes on to provide instances of black women's discourse that constantly frame race and gender identities and conflicts. It demonstrates how language not only represents but also is acted on and reconstituted to reveal, critique, and include a place and space for all women.

## Not White and So Not Quite Women

It is true for many women, and especially for African American women, that the notion of a woman's place is a harrowing concept. Many historians have detailed how black women were treated as property under slavery and denied rights to their bodies as well as to femininity, family, and mother-hood. While the place of black women in legal history concerning women's rights is disturbing, the language of black people was regulated to further limit women to this precarious place. During U.S. slavery and until the 1960s in the South, blacks could not exhibit linguistic agency nor could they initiate verbal interactions with whites (Morgan 2002). In addition, submission to white supremacy was required in nonverbal communication. In many respects, black communication with whites in general was treated as powerless, agentless, childlike, and feminine in that it was constantly under the surveillance of white men. Interactional styles included nearly every one of the verbal and nonverbal expectations of women's speech described by Lakoff: politeness (use formal address when speaking to a white person), passivity (do not speak unless spoken to), insecurity (use hedges and tag questions), and so on. Thus the linguistic and conversa-tional cues of subservience and dependence associated by Lakoff with women's language were also necessary to perform the identity assigned to African Americans under slavery and segregation.

While many identify the Black Power movement as the end of dis-cursive compliance with white supremacy, the actual reconfiguration of the discourse of African Americans occurred during the civil rights move-ment, where agentive and assured speech replaced tentative and self-effacing discourse. Once the Black Power movement sought to move the struggle for civil rights to one that argued for the same entitlements as whites, a discourse style was ushered in that did not simply address, con-front, and resist compliant African American discourse. The new discourse annihilated the old and left it a symbol of a self-hating slave mentality. The new discourse style confronted white supremacy and neither complied with it nor demanded rights within it. Instead, the discourse style asserted a black presence on its own terms, one that reflected a different consciousness and a sense of entitlement. As a result, African American speech in white-dominated contexts has gone from being depicted as childlike, feminine, overly polite, and self-effacing to being viewed as aggressive, impolite, di-rect, and threatening.

Black women found themselves caught in the crevices of the shift from powerless and feminine discourse to a style symbolizing a powerful black masculinity that challenges, threatens, and competes with white mas-culinity. To assert equal entitlements meant the negotiation of both femi-nine and masculine discourses, with racist and sexist baggage embedded in both. Thus, while this discursive space is potentially a powerful one, it is also one of unending contestation and mediation.

However, explorations into the particular issue of African Diasporic women's language and identity have been few (e.g., Etter-Lewis 1993; Fos-ter 1995; Morgan 1991; Stanback 1985). It is not surprising that at the core of black communities are women who were prepared and compelled to confront racial, class, and gender injustice. There are rewards for women who are adept at handling discourse concerning these subjects. And there is punishment for those who are naïve and fail to recognize the power they and those in power have over their words. As a result, there are two functions of African American women's discourse. One is associated with cultural identity and the other is a powerful discourse about racial, gender, and class injustice. In this discourse, any critique of gender hegemony is also a critique of racial hegemony.

## Our Best Features Forward

When black women index race, class, and gender, they may do so by choosing marked features that, at least for them, invoke hegemony. Thus in many cases, they not only index them as cultural and social identities but also as a critique of racism, sexism, and social-class elitism as well. Reading dialect, for example, occurs when members of the African American community contrast, index, or otherwise highlight what they consider to be obvious contrasting features of AAE and General English in an unsubtle and unambiguous manner to make a point (Morgan 2002). In this way, the "hypercorrect" language associated with white women (*LWP* 80) becomes a resource for identity and critique by black women.

Table 1 lists additional linguistic resources—both those associated with "women's language" in *LWP* and others—that may index race, gender, and class through grammatical or conversational indexing. In other words, such resources index sometimes race, sometimes gender (see Smith 1998). It is important to note that the resources associated with white women's speech take on different meanings when used by black women. For example, *smart talk* refers to women talking with an attitude while *cross talk* highlights overlaps and floor-taking in conversations among Caribbean women. *Small talk*, however, refers to polite, somewhat feminized conversation marked as meaningless. Meaningless and empty adjectives, an element of "women's language" as described by Lakoff (*LWP* 78), may index highly feminine and/or stereotypical whiteness and the performance of femininity, and they are frequently used among African American comedians to portray gay characters in stand-up routines. Vowel length may signal a black female identity as well as indicating signifying and gossip episodes (Morgan 1996), whereas intonation may index racial stance and identity as well as a white or black woman's stance. In contrast, hedges nearly always index white women, although they also imply insincerity rather than a lack of power. As mentioned above, grammatical contrasts or reading dialect as well as signifying and embedding may index racial or gender identities, sometimes insultingly. Interruptions and latching may also signify disrespect or a negative opinion about the topic (Morgan 1996; Troutman 2001). Finally, diminutives serve to highlight and dismiss mindless feminine stereotypes.

Table 1. Indexes of Gender, Race, and/or Class in African American Women's Speech

| Feature | Example | Social Context | Function |
| --- | --- | --- | --- |
| Metalinguistic words and phrases | *Smart talk, cross talk, small talk* | Across social situations | Identifies conversational strategy |
| Empty adjectives and expressions | *Oh my goodness,* etc. | Across genders and social groups | Signals feigned stereotyped weak feminine style |
| Vowel length | *Girl, ho::ney!!* | Among black women | Signals opinions, social assessments, and gossip |
| Intonation | Rising or falling: *I think I like you.* | Across cultures, social groups, and genders | Rising: dishonesty, mindlessness Falling: honesty, resignation |
| Hedges | (a) *I think maybe I might could think about it.* (b) *I guess I might think about it.* | Across cultures, social groups, and genders. (a) indexes a gender stereotype of black women and (b) indexes white | Feigns extreme uncertainty |
| Grammar | (a) Hypercorrect: *I will be leaving soon.* (b) Hypocorrect: *I be leavin' real soon.* | (a) Across cultures, genders, and classes (b) Directed to black listeners only | (a) Hyper-middle-class, stereotypical woman's speech (b) Signifying on stereotypical black woman's speech |
| Signifying and embedding | *I like your hair.* (when the speaker means the opposite) | Across all groups | Indexes black women's identity in conversation across races |
| Interruption, overlap, latching | | Across both genders, mainly in conversations within the speech community | Shows either agreement or disagreement in content |
| Diminutives | *They gave a little party.* | Across cultures, social groups, and genders | Signals dismissive and negative attitude of the speaker |

## There's No Place Like Home

As bell hooks (1990), Kamala Visweswaran (1994), Valerie Smith (1998), Dorinne Kondo (1997), and others maintain, feminist theory must be situated at home. To explore this place is crucial, for the intersection of many factors greatly affects linguistic analysis in general as well as descriptions of language use among women, and African American women in particular. But as these scholars argue, home is not always a place we fully experience and it is not a place without its problems. It is simply all that we have and where we must start.

This essay argues for a paradigm shift that increasingly incorporates a definition of women that assumes class, ethnic, and racial diversity. In order to ensure that we represent the complexity of women's place, we must "expose the role of race as a metalanguage by calling attention to its powerful, all-encompassing effect of the construction and representation of other social and power relations, namely, gender, class, and sexuality" (Higginbotham 1992: 3–4). Just as Lakoff's examination of her own speech and that of her peers may have been the jumping-off point for the feminist analysis of language, the actual linguistic and discursive practices of women of color offer a framework from which to examine all women's language. There is no place for the black woman if she is not also everywoman.

REFERENCES

Etter-Lewis, Gwendolyn (1993). *My soul is my own: Oral narratives of African American women in the professions.* New York: Routledge.

Folb, Edith (1980). *Runnin' down some lines: The language and culture of black teenagers.* Cambridge, MA: Harvard University Press.

Foster, Michèle (1995). "Are you with me?" Power and solidarity in the discourse of African American women. In Kira Hall & Mary Bucholtz (eds.), *Gender articulated: Language and the socially constructed self.* New York: Routledge. 329–350.

Henley, Nancy(1995). Ethnicity and gender issues in language. In Hope Landrine (ed.), *Bringing cultural diversity to feminist psychology: Theory, research, and practice.* Washington, DC: American Psychological Association. 361–396.

Higginbotham, Evelyn Brooks (1992). African-American women's history and the metalanguage of race. *Signs* 17:251–274.

hooks, bell (1990). *Yearning: Race, gender, and cultural politics.* Boston: South End Press.

Kochman, Thomas (1981). *Black and white styles in conflict.* Chicago: University of Chicago Press.

Kondo, Dorinne (1997). *About face: Performing race in fashion and theater.* London: Routledge.

Lakoff, Robin (1975). *Language and woman's place.* New York: Harper & Row.

Mitchell-Kernan, Claudia (1971). *Language behavior in a black urban community.* Berkeley, CA: Language Behavior Research Laboratory.

Morgan, Marcyliena H. (1996). Conversational signifying: Grammar and indirectness among African American women. In Elinor Ochs, Emanuel Schegloff, & Sandra A. Thompson (eds.), *Interaction and grammar.* Cambridge: Cambridge University Press. 405–433.

———— (2002). *Language, discourse, and power in African American culture.* Cambridge: Cambridge University Press

Scott, Patricia Bell (1974). The English language and black womanhood: A low blow at self-esteem. *Journal of Afro-American Issues* 2:218–224.

Smith, Valerie (1998). *Not just race, not just gender.* New York: Routledge.

Smitherman, Geneva (1977). *Talkin and testifyin: The language of Black America.* Boston: Houghton Mifflin.

Stanback, Marsha Houston (1985). Language and black woman's place: Evidence from the black middle class. In Paula A. Treichler, Cheris Kramarae, & Beth Stafford (eds.), *For alma mater: Theory and practice in feminist scholarship.* Urbana: University of Illinois Press. 177–196.

Troutman, Denise (2001). African American women: Talking that talk. In Sonja Lanehart (ed.), *Sociocultural and historical contexts of African American English.* Philadelphia: John Benjamins. 211–238.

Visweswaran, Kamala (1994). *Fictions of feminist ethnography.* Minneapolis: University of Minnesota Press.

# 20 ::

# The Anguish of Normative Gender

## Sociolinguistic Studies among U.S. Latinas

NORMA MENDOZA-DENTON

An enduring puzzle for the study of language and gender among minority populations is the extent to which the gendered behavior observed in majority populations (on which theory is usually based) is generalizable to minority groups. In particular, my concern in this essay is the following: How do Latina women negotiate contradictory ideologies coming from Latina/o communities, on the one hand, and from dominant-culture ideologies for women in general and Latina women in particular, on the other hand?

In her book *Borderlands/La Frontera: The New Mestiza* (1987), Gloria Anzaldúa comments on the links between Latinas' gendered linguistic transgression and Standard English usage:

> I remember being caught speaking Spanish at recess—that was good for three licks on the knuckles with a sharp ruler. I remember being sent to the corner of the classroom for talking back to the Anglo teacher when all I was trying to do was tell her how to pronounce my name. If you want to be American, speak American. If you don't like it, go back to Mexico where you belong. *"I want you to speak English. Pa' hallar buen trabajo tienes que saber hablar inglés bien. Qué vale toda tu educación si todavía hablas inglés con un ac-*cent?," my mother would say, mortified that I spoke English like a Mexican. At Pan American University, I, and all the Chicano students were required to take two speech classes. Their purpose: to get rid of our accents. . . . En boca cerrada no entran moscas. "Flies don't enter a closed mouth" is a saying I kept hearing when I was a child. Ser *habladora* was to be a gossip and a liar, to talk too much. *Muchachitas bien criadas,* well-bred girls don't answer back. *Es una falta de res-peto* to talk back to one's mother or father. *Hocicona, repe-*

> *lona, chismosa,* having a big mouth, questioning, carrying
> tales are all signs of being *malcriada.* In my culture they are
> all words that are derogatory if applied to women — I've never
> heard them applied to men. (53–54)

Anzaldúa's work echoes Robin Lakoff's observations on ladylike speech in *Language and Woman's Place* (*LWP*) (1975) but with a twist: when more than one language is involved, the very act of switching between them carries gendered implications.

The work on language and gender among U.S. Latinas has thus far been characterized by attention to actual or perceived adherence to normative gendered expectations, what I call the "Anguish of Normative Gender" (cf. Baugh 1984). The anguish resides in the very act of linguistic implementation; speakers must address two, and more often three or four, sets of norms for gendered linguistic behaviors at the collective and individual levels. Consider Ana Celia Zentella's (1987: 169–171) rhetorical questions of identity conflict that young Puerto Ricans pose for themselves, questions that recognize different possible avenues for identity production and alignment: "WHAT AM I? PUERTO RICAN OR AMERICAN? . . . WHAT COLOR AM I? WHITE OR BLACK? . . . WHICH LANGUAGE SHOULD I SPEAK? SPANISH OR ENGLISH? WHICH SPANISH SHOULD I SPEAK, PUERTO RICO'S OR SPAIN'S? WHICH ENGLISH SHOULD I SPEAK, BLACK OR WHITE?" Adding in gender and sexual orientation, while dealing with what W. E. B. Du Bois (1903: 2) termed *double consciousness,* "this sense of always looking at one's self through the eyes of others," creates a veritable hall of mirrors for Latinas in the United States.

In this essay I sketch some paradoxes of research in the field, keeping in mind, as Deborah Cameron (1992) admonishes, that we must look not only at gender differences but also at the difference that gender makes. I begin by outlining some of Lakoff's arguments on gendered ideologies of language and politeness, of conservatism and innovation, and proceed to show how those ideologies set up contradictions for Latinas (my essay, though dealing mostly with women, also advocates the theorizing of Latino masculinity and language behavior; cf. Cintron 1997). I conclude by presenting a case study from my own research, which investigates issues at the intersection of class and gender among Latina youth.

## Lakoff's Legacy and Its Relation to Current Debates

*LWP* has proved not only groundbreaking but also downright uncanny: a number of Lakoff's theoretical analyses of gendered language behavior would later find statistical support in certain quarters of quantitative sociolinguistic study (Labov 1990). Lakoff's list of the features that comprise women's language includes the use of hypercorrect and superpolite forms:

> 6. Hypercorrect grammar: women are not supposed to talk rough. It has been found that, from a very young age, little boys [engage in nonstandard language behavior] more than do little girls . . . [and] are less apt . . . to be scolded [for doing so]. Generally women are viewed as being the preservers of literacy and culture, at least in Middle America, where literacy and culture are viewed as being somewhat suspect [i.e., effeminate, cf. *LWP* 44] in a male. . . . In cultures where book larnin' is the schoolmarm's domain, this job [of preservation] will be relegated to women. [Lakoff goes on to suggest that women are less prone to neologisms and are less likely to be the source of linguistic innovation than men.]
>
> 7. Superpolite forms. . . . This is related to [women's] hypercorrectness in grammar, of course, since it's considered more mannerly in middle-class society to speak "properly." But it goes deeper: women don't use off-color or indelicate expressions. (*LWP* 80)

Lakoff's work launched a thousand ships in the field of variationist studies of language and gender: Can women in general be shown to be more conservative and status-seeking in their linguistic behavior than men? (For highlights of the debate, see Eckert 1989, this volume; Eckert & McConnell-Ginet 2003; Labov 1990; Trudgill 1972.) And yet the question remains paradoxical when applied to Latinas: How should we evaluate a claim of female conservatism and prestige-mindedness where the language that might be thought to be the conservative language, Spanish, is marginalized in practice and its maintenance discouraged? How do we reconcile the larger social stigmatization of Spanish-based linguistic resources (Hill 2001; Ramírez 1981) with positive language attitudes on the part of U.S. Latinos (García et al. 1988)?

## Swearing and the *Abuelitas* (Grandmothers)

In his essay "Me Macho, You Jane" (1996), Dagoberto Gilb recounts watching an Anglo basketball coach repeatedly and unfairly scolding his ten-year-old son. Gilb blurts out: "Motherfucker, you leave him alone!" The author continues:

> The coach glared at me, appalled. Worse yet, I caught something else too. An I-told-you-so smirk. Now he had confirmed that I was from the crass, violent, low-class, vulgar, gang-ridden, unfit-to-lead culture he so clearly was not from. I'd

justified him in his self-righteous fundamentalism. But I was shamed equally about being an American, the ugliest kind. *Abuelitas*, sitting gracious and gently near me, dressed with Sunday shawls over their shoulders, watching their sweet *nietecitos* [grandkids] playing, being nothing but young and sweet, leaned forward, stunned, disgusted, like I'd hocked one onto the foot of the Virgen de Guadalupe. Two little girls on the other side of them got off their seats to step out onto the court to look at the face of the goon. Their innocent mouths were open. . . . If I could've left I would have. It was that I was in the corner and the door was at the other end, and I couldn't. (14–15)

This excerpt illustrates linguistic double consciousness, with its paradoxical overlapping frames of reference across gender, class, and ethnicity: swearing marks the narrator as boorishly American to the Latina *abuelitas* and little girls, while simultaneously confirming stereotypes of slum-dwelling Latino male riffraff to the Anglo coach. The same speech event is interpreted, unfortunately for Gilb, in diversely unflattering yet consistently gendered ways by both Anglos and Latinos.

Marcia Farr (1994) defines *relajo* as the suspension of seriousness that for the women in her study distinguishes the decorum and social norms of the public sphere from the freedom from those norms in the private sphere. Her transgenerational study of a Michoacán (Mexican) transnational community in Chicago places *relajo* within a cline of social activities that connect the individual to the social and that range in scale from the festival through the smaller carnival, *fiesta, relajo, desmadres*, and the double entendre of the single-word *albur* (innuendo). According to Farr, these events constitute transformative experiences and entail the expression of verbal-art genres valued within the community. Joking during *relajo*, for instance, involves criticism of the common gendered moral code. Many of the teasing routines that Farr documents deal with gender-role and ideological differences between Michoacán and Chicago. *Echar desmadres* ('to joke around'; literally, 'to throw unmothers'!), an even more carnivalesque and heightened form of *relajo*, deals almost exclusively with sexually oriented double entendre, and is documented by Farr among the *abuelitas* of the community. If *relajo* among the women in Farr's study occurs only in the private sphere, *desmadre* involves the most intimate of circles within that sphere, and the sexually explicit nature of this speech routine relies precisely on such intimate, gendered settings. Imagining Gilb's shawl-wrapped *abuelitas* getting together at home to become Farr's ribald jokers reminds us to consider contextual dependency not only in the interpretation of speech acts such as swearing but also in our theorizing of gender roles.

In ethnographic studies of Latinas' gender transgression, we see that the stigma in the use of taboo words and expletives serves to keep women in Lakoff's figurative linguistic place. Letticia Galindo's work (see, e.g., Galindo 1999) investigates the public speech of East Austin, Texas, *pachucas* (Mexican American female street-gang associates, following the *pachuco* style in vogue in the 1940s through 1970s), focusing on their use of *caló* (a form of slang that involves nonstandard language and codeswitching), taboo words, and expletives. Galindo regards the *pachucas* with whom she conducted her research as innovative, uninhibited, assertive speakers breaking with traditional patriarchal structures through words that are off-limits to "ladies" (cf. Bean & Johnstone, this volume). Galindo contends that the use of *caló* and taboo language as a lingua franca among the *pachucas* facilitates the performance of particular speech acts traditionally associated with males (boasting, challenging, and insulting), arguing that these acts serve the social functions of conveying intimacy and camaraderie.

A parallel to this work, also conducted in Texas but among men, is the research of José Limón (1994), which deals with *carnalismo*—the combination of bawdiness and talk about food—in the casual conversation of Mexican men in south Texas. The exaggerated masculinity, homoerotic innuendo, and grotesque-realistic degradation (Bakhtin 1984: 21) inherent in *carnalismo* (a three-way ambiguity we may gloss as 'sharing [sexual] meat' and 'fictive-kin brotherhood') is understood by Limón as an instance of class-contestative ideology, opposing it to the ruling bourgeois official culture of both Anglos and upper-class Mexican Americans. Thus the *pelado's* (Mexican lower-class man's) hypermacho discourse of sexuality, the body, and low-prestige food ("Mexican leavings," as an Anglo rancher told Limón) "acts as a counterpoint to the repression and affectation of the ruling sectors throughout the region" (Limón 1994: 136).

## Gender, Ethnicity, Class, and Language Choice among California Latina Youth

In my own work, which is indebted to all these scholars, I seek to address issues at the intersection of class, gender, and ethnicity, with emphasis on personae as the carriers of linguistic style (cf. Eckert 2000). In an ethnographic and sociolinguistic study of social networks and linguistic behavior among Latina high school girls in the Bay Area of northern California, conducted over the course of two-and-a-half years in the mid-1990s (Mendoza-Denton 1997, 1999, forthcoming), I have examined the linguistic patterning and social differentiation of several distinct self-identifying groups of Latina girls. Latina and Latino students accounted for approximately twenty percent of the 1,200 students at Sor Juana High School (a pseudonym) and were subdivided into Chicanas, Mexicanas, and recent immigrants from other Latin American countries. Within these groups, cross-cutting allegiances divided students along the lines of nation, ethnicity, socioeconomic status (SES), and immigration history. For the purposes of this essay I shall discuss only one of the groups, the Spanish-speaking *Piporras*, mestiza (mixed Native Mexican–European–African) girls from the countryside (for a fuller account, see Mendoza-Denton 1997, 1999).

As with all ethnography, the participant-observer's perspective merits mention as inherently embedded in the social and power relationships emerging in the larger society and in the enterprise of anthropology. Like the girls that I interviewed and who allowed me to participate in their social networks, I was a Spanish-speaking *mestiza* who left Mexico in early adolescence. Like the *Piporras*, I was a native Mexican Spanish speaker, and had extensive family networks in Mexican rural areas. Unlike them, I was from a large Mexican city, middle-class, had wide access to the dominant European American culture, and spoke a more standard variety of English (albeit as a second language). This range of similarities and differences made me an insider-outsider, and allowed me to participate as teacher/ older sister/fictive kin depending on the circumstance.

One of the largest groups among the Latinas at Sor Juana High School, *Piporras* were recent-immigrant adolescents from Mexico's countryside, sometimes monolingual Spanish speakers and sometimes bilingual in Mexican indigenous languages. Coming from rural Mexican families, many of them worked as itinerant farm workers and were often absent from school to pick produce on California farms alongside their parents. As the most recent immigrants from Mexico, *Piporras* were the girls that other Latinas in the school sometimes complimented, sometimes taunted, as being "traditional Mexican girls." Immigrant *Piporras* were expected to hold down the proverbial fort of traditional values, while U.S.-born Chicanas were indulged by teachers and parents with more freedom and less reproach for social experimentation. At school, *Piporras* became vested with the role of keepers of feminine virtue and traditions of the motherland; they were often asked and sometimes just expected to participate in activities that reproduced versions of Mexican gendered identities. The feminine arts fell squarely on their shoulders. Thus it was often *Piporras* (and their mothers) who would volunteer or be asked to cook Mexican food for school events, and *Piporras* also who were recruited as primary participants in Ballet Folklórico, the Mexican folk-dance group at the school (and their mothers who had to sew the sequined dresses). Tracked into beauty school ostensibly because of their limited English skills, at home *Piporras* were held to rigorous feminine standards that involved housework and child care, and that encouraged their relative seclusion even from school-sponsored activities like physical-education classes. Even at lunch, these girls stood in line in the cafeteria, retrieved their rations, and ate isolated in a separate room, inhabiting a private, quasi-domestic sphere within the public school system.

Immigrant and culturally distinct communities offer cases where the expectations of the school, of parents, and of society may not only fail to converge but also in effect may create contradictory demands. Thus the *Piporras'* refusal to swim during their menstrual periods, while accurately aligned with parental authority and expectations, went deeply against the grain of what is commonly required of an American high schooler, creating no end of conflict between parents and the school. The girls' negotiation and balancing of parental, cultural, and school expectations was especially complex, since contradictions sprang up in almost every arena—not only with respect to sports but also with respect to how much and how late a girl may stay at school or fraternize with boys, and certainly with respect to how much girls should be taught about sex.

Linguistic expectations from teachers and classmates that dogged *Piporras* included the presumption of lesser English and greater Spanish proficiency. Because the *Piporra* designation subsumes ethnicity and class as well as gender, it functions as an excellent test case for issues of women's conservatism and of linguistic change. In contrast to the *Piporras*, the more "Westernized" groups of recent immigrant girls, those coming from European families and higher SES in the big metropolises of Mexico, were regularly assumed by teachers to speak less Spanish than the *Piporras* (despite the fact that they were often more "standard" speakers). With more social freedoms and fewer responsibilities for the defense of traditional Mexican womanhood, the higher-SES girls were quickly promoted out of "English as a Second Language" classes. Subsequently, through exposure to mainstream curricula and the accompanying negative attitudes toward Spanish preservation they also experienced greater language shift, thus fulfilling the assumption of greater English-speaking ability that others had of them from the beginning. *Piporras*, however, tended to maintain Spanish while they acquired English. Phenotypic Indianness and lower SES functioned as the ratification of their authenticity as Mexican, and placed them under chronic stereotype threat, with interlocutors expecting their phenotype to correlate to linguistic choices.

As this brief discussion suggests, my own work in the field of language and gender owes a great debt to Robin Lakoff. Linguists' understanding of the social phenomenon of gendered conservatism that she described continues to be enhanced by extending her insights to new populations and taking into account the intersecting axes of class and ethnicity.

REFERENCES

Anzaldúa, Gloria (1987). *Borderlands/La frontera: The new mestiza*. San Francisco: Aunt Lute Books.
Bakhtin, Mikhail (1984). *Problems of Dostoevsky's poetics*. Minneapolis: University of Minnesota Press.
Baugh, John (1984). Chicano English: The anguish of definition. In Jacob

Ornstein-Galicia (ed.), *Form and function in Chicano English*. Rowley, MA: Newbury House. 3–13.

Cameron, Deborah (1992). "Not gender difference but the difference gender makes": Explanation in research on sex and language. *International Journal of the Sociology of Language* 94:13–26.

Cintron, Ralph (1997). *Angels' town: Chero ways, gang life, and the rhetorics of the everyday*. Boston: Beacon.

DuBois, W. E. B. (1903). *The souls of Black folk*. New York: New American Library.

Eckert, Penelope (1989). The whole woman: Sex and gender differences in variation. *Language Variation and Change* 1:245–267.

———— (2000). *Language variation as social practice*. Oxford: Blackwell.

Eckert, Penelope, & Sally McConnell-Ginet (2003). *Language and gender*. Cambridge: Cambridge University Press.

Farr, Marcia (1994). *Echando relajo*: Verbal art and gender among Mexicanas in Chicago. In Mary Bucholtz, Anita Liang, Laurel Sutton, & Caitlin Hines (eds.), *Cultural performances: Proceedings of the third Berkeley Women and Language Conference*. Berkeley, CA: Berkeley Women and Language Group. 168–186.

Galindo, D. Letticia (1999). Caló and taboo language use among Chicanas. In D. Letticia Galindo & María Dolores Gonzales (eds.), *Speaking Chicana: Voice, power, and identity*. Tucson: University of Arizona Press. 175–193.

García, Ofelia, Isabel Evangelista, Mabel Martínez, Carmen Disla, & Bonifacio Paulino (1988). Spanish language use and attitudes: A study of two New York City communities. *Language in Society* 17:475–511.

Gilb, Dagoberto (1996). Me macho, you Jane. In Ray Gonzalez (ed.), *Muy macho: Latino men confront their manhood*. New York: Anchor.

Hill, Jane H. (1995). Mock Spanish, covert racism, and the (leaky) boundary between public and private spheres. In Susan Gal & Kathryn Woolard (eds.), *Language and publics: The making of authority*. Manchester: St. Jerome. 83–102.

Labov, William (1990). The intersection of sex and social class in the course of linguistic change. *Language Variation and Change* 2:205–254.

Lakoff, Robin (1975). *Language and woman's place*. New York: Harper & Row.

Limón, José (1994). *Dancing with the devil: Society and cultural poetics in Mexican-American South Texas*. Madison: University of Wisconsin Press.

Mendoza-Denton, Norma (1997). Chicana/Mexicana identity and linguistic variation: An ethnographic and sociolinguistic study of gang affiliation in an urban high school. PhD diss., Stanford University.

———— (1999). Turn-initial *no*: Collaborative opposition among Latina adolescents. In Mary Bucholtz, A. C. Liang, & Laurel A. Sutton (eds.), *Reinventing identities: The gendered self in discourse*. New York: Oxford University Press. 273–292.

———— (forthcoming). *Homegirls: Symbolic practices in the making of Latina youth styles*. Oxford: Blackwell.

Trudgill, Peter (1972). Sex, covert prestige, and linguistic change in the urban British English of Norwich. *Language in Society* 1:179–195.

Ramírez, Arnulfo G. (1981). Language attitudes and the speech of Spanish-

English bilingual pupils. In Richard Durán (ed.), *Latino language and communicative behavior.* Norwood, NJ: Ablex. 217–232.

Zentella, Ana Celia (1987). Language and female identity in the Puerto Rican community. In Joyce Penfield (ed.), *Women and language in transition.* Albany: SUNY Press. 167–179.

# 21 ::

# Contradictions of the Indigenous Americas

## Feminist Challenges to and from the Field

SARA TRECHTER

## The Field

Robin Lakoff's *Language and Woman's Place* (*LWP*) (1975) called linguists
to realize their obligation to analyze and transform the place of women in
English. Recognizing that language cannot solely determine social reality,
Lakoff nevertheless encourages the linguist to take an active role in social
transformation because of her understanding of how language reflects "the
weaknesses and strengths of a culture" (*LWP* 75; see also Ehrlich, this
volume). In the same year that Lakoff's work was published, Anne Bodine
(1975) surveyed the languages of the world that overtly encoded "sex differentiation" in their phonology or grammar; that is, languages that contained linguistic structures indicating the gender of the speaker, the listener, or both (cf. Matsumoto, this volume). Sixty percent of the languages
she cited were indigenous languages of the Americas.

Twenty-eight years later, the response of most researchers of Native
American languages to the opportunities created by this work is an equivocal stance. For over a century, Americanists have scientifically identified
and more often reified difference in women's and men's language but have
often failed to probe how the identification of gender connects with gender
*identity*. With a few exceptions (Deloria 1937; Kimball 1987; Luthin 1992;
Trechter 1999), linguists have seemingly forgotten in their representations
of indigenous languages that Ferdinand de Saussure's arbitrariness of the
sign does not necessarily extend to encoded gender, which is deeply en-
meshed within the ideological construction and interpretation of social
behavior. It is even more rare to encounter a treatment of how such linguistically constructed identities may or may not constitute and reflect gender inequality (for an exception, see Medicine 1987). In the gender and
language literature in the Americas, linguistic anthropologists have focused
on the interplay of style, language shift, or genre differences rather than
on linguistic features that are recognized as markers of gender identity by

indigenous peoples (Brown 1980; Hill 1987; Sherzer 1987). As linguistic anthropologists delve into the relationship between language, social identity, and socioeconomic and human rights—the issues involved in language endangerment and language rights throughout the world—the cultural-linguistic place of indigenous women becomes vital. However, those on the front lines of work with indigenous language grammars, descriptive linguists, often do not provide a sociocultural and contextual perspective on gendered languages.

Such gaps are obvious to many linguistic fieldworkers, who realize that even a structural description and dictionary are not easily produced. They recognize the difficulty of addressing basic grammar and vocabulary adequately, especially since the structures of a threatened language often suffer from attrition through the influence of other languages. However, sociocultural lacunae should not be too easily explained away. They also emerge from the history and culture of linguistics and the structuralist and apolitical approaches to language exploration that Lakoff rightly objected to: "If [the linguist] does not examine the society of the speakers of the language along with the so-called purely linguistic data, he [or she] will be unable to make the relevant generalizations, will be unable to understand why the language works the way it does. He [or she] will, in short, be unable to do linguistics" (*LWP* 75). Sociocultural gaps can become an unintended imposition of the linguist's own culture because of her prominent role in language maintenance through the cocreation of grammars, dictionaries, and pedagogical materials with native speakers. For instance, a linguist who is used to acknowledging only two genders, female and male, might well describe cultures that overtly recognize three or four distinctive genders in only binary terms. Anything else would be "deviant" from the pattern rather than worthy of description in its own right. Unless the writer of a grammar specifies the sociocultural context of gendered language— who uses it, when, and with what meanings—she will establish a sex-based norm for women and men across the board. This is especially problematic in pedagogical materials designed to teach the language in which the "basics" of appropriate communication are initially oversimplified. In addition, as the reader unconsciously fills in the spaces based on her own cultural background, the resulting uptake is often one that simultaneously exoticizes the other and reinforces the ideology of gender as an absolute binary (Trechter 1999). Thus, the purpose of this essay is to explore the gender gaps in indigenous language accounts of the Americas, their causes, and how they are being addressed. Although the diversity of voices in indigenous languages can be silenced in linguistic accounts, they are becoming increasingly more prominent in the fieldwork context. The process of examining Lakoff's sociopolitical challenges to the study of indigenous American languages and gender therefore has an added benefit. It returns the challenges of those voices from the field to feminist linguistics.

## The Tradition

The study of gender in the indigenous languages of the Americas has a lengthy history. Linguistic differences between women and men were noted in grammars from the Amazon to the Arctic: Karajá (Brazil), Carib (Caribbean), Koasati (Louisiana), Yana (Northern California), and Chukchee (northeastern Siberia), to name a few. Sometimes variable uses of these gender indicators were also mentioned, such as in Haas's (1944) description of men using women's pronunciation when quoting female characters in a folktale. However, the structuralist focus of the times emphasized encoded distinctions in meaning at or below the level of the sentence. Textual or discourse examples accompanying such descriptions served to highlight grammar in a meaningful context rather than make discourse grammar an object of analysis and description. Formalist approaches perpetuated such a limited focus, except that encoded gender because of its social connotations became even less relevant for those working on a universal grammar.

In each of these cases, the linguist was also deterred from a proactive description of any gender bending in the language by the notion that she should not be advocating change or even emphasizing alternative voices because this would violate a basic maxim of the linguistic enterprise: to describe rather than prescribe. Barrett (1997) points out the deceptiveness of this maxim. He argues that a description of a speech community's majority group reifies one norm and proscribes alternative expressive meanings. Indeed, if we report that a language has an encoded (phonological or morphological) gender distinction but that certain factions of the society violate that code, these are automatically considered at best dialect differences and at worst deviant.

Once the concept of gender is invoked, it presupposes a cultural analysis of what gender is: women and men are culturally defined as having certain abilities, responsibilities, stances, and ranges of actions. However, if a grammar states that women have a certain way of speaking in a language because that way of speaking is part of being a woman, little meaningful description is accomplished. We have done nothing toward examining the meaning of gender in language; we have merely established an indexical relationship between two social facts, speech practice and gender. This is the barest of grammatical description. Such work is a first step, but because languages and cultures signify and define gender differently, the description is far from complete.

In addition to such narrow definitions of an adequate descriptive grammar, field linguists were (and still are) plagued by the very real exigencies of linguistic fieldwork. Language attrition and the deaths of some of the last speakers of the language, inadequate funding, the immediate demands of language preservation, and the thorny political problems of working with indigenous languages often make anything but minimal grammatical description impossible. Despite their best intentions, some fieldworkers do not have the opportunity to work with both female and male consultants, much less to witness different discourse genres. When a threatened language is used in fewer and fewer contexts, stylistic choices that indicate the stance and attitude of the participants as well as gender become less fluid. Indeed, when the *socio* half of sociolinguistics is irrevocably reduced, there is some excuse for less than thorough attention to gender.

Nevertheless, it is in precisely these circumstances that researchers need to be particularly careful in their representation of gendered language, for they risk unintentionally inscribing a stereotypic representation that could stand on the linguistic record indefinitely. Since 1975, inspired by feminist work on the social complexity of gender, several linguists have returned to some of the most famous accounts of gendered language difference in the Americas. Through an examination of textual materials, they defined the meaning of gendered speech in these languages. For instance, Luthin (1991) found that men's phonologically differentiated speech to other men in Yana (first described by Sapir 1949) was also used with women on formal occasions. Kimball (1987) found that in Koasati men's use of [-ʃ] instead of the more nasal pronunciation of women was actually a discourse marker, which was also used by speakers of higher status regardless of gender. In my own work on Lakhota, I found that gendered morphological indicators in context were not direct indicators of the sex of speaker, but rather indexed a meaningful stance toward the content of the proposition. Certain stances became strongly associated with female versus male speech through their use and appropriateness in different discourse genres (Trechter 1999). Even in cases of limited data, sociolinguistic complexity is retrievable.

## The Contradictions

Yet none of these advances have led to overt recognition of sexism or recommendations for changing an indigenous language. Combined with the notion that linguists should not prescribe is the ironic implication that we should also not become political, at least in the area of our expertise. In the past twenty years, however, Americanists have stepped firmly into the realm of language politics by acknowledging some responsibility for maintaining the objects of their study (Hale et al. 1992). The ideology implicit in the discourse of language endangerment is that the linguist is akin to a salvage worker, rather than an activist who promotes innovation and development of the language in new directions. The endangerment frame confronts both the researcher/activist and the indigenous linguist with a contradiction: living, vital languages are natural hybrids in a constant change of state and development, but it is important to preserve and conserve the richness of linguistic structure that is fast disappearing in the world. Brigham Golden (2001: 2) reflects this conflict differently in his discussion of indigenism, which he defines as "an ethic and logic of preservation." He demonstrates that indigenous women may fight cultural preservation efforts, especially if these are seen as threatening to their own empowerment. However, indigenous women may also wish to move in directions that challenge existing feminist tenets.

It is no surprise that other linguists' response to the murky difficulties of deciding "weaknesses and strengths" has remained equivocal. Yet gender prescriptivism in the indigenous language context still lies squarely where it has traditionally — in the guise of pedagogical materials, dictionaries, language education programs, and the training of native-speaker linguists. The linguist may be wary of engaging in prescriptivism, but she actually has little control over how people take up, interpret, and use such materials. Books that instruct or provide a model will most likely be interpreted as offering a language prescription. For this reason, it is vital to capture how native speakers ideologically construct gender in their language as well as different discourse examples that show how it actually plays out.

Of course, to be taken up at all, descriptive and prescriptive projects that are completed dialogically are more viable (though perhaps initially less efficient). Unlike mere involvement in a project, when a community has the ability to determine the project's scope, purpose, and products, it is more likely to become a continuing community issue in which members can recognize themselves. This is very apparent in a successful language project among Qom (Toba Daviaxaiqui) community members (Toba Daviaxaiqui community, pers. comm. November 2002) in Buenos Aires, who stress the value in maintaining a living language:[1]

> Algunos lingüistas y antropólogos han realizado interesantes
> investigaciones sobre nosotros, pero los artículos y los libros
> que escribieron no son suficientes, no hablan, no caminan,
> no tienen espíritu y por lo tanto, no pueden llegar profunda-
> mente al corazón de nuestros hijos. En cambio, nosotros mis-
> mos somos el "libro."
> (Some linguists and anthropologists have completed interest-
> ing research about us, but the articles and books they wrote
> are not enough; they don't speak, walk, or contain our spirit,
> and therefore they cannot reach deeply into the hearts of our
> children. Rather, we ourselves are the "book.")

Another example of a dialogic research process is seen in the construction of a monolingual picture dictionary in Coatzospan Mixtec in northern Oaxaca, in which the final product was produced only after multiple sessions with different groups in the village at Catholic and evangelical churches, basketball courts, the common clothes washing area, the health clinic, the local store, in people's homes, and elsewhere (Gerfen & Vance 2002). Village members made suggestions for orthography and appropriate photographs. In addition, they opted to represent "men's" speech as the basic vocabulary form in instances where "women's" speech has a palatalized consonant before front vowels (/t/ vs. /tʃ/ and /nd/ vs. /ndʒ/). Despite the fact that many people commented that they preferred the sound of "women's" pronunciation, they opted for men's because it preserved a distinction between words that had become homophonous in "women's" pronunciation.

Although such labor may not fulfill every feminist's vision of proactive gendered language change, it is a feminist approach to language. Both the native speakers and the linguists were empowered through the dialogic process to achieve a deeper linguistic understanding of Mixtec and participate in the cocreation of literate culture. Much like a conversation—an apt linguistic metaphor for feminist fieldwork—no single participant knew or had ultimate control over the end product, nor will participants interpret that product in the same way. And like a good conversation, aspects of this dialogic research process may be repeated in new contexts and potentially transformed.

## Conclusion

The description of gendered language in the Americas continues among researchers with a feminist agenda and those who see the importance of gender to complete grammatical description (Ribeiro 2001). Lakoff's recommendations thus represent unique challenges and opportunities for a feminist linguistics in general and indigenous gender and language in particular. Researchers have been forced to rethink the nature and politics of the linguistic field and the degree of control that experts should have. Some scholars have moved toward a linguistics of empowerment, in which they do not necessarily seek to relinquish control, yet nevertheless empower others through the research process (Cameron et al. 1992). The issue of who embodies and lives a language is highly relevant to indigenous people and is therefore becoming more relevant to the linguists who depend on them. That successful feminist language change or prescriptivism should involve working with community members, whose voices and opinions codetermine the ultimate product or analysis, is one possibility. This type of political obligation may be seen as extreme to those who work in English-speaking communities. However, such a notion is no more radical than Lakoff's suggestion in the formalist 1970s that linguists should have an understanding of a society—including "the weaknesses and strengths of [its] culture"—in order to write an adequate grammar of its language.

NOTE

I would like to thank Mary Bucholtz for her support, excellent suggestions, and astute editing.

1. This excerpt is from a letter composed by the Toba Daviaxaiqui in support of their nomination for the Society for the Study of the Indigenous Languages of the Americas' Ken Hale Prize, which they received in 2003.

REFERENCES

Barrett, Rusty (1997). The "homo-genius" speech community. In Anna Livia & Kira Hall (eds.), *Queerly phrased: Language, gender, and sexuality*. New York: Oxford University Press. 181–201.

Bodine, Anne (1975). Sex differentiation in language. In Barrie Thorne & Nancy Henley (eds.), *Language and sex: Difference and dominance*. Rowley, MA: Newbury House. 130–151.

Brown, Penelope (1980). How and why women are more polite: Some evidence from a Mayan community. In Sally McConnell-Ginet, Ruth Borker, & Nelly Furman (eds.), *Women and language in literature and society*. New York: Praeger. 111–136.

Cameron, Deborah, Elizabeth Frazer, Penelope Harvey, Ben Rampton, & Kay Richardson (1992). *Researching language: Issues of power and method*. London: Routledge.

Deloria, Ella (ca. 1937). Dakota autobiographies. Boas Collection, MS 30 (x8a.6). Philadelphia: American Philosophical Society.

Gerfen, Chip, & Kelley Vance (2002). Ka'u o: An orthography and picture dictionary for Coatzospan Mixtec. Paper presented at the annual meeting of the Society for the Study of the Indigenous Languages of the Americas, San Francisco, January.

Golden, Brigham (2001). Lawrence says, "life was better then"; Agnes says, "life is better now": The lessons of "indigenous" women for theory and activism in feminist anthropology. *Voices: A Publication of the Association for Feminist Anthropology* 5:1–8.

Haas, Mary (1944). Men's and speech in Koasati. *Language* 20:142–149.

Hale, Ken, Michael Krauss, Lucille Watahomigie, Akira Yamamoto, Colette Craig, LaVerne Masayesva Jeanne, & Nora England (1992). Endangered languages. *Language* 68:1–42.

Hill, Jane (1987). Women's speech in modern Mexicano. In Susan Philips, Susan Steele, & Christine Tanz (eds.), *Language, gender, and sex in comparative perspective*. Cambridge: Cambridge University Press. 121–160.

Kimball, Geoffrey (1987). Men's and women's speech in Koasati: A reappraisal. *International Journal of American Linguistics* 53:30–38.

Luthin, Herbert (1991). Restoring the voice in Yanan traditional narrative. PhD diss., University of California, Berkeley.

Medicine, Beatrice (1987). The role of American Indian women in cultural continuity and transition. In Joyce Penfield (ed.), *Women and language in transition*. New York: SUNY Press. 159–165.

Ribeiro, Eduardo Rivail (2001). Female and male speech in Karajá. Paper presented at the summer meeting of the Society for the Study of the Indigenous Languages of the Americas, Santa Barbara, July.

Sapir, Edward (1949). Male and female forms of speech in Yana. In David Mandelbaum (ed.), *Selected writings of Edward Sapir.* Berkeley: University of California Press. 206–212.

Sherzer, Joel (1987). A diversity of voices: Men's and women's speech in ethnographic perspective. In Susan Philips, Susan Steele, & Christine Tanz (eds.), *Language, gender, and sex in comparative perspective.* Cambridge: Cambridge University Press. 95–120.

Trechter, Sara (1999). Contextualizing the exotic few: Gender oppositions in Lakhota. In Mary Bucholtz, A. C. Liang, & Laurel A. Sutton (eds.), *Reinventing identities: The gendered self in discourse.* New York: Oxford University Press. 101–122.

# 22 ::

# Language and Woman's Place

*Blueprinting Studies of Gay Men's English*

WILLIAM L. LEAP

I own two copies of Robin Lakoff's *Language and Woman's Place* (LWP) (1975). The first is a relatively new edition, part of a book order from a recent course in gender studies. The second copy is much older. Its now-browned pages give off a faint musty smell and the binding makes crackling sounds. This is a first printing, and it was one of the first books on language, sexuality, and gender that I added to my library. Today, it is surrounded by many other volumes addressing similar themes. But in 1975, when I purchased this copy, it occupied a more solitary place on the sociolinguistic bookshelf because of its subject matter and because of the approach to research that it details. Both of these anomalous qualities attracted me to LWP, and, as I explain below, they have continued to provide valuable orientation for my own work with language and sexual sameness.

## The Subject and Method of LWP

Prior to the publication of *LWP*, there had been some discussion of "women's language" and "men's language" in the anthropological literature, but frequently these sources simply repeated the idea that in a given (and usually non-European) cultural context, women (as a group) use language differently from men (as a group) (see Trechter, this volume, for further discussion). Typically, these sources cited specific items in inflectional morphology or word-order patterning as evidence of the differences. Some of them suggested that women might command their own "dialect" of the "local language" in question or that women might even constitute a separate speech community. In the main, the focus in these discussions was the issue of sex differences in language. Certainly, this was an important point, but its discussion left unanswered many of the questions that more recent research and political interests obligate linguists to address.

Like these earlier sources, *LWP* also directs attention to linguistic reflections of female-male sex differences. But Lakoff's discussion of those reflections did not center on "language-as-structured" so much as on "language-as-situated" within the material conditions and practical workings of ideology, in terms of which speakers of the language in question constitute their everyday lives. Today, we recognize this argument as a fundamental stance in cultural studies, and the similarities are striking between the discussion of language in *LWP* and in Paul Goodman's *Speaking and Language: Defense of Poetry* (1973), Raymond Williams's *Marxism and Literature* (1977), and other classics in cultural studies from this period. Lakoff did not make use of a cultural-studies vocabulary when framing her reflections on the material and ideological quotidian, but she built her argument within a similar frame of reference, raising questions about the social and cultural factors that determine (in the sense of Williams 1977: 85) linguistic practices and about the erasure of voice and its connections to inequality, dominance, and limited opportunity.

Of course, subsequent research has refined some of Lakoff's initial claims about the interplay of language, context, and politics that gives rise to "women's language." For example, we now have a sharper sense of why a woman's use of tag questions may reflect her "not being really sure of [her]self, . . . looking to the addressee for confirmation, . . . having no views of [her] own" (*LWP* 49) within a particular conversation. But refinements are not refutations. Lakoff never claimed that *LWP* offered the final statement regarding the relationship between language, gender, and sexuality in everyday life; she intended only to introduce arguments that others might continue to explore. Nothing in what we have now learned about language, sexuality, and gender has undermined the vision embedded in Lakoff's initial argument: "to provide diagnostic evidence from language use for one type of inequity that has been claimed to exist in our society: that between the roles of men and women" (*LWP* 39). And nothing has detracted from the inspiration that Lakoff provided to the rest of us by articulating this vision so straightforwardly in 1975.

Many of Lakoff's examples were derived from her own experience with the regulatory power of language or from her own readings of the regulatory messages underlying the linguistic experiences of others. In one sense, there was nothing unique in this practice. Linguists had been using personal experiences and reflections to guide their studies of linguistic structure and pattern since the heyday of phonemic analysis, if not before (see also Lakoff's introduction to this volume). But using the self as an informant raised all sorts of questions about objectivity, reliability, and replication, and Lakoff addressed this point explicitly in *LWP*:

> The data on which I am basing my claims have been gathered mainly by introspection: I have examined my own speech and that of my acquaintances, and have used my own intuitions in analyzing it. I have also made use of the media.

> ... [Those] familiar with what seem to [them] more error-proof data-gathering techniques ... may object that these introspective methods may produce dubious results. But ... *any* procedure is at some point introspective.... [And] if we are to have a good sample of data to analyze, this will have to be elicited artificially from someone; I submit I am as good an artificial source of data as anyone. (*LWP* 40)

The position that Lakoff detailed here was at odds with the neopositivist linguistic practice so vigorously promoted by generative grammar and mainstream sociolinguistics during the 1970s, and when it first appeared *LWP* received much criticism for its so-called failure to maintain rigorous standards of proof. But subjective reading is a hallmark feature of cultural studies, and hence another example of *LWP*'s important connections to this intellectual domain. Moreover, a responsible use of researcher positionality is equally central to current-day interests in language, political economy, and ideology and to studies of language, sexuality, and gender that are informed by those interests. In that sense, Lakoff's work foregrounded what, for many of us, has become a valued approach to real-life linguistic description (see also Queen, this volume).

## "Women's Language" and Gay Men's English

Lakoff's understanding of language outlined in *LWP*, her proposal to use linguistic data as "diagnostic evidence" for broader conditions of inequality, and her willingness to use her own experience as part of her database — and to be quite up-front about doing so — are three ways in which this book has been important to my work with gay men's English and to the broader study of language and sexual sameness with which that work is closely associated.

Initially, I was attracted to Lakoff's decision to use certain structural features associated with women's use of language as the entry point for her discussion, and I tried to follow her lead in my earliest work with gay men's English. Quite quickly, I realized that the structural features that were relevant to gay men's linguistic practices could not be understood independently of social and cultural contexts or of the workings of power that unfold there. Lakoff had said as much in *LWP*, but I did not take that part of her message to heart when writing my own book, *Word's Out: Gay Men's English* (1996). As a result, while acknowledging the need to consider differences in linguistic practices (see, e.g., pp. xvii–xxii), I chose to focus the discussion in *Word's Out* primarily on linguistic domains accessible to me (a white, middle-aged, academic, partnered resident of Washington, DC) and to leave discussions of language use in other domains to researchers already situated there. By adopting this position, I was endorsing Lakoff's argument that "I am as good an artificial source of data as anyone" (*LWP* 40). But because the data were largely derived from my own domains of experience, adopting this position also meant that the database for this project became deeply embedded in whiteness and the middle class.

Critics have rightly complained about the absence of voices of color in *Word's Out*'s arguments and examples, and work by E. Patrick Johnson (2001, 2004), Philip Brian Harper (1993), Martin F. Manalansan (1994, 1995), and other scholar/activists has begun to bring those voices into the discussion of "gay English." My recent work in Washington, DC (Leap 2002a, forthcoming), and in Cape Town, South Africa (Leap 2002b, 2004), now incorporates a much broader perspective on language, race, and class, and certainly benefited from doing so.

But reading *Word's Out* as a book about whiteness and white privilege does not erase its usefulness as a discussion of the political and ideological dimensions of this component of gay men's language use. In fact, reading *Word's Out* strictly in terms of its limited framework will situate the book's discussion more clearly within the relevant social context; doing so will also encourage interested readers to consider how social context situates their interests in gay men's English and, I hope, invite them to pursue their own interests accordingly. Presenting a suggestive argument in hopes that others will develop it further was a central theme in *LWP* and was a part of Lakoff's argument that I did remember to take to heart.

More important to *Word's Out*, and to my subsequent work with gay men's English (Leap, 1997, 1999, 2002a, 2002c, forthcoming), was the prominent position that Lakoff gave to her own experiences and perspectives in her database. As I mentioned earlier, this was something that I did frequently in *Word's Out* and that has also been a topic of criticism. But I do not regret adopting this position, and I continue to maintain it. As a gay man who enjoyed the benefits of male privilege in academe by keeping my sexuality deeply hidden from public discourse (OK, maybe the masquerade wasn't that effective, but I worked hard for many years to maintained the formalities of the closet), then reacted in anger when faced with the AIDS pandemic and the public indifference in response to it, I bring to the table a familiarity with gay terrain, private and public, that is as credible, in its own way, as that of many other gay men of comparable location and background. If I am asking other gay men to talk personally and powerfully about language in daily life, how can I not impose the same requirement on myself?

Would I have written *Word's Out* as I did, and made use of my own gay career as a database, if *LWP* had not served as the project's phantasmic original? I don't know. But just as is true for many other scholars, I do know that *LWP* provided a useful blueprint and strong incentive as I began my own exploration of language and (homo)sexual experience. It is heartening to know that a revised edition of *LWP* is now available and accessible to younger scholars; it is an honor to be able to make a small contribution to that end.

REFERENCES

Goodman, Paul (1973). *Speaking and language: Defense of poetry.* Chicago: University of Chicago Press.

Harper, Philip Brian (1993). Black nationalism and the homophobic impulse in response to the death of Max Robinson. In Michael Warner (ed.), *Fear of a queer planet: Queer politics and social theory.* Minneapolis: University of Minnesota Press. 239–263.

Johnson, E. Patrick (2001). Feeling the spirit in the dark: Expanding notions of the sacred in the African American gay community. In Delroy Constantine-Simms (ed.), *The greatest taboo: Homosexuality in black communities.* Los Angeles: Alyson Books. 88–109.

———— (2004). Mother knows best: Black gay vernacular and transgressive domestic space. In William L. Leap & Tom Boellstorff (eds.), *Speaking in queer tongues.* Urbana: University of Illinois Press. 251–277.

Lakoff, Robin (1975). *Language and woman's place.* New York: Harper & Row.

Leap, William L. (1996). *Word's out: Gay men's English.* Minneapolis: University of Minnesota Press.

———— (1997). Performative effect in three gay English texts. In Anna Livia & Kira Hall (eds.), *Queerly phrased.* New York: Oxford University Press. 310–325.

———— (1999). Language, socialization, and silence in gay adolescence. In Mary Bucholtz, A. C. Liang, & Laurel A. Sutton (eds.), *Reinventing identities: The gendered self in discourse.* New York: Oxford University Press. 259–272.

———— (2002a). Not entirely in support of queer linguistics. In Kathryn Campbell-Kibler, Robert J. Podesva, Sarah J. Roberts, & Andrew Wong (eds.), *Language and sexuality: Contesting meaning in theory and practice.* Stanford, CA: Center for the Study of Language and Information. 45–64.

———— (2002b). "Strangers on a train": Sexual citizenship and the politics of public transportation in apartheid Cape Town. In Arnaldo Cruz-Malave and Martin F. Manalansan IV (eds.), *Queer globalizations: Citizenship and the afterlife of colonialism.* New York: New York University Press. 219–235.

———— (2002c). Studying lesbian and gay languages: Vocabulary, text-making, and beyond. In Ellen Lewin & William L. Leap (eds.), *Out in theory: The emergence of a lesbian and gay anthropology.* Urbana: University of Illinois Press. 128–154.

———— (2004). Language and (homo)sexual citizenship in post-apartheid South Africa. In William Leap & Tom Boellstorff (eds.), *Speaking in queer tongues.* Urbana: University of Illinois Press. 134–162.

———— (forthcoming). *Gay city: Sexual geography, the politics of space, and the language of sites in Washington, DC.* Minneapolis: University of Minnesota Press.

Manalansan, Martin F., IV (1994). Searching for community: Gay Filipino men in New York City. *Ameriasia Journal* 20:59–74.

——— (1995). "Performing" the Filipino gay experiences in America: Linguistic strategies in a transnational context. In William L. Leap (ed.), *Beyond the lavender lexicon*. Newark, NJ: Gordon & Breach. 249–266.

Williams, Raymond (1977). *Marxism and language*. London: Oxford University Press.

# 23 ::

# The Way We Wish We Were

*Sexuality and Class in* Language and Woman's Place

RUDOLF P. GAUDIO

It's no wonder I became an academic. As an Ivy League–educated gay man who came of age just a few years after Robin Lakoff's *Language and Woman's Place* (*LWP*) (1975) was published, I couldn't possibly have gone into hairdressing or interior decorating. What a waste of a good education, and what would my parents tell their friends? Nor could I enter the more manly professions of banking, law, or medicine, where I'd have to repress my emotions, hide my knowledge of color terms, and tell dirty jokes during happy hour. Fortunately, the unmacho world of academia offered me a place where I could use words like *fuchsia* and *taupe, lovely* and *fabulous* without having to worry about my reputation. I could be polite and employ a wide range of intonational patterns and still keep my job. Academic men were like priests, you see (which is what I'm sure I would have become if my father and grandparents had never left southern Italy); having given up the swaggering competitiveness of the real world for careers of the mind and soul, they could afford to come across as a bit womanish. This was important to me because, as a post-Stonewall homosexual, I had rejected the American masculine image (but not my class privileges), and I was naturally sympathetic with the goals of the women's liberation movement. In addition to letting me talk as queerly as I wanted, academia allowed me to have prestige, liberal ideas, and a steady if modest income, and no one would question me or my parents about my sexuality—at least not openly.

The preceding account of my professional history is clearly tongue-in-cheek, but it is not entirely baseless. A similar characterization might be offered of *Language and Woman's Place.* After three decades of research and writing on language and gender—much of it inspired by *LWP*—critics of the book have identified its shortcomings and refuted many of Lakoff's claims, yet its exploration of the linguistic and psychological ramifications of sexual inequality still conveys powerful truths. By this I do not mean simply to endorse Lakoff's claims as true in a positivistic sense, but rather to highlight the ongoing political and philosophical importance of the kinds of questions she encourages us to ask. In addition to the book's open-ing line — "Language uses us as much as we use language" (*LWP* 39) — one of its most enduringly instructive passages is this: "Stereotypes are not to be ignored: first, because for a stereotype to exist, it must be an exag-geration of something that is in fact in existence and able to be recognized; and second, because one measures oneself, for better or worse, according to how well or poorly one conforms to the stereotype one is supposed to conform to" (*LWP* 94). I highlight this passage because the problem of facts versus stereotypes lies at the heart of the challenges I have faced not only as a gay male reader of *LWP* but also as a student and teacher of language and gender. Like many others, I have sometimes discounted Lak-off's emphasis on stereotypes as detracting from the empirical accuracy of her work, but a careful reading of the way Lakoff selects and treats certain stereotypes offers insights into her relationship with the progressive socio-political movements that were active in the time and place in which she wrote. While the rhetoric associated with those movements might seem dated now, the goals they sought to achieve — and Lakoff's particular focus on the role of language in pursuing (or impeding) those goals — are no less relevant for activists and scholars engaged in the progressive struggles of our day.

I first taught *LWP* in the winter of 1997 when, as a neophyte assistant professor at the University of Arizona, I assigned the students in my un-dergraduate "Gender and Language" class the task of writing a three-page essay critically evaluating Lakoff's arguments. One of the best essays was written by a male student who came out in class as gay several weeks later in the semester. Although "Mark" appreciated the pioneering work Lakoff had done in calling attention to the connection between language and gender inequality, he disagreed strongly with her representation of gay men. Whereas Lakoff's references to "homosexuals" are brief, sporadic, and matter-of-fact, Mark's criticisms were defensive and occupied a significant portion of his essay; although he did not say so explicitly, he seemed of-fended by the way she equated gay men's speech with that of women. I gave him an A on his paper, but in my comments I felt compelled to defend Lakoff by reminding him that she had written the text in a different era and that women, not gay men, were the focus of her argument. Yet as a graduate student my own initial response to *LWP* had been very much like Mark's. In my marginal notes I had underlined and commented on Lakoff's references to "homosexual" men with far more consistency than I devoted to any other theme, and I was intensely critical of the way she seemed to affirm the stereotype of gay men's effeminacy.

The disjunctures between my responses to *LWP* at two different stages in my academic career reveal strengths and weaknesses in the book's rhetoric that make it both risky and valuable to use in undergraduate classes. On one hand, my coolly professorial response to Mark's passionate rejection of *LWP*'s portrayal of gay men belies Lakoff's claims about both gay and academic men as "reject[ing] the American masculine image" (*LWP* 44), for what could be more hegemonically masculine than my use of the language of scientific objectivity to discount an argument that was motivated (I assumed) by the writer's emotion? The irony in this case is that while I was using the language of science to defend *LWP*, Mark's arguments were scientifically unassailable: there is no empirical evidence for Lakoff's assertions about gay men's speech, and even many claims she makes about women's speech have been disproven or remain statistically unverified. One way to avoid this problem would have been for Lakoff to mitigate her assertions but that would have contradicted one of her main arguments, namely, that women are too inclined to mitigate! Lakoff's assertiveness can thus be seen as a performative instantiation of her commitment to speaking (and writing) less like a "lady" and more like the men whose power she sought to share. If ganders such as Noam Chomsky and Erving Goffman can theorize without backing up their claims with empirical facts, why can't the goose?

On the other hand, the fact that both Mark and I myself as a graduate student responded so passionately to Lakoff's depiction of "homosexuals" as "ladylike" indicates that the negative connotations of that image still wielded power over us. More than twenty years after *LWP*'s publication, and in the immediate wake of political movements like ACT UP and Queer Nation, Mark read the book's stereotypical representations of gay men's speech not as a historical artifact but as a contemporary-sounding expression of homophobic prejudice. To paraphrase the passage I quoted above: both for Mark and for me as a grad student, two twenty-something gay men in the 1990s, the stereotype of the swishy homosexual remained a powerful image that we continued to measure ourselves by—hopefully insisting that we did not, and would not, conform to it. The fact that we not only disagreed with Lakoff's repetition of that stereotype but also took offense at it was due to our fear that, given the book's exalted status and wide audience, it would only reinforce that image in the mind of the general public and thereby perpetuate our suffering. Indeed, because Lakoff frequently does not distinguish normative gender stereotypes from claims about how real women and men talk, there are always a few students in my undergraduate classes who accept her assertions as factual—despite my own attempts at qualifying them or the astute criticisms of fellow students like Mark.

Contemporary readers can productively address the rhetorical problems in *LWP* by approaching the text dialogically, in the sense described by Mikhail Bakhtin (1986). While Bakhtin focuses primarily on the artful use of language and voice in nineteenth-century European novels, a similar literary-historical consideration of the sociolinguistic stereotypes that Lakoff chose to analyze reveals her critical engagement with the ideologies, movements, and slogans that were salient in the time and place in which she wrote. For example, as many critics have noted, many of Lakoff's claims about women's and men's linguistic behavior reproduce stereotypes that were prevalent among conservative, middle-class, white Americans in the post–World War II era. Although the empirical validity of those stereotypes was always dubious, Lakoff's account of the psychological and social harm they inflicted on women of her generation and social class remains compelling. Another sign of Lakoff's involvement in the sexual politics of her era is her assertion, quoted above, that (male) homosexuals "reject the American masculine image." Such a rejection was in fact one of the stated goals of the gay liberation movement, which was especially strong in the San Francisco Bay Area where Lakoff lived and worked (and still does). Unfortunately, although drag queens, transgendered women, and other unmasculine types were at the forefront of numerous gay liberation protests in the late 1960s, and although gender nonconformity has also been at the heart of such movements as the Radical Faeries, ACT UP, and Queer Nation, gay men's commitment to the goal of rejecting hegemonic masculinity has never been as strong or monolithic as Lakoff suggests: think of obsessively muscular gym clones and gay activists in business suits, not to mention Mark's and my own initial hostility toward the image of effeminate homosexuals.

A more surprising assertion in *LWP* is that male academics have similarly rejected the "American masculine image" and that they too speak "women's language." Although this claim is even more empirically dubious than Lakoff's portrayal of gay men—she cites the hypothetical, and implausible, example of a (presumably heterosexual) male professor exclaiming, "What a lovely hat!" (*LWP* 47)[1]—its inclusion in *LWP* highlights the political-economic and ideological dimensions of the relationship between gender and language. In particular, while gay men's rejection of hegemonic masculinity is implicitly attributed to the stigmatization they endure because of their supposed propensity for stereotypically feminine activities, academic men are described as a politicized class that has "ostensibly at least, taken itself out of the search for power and money" (*LWP* 47). As a result, Lakoff concludes, "academia is a more egalitarian society than most, in terms of sex roles and expectations" (*LWP* 82). If this conclusion seems idealistic, it is also unsurprising given the time and place in which Lakoff issued it—as a young professor at the University of California at Berkeley, one of the most famously radical campuses in the United States in the late 1960s and early 1970s. However, the idealism that infuses Lakoff's analysis leads to confusing implications, for according to her, whereas academic men employ "women's language," academic women do not! The reason Lakoff offers for this is that, because academic men are generally unconcerned with the real-world pursuit of wealth and power, academic women are less inclined to feel insecure in their male colleagues' presence and are therefore "less apt to have to resort to women's language" (*LWP* 82; see also discussion in Hall, this volume). Yet if "women's language" is, as Lakoff argues, a reflection of speakers' insecurity, it is not clear why it would be used by academic men, whose day-to-day lives do not normally require them to subordinate themselves. Answering this question requires a more systematic comparison and analysis of actual situations of language use than Lakoff provides, due to her reliance on the abstract generalizations and introspective methodology that were—and to a great extent still are—standard in theoretical linguistics.

As a gay male academic whose professional life has included several experiences of antigay prejudice and who well understands the degree to which academics of both sexes are financially undercompensated compared to, say, doctors, lawyers, and corporate executives, I am sympathetic to Lakoff's claims about the relative nonconformity of gay and academic men to hegemonic gender norms. However, although many of my heterosexual male colleagues are firmly supportive of feminism, gay rights, and economic justice, there is no objective comparison between the social, political, and economic disfranchisement faced by gay men (and other queers) and the sociopolitical status of professional academics, which far outstrips their merely middle-class salaries. And while unsympathetic listeners might occasionally characterize the linguistic performances of some erudite or politically progressive male professors as "unmasculine," "womanish," or "wimpy," the use of such gendered epithets needs to be analyzed critically as the expression of a cultural ideology that construes a certain misogynistic, homophobic stereotype of working-class heterosexual male behavior as iconic of American masculinity at large. The fact that such epithets are today being deployed by politically conservative elites, especially the warmongering supporters of President George W. Bush, underscores their ideological function.

A critical, dialogical analysis of the ways gay and academic men are represented in *LWP* reveals Lakoff's incipient engagement with what subsequent scholars have called the performative coarticulation of gender with other key modes of social organization, especially sexuality and class. (Lakoff's intermittent references to her own whiteness and to the black civil rights movement suggest that race and ethnicity are also relevant, but that is beyond the scope of this essay; see also Livia, this volume.) If Lakoff's failure to fully problematize this coarticulation were to imply an uncritical endorsement of gender, sexual, and class inequalities, I would have to agree with the sentiment (but not the misogynistic word choice) of a gay male colleague who has described Lakoff as a "succubus" who seduces naive readers into espousing an outmoded, binaristic model of gender and language (Kulick 1999: 606). But that characterization is clearly unfounded: it overlooks Lakoff's explicitly progressive intentions, and it fails to examine her claims in light of the time and place in which she wrote. The fact that Lakoff does not adequately historicize her arguments is unfortunate, yet that is true of most linguistic theorizing from the 1970s, and to a great extent even today. And like many of her linguistic colleagues, past and present, Lakoff does not systematically distinguish empirical facts from normative judgments, whether these take the form of conservative stereotypes or radical slogans. This oversight leads not only to her emphasis on gender binarism but also to her overly optimistic view of gay men and male academics as feminist — and feminine — partisans in the struggle against patriarchal oppression. As a gay male academic who happens (or at least imagines himself) to embody some of the sociolinguistic and political generalizations about "unmasculine" men contained in LWP (and whose fears of being identified as such have greatly receded since I first read it), I wish I could agree with her progressive portrayal of me and my sexual and professional brothers. But alas, that coalition — however ascendant it might have seemed in the early 1970s — has yet to achieve the institutional power that the activists of that era were seeking. Yet who can fault Lakoff, or any of us, for hopefully imagining otherwise?

NOTE

1. My sense of this example as implausible — or at least highly marked — has been confirmed by several straight and gay male informants.

REFERENCES

Bakhtin, Mikhail (1986). The dialogic imagination. Ed. Michael Holquist. Trans. Caryl Emerson & Michael Holquist. Austin: University of Texas Press.
Kulick, Don (1999). Transgender and language. GLQ: A Journal of Lesbian and Gay Studies 5:605–622.
Lakoff, Robin (1975). Language and woman's place. New York: Harper & Row.

# 24 ⠶

## "I Am Woman, Hear Me Roar"

*The Importance of Linguistic Stereotype for Lesbian*

*Identity Performances*

ROBIN QUEEN

When I was six, I believed that I had been born a boy. It wasn't that I questioned my apparent girlness, nor was I unhappy being a girl. I just assumed that the delivering doctor had performed a medical intervention because my parents really wanted a girl and were disappointed when a boy emerged. I was happy that I had become what my parents wanted, but I thought that a bit of boy must have lingered inside me. I understood that my longing to be loud and obnoxious, always right, physically powerful, and often very dirty was not quite in line with what my body seemed to predict for my behavior, and so I simply believed that my body and my gender didn't quite map onto each other. A year or so later, having figured out the implausibility of my story, I created an older brother, who encouraged me to play football, go on bug-hunting adventures, find the scariest hills for riding my bike, and cuss like a sailor. Through this fictional older brother, I remained able to explain why I didn't really act like other girls I knew.

By the time I crossed that heterosexual threshold known as junior high school, I desperately wanted to be an unequivocal girl. Even though my upbringing as a middle-class Southern girl should have made me a shoo-in, I never quite seemed to pull it off. I blow-dried and curled my hair, wore mascara, wobbled on one-inch Candies shoes, carried my books cradled in my arms rather than slung at the hip, and tried hard not to cuss. Once in a while I wore a skirt. At the same time, I couldn't tell the difference between midnight red and savage red nail polish, chose my lip gloss based on flavor rather than color, and often forgot (as I still do) whether chartreuse was in the green or the pink family. My attempts not to cuss were more or less futile, and I was far more interested in playing football with the boys than in watching or cheering as they played football without me. I (and my parents) felt tortured by my apparent failure at being a girl. It took some time for me to realize that rather than being a failed girl, I was a failed heterosexual girl. I was, however, a rather successful lesbian.

At the risk of indulging in a bit of myopia, I offer my experiences as an illustration of one of the more vexing problems of addressing the interplay of sexual identities and gender identities. Couple this general problem with the somewhat more specific problem of figuring out where language fits within such a vortex of identity management, and the task of working out the interactions between language and the social facts surrounding gender and sexual identities can seem insurmountable. Given that recent research (e.g., Bucholtz, Liang, & Sutton 1999; Kroskrity 2000; Eckert & Rickford 2001; Schieffelin, Woolard, & Kroskrity 1997) has repeatedly shown that the indexical power of language is highly local, deeply context-bound, fluid, and ever-shifting, it might seem as if generally tying language to lesbian identities (or to any particular identity) is largely a fool's errand.[1] Yet I would argue that it is precisely such generalizations that are critical to understanding how speakers juggle their multiple identities as well as the linguistic cues that may be tied to those identities. Thus, I follow Robin Lakoff in *Language and Woman's Place* (*LWP*) (1975) in asserting that "one measures oneself, for better or worse, according to how well or poorly one conforms to the stereotype one is supposed to conform to" (*LWP* 94). In the remainder of this essay, I follow Lakoff in other ways as well, exploring how various analytic and methodological arguments found in *LWP* reveal surprising insights into the linguistic resources speakers might use for revealing and performing a lesbian sense of self and into the linguistic resources that may be used to represent lesbians. Before going too much further into these issues, however, it is important to digress slightly into a discussion of what I do and don't mean when I use the term *identity*.

My desk dictionary provides the following definition of identity: "The fact or condition of being the same or exactly alike." This definition highlights the seemingly unavoidable focus on sameness, and the static categorization implied therein, that underlies the strongest critiques of using *identity* to identify or explain social phenomena. Identity labels often fail because they can't possibly capture the nuances and intricacies involved in the emergence and performance of our social selves. We orient around differences as well as similarities, and we blend multiple aspects of ourselves into social selves that shift according to context, situation, and desire.

It is, however, important to reconcile the undeniable flexibility with which we adjust ourselves in the social world with the equally undeniable observation that we orient, make judgments about, and sort ourselves and others based on social categories. How else could I have had the sense that I was a failed girl or that my sister was a stunning success? By using social categories like "lesbian" or "woman" for exploring the connections between language use and specific ways of orienting the self in the social world, I intend "an internal organization of self-perceptions concerning one's relationship to social categories . . . that also incorporates views of the self perceived to be held by others" (Stein 1997: 211). I find this description useful because it leaves room for exploring the importance of intragroup as well as intergroup variation. The social category "woman" thus becomes something other than a category that sits in contradistinction to the category "man." Multiple ways of inhabiting "woman" open up, and understanding the category and people's orientation to it no longer depends on the assessment of success or failure to adhere, but rather on the kaleidoscopic means through which people take the category on while at the same time relying on stereotypical configurations of it (see also Bean & Johnstone, this volume).

Of the many lesbians to whom I have spoken about their perceived relationship to the social category "woman," none has ever claimed that it was a category that did not apply to her.[2] Most have expressed the essentialness of a deep connection to the category "woman," both for themselves and for those whom they love. Many expressed far more affiliation with women of all sorts than with men who shared their sexual identities as "queers," and they often noted that gay men were culturally so different that there was really no basis for interaction beyond very specific kinds of political action. Bearing this affiliation in mind, my use of the term *lesbian* is intended to highlight the salient ties to a specifically female gender identity and to a specifically same-sex sexual identity (see Epstein 1991 for a discussion of the differences in *sexual orientation, sexual identity,* and *sexual preference*). As for the place of language within this morass, I follow current sociolinguistic norms in assuming that variability in language constitutes a social practice that is tied to the creation, maintenance, and performance of social selves (Eckert 2000; Milroy & Gordon 2002; Ochs 1992). I also assume, following Lakoff, that it is explicitly the stereotypical associations made between language and social categorization that allow language variation to function in this way, recognizing of course that these associations easily shift both in their social meanings and in their overall constitutions.

Lakoff based her insights on introspection and intuition, with the stipulation that they were founded on white, educated, middle-class women's speech and on media representations. Bucholtz and Hall (1995) have noted that her choice of method was well within the boundaries of linguistic practice at the time (and it still is in several areas of linguistics) and thus is not in and of itself open to reasonable critique. Lakoff herself rebuts critiques of this method by noting that all methods are introspective in one way or another and that, though partial, her choice of data source "is still of use . . . in providing a basis for comparison, a taking-off point for further studies" (*LWP* 40; see also Leap, this volume). However, it is possible to make a much stronger counterargument to critiques of Lakoff's method. It provided an analytic window that constructed and constrained "woman's" linguistic stage, offering a set of features that operated stereotypically and en masse to help index "woman." Although it may seem counterintuitive, this method ultimately encourages multiple stances to the category itself. For instance, the stereotypical user of this package was posited as a middle-class, white, presumably heterosexual woman, a characterization that serves to highlight intricate patterns of gender, sexual, ethnic, and social-class identities. The linguistic resources Lakoff bound together commented just as strongly on racial, social-class, and sexual-identity stereotypes as they did on gender. They also became a codified trope available to a wide variety of speakers who want to take a stance vis-à-vis the category "woman" (Barrett 1997; Hall & Bucholtz 1995; Queen unpublished ms.).

I have found that the exploration of language use among lesbians is made easier by considering how language is presented in representations of lesbians and how those representations take linguistic stances that incorporate elements of Lakoff's linguistic package. In general it seems clear that representations of lesbians creatively adopt and reject different elements of this package, often combining them with other linguistic packages that reveal further stereotypes, such as those tied to masculinity. In Queen 2001, I demonstrate how the television situation comedy *Ellen* linguistically distinguished lesbian characters from nonlesbian characters through the same linguistic patterns that were used to distinguish male characters from female characters more generally. Similarly, data from the characters in the zine *Hothead Paisan, Homicidal Lesbian Terrorist* showed an intricate interplay between multiple linguistic tropes of gendered and sexual identities, many of which revolved around competing models of femininity and masculinity (Queen 1997).

Though similar in some ways, these two sets of representations differed in being geared to radically different audiences, and the means through which lesbians were linguistically represented in each tended to reflect the expectations of their audience. *Ellen*, shown on network television during primetime, was clearly aimed at a general audience, while *Hothead Paisan*, which was available primarily through subscription or in bookstores oriented to queer audiences, was clearly aimed at a queer, primarily lesbian, audience. The linguistic representations on *Ellen* engaged in what Irvine (2001) and Gal and Irvine (2000) have called *fractal recursion*, in which the oppositions between groups may be projected onto seemingly similar intragroup differences. This means of representation, particularly in media outlets not aimed specifically at a lesbian (or otherwise queer) audience, tends to present lesbians as the masculine counterpart to heterosexual femininity from within the social category "woman." For example, since the early 1990s, it has been exceedingly rare to find an overtly masculine woman portraying an explicitly heterosexual woman. *Hothead Paisan*, however, represents multiple lesbian and transgendered identities, while the portrayals of heterosexuals are caricatures of hyperfemininity and hypermasculinity with predictable (i.e., stereotypical) patterns of language use. In both of these cases, the lesbian characters are represented as unequivocally female, and in both cases stereotypes about the linguistic creation and expression of gender are central to those representations.

Performances of femininity and masculinity play themselves out on lesbian bodies and in lesbian mouths, and for many lesbians the appeal of masculinity is specifically in being masculine women (see Halberstam 1998). Masculine women tend to be read, at least initially, as lesbians, while feminine lesbians tend to be read as heterosexuals (and something analogous seems true of gay men as well). Having learned to recognize femininity and masculinity in the South, I have often found myself doing a double-take when I see a midwestern woman, whose semiotics scream "dyke" to me, begin talking to her husband as he steps out of the minivan. This causes my partner, a native midwesterner, unending amusement; however, it also illustrates how strongly stereotypes of gender expression guide our assessments and categorizations of those who enter our social worlds, even as those assessments remain tightly bound to local contexts, interactions, and moments in time. It is hardly surprising that queers and nonqueers alike look to stereotypes of gender as a means of constructing, performing, and orienting around myriad acts of social and linguistic identity. Similarly, it is unsurprising that queer theoretical inquiry has largely emerged out of the exploration of the ways in which gender itself is called into question by those for whom gender and sexual identities, orientations, and practices are not in the stereotypical alignment.

Lakoff's focus on the overt description of stereotypical features of "woman's language" has thus been immensely useful for me as I have worked to understand more about the place of language in the expression of lesbian identities. She made it clear that the issue of "woman's language" (and the issue of how language is used to represent women) has less to do with the actual social category "woman" and much more to do with assumptions about gender in the social world. She recognized that there would be differences in the degree to which different women made use of the features she identified. For instance, she hypothesized that academic women would be less likely to use these forms with the same frequency or in the same combinations than would nonacademic women (*LWP* 82). She presented an early shift in the analytic landscape of language by arguing that the social category "woman" is constructed both through conventions of language (e.g., representation) and through conventions of language use. Although she came to her description as a generative semanticist, she also provided a way of thinking about "woman" as a social rather than demographic (and hence discrete) category. This conceptualization complemented and enhanced the burgeoning field of sociolinguistics, which tended (and in some cases still does) to assume that social categories existed independently of speakers (cf. Eckert 2000). In opening up the study of language and gender to include the meanings associated with being "woman," Lakoff also opened up the possibilities for thinking about sociocultural variations on gender identities that moved beyond the strict binarity of woman/man. And in presenting "woman" as tied to stereotype, she indicated the limitations of relying solely on quantitative analysis for an understanding of the ties between language and gender, noting that "a stereotypical image may be far more influential than a (mere) statistical correlation" (*LWP* 83). Understanding the influence of stereotypes has not only helped me explore the ways in which such stereotypes are tied to the linguistic expression of lesbian identities. It has also helped me reconcile my early confusion about being a girl, and it has allowed me to find a space for being a lesbian who loves cats but owns no flannel shirts.

NOTES

1. In fact, some have argued that it is such a fool's errand as to be unworthy of pursuit (e.g., Kulick 2000).

2. I was lucky to interview a number of lesbians in northeastern Ohio as part of a long-term research project concerned with the place of language in the projection of lesbian identities. I offer great thanks to the thirty lesbians who spent the time to educate me on just how important being women was to their sense of being lesbian.

REFERENCES

Barrett, Rusty (1997). The "homo-genius" speech community. In Anna Livia & Kira Hall (eds.), *Queerly phrased*. New York: Oxford University Press. 181–201.

Bucholtz, Mary, & Kira Hall (1995). Introduction: Twenty years after *Language and Woman's Place*. In Kira Hall & Mary Bucholtz (eds.), *Gender articulated: Language and the socially constructed self*. New York: Routledge. 1–18.

Bucholtz, Mary, A. C. Liang, & Laurel A. Sutton (eds.) (1999). *Reinventing identities: The gendered self in discourse*. New York: Oxford University Press.

Eckert, Penelope (2000). *Linguistic variation as social practice*. Malden, MA: Blackwell.

Eckert, Penelope, & John Rickford (eds.) (2001). *Style and sociolinguistic variation*. Cambridge: Cambridge University Press.

Epstein, Steven (1991). Sexuality and identity: The contribution of object relations theory to a constructionist sociology. *Theory and Society* 20:825–873.

Gal, Susan, & Judith Irvine (2000). Language ideology and linguistic differentiation. In Paul Kroskrity (ed.), *Regimes of language*. Santa Fe, NM: School of American Research Press. 35–84.

Halberstam, Judith (1998). *Female masculinity*. Durham, NC: Duke University Press.

Hall, Kira, & Mary Bucholtz (eds.) (1995). *Gender articulated: Language and the socially constructed self*. New York: Routledge.

Irvine, Judith (2001). Style as distinctiveness: The culture and ideology of linguistic differentiation. In Penelope Eckert & John Rickford (eds.), *Style and sociolinguistic variation.* Cambridge: Cambridge University Press. 21–43.

Kroskrity, Paul (ed.) (2000). *Regimes of language.* Santa Fe, NM: School of American Research Press.

Kulick, Don (2000). Gay and lesbian language. *Annual Review of Anthropology* 29:243–285.

Lakoff, Robin (1975). *Language and woman's place.* New York: Harper & Row.

Milroy, Lesley, & Matthew Gordon (2002). *Sociolinguistics: Method and interpretation.* Malden, MA: Blackwell.

Ochs, Elinor (1992). Indexing gender. In Alessandro Duranti and Charles Goodwin (eds.), *Rethinking context.* Cambridge: Cambridge University Press. 335–358.

Queen, Robin (1997). "I don't speak Spritch": Locating lesbian language. In Anna Livia & Kira Hall (eds.), *Queerly phrased.* New York: Oxford University Press. 233–256.

———— (2001). Sexual identities, language, and popular culture: The case of Ellen. Paper presented at the 29th Conference on New Ways of Analyzing Variation, Lansing, MI, October.

———— (unpublished ms.). The days of our lives: Language and the commercial imperative on a daytime television drama.

Schieffelin, Bambi, Kathryn Woolard, & Paul Kroskrity (eds.) (1998). *Language ideologies: Practice and theory.* Oxford: Oxford University Press.

Stein, Arlene (1997). *Sex and sensibility: Stories of lesbian generation.* Berkeley: University of California Press.

# 25 ::

## As Much as We Use Language

*Lakoff's Queer Augury*

RUSTY BARRETT

A few days before I was to finish third grade, a tornado destroyed my family's home in Arkansas, and we had to move to a new house across the street from the scariest girl in school. One day that summer, she tied her younger brother to a tree and spent the afternoon throwing a small axe at him like a knife thrower at the circus. When I screamed for her to stop before she hurt him, she simply glared at me and said, "Go to hell, you motherfucker." When I ran to tell my mother what was happening at the neighbor's house, I was careful to say "H-E-double-hockey-sticks" rather than utter the word *hell* (which I knew to be a "bad" word), but I said *motherfucker* with no self-censorship, having never heard the word before. My mother was on the phone as I ran in, and she laughed hysterically, telling her friend what I had said. For the next several days I heard my parents repeating the event to all their friends and laughing about it. My personal terror and concern for the boy across the street went largely ignored and the focus of the event (for my parents at least) seemed to be the fact that I had said the "F-word" for the first time and that a girl had learned the word before me. I demanded to know what the word meant. Not wanting to tell me about sexual intercourse, my parents told me that it meant "to love someone." "But I love my mother, so I must be a motherfucker," I protested. The reply, "No, *fuck* means to love Mommy like *Daddy* loves Mommy," left me utterly bewildered. I was angry and confused by the fact that I had not been taken seriously simply because I didn't know a particular grown-up word — a word I still didn't understand.

I saw my first Shirley Temple movie later that summer, and I was enthralled. My fascination was not with Shirley Temple herself, but with the way that she was treated by the adults around her. They talked to her as if she were an equal, and she seemed to hold power over them in some way. I may have been just looking for justification for something I wanted to do anyway, but I convinced myself that the best way to gain respect from adults would be to act as much like Shirley Temple as possible. That evening, when my father took me to purchase school supplies, he asked if I liked a particular set of pencils. Seizing my chance at gaining adult respectability, I looked him in the eye and said, "Oh, Father, they're *lovely!*" My father stood in shock for a moment, showing a fear I'd never seen in him—a fear that could only come from seeing the son who bears your name voluntarily perform a Shirley Temple impersonation in the middle of a crowded Wal-Mart store. He grabbed me tightly by the shoulders, lifting me off the ground. Trying to remain calm, he said, "Don't *ever* use that word again. That's a *girl's* word." I knew what word he meant, but I felt as though I had been tricked by some horrible grown-up conspiracy. How could my utterance of *fucker* (which was obviously something adults didn't want me to fully understand) produce laughter, but a seemingly harmless word like *lovely* create such fear and rage. I understood for the first time what it means to be used by language.

Robin Lakoff begins *Language and Woman's Place* (LWP) (1975) by noting that "language uses us as much as we use language" (39). Lakoff's assumptions foretell many of the theoretical foundations of queer theory that would emerge some twenty years later. Judith Butler's (1990: 136) view of gender as a "performance without an original" is strikingly similar to Lakoff's view of how one "becomes" a lady through a particular linguistic performance. Lakoff highlights the incredible power of social normativity in regulating the ways in which we use language and the ways in which language uses us. A crucial (and often neglected) point in Lakoff's arguments is that social norms *precede* the linguistic forms that reflect social inequalities:

> The speaker of English who has not been raised in a vacuum *knows* that all of these disparities exist in English for the same reason: *each reflects in its pattern of usage the difference between the role of women in our society and that of men.* If there were tomorrow, say by an act of God, a total restructuring of society as we know it so that women were in fact equal to men, we would make certain predictions about the future behavior of the language. One prediction we might make is that *all* these words, together, would cease to be nonparallel. . . . If their peculiarity had nothing to do with the way society was organized, we would not expect their behavior to change as a result of social change. (*LWP* 74; original italics)

Lakoff's prediction is founded on the assumption that the social determines the linguistic, specifically claiming that language change follows (rather than causes) social change. In contrast, by accepting the *linguistic turn* (the idea that social reality is created through the use of language), queer theorists often assume that forms of social domination emerge through the performative power of language. Both Lakoff and Butler recognize the relationship between identity categories and individual expres-

297

sions of identity. Lakoff argues that it is through behaviors such as using women's language that a "woman" becomes a "lady," while simultaneously demonstrating that the category "lady" is an imagined euphemism. Apart from the assumptions about the relationship between the social and the linguistic, Butler's view of gender as performative is quite similar to Lakoff's original proposal.

Butler takes the notion of performativity from J. L. Austin's (1962) theory of performative speech acts (see Meyerhoff, this volume). Rather than simply convey meaning, performative utterances cause an actual change in the world. Regardless of speaker intent, the felicity conditions proposed by Austin for particular performatives are only relevant in so far as the listener recognizes that the conditions have been met. This is true both for behavioral performatives (like women's language) and for identity labels (such as *lady* or *queer*).

The relative importance of speaker and listener can be seen in my experiences of being used by language as a child. Both cases can be seen as performative language. My failure to recognize the term *motherfucker* as an obscenity indexed the identity of a naive and inexperienced child, while my use of *lovely* was an instance of nonnormative gender behavior, indexing an identity lacking in masculinity. Neither of these identities is one that I intended to convey or create, but they were clearly felicitous performatives given the reactions of the listeners involved. The fact that unintentional performatives may be felicitous makes it clear that the listener's assumptions about "citationality" and authority are the crucial factor in determining whether or not a performative succeeds.

Studies in linguistics have demonstrated that a listener's stereotypes about a speaker are capable of overriding speech perception. Donald L. Rubin (1992) and Nancy Niedzielski (1999), for example, both demonstrate that listeners will perceive their native dialect as "accented" when they assume that the speaker is from a different dialect or is a nonnative speaker. Thus, it seems clear that the felicity of a performative is dependent on the *listener's* recognition of the citation and perception of the speaker's authority. Because the listener's perception will always be regulated by social normativity, a seized citation will only succeed as a new performative when the social context has become one in which listeners are willing to accept the performative as felicitous. Thus, debates over identity categories and offensive or sexist language can be seen as attempts to gain the listener's acceptance of a social reality in which the performative is actually valid (or has ceased to be valid). As Sally McConnell-Ginet (2002: 158) suggests, the process of "defining is an attempt to direct thought along certain theoretical lines, to push a particular strategy for political action."

Lakoff understood the primary role of the listener and recognized that listeners use their inherent knowledge of social norms when they interpret the meaning of utterances. In fact, one of her main points about linguistic theory is that Chomskyan linguistics fails to take the importance of social normativity into account in its models of language as a cognitive system. As she expected, Lakoff's imagined future world of gender equality has not emerged since the publication of *LWP* (see also Livia and Holmes, both this volume). Even so, there have been sufficient changes in the use of many of her examples to see how Lakoff's predictions about the social preceding the linguistic have been fulfilled.

Many of Lakoff's examples seem archaic thirty years later. The term *lady doctor* (*LWP* 54) sounds condescending if not outright silly. Similarly, saying that a woman is *a professional* (*LWP* 59–60) no longer automatically conveys that she is a prostitute. One of the primary accomplishments of the feminist movement has been the acceptance of women as professionals in a variety of careers. Speakers now accept the validity of *professional* as a citation that can refer to women in the same way that it refers to men. A doctor who happens to be a woman is now more likely to be referred to as *a doctor,* suggesting that listeners now recognize *doctor* as an equally valid citation regardless of whether the referent is female or male. Interestingly, the parallel term *male nurse* is still common, suggesting that *nurse* continues to be perceived as referring to women. Terms for women that refer to marital status, however, have not fared so well in the last thirty years, and the move to use *Ms.* as a title for women has met with limited success (Holmes 1994; Kelly 1998; Lakoff 1990; Penelope 1990). In all of these cases, the linguistic change over the last thirty years has followed changes (or lack of change in the case of *male nurse*) in social norms.

The success of instilling new citations has been successful only in cases when there are corresponding changes in social norms. Even in cases where a nonsexist term has been accepted, the continued presence of sexist societal norms may force the term to be reinterpreted in a sexist manner. The evidence suggests that Lakoff's predictions were correct in recognizing the ways in which societal norms constrain the possibilities for language change.

In stark contrast to Lakoff, Butler (1993, 1999) argues that because the performative nature of language creates social reality, it is possible to change society through the intentional "misuse" of a citation such as *queer* to refer to anyone with a nonnormative gender or sexual identity. In Butler's view, the repetition of *queer* in a redefined context exposes the heteronormative character of society and eventually leads to more acceptance for nonnormative sexual and gender identities. Much like the case of *Ms.,* the recent debates about *queer* can be seen as an attempt to convince listeners that the term meets the felicity conditions of citationality and authority.

In his critique of *queer linguistics,* Don Kulick (2002) focuses on the validity of the citation, claiming that *queer* has no "real-world" referent because the range of identities falling under the *queer* umbrella do not form a coherent social group. Kulick claims that the absence of a "real" *queer* social category leads *queer* to be used as a stand-in term for *gay and lesbian,* which he sees as a more realistic social category. Yet a *gay and lesbian* identity can be no more or less "real" than a *queer* identity, as all identity labels reflect imagined communities that exist primarily in the minds of speakers.

While Kulick questions *queer*'s citational validity, William Leap (2002) argues against the performative power of *queer* with regard to speaker authority. Leap feels that the use of *queer* as a label for individuals who may not self-identify as *queer* denies those individuals the right to self-naming. Because the majority of "gay" men identify as *gay* rather than *queer*, Leap sees *queer* as an attempt to gain authority over those who self-identify as *gay* by imposing an identity (and corresponding identity label) that they may very well reject. For those who choose to refer to themselves as *gay*, the use of *queer* disrespects their personal preferences for describing their own identities. Leap (2002: 61) holds that queer theorists don't have the authority to invent and impose identity labels because it is "ethically unacceptable" to usurp the authority for self-naming. Although it should not be surprising to find that a recently introduced term is not in widespread usage, this fact forms the basis for Leap's claim that using *queer* is an attempt to gain authority over individuals who wish to be called "gay men."

The reactions of both Kulick and Leap demonstrate that speaker intention has little impact on whether or not a performative is felicitous. As listeners, Kulick and Leap view *queer* as infelicitous based on their individual understandings of the social norms that restrict citationality and authority. Listeners often reject or redefine proposals for language change based on an a priori acceptance of social norms. Reclamations like *queer* are always contested not because they have no rational basis, but because of the gut reaction to the words' citational history as a potential form of hate speech.

As an acceptable identity category *queer* seems to be infelicitous for many listeners, but in academic contexts terms like *queer theory* continues to be accepted and widely used. Few would question scholars' right to choose the name for their own theory. Thus, *queer* in *queer theory* is subject to a different set of social norms that *queer* as a more widespread identity category. The case of *queer* supports Lakoff's prediction that social norms constrain the possible directions of language change.

The potential rejection of *queer* as an identity category does not mean that the "queer experiment" has been a failure. Criticisms of queer theory often seem to assume that widespread acceptance of *queer* as an identity label was the primary motivation for the original reclaiming of the term. Butler (1993, 1997) is quite clear that the primary goal of *queer* was to question the role of authority and normativity in the formation of identity categories by proposing a reclaimed label for a community defined on the basis not of shared social practice, but of shared rejection of (hetero)normativity. Whether or not *queer* succeeds as a new identity label, it has validated theoretical stances that question the meaning of identity labels and the inherent exclusivity of identity categories. The "queer experiment" has tested our potential for controlling the ways in language uses us. In this sense, queer theory follows the tradition so eloquently established by LWP.

The unintentional performatives of my childhood suggest that regardless of our intentions, speakers cannot always control the ways in which they use language. The inclusion of language change in struggles for social and political change emerges from our desire to assert control over the language that defines our identities. The queer fulfillment of Lakoff's prediction suggests that the degree to which we can assert this control is constrained by the degree of success in the struggle for social equality. By raising discussion about the ways in which social inequalities are reflected and reproduced through language, the work of both Butler and Lakoff becomes a strategy in the struggle for social change.

Although language change does not create social change, the examination of inequalities in language structure may become an important tool in struggles for social change by stimulating symbolic discussions of social injustice. As much as we use language, we cannot depend entirely on language in the struggle for social change. As much as language uses us, the discussions sparked by *Language and Woman's Place* continue to be a crucial component in the realization of social change.

REFERENCES

Austin, J. L. (1975). *How to do things with words.* Cambridge, MA: Harvard University Press.
Butler, Judith (1990). *Gender trouble: Feminism and the subversion of identity.* New York: Routledge.
———(1993). *Bodies that matter: On the discursive limits of "sex."* New York: Routledge.
———(1997). *Excitable speech: A politics of the performative.* New York: Routledge.
———(1999). Performativity's social magic. In Richard Shusterman (ed.), *Bourdieu: A critical reader.* Oxford: Blackwell. 113–128
Holmes, Janet (1994). Inferring language change from computer corpora: Some methodological problems. *International Computer Archive of Modern English Journal* 18, http://www.hit.uib.no/icame/ij18/.
Kelly, Barbara F. (1998). She's married, she's divorced, she's old, she's gay: Folklinguistic attitudes to use of the address term *Ms.* In Suzanne Wertheim, Ashlee C. Bailey, & Monica Corston-Oliver (eds). *Engendering communication: Proceedings from the fifth Berkeley Women and Language Conference.* Berkeley, CA: Berkeley Women and Language Group. 247–258.
Kulick, Don (2002). Queer linguistics? In Kathryn Campbell-Kibler, Robert J. Podesva, Sarah J. Roberts, & Andrew Wong (eds.), *Language and sexuality:*

*Contesting meaning in theory and practice.* Palo Alto, CA: CSLI Publications. 65–68.

Lakoff, Robin (1975). *Language and woman's place.* New York: Harper & Row.

———(1990). *Talking power.* New York: Basic Books.

Leap, William L. (2002). Not entirely in support of a queer linguistics. In Kathryn Campbell-Kibler, Robert J. Podesva, Sarah J. Roberts, & Andrew Wong (eds.), *Language and sexuality: Contesting meaning in theory and practice.* Palo Alto, CA: CSLI Publications. 45–64.

McConnell-Ginet, Sally (2002). Queering semantics: Definitional struggles. In Kathryn Campbell-Kibler, Robert J. Podesva, Sarah J. Roberts, & Andrew Wong (eds.), *Language and sexuality: Contesting meaning in theory and practice.* Palo Alto, CA: CSLI Publications. 137–160.

Niedzielski, Nancy. 1999. Social factors in the perception of variation. *Journal of Language and Social Psychology* 18:62–85.

Penelope, Julia. 1990. *Speaking freely: Unlearning the lies of the fathers' tongues.* Oxford: Pergamon.

Rubin, Donald L. (1992). Nonlanguage factors affecting undergraduates' judgements of nonnative English-speaking teaching assistants. *Research in Higher Education* 33:511–531.

# Index

For enquiries or renewal at
Quarles LRC
Tel: 01708 455011 – Extension 4009